'How has the EU managed to navigate a reconfigure
In this exciting new book, Richard Youngs offers a s
an "outside-in" perspective and new enlightening c
tual framework provides a clear thread through a rich
approach to external action in the last decade. An in
standing of Europe's changing role in the world for yea

, of Oxford, UK

'At last, a course book on the European Union and the ___ that is comprehensive, intelligible and attuned to the realities of a world in transformation. Richard Youngs' accessible and informative writing succeeds in merging scholarly rigor with policy sensibility. Much of the existing literature on this subject takes the "inside-out" approach of looking at European Union instruments and policies. Youngs does a real service by tackling the subject from the opposite viewpoint, how the EU's external action fares in selected world regions or substantive thematic areas. With the COVID-19 pandemic challenging so many of our pre-existing assumptions, *The European Union and Global Politics* could not come a moment too soon.'
– Fabrizio Tassinari, *European University Institute, Italy*

'Most of the literature on the EU's foreign policy is concerned with the nitty-gritty of its institutional development and with endless debates of what kind of power the EU is. This book takes a different stance and focuses on what the EU actually does in global politics at a time when world politics is in almost constant turmoil. Youngs provides a most welcome comprehensive overview of how the EU responds to the many external challenges with which it is confronted. A well-written must-read!'
– Thomas Risse, *Free University of Berlin, Germany*

'A fresh and refreshing analysis of EU foreign policy – of what it is and what it does. The book contributes both in conceptual and empirical terms, and examines EU foreign policy in a specific systemic setting. It avoids the pitfalls of meta-theorising and addresses all the relevant contemporary cases to illustrate its highly accessible arguments. A useful volume for all engaged with the study of European foreign policy.'
– Spyros Economides, *London School of Economics, UK*

THE EUROPEAN UNION SERIES
Series Editors: Simon Bulmer, Neill Nugent, Frank Schimmelfennig

The European Union Series provides an authoritative library on the European Union ranging from general introductory texts to definitive assessments of key institutions and actors, policies and policy processes, and the role of member states.

Books in the series are written by leading scholars and reflect the most up-to-date research and debate. Particular attention is paid to accessibility and clear presentation for a wide audience of students, practitioners and interested general readers.

The series editors are **Simon Bulmer**, Professor of European Politics at The University of Sheffield, UK, **Neill Nugent**, Emeritus Professor of Politics at Manchester Metropolitan University, UK, and **Frank Schimmelfennig**, Professor of European Politics at ETH Zurich, Center for Comparative and International Studies, Switzerland. Previous co-editors of the series were **Vincent Wright** and **William E. Paterson**.

General textbooks
Published

Laurie Buonanno and Neill Nugent **Policies and Policy Processes of the European Union (2nd edn)**

Desmond Dinan **Encyclopedia of the European Union** [Rights: Europe only]

Desmond Dinan **Europe Recast: A History of the European Union (2nd edn)** [Rights: Europe only]

Desmond Dinan **Ever Closer Union: An Introduction to European Integration (4th edn)** [Rights: Europe only]

Mette Eilstrup Sangiovanni (ed.) **Debates on European Integration: A Reader**

Simon Hix and Bjørn Høyland **The Political System of the European Union (3rd edn)**

Dirk Leuffen, Berthold Rittberger and Frank Schimmelfennig **Differentiated Integration**

Paul Magnette **What is the European Union? Nature and Prospects**

John McCormick **Understanding the European Union: A Concise Introduction (8th edn)**

Brent F. Nelsen and Alexander Stubb **The European Union: Readings on the Theory and Practice of European Integration (4th edn)** [Rights: Europe only]

Neill Nugent (ed.) **European Union Enlargement**

Neill Nugent **The Government and Politics of the European Union (8th edn)**

John Peterson and Elizabeth Bomberg **Decision-Making in the European Union**

Ben Rosamond **Theories of European Integration**

Sabine Saurugger **Theoretical Approaches to European Integration**

Ingeborg Tömmel **The European Union: What it is and How it Works**

Esther Versluis, Mendeltje van Keulen and Paul Stephenson **Analyzing the European Union Policy Process**

Richard Youngs **The European Union and Global Politics**

Hubert Zimmermann and Andreas Dür (eds) **Key Controversies in European Integration (3rd edn)**

Also planned

The Government and Politics of the European Union (9th edn)

The Political System of the European Union (4th edn)

The Foreign Policy of the European Union (3rd edn)

Differentiated Integration (2nd edn)

The major institutions and actors
Published

Renaud Dehousse **The European Court of Justice**

Justin Greenwood **Interest Representation in the European Union (4th edn)**

THE EUROPEAN UNION AND GLOBAL POLITICS

Richard Youngs

 macmillan international HIGHER EDUCATION

 RED GLOBE PRESS

First published 2021 by
RED GLOBE PRESS

Red Globe Press in the UK is an imprint of Macmillan Education Limited, registered in England, company number 01755588, of 4 Crinan Street, London, N1 9XW.

Red Globe Press® is a registered trademark in the United States, the United Kingdom, Europe and other countries.

ISBN 978-1-352-01195-1 hardback
ISBN 978-1-352-01188-3 paperback

This book is printed on paper suitable for recycling and made from fully managed and sustained forest sources. Logging, pulping and manufacturing processes are expected to conform to the environmental regulations of the country of origin.

A catalogue record for this book is available from the British Library.

A catalog record for this book is available from the Library of Congress.

Commissioning Editor: Peter Atkinson
Assistant Editor: Becky Mutton
Cover Designer: Laura de Grasse
Production Editor: Elizabeth Holmes
Marketing Manager: Amy Suratia

Contents

List of Figures

List of Tables

List of Boxes

Preface

Editors at Macmillan commissioned me to prepare an updated course book on EU foreign policy in September 2018. The thinking was that a text structured around some of the international challenges crowding in on the European Union would provide a necessary complement to other volumes covering EU external relations. In the two years that followed, this rough germ of an idea became even more relevant than could have been imagined, as the EU's external challenges mounted and became even more taxing. The idea was to look to a writer with a somewhat unusual, split presence in both academia and the policy-linked think-tank environment in Brussels. In line with this, I have expressly sought to marry these analytical and more policy-oriented worlds to offer a course book that is accessible and informative of real-world events while also reflective of the subject area's main analytical debates. In this endeavour I was expertly guided by Macmillan editors, initially Andrew Malvern and then Peter Atkinson, who offered detailed input in shaping the manuscript.

As head of Politics and International Studies at the University of Warwick, Nick Vaughan-Williams provided support for my work and involvement at the department. At the Carnegie Endowment for International Peace, Thomas Carothers provided expert advice on this and many other of my projects. The book draws on the multiple research projects I have undertaken in Carnegie Europe that have given insightful access to insider debates among diplomats in Brussels. The Carnegie Europe team in Brussels have provided extensive support for these various strands of ongoing work.

My work has benefitted in recent years from the support that several foundations have provided to the Carnegie Endowment for International Peace. They include the Ford Foundation, the Hewlett Foundation and the Charles Stewart Mott Foundation. I am grateful for this support but of course remain solely responsible for the views expressed in this book.

Different parts of the text benefitted from advice and input from colleagues and experts working either on general EU foreign policy debates or on specific thematic challenges. These include Richard Whitman, Michael Smith, Pol Morillas, Giovanni Grevi, Neill Nugent, Kristina Kausch, Özge Zihnioğlu, Elene Panchulidze, Gergana Noutcheva, Anna Herranz-Surrallés, Olivia Lazard, Michael Emerson, Stefan Lehne, Pierre Vimont, Ken Godfrey, Erik Brattberg and Rosa Balfour. Magdalena Segre and Maria Koomen helped in particular with the design of the book's graphics. Three anonymous reviewers also provided extremely helpful suggestions.

If the constraining impact of international challenges sits at the heart of the book's perspective on EU external action, such disruption also complicated the preparation of the book itself. I worked to finalise the text under COVID-19 lockdown at home in Madrid, like so many others suddenly deprived of the pan-European life upon which I had come to depend so heavily. I am grateful to diplomats and experts for helping out with final rounds of conversations, meetings and interviews conducted virtually during those unsettling months. The book offers coverage of the EU's response to the COVID-19 pandemic and reflects upon what this is likely to mean for Europe's place in the world. Yet, finished in winter 2020 the book can offer no more than a preliminary examination of this issue. The aftershocks of COVID-19 will be felt for many years and undoubtedly act as a major shaper of EU external action that will need to be chronicled in depth for some time ahead. If the pandemic added a challenge to finishing the book, it is also likely to reinforce many of its main propositions about the EU's need to adapt to external challenges.

Madrid, December 2020

Abbreviations

ACP	African, Caribbean and Pacific states
AI	Artificial Intelligence
AKP	Justice and Development Party, Turkey
ASEAN	Association of South-East Asian Nations
ASEM	Asia–Europe Meeting
BiH	Bosnia Herzegovina
CARD	Coordinated Annual Review of Defence
CEPA	Coordination and Enhanced Partnership Agreement, with Armenia
CFSP	Common Foreign and Security Policy
CivCom	Committee for Civilian Aspects of Crisis Management
COP	Committee of the Parties
CSDP	Common Security and Defence Policy
CSO	Civil Society Organisation
CT	Counter-Terrorism
D10	10 Democracies Initiative, UK
DCFTA	Deep and Comprehensive Free Trade Area
DG Clima	Directorate-General for Climate Action
DG DevCo	Directorate-General for Development Cooperation
DG NEAR	Directorate-General for Neighbourhood and Enlargement Negotiations
DRC	Democratic Republic of the Congo
EaP	Eastern Partnership
EBRD	European Bank for Reconstruction and Development
EC	European Communities
ECHO	Directorate-General for Civil Protection and Humanitarian Aid Operations
EDF	European Defence Fund
EEAS	European External Action Service
EED	European Endowment for Democracy
EEU	Eurasian Economic Union
EIB	European Investment Bank
EIDHR	European Instrument for Democracy and Human Rights
EII	European Intervention Initiative
EMP	Euro-Mediterranean Partnership
ENISA	European Agency for Cyber-Security (previously, Agency for Network Information Security)
ENP	European Neighbourhood Policy
ESDP	European Security and Defence Policy
ETS	Emissions Trading Scheme
EU	European Union

FCAS	Future Combat Air System
GDP	Gross Domestic Product
GDPR	General Data Protection Regulation
GNA	Government of National Accord, Libya
GSP	Generalised System of Preferences
IAEA	International Atomic Energy Agency
IcSP	Instrument contributing to Security and Peace
IMF	International Monetary Fund
IPCC	Intergovernmental Panel on Climate Change
IS	Islamic State
JCPOA	Joint Comprehensive Plan of Action
MENA	Middle East and North Africa
NATO	North Atlantic Treaty Organisation
NGO	Non-Governmental Organisation
ODA	Overseas Development Assistance
OECD	Organisation for Economic Cooperation and Development
PESCO	Permanent Structured Cooperation
UfM	Union for the Mediterranean
UN	United Nations
WHO	World Health Organisation
WTO	World Trade Organisation

1 Introduction

European governments made their first, tentative efforts to coordinate foreign policies fifty years ago, in the early 1970s. Since then, European Union (EU) external policy processes and instruments have developed but have done so slowly and mostly without dramatic change. Coordination between EU states has deepened incrementally in some areas of external policy, while distinctive national foreign policies and elements of clear discrepancy between member states endure. Yet the challenges pressing in on the Union from outside have transfigured its external policy agenda. In contrast to the low-key, incremental advance of the EU's internal policy processes, the external world has changed almost beyond recognition in the last half-century. These changes have increased the salience of external challenges and required important adjustments in the way the EU engages with the world. This book offers a comprehensive overview of how EU external policies have adapted to these global challenges over time.

A new normal

In the span of the last fifty years, the EU's external policy challenges have shifted through several phases. European foreign policy coordination was born at the height of the Cold War. In this period, the then European Communities faced an apparently existential threat, within a relatively fixed international system of strategic bipolarity. This system anchored Europe's geopolitical bearings within a Western camp led by the United States. International issues were coloured by, and generally subordinate to, the binary confrontation of the Cold War. The international sphere exerted a powerful influence over European integration, and it lessened both the possibility of and need for an independent European foreign and security policy.

After the end of the Cold War, these constraints loosened as the 1990s progressed. This was a phase of new opportunity, in which the EU's aspirations to a united and distinctive international presence became more powerful. The rules and norms of liberal international order appeared to attain a more global reach. The EU was able to move with this tide in projecting outwards its own multilateral notions of economic and security cooperation. An increasing number of countries embarked on democratic transitions, and often sought European assistance to take these processes of reform forward. Regional security challenges arose, and often called for EU involvement separate from US strategic leadership. Trends in national-level politics around the world combined with the post-bipolar structure of the international system to give a fillip to EU external action – in terms of both its internal cohesion and its substantive liberal goals.

From the late-2000s, it became evident that the core features of this post-Cold War era were giving way to other trends. A range of security risks intensified. The shift of global power away from Western advanced economies accelerated. Many rising powers challenged the patterns and rules of the liberal international order. Fiercer geopolitical rivalries displaced notions of cooperative security. While economic interdependence continued to deepen, a pushback grew against globalisation. The spread of democracy stalled and in some countries authoritarianism returned. US leadership weakened; in the years after President Trump was elected the United States in some respects became another foreign policy problem as opposed to core security provider to Europe. The EU's own loss of power was compounded by a decade of economic crisis and then by the UK's decision to leave the bloc. In 2020 the COVID-19 pandemic both presented an additional challenge and accentuated many of the global dynamics that had been accumulating during the 2010s.

Into the 2020s a whole series of global changes was no longer prospective but had become a new normal. Not everything about this new normal was necessarily adverse. While the EU lost power and geopolitics became more competitive, opportunities emerged as well, in the shape of new partners, alliances and markets. Digital technology changed international relations, in both positive and less positive ways. And while accounts tended to talk of the emergent uncertainties being unprecedented, in some ways the threats of many previous periods were at least as daunting. Yet the crucial starting point for this book is that the new normal had already left its mark on the EU's external policies. The Union has already spent several years repositioning its role in global affairs. And this suggests a need to re-examine longstanding ways of conceptualising the EU's relations with the wider world.

An outside-in approach to EU foreign policy

This backdrop calls for an updated coverage of Europe's role in global politics. This book adds to existing overviews of EU foreign and security policy by tackling the topic from a different angle. It is written around an overarching theme: the EU has in recent years needed to work hard to retain its international influence in a more challenging world and to harness the positive opportunities that might enable it to do so. While most existing analysis of EU foreign policy has tended to focus on how internal coordination does or does not take place between EU member states and institutions, or on the EU using its own models and rules to transform other countries, this book places greater emphasis on understanding how the EU has reacted to the battery of international challenges and constraints it has come to face.

Accounts of EU external policy have traditionally centred heavily around the question of whether the Union can be considered as an international power and how its unique ways of acting globally can best be described. Much of the focus has been on dissecting the EU's formal institutional processes and the internal policy-making dynamics of its foreign and security policy coordination. This book reports on the latest developments and academic debates with respect to these (still important) issues, but places rather greater stress on *substantive* external policy challenges. It aims to provide the student and other readers with a full and up-to-date appreciation of the real-world dilemmas that EU external policy confronts as it has adjusted to the new normal.

This can be termed an 'outside-in' approach to studying the EU's role in global politics. That most work on EU foreign policy has focused on internal, institutional questions is understandable. Yet this can also begin to look somewhat self-indulgent in light of the pressing challenges that have taken shape globally. The self-confident focus on conceptualising the EU's status as a unique power may have been to some extent justifiable while the Union was building up its external instruments and developing the parameters of its international identity. As the EU has had to respond to acute and constricting exogenous challenges, however, an outside-in perspective is today needed to complement inside-out analysis. This focuses on how the bloc has positioned itself towards a reshaped global scenario and whether its external strategies have had meaningful effect or not. The book adopts this conceptual lens on EU 'external action', which is understood to embrace the wide range of international policies, including but extending beyond standard foreign policy (as defined in Box 1.1).

Box 1.1 Definitions

The book uses the concept of EU external action. This is defined to include the standard diplomatic issues of foreign policy and the core military instruments of traditional security and defence policy, but also policy areas such as trade, geo-economics, technology, climate and energy that have important external dimensions. The book pays special attention to how these wider sets of issues relate to core strategic goals and interests. In this sense, it uses a broad notion of security that includes but is not limited to military and defence issues.

The book is concerned with EU external action in the comprehensive sense of common EU-level initiatives combined with member states' national external policies. National policies can drive EU-level positions forward and give them tangible substance or hold back coordination. EU external action can be national actions supported by EU institutions, or the reverse.[1] Instead of trying to hold separate what is strictly 'national' and what is 'EU' policy, experts have increasingly suggested that 'EU external action' needs to be understood as a holistic fusion of the two levels.[2] The book acknowledges that European policy has become more multilayered, with the national level of external agency influential in many areas.[3]

The UK is covered as an EU member state up to 2020; the book also examines some of the external policy implications of it no longer being a member from that point.

A conceptual framework for the new normal

The book sets the scene for this outside-in perspective by providing an outline of the historical evolution and institutional processes of EU external action (Chapter 2). It then explains (in Chapter 3) why the changing nature of international politics requires a shift in analytical approaches and unpacks the outside-in conceptual framework. The book then applies this framework to the main themes that have dominated EU external action. Chapter 4 assesses how EU policies have adapted to the changing shape of global order. Chapter 5 examines the different dimensions of 'protective security' that have become more prominent drivers of EU policies. Chapter 6 outlines EU geo-economic strategies and stresses the bloc's evolving approaches to trade and investment. Chapter 7 investigates the special place of enlargement in EU external action and how this may have reached its limit. Chapter 8 unpacks the different elements of EU policies on climate change and energy security, while Chapter 9 assesses how EU support for democracy and human rights has evolved.

The book then looks in detail at challenges facing the EU in two regions. While the book focuses mainly on key cross-cutting themes and purposely does not run through a list of each and every geographical region in turn, two regions merit their own chapters. The Middle East and North Africa have generated multiple security concerns that have had a profound impact on EU interests. To the east, war in Ukraine and Russia's broader assertiveness have become equally important and taxing priority concerns. Chapters 10 and 11 outline the evolution of EU policies in these two regions over the years, highlighting their resonance with the outside-in conceptual framework. Reflecting the outside-in theme that runs through the book, each thematic and geographical chapter starts by laying out the main challenges facing the Union and how these have evolved in recent years.

The outside-in framework helps uncover five significant adaptions to EU external action in recent years:

External challenges. Powerful international challenges and crises have driven an evolution in EU external action. The Union has moved in significant ways to adjust to the new normal of global politics; such readjustment is no longer a pending imperative but has been ongoing over several years. The EU has had to deal with an unenviable cocktail: the apparent loosening of the international order's foundations; specific crises and conflicts, like those that have shaken Ukraine, Syria and Libya; and all-embracing thematic challenges like climate change, migration, the geopolitics of digital technology, and from 2020 the COVID-19 pandemic. These challenges have become defining issues in their own right and have also altered the dynamics of EU external action: the weight of external factors in explaining EU policies has increased relative to internally embedded identities, processes and modes of action.

Unity-with-diversity. In some areas of external action, EU coordination has deepened progressively over the years. In other areas, European governments have put greater emphasis on their national foreign policies and on non-EU levels of international cooperation. While this co-existence of contrasting dynamics is neither new nor surprising, a striking curiosity is that convergence and divergence have both intensified in recent years, rather than these being mutually exclusive trends. The new array of external challenges has pulled European governments together in some instances, but has prompted more flexible, non-EU responses in others. As global politics have become more clearly multi-level, so too has European external action.

A less distinctive power. The EU has remained a *sui generis* international actor in notable ways. Yet whole areas of its external action have come increasingly to resemble more traditional diplomatic and commercial strategies. The tools and instruments the EU deploys internationally have mixed quintessentially EU policy frameworks, based around the extension of the Union's own cross-border norms and rules, with more standard forms of conducting foreign relations. The EU has become less unique as an international actor than it once was and certainly than its own rhetoric has long claimed. Its external policies have increasingly been built around a mix of old- and newer-style approaches and ways of acting – a kind of hybrid style of geopolitics.

Protective security. What can be termed 'protective security' has become a more notable priority for EU external action. While this is not the term it uses officially, the EU's clear priority in recent years has been one of self-protection rather than seeking 'transformative power' over other countries. The balance has shifted from policies aimed at extending EU presence outwards to minimising the internal impact of external trends. This shift has not been absolute or germane to every issue in all third countries, but it has been decisive. The COVID-19 crisis has most recently pushed this protective logic clearly to the forefront. Protective security has involved a change in how the EU defines its strategic priorities, towards a more immediate or proximate and less diffuse understanding of self-interest. The traditional debate about the balance in European policies between values and interests does not quite capture this shift: the EU has always pursued its interests but has over time redefined what is required to advance these.

A new metric of European influence. Policy-makers and analysts have tended to apply a metric for Europe's foreign policy impact based on other countries incorporating EU norms and the Union demonstrating its standing as a major power. The changed contours of EU external action call for a reworked measure of effectiveness. The impact of European external action has still sometimes been highly consequential, but in general has become more modest. The EU has in broad terms moved to a more realistic notion of its own power and curtailed its level of ambition in global affairs. While in many ways this is no bad thing, in multiple areas the EU has failed to prevent challenges becoming more acute in circumstances where it could have had more impact. What counts as success in EU external policy has changed and become more difficult to assess.

These five themes form the spine of the book and are addressed in each of the chapters that follow. Each thematic chapter concludes with a brief summary of what light it sheds on each of the five themes. The concluding chapter brings together these different elements of the outside-in conceptual framework and draws out a common theme: the need to update some of the received wisdom that has accumulated around European external action over the years. These conclusions highlight how EU external action has gradually diverged, at least to a degree, from some of its previously defining features. The book is not devised as a critique of everything that may be wrong with European policies; rather, it is a more even-handed mapping of how the EU has adjusted to a new normal in international relations. This raises interesting and, in some cases, counter-intuitive conceptual pointers for how the EU has positioned itself as an international actor into the 2020s.

PART I
BACKGROUND

2 The Evolution and Institutions of EU External Action

Although this book keeps its main focus on contemporary and substantive international challenges, some initial scene-setting background is required on the EU's history and institutional structures. This chapter describes how EU external action developed in stages from the early days of the European Communities, through the creation of the Common Foreign and Security Policy in the 1992 Maastricht Treaty, to the new structures introduced by the Lisbon Treaty in 2009. The chapter explains the basic policy-making structures and institutional processes that govern EU external action. It charts how in recent years the broader context has evolved, looking in particular at how the last decade of internal European crisis and the ongoing shifts in global power have impinged upon EU interests and influence. In recent years, governments and EU leaders have begun to deploy a new framing narrative that casts more assertive and united European external action as essential to ensure the Union's survival. The chapter notes how the general arc of EU policy development has, in some senses, returned to the European project's original concerns to shore up and protect a fragile continent.

Shaped by history: 1950 to 2010

Core EU foreign policy took shape in an incremental manner over many years. While some areas of external action developed early, foreign policy proper became a significant feature of EU cooperation from around the late 1990s, forty years after the launch of the European Communities (EC).[1] The EC's founding rationale was primarily about internal reconciliation between member states and post-war economic regeneration, rather than external objectives. The treaties establishing the European Communities did not establish competence in foreign policy. Foreign policy was too controversial and too entwined with the essence of national sovereignty for far-reaching integration to be immediately feasible in this sphere. In the early 1960s, the French government proposed a European foreign and security policy; the plan elicited opposition from within the French parliament and other member states and was dropped.

The EC's international presence was instead forged through a network of trade agreements. The EC signed a raft of such accords through the 1960s and 1970s. Many of the earliest trade agreements were with former European colonies, especially in Africa. This led the EU to design innovative agreements that combined trade preferences with development aid. In this way EU external action began through a trade and development lens, rather than from a military, hard security or overtly geopolitical angle. This particular historical path embedded an external identity that continues to condition European approaches to global issues today.[2]

In the 1970s, European governments began to develop a process of dialogue on foreign policy proper. This so-called European Political Cooperation took the form of informal consultations between European foreign ministers, outside the formal EC framework. The aim was modest: foreign ministers met once a month for general discussions on world affairs, with a view to improve communication, reduce misunderstandings and temper differences between European countries. This did not generate common approaches to the main international issues of the 1970s. Atlanticists like the UK, the Netherlands and Portugal diverged from France's strategic worldview. However, on select issues member states did begin to fashion common and distinctive positions. In 1980 they declared their support for Palestinian self-determination, in the face of opposition from the United States. They pressed for détente and rapprochement with the Soviet bloc through the Conference on Security and Cooperation in Europe. European states also coordinated sanctions against South Africa's apartheid regime.[3]

Until the early 1990s, the bipolarity of the Cold War militated against European autonomy in foreign and security policy. With international relations conditioned almost in their entirety by the Cold War, little strategic space existed for an independent European foreign policy. Europe was clearly under the US's security umbrella and subordinate to its leadership. Even those critical of Atlanticist states did not seek to challenge the security primacy of the North Atlantic Treaty Organisation (NATO). This was the unchallenged vehicle for European security policy, under the US's strategic protection. The US itself had a low opinion of European coordination efforts, reflected in the much-cited quip from US secretary of state, Henry Kissinger, that 'Europe' had no single telephone number for him to call.

As the 1990s began, changes occurred that fundamentally altered the political context and propelled more broadly conceived external action to the top of the European agenda. This was due to both internal and external factors. It was at this moment that the EC moved towards creating its single internal market. As it began to operate as a truly single economic system, so the need for accompanying unity in external relations became more germane. The Single European Act brought foreign policy formally into the treaties, giving it a legal base. By the beginning of the 1990s, the EC's combined structural weight in international relations was becoming more apparent as the broad 'European project' picked up steam: the bloc was by now the world's largest trading entity, its largest provider of development assistance and its largest source of foreign direct investment.

As these internal dynamics gathered pace, the structural parameters of international relations changed completely. The fall of the Berlin Wall opened both the opportunity and the need for more European foreign policy action and autonomy. The Cold War was the glue that held Europe and the US together; against a backdrop of superpower rivalry, Europeans naturally fell into the shadow of American primacy. When the Soviet Union collapsed, and the international system went from bipolar to unipolar, there was more onus on the EC developing its own external identity and positions.[4]

The challenges that emerged in the immediate aftermath of the Cold War seemed to place Europe more than the US in the frontline. The EC was called upon to take the lead in helping the newly independent states of Eastern Europe stabilise and democratise. As some talked of a 'clash of civilisations' with the Muslim world replacing the West's ideological battle with Communism as international relations' main faultline, it was on Europe's doorstep that tensions in the Middle East and North Africa rose to the surface. And, as the end of the Cold War brought in its wake the violent break-up of Yugoslavia, here were new conflicts emerging within Europe itself that begged for strong European leadership.[5] In short, a combination of internal and external – endogenous and exogenous – factors intensified European governments' political will to deepen and improve their external policy coordination.

While the 1993 Maastricht Treaty is remembered mainly for setting in train economic and monetary union – and renaming the European Communities as the European Union – it also created the Common Foreign and Security Policy (CFSP). Governments made a decisive move in foreign and security policy and put in place the institutional processes of a comprehensive system of 'external action'. The CFSP framework obliged member states to consult on external issues and defined a set of common objectives. It gave EU diplomacy access to the financial resources of other areas of external action. The process was still largely intergovernmental, with member states the primary protagonists. Decision-making was consensus-based and member states would still pursue national foreign policies of their own alongside common EU efforts. In 1999, a High Representative began work as the visible face and quasi-minister responsible for European foreign policy.

International challenges in the years following the Maastricht Treaty prompted a number of new developments. Against the backdrop of conflict in Kosovo, in 1999 EU governments committed to a European Security and Defence Policy (ESDP) that became operational in 2001; this was later rechristened the Common Security and Defence Policy (CSDP). Chastened by their inability to contain violence in the Balkans, governments set themselves targets for boosting jointly deployable peacekeeping and conflict resolution capacities. This shifted such tasks away from a separate organisation, the Western European Union, that had previously kept such security matters out of the EU's formal remit. A key agreement was negotiated that would allow CSDP access to NATO military assets and command structures. While initially debates predominated about the precise relationship between CSDP and NATO, these concerns somewhat fell away as EU missions gradually developed their own track record.[6]

As conflict in the Balkans diminished, a new challenge emerged in the wake of the 9/11 terrorist attacks in September 2001. These gave rise to thorny questions about how the EU should tackle both the acts and roots of international terrorism. They also led to the US-led invasion of Iraq and one of the most serious ever episodes of European disunity in international affairs. Not only did some member states participate in the invasion and others oppose it, but they aired their disagreements publicly, and with some vitriol, in the United Nations. While the conflicts in Iraq and Afghanistan were the subject of major disagreements between member states, however, they also pushed European governments to take a harder look at their military shortfalls and the need to strengthen counter-terrorism coordination.

In 2003, these international events acted as a catalyst for the publication of a European Security Strategy. This was the first time the EU mapped out something akin to a strategic vision. It stressed a number of core principles, including support for 'effective multilateralism' and 'preventive engagement'. Partially an attempt to repair the damage caused by tensions over Iraq, the strategy became something of a founding document for EU strategic philosophy. It was broader in scope than a US security strategy drawn up at the same time and resonated with a multi-pronged concept of EU external action wider than traditional security policy.[7] After CFSP momentum gathered during the decade, in 2009 the Lisbon Treaty improved and deepened EU external action decision-making rules and institutional capacities.[8]

Crisis years and beyond: 2010 to 2020

Until this moment, there was a widespread narrative of gradually accumulating EU influence and innovative forms of European external action. In the 2010s, this backdrop changed. While the Lisbon Treaty added many elements to the formal institutional framework governing EU external action, its implementation coincided with the financial crisis that lasted for nearly a decade and took the EU to the verge of collapse. In these years, the EU struggled to come to terms with two parallel dilemmas, as its long-term relative decline in the world was superimposed with a crisis that seemed dramatically to accelerate adverse trends. The narrative switched from one of the EU gradually taking shape as an emergent superpower to one of minimising the fall-out from these twin challenges.

While the EU's share of global GDP began declining in the late 1980s, this decline deepened in the 2010s. From generating over a quarter of world GDP in the mid-1990s, post-crisis trendlines had the EU share falling under 10 per cent by 2050 – Figures 2.1 and 2.2 show this decline in detail.[9] The crisis left many EU states more

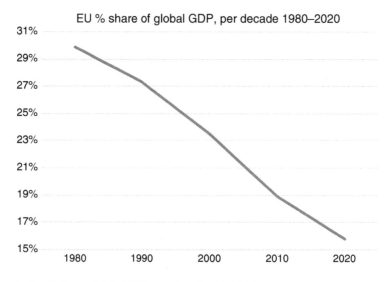

Figure 2.1 EU share of global GDP, per decade 1980–2020
Source: IMF database www.imf.org/en/Data

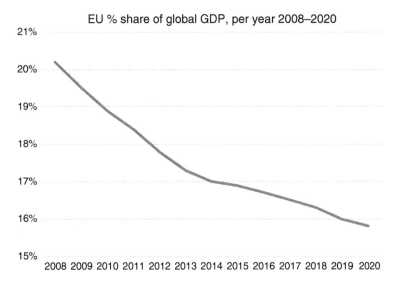

Figure 2.2 EU share of global GDP, per year 2008–2020
Source: IMF database

dependent on capital flows from China, other Asian economies and the Gulf. European governments' request for Chinese funds to save the euro represented a fundamental and pivotal reversal of centuries-old power dynamics.[10] The G20 displaced the G8 as the pivotal international economic forum, diluting European influence. The international appeal and reputation of EU financial regulations suffered; the Union was suddenly a source of instability rather than provider of model standards.[11] The EU's development and defence spending both declined during the crisis years.

In addition to its negative impact on EU finances and external resources, the crisis also seemed to open new divisions between member states. The bitter internal divides over economic policy bled into the realm of foreign policy.[12] Experts talked of the years of crisis producing a 'renationalisation' of states' foreign policies.[13] Many believed that EU foreign policy came out of the crisis more fragmented and more inward-looking.[14] And, less tangibly, the crisis undercut the EU's appeal as a normative model and as a reference point for the democratic management of interdependence. The EU was suddenly a problem for the rest of the world to contain as much as it was an actor offering solutions to global problems. Even if many within and beyond Europe exaggerated this aspect of the EU's woes for their own agendas, the Union had undoubtedly suffered a certain fall from grace in the eyes of the world.

After years of dramatic and fraught crisis management the EU gradually emerged from the worst years of crisis. From around 2017, the European project stabilised and even began to regain a degree of momentum. The crisis left the EU contending with a series of new challenges and weaknesses but also acted as a catalyst for deeper cooperation in at least some areas of policy. As European governments agreed cooperation in several economic domains as part of their efforts to contain the Eurozone crisis, so new debates opened up about deepening cooperation in foreign policy too. The very problems that hit the EU so hard after 2009 made it clear that European governments needed to stick together and that they all shared a common fate in the global system.[15]

As the 2010s progressed, multiple efforts were made to reform the CFSP. In 2016, the EU presented a new Global Strategy. This was built around a narrative that more active external policy would be needed to help the EU project survive – a reversal from foreign policy being framed as an outgrowth of the success of integration.[16] Trade flows and external resources slowly began a post-crisis rebound. EU exports recovered in the late 2010s and the Union was still the world's largest trade bloc at the end of the decade (a trend detailed in Chapter 6). After recession-period cuts, by 2017 the EU was back to providing over half global development aid – Figures 2.3 and 2.4 detail donors' aid totals.[17] Member

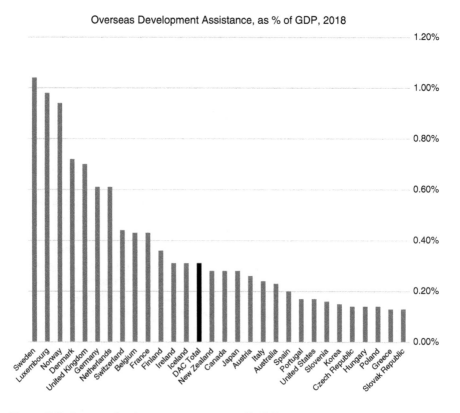

Figure 2.3 Overseas development assistance, as % of GDP, 2018
Source: OECD Donor Tracker https://donortracker.org/

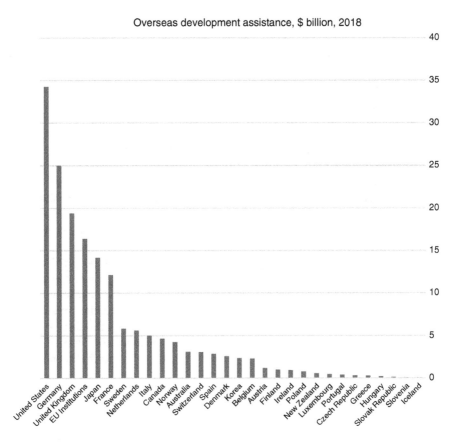

Figure 2.4 Overseas development assistance, $ billion, 2018
Source: OECD Donor Tracker https://donortracker.org/

states tentatively began to increase their military spending too from around 2017 (as outlined in Chapter 5).

In 2018, Commission president Jean-Claude Juncker said the EU needed 'Weltpolitikfahigkeit' – the ability to play an assertive and meaningful role in world politics.[18] In 2019 the Franco-German Aachen Treaty made several commitments to deepen foreign-policy cooperation, including through joint military missions. President Emmanuel Macron's 'European Renaissance' proposal presented in February 2019 included several foreign policy ideas, including a new European Security Council and a new defence treaty.[19] France and Germany presented the European Security Council idea partly as a means of maintaining tight strategic coordination with the UK as the latter left the European Union; so-called E3 cooperation intensified from 2018, France and Germany seeing this as a 'light touch' way of working with the UK.[20]

Commitments to more effective external-policy coordination also came with a reframed narrative that focused on the need to redress the Union's vulnerability to other powers. President Macron's stated aim was to make the EU 'an autonomous power equal to others' and prevent the bloc becoming 'the plaything of great powers'.[21] He and other leaders began ritually using a refrain of Europe needing to 'regain its sovereignty'. At the end of 2019 the incoming Commission president, Ursula von der Leyen, promised a 'geopolitical Commission' and made foreign policy a higher priority than it had been in the 2014–2019 institutional term.[22] She set up a new committee under her control to pull all areas of policy together in pursuit of geopolitical goals. Incoming High Representative Josep Borrell insisted 'we need to nurture a culture of thinking geopolitically' and urged the EU to 'relearn the language of power'.[23]

The COVID-19 emergency gave rise to further commitments to strengthen the EU's global actions and presence. Despite plentiful warnings of a probable pandemic, European governments were caught off-guard by COVID-19 and initially scrambled to respond through mainly national measures with little EU-level coordination. French foreign minister Jean-Yves Le Drian insisted the pandemic must and would 'accelerate the re-founding of Europe's international power.'[24] The EU made some notable attempts to coordinate international responses to the pandemic, for example on the development and distribution of a vaccine. Yet no major changes were made to the basic institutional structures of EU foreign and security policy. Amid acrimonious debates over post-Covid recovery funding, member states whittled down the Commission's proposed allocations for external action within a new EU budget and pushed to switch these funds to internal spending.

National foreign policies

As EU-level commitments have evolved in response to emerging challenges and crises, so in parallel have member states' national foreign policies shifted in recent years. Perhaps most significant has been Germany's increasingly dominant role in Europe. Some argue that Germany has been guilty of 'leadership avoidance' and of functioning as a rather soft 'facilitator' in global politics rather than a power with real strategic purpose.[25] However, most see the country gradually seeking more of a lead role in EU external action, while also scaling up its national foreign-policy capacities.[26] German foreign policy has become slightly tougher-edged, remaining multilateralist and Europeanist, but less reluctant than previously to act against such declared principles.[27] In a much-cited quip, then foreign minister Sigmar Gabriel expressed concern that Germany should not be left as 'the only vegetarian in a world of carnivores'.[28] Germany has acted through more ad hoc coalitions in recent years and at a number of different levels as it exerts leadership rather than being quite so wedded to EU unity as an end in itself.[29]

For many years, France was beguilingly both lead proponent of European foreign policy cooperation and the country that most resolutely defended its national influence and interests. President Chirac's opposition to international intervention in Iraq in 2003 was a notable apogee of the traditional quest for strategic independence. The general view was that under presidents Nicolas Sarkozy and François Hollande French foreign policy lost some of its customary global ambition. From

2017, President Macron promised to reverse this. Macron was more instinctively pro-European than his predecessors and stressed a commitment to deepen EU cooperation. Yet his presidency also swung back to focus on France's hard security priorities and what Macron called the 'aggressive pursuit' of France's national economic interests in the world – a return to the tradition of 'external Gaullism'.[30] The French proposal for a European Security Council aimed to strengthen the role of national governments relative to EU institutions. Macron has sought to position himself as the world's mediator; under his presidency France has orchestrated an unmatched range of diplomatic initiatives to engage with different sides to conflicts, with difficult regimes and with intractable policy issues. Other member states became concerned at Macron's tendency to launch ideas without consultation and to present French interests as synonymous with European views.

The UK has recast its foreign policy aims due to Brexit. After the 2016 Brexit referendum, the UK government drew up a Global Britain strategy and worked to shore up its international presence, extending its network of bilateral strategic partnerships with countries around the world and expanding its diplomatic service through several hundred new positions. In early 2019 then foreign secretary Jeremy Hunt suggested that the UK could play the role of 'an invisible chain linking together the democracies of the world'.[31] A 'fusion doctrine' aimed to get all UK policy instruments more directly targeted on high-level strategic foreign policy interests.[32] In 2020 the new Conservative government announced the country's most comprehensive security and defence review since the Cold War. It also merged the Department for International Development into the Foreign and Commonwealth Office with the aim of using resources in a more pointedly strategic manner. The British government sent mixed signals to the EU, saying it wanted to maintain unity with the bloc but also indicating a desire to take up independent foreign policy positions.[33] It rejected a formal agreement with the Union on foreign and security policy, preferring informal E3 coordination with France and Germany outside EU structures. In all this there was serious strategic rethinking mixed with less convincing attempts to offset Brexit.[34]

The international ambitions of other European states have generally remained more modest. Italy's international presence diminished appreciably during the Eurozone crisis as the country had fewer resources to invest in external policies. Yet, as the country was hit by the migration surge after 2015, Italy played a disproportionately impactful agenda-setting role in getting migration issues mainstreamed into EU external action. Under the coalition between the Lega and Five Star Movement that took power in 2018, Italy committed to a foreign policy more oriented towards immediate national interests rather than EU coordination. It was especially combative towards France and President Macron. The government curiously sought improved relations with the US, Russia and China simultaneously, in each case outside some of the parameters of common EU positions.[35] When the Lega left government and a new coalition between Five Star and the centre-left Partito Democratico took office, Italy tilted back towards its more traditional positioning. However, the internal constraints on its strategic input to EU deliberations remained severe.

Spain also punched below its weight for most of the 2010s. From 2018, and especially under a new Socialist government, the country looked for a way to regain international influence. After years of punishing austerity, the Spanish government committed to increase military and aid budgets, although the country remained a below-average player in both these areas. A leading edge of Spain's effort to regain international standing was España Global, a public relations initiative aimed at improving the country's image, mainly against Catalan self-determination. Under the new Socialist government from 2019 this morphed into a strategy aimed more at Spain's geo-economic and geopolitical national interests. Spain defined itself as a 'nodal power' seeking a foreign policy based on linking together different regions and networks of influence. The country remained firmly pro-European but also began to foreground its own national interests to a slightly greater extent than previously.[36]

Other member states have also developed more active national foreign policy strategies; the book's thematic chapters will cover these in each specific area. The very brief country snapshots serve to register the analytically significant point that member states have increasingly sought to strengthen elements of their national diplomacy and to protect their national room for strategic manoeuvre. Even as most governments look for deeper EU cooperation, they have simultaneously beefed up their own separate foreign policy initiatives, while also wielding de facto national vetoes with increasing frequency.

The EU external relations system

This historical arc of developments at European and national levels has left the EU with a very particular institutional framework. The conjoining of internal and external forces has generated a complex *sui generis* institutional framework. This was designed in the early 1990s and has since been modestly upgraded and remoulded on the occasion of several treaty revisions; the 2009 Lisbon Treaty sets out the currently applicable provisions for external action (see Box 2.1). The EU's institutional framework divides responsibilities for different elements of external relations in different ways – with multiple dividing lines within and across the EU institutions and the member states.[37] Figure 2.5 provides a graphic representation of the main areas of EU external action. Taking each strand in turn, the external action system can be summarised as follows:

Foreign policy positions and core diplomacy

European leaders set the broad parameters of EU foreign policy in the European Council. Foreign ministers undertake the bulk of coordination work in the Foreign Affairs Council, where they take operational decisions. Member state ambassadors in the Political and Security Committee provide day-to-day support to foreign

Box 2.1 Foreign and Security Policy provisions of the Lisbon Treaty

Select extracts

Article 21 lists very general aims of EU foreign and security policy, these being for the Union to:

'(a) safeguard its values, fundamental interests, security, independence and integrity;
(b) consolidate and support democracy, the rule of law, human rights and the principles of international law;
(c) preserve peace, prevent conflicts and strengthen international security;
(d) foster the sustainable economic, social and environmental development of developing countries...;
(e) encourage the integration of all countries into the world economy, including through the progressive abolition of restrictions on international trade;
(f) help develop international measures to preserve and improve the quality of the environment and the sustainable management of global natural resources;
(g) assist populations, countries and regions confronting natural or man-made disasters; and
(h) promote an international system based on stronger multilateral cooperation and good global governance.'

Article 26 stresses member states' role: 'The common foreign and security policy shall be put into effect by the High Representative and by the Member States, using national and Union resources.'

Article 42: 'The common security and defence policy shall ... include the progressive framing of a common Union defence policy. This will lead to a common defence, when the European Council, acting unanimously, so decides.'

'Those Member States whose military capabilities fulfil higher criteria and which have made more binding commitments to one another in this area with a view to the most demanding missions shall establish permanent structured cooperation within the Union framework.'

'If a Member State is the victim of armed aggression on its territory, the other Member States shall have towards it an obligation of aid and assistance by all the means in their power.'

Article 43. The security and defence policy can include 'joint disarmament operations, humanitarian and rescue tasks, military advice and assistance tasks, conflict prevention and peace-keeping tasks, tasks of combat forces in crisis management, including peace-making and post-conflict stabilisation. All these tasks may contribute to the fight against terrorism, including by supporting third countries in combating terrorism in their territories.'

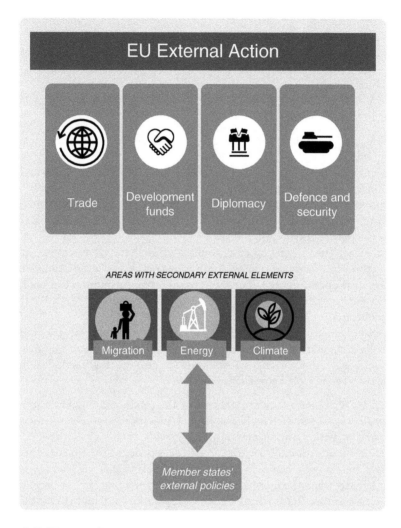

Figure 2.5 EU external action system

ministers. Below this run a large number of geographical and thematic working groups. Member states take first-order, substantive decisions by unanimity. Qualified majority votes are possible for measures that implement these decisions; in practice, this provision is not regularly used. Through so-called constructive abstention a state is able to not apply an EU foreign policy position in return for not blocking other states.

The High Representative can make proposals, alone or with the Commission's support. The High Representative represents the EU and is charged in particular with bringing about consistency between the different elements of external action, especially by chairing the Commissioners Group on External Action, a key innovation of the Lisbon treaty. The European External Action Service (EEAS) began work in late 2010 as a proto-diplomatic service (several governments insisting it was named a 'service' to them rather than given a name more redolent of a ministry). It oversees around 140 delegations across the world, representing both member states and the Commission. The EU publicises the EEAS as the biggest diplomatic service in the world. The European Neighbourhood Policy is managed outside the EEAS by a separate directorate, DG NEAR.

Security and conflict interventions

Defence and security policy have long been the strand of external action over which member states retain their strongest hold. However, it is also the strand that has developed most significantly in recent years. The CSDP provides an umbrella for the deployment of military and civilian missions to conflict scenarios around the world. These missions can take on the full range of peacekeeping and conflict resolution tasks. As of 2020, there had been 34 CSDP missions, the largest number providing police training or border patrols – see Figure 2.6. A Military Committee comprised of member state representatives addresses conflict and security issues,

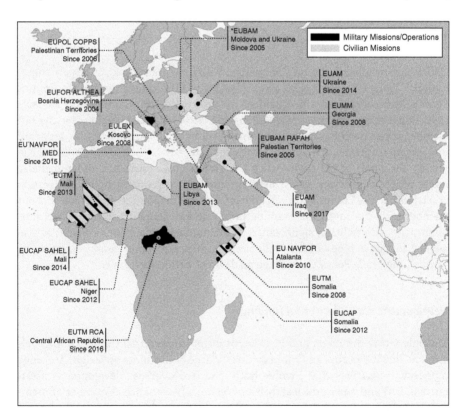

Figure 2.6 CSDP missions, as of 2020
Source: European Union (2019), p. 34

reporting to the High Representative. A number of EU Special Representatives cover various conflicts around the world. The Military Committee and a Committee for Civilian Aspects of Crisis Management (known as CivCom, made up of member state representatives) cover conflict resolution, peacekeeping and post-conflict stabilisation. A group of lower-order bodies covers the core areas of security, including the EU Military Staff and a Joint Situation Centre.[38]

While NATO is still the principal security alliance involving European states, the EU has gradually carved itself a modest role in defence policy. The Lisbon Treaty provides for 'enhanced cooperation': a minimum of nine member states can move forward to enhance their defence capabilities together, without the involvement of all member states. This has been supplemented with the so-called PESCO (Permanent Structured Cooperation) process through which the EU coordinates member states' cooperation in jointly strengthening military capabilities. The Commission oversees a Defence Fund that was created in 2018. The Lisbon Treaty also included a rather non-specific 'solidarity clause' under which member states are to provide security support to any EU state hit by a terrorist attack or other disasters.

Trade policy

Under the so-called Common Commercial Policy, EU trade policy is largely supranational. Trade is one of the few areas of exclusive EU competence, and the Council decides trade agreements by qualified majority vote. The Commission has sole right of initiative over most trade issues and leads trade negotiations for the EU; member states need to approve any final deal, by qualified majority for standard international agreements, but unanimity for agreements that include political elements. The remit of EU trade policy has gradually widened, and today includes issues related to services, investment and intellectual property rights. On certain crucial issues, the Commission can take retaliatory trade action on its own without member state approval, for example imposing anti-dumping duties – decisions potentially with political significance. The European Parliament's consent is also needed for most types of EU trade accords. Member states retain engagement through the Trade Policy Committee made up of national officials.

Development aid and external funding

Multiple actors decide on and implement European external funding and development aid. The European Commission is a large donor in its own right and runs numerous initiatives that involve both standard overseas development assistance (ODA) and more political forms of technical assistance. A number of member states have reasonably large bilateral development aid programmes: Germany, the UK, France, Sweden and the Netherlands generally allocate over 5 billion euros a year; Denmark and Luxembourg are also generous donors in relative terms, and, to a lesser extent, Belgium, Finland and Ireland; other states give small amounts of 0.2 per cent of GDP or less. Taken together, the Commission and member states provide just under 60 per cent of global ODA – not taking Brexit into account. Commission aid is normally about 20 per cent of the total EU aid budget.

In the last decade, the UK and Germany have been the largest providers of aid in absolute terms. In the 2010s the world's biggest single donors were, in order: the US, Germany, the UK and the European Commission. In 2018 (only) Denmark, Luxembourg, Sweden and the UK met the commitment for aid to be a minimum of 0.7 per cent of GDP. (In 2020 the UK reduced its allocation to 0.5 per cent).[39] Part of the Commission's external funding goes through the European Development Fund which is outside the main EU budget and not subject to European Parliament control. The rest is split between two separate directorates, DG Devco and DG NEAR, while the European External Action Service sets overarching programming objectives for aid. The directorate-general for Civil Protection and Humanitarian Aid Operations (ECHO) manages humanitarian aid separately. Tables 2.1 and 2.2 show the breakdown of Commission external funding (Box 2.2).

Table 2.1 European Commission, external aid instruments, euros million, 2014–2020

Instrument for Pre-accession Assistance (IPA)	11,699
Humanitarian Aid Instrument	148
European Neighbourhood Instrument (ENI)	15,433
Development Cooperation Instrument (DCI)	19,662
Partnership Instrument (PI)	955
Instrument Contributing to Stability and Peace (IcSP)	2,339
European Instrument for Democracy & Human Rights (EIDHR)	1,333
Common Foreign and Security Policy	2,339
Asylum, Migration and Integration Fund	3,137

Source: European Commission

Table 2.2 European Commission, external aid instruments, euros million, 2021–2027

Instrument for Pre-accession Assistance (IPA)	12,565
Humanitarian Aid Instrument	10,260
Neighbourhood, Development and International Cooperation Instrument	70,800
Common Foreign and Security Policy	2,375
Migration and border management	22,671
Security and defence	13,185

Source: European Commission

Box 2.2 External relations portfolios in 2019–2024 Commission

High Representative for Foreign and Security Policy – Josep Borrell, Spain
Trade – Phil Hogan, Ireland; replaced in October 2020 by Valdis Dombrovskis, Latvia.
Neighbourhood and Enlargement – Oliver Varhelyi, Hungary
International Partnerships – Jutta Urpilainen, Finland
Crisis Management – Janez Lenarcic, Slovenia

Several other portfolios that are not mainly concerned with external policies have external elements or read-overs, including:

Energy – Kadri Simson, Estonia
European Green Deal – Frans Timmermans, Netherlands
A Europe fit for the Digital Age – Margrethe Vestager, Denmark

---

Conclusion

EU external action has gone through very specific processes of historical evolution and institutional development. The overall arc of EU policies has not been one of smooth, ever-accumulating unity. Rather, member states reached a certain degree of cooperation – not complete, but also not inconsequential – and then remained more or less at that level. Within a relatively fixed institutional framework since the early 1990s, many of the EU's external action policy-making dynamics appear deeply rooted. The institutional features that define and shape EU external action have been more enduring and settled than many predicted would be the case. They have not collapsed in effectual failure and, in many areas, have proven workable as a framework for everyday decision-making. Yet neither have they served as a staging post towards a more fully Europeanised external policy machinery.

The EU's institutional structure is highly complex and varied in the way that decisions are made and power articulated in the different policy areas that make up the totality of its external action. The balance of power between states and EU-level institutions differs across policy areas. Many different actors have a role in and hold over the Union's international presence, identity and influence – and these unsurprisingly have different views and approaches to global challenges. These differences are not an anomaly or a surprising aberration, but hardwired into the very design of the external relations system and a predictable part of its routine functioning. This complex system has not moved in any single direction. Some of the modest fine-tuning agreed in the last decade has increased the weight and influence of the EU institutions and supranational dynamics; some has rather shifted the centre of gravity to national governments.

Paradoxically, while the EU's institutional structures have remained relatively unchanging for three decades, the world around Europe has changed fundamentally and with much turbulence. In the 2000s and early 2010s, the EU struggled to come to terms with deep structural change in global politics and with crises in Europe itself. By the late 2010s, these changes were no longer just-emerging developments, but represented a fairly well-established new normal. This opened the doors to an era in which the focus would be on how well the EU was adjusting to the new international context. This has been evident within the trajectory of member states' national foreign policies as much as at the EU level. In the last decade, the EU has lost some of its relative power; this is by no means all the Union's fault but simply a natural result of other powers' growth and foreign policy activism, and it is not necessarily entirely negative. Yet it has pushed EU external action into different terrain.

Curiously, this new focus returns the EU to some of its original ethos. When the European project started it was to rebuild and overcome Europe's destruction, and in the Cold War era give it some solidity and standing when the West faced a clear systemic threat. Then for some time from the early 1990s the agenda and narratives were more ambitious and outward-looking, and more about remoulding other powers and the whole global system. Debates were at this point about how far the EU could extend its burgeoning power and normative visions. Yet recent years have seen this inverted once more. The increasingly pre-eminent narrative has centred on stopping the EU becoming subservient to other powers. The tragedy of the COVID-19 virus has acted as the latest ratchet in this direction. Although it has remained unclear what the EU means by acting more 'geopolitically' or recovering 'European sovereignty', the change in language has been significant. Notwithstanding the obvious differences between the post-war and current geopolitical contexts, there is at least a degree of circularity in the EU returning to a concern with protecting itself from other powers and a febrile outside world.

3 An Outside-in Framework for EU External Action

This chapter sets the conceptual framework around which the book is organised. It first outlines the main traditional analytical approaches to the study of EU external action, before arguing that a different kind of 'outside-in' conceptual framework is required. Traditionally, three broad analytical concerns have dominated the study of EU external action: explaining coordination between European governments on international issues; capturing how the EU has developed a distinctive kind of power; and showing how the EU acts internationally by externalising its own internal rules and norms. The chapter draws on work calling for a reworked analytical lens that builds on but moves beyond these traditional concerns. It outlines an outside-in conceptual framework that places greater emphasis on the study of European responses to identifiable events and challenges, as opposed to how certain policies emerge out of particular EU internal dynamics and instruments. The framework entails a focus on five themes: strategic adjustments to identifiable external challenges; external drivers of EU unity and discord; the EU's move away from being such a distinctive international power; a notion of protective security; and a reworked measure of EU influence over international events. These five themes form the spine of the book's thematic and geographical chapters.

Traditional analytical approaches

Three analytical approaches and debates have dominated the study of EU external action. While there are many other sub-branches of theoretical enquiry and analytical frameworks fixed on explaining very particular elements of EU external action, three broad areas of concern have been traditionally pre-eminent. These have focused on, respectively: internal EU convergence; distinctive EU power; and EU external governance.

Internal EU convergence

If at a policy level there has often been disappointment and frustration with the performance of European foreign policy coordination, much analytical work has focused on explaining the deepening of EU cooperation. From a variety of different theoretical perspectives, analysts have pointed to the EU's success in mitigating divergences between member states and EU institutions. The highly influential theoretical framework of liberal intergovernmentalism – rooted in a liberal theory of cooperation between states – holds that governments have seen enough value in cooperating for the EU to establish a notable presence in international affairs. It sees member state governments driving a process of coordination in external action as they perceive the rational value of combining their efforts and resources. Some theorists believe this kind of intergovernmental bargaining has led to the EU becoming a 'second superpower' in international relations and that rational interest calculations have led governments to find the right level of coordination to tackle foreign policy challenges.[1]

While the focus on national governments' primacy has been a mainstay for many years, most analytical work has explored the emergence of coordination dynamics beyond the strict control of and bargaining between national governments. Theorists refer to a number of different reasons for European-level foreign policy convergence and coordination. Some point to an internal process of ideational socialisation around certain cooperative security norms. Constructivist accounts of international relations seem especially relevant to the European Union as EU policy-makers' views and values have gradually been reshaped by regular interaction. Constructivists argue that such common EU policy identities have come to outweigh national calculations of narrow self-interest. For many years the fairly standard take on EU foreign policy has stressed how far such ideational convergence has propelled the Union towards a more united and influential global role.[2]

From a different, but overlapping analytical angle, institutionalist perspectives hold that states follow norms that have built up and embedded themselves in policy processes over time. Institutionalists emphasise how years of regularised processes of coordination have bred common outlooks between member states around rule-based international action and the EU's complex institutional processes have helped the formulation of such shared positions. The decades-long experience of coordination has created a cooperation reflex. National interests themselves are formulated with the European dimension in mind; agreeing European positions is itself part of the national interest calculus. Member states have regularised reciprocal compromise to ensure common positions.[3]

Some point to a dynamic of 'collective securitisation': the EU acts as a site of 'security governance' that shapes common perceptions of external strategic challenges. This goes beyond the chance coinciding of member state interests; it gives the EU institutions autonomous agency in defining the security agenda and influence in coalescing member state positions.[4] This helped ensure that EU foreign policy cooperation did not entirely wither away during the post-2009 economic crisis: the bloc's identity as a strongly embedded 'security community' was able to withstand economic divisions and keep the EU relatively united in foreign affairs even as the whole European project seemed to teeter on the brink of collapse.[5] All such arguments differ from what the standard realist international-relations framework would predict. The realist tradition has not been predominant in the study of European foreign policy cooperation and when analysts have formulated realist-inspired accounts it has been to cast doubt on the significance of EU foreign policy processes.[6] For realist thinkers EU external action in general remains a puzzling enigma.[7]

Distinctive power

A closely related, second strand of conceptual debate has been analysts' focus on describing and explaining why the EU wields a distinctive kind of power in international relations. A commonly held view among both analysts and diplomats is that the EU embodies a novel kind of international power. Over the years, writers have suggested many original terms and metaphors to capture this situation, describing the EU variously as a normative, civilian, soft or ethical power.[8] All such notions, which dominate the accumulated academic literature on European foreign policy, reflect the similar notion of the EU being a uniquely cosmopolitan, liberal power.

Analysts refer to a number of traits that make up this supposed identity. They assert that the EU wields power by example rather than by military might, and offers a fundamentally different vision of international relations, in particular compared to that pursued by the United States. The EU's approach to security has focused on promoting global public goods, or milieu rather than possession goals. EU foreign policy has worked on the belief that security is best pursued by assisting other states rather than by seeking more relational power over them. It is widely assumed that the EU has rejected standard forms of competitive, power-maximising geopolitics and has instead been drawn to security based on cooperative inclusion.

In this sense, the EU is often said to be a post-Westphalian actor as it does not act in accordance with conventions of national sovereignty and interests. The US may often support global deals on trade, security or human rights, but it habitually pursues such liberal end-goals through the instruments of geopolitical power. The EU has supported multilateral process as desirable in itself. The EU's core approach to global issues has been to search for 'settled frameworks' through which to pursue rule-based relationships with third countries.[9] It is often described as a post-modern power because its international actions are predicated on persuasion, cognitive change and the importance of law and rules. In part this distinctive external identity comes from the centrality of such principles to the EU's own existence and internal integration model.[10] A common view is that the EU has stood as a liberal power in an increasingly non-liberal world.[11] Sceptics argue that the EU uses this post-modern narrative simply because it has been unable to develop more powerful geopolitical strategies.[12]

Externalising the EU

A more precise follow-on from these concepts is the conviction that EU external action is based in large measure on the Union externalising its own rules and governance norms. This has generated a distinctive analytical perspective of EU 'external governance' – a form of influence that is very different from traditional concepts of power projection. This conceptualises EU external action and influence as being based on the outward extension of the Union's own internal legal rules. This kind of 'governance-power Europe' or 'functional-power Europe' conveys the notion of the EU effectively exporting very functional or technical rules and regulations to other countries.[13] A related concept of 'market-power Europe' holds that the 'EU most consequentially affects the international system by externalising its internal market-related policies and regulatory measures.'[14]

The EU's ability to extend the scope of its own area of shared governance rules gives it a series of foreign policy tools that standard nation-state powers do not have. The EU is able to get under the skin of third-country governments and alter the whole nature of their economic models, political systems and societal norms. This represents a 'structural' approach to foreign policy that contrasts with powers that seek 'relational' power gains over other countries. The EU uses its own norms and laws to develop rules and structures in and for other states that it believes provide the most sustainable means of security and stability.[15] This resonates with theories that highlight the roles played by 'transnational institutionalist' forms constitutive of the Union's internal forms of cooperation.[16]

These notions have been especially prominent in accounts of policies towards candidates for accession to the EU and other states that are part of the so-called European Neighbourhood Policy. Here, most analytical work on EU foreign policy has been on neighbouring countries' compliance with EU rules. The primary analytical focus has been on the factors that determine other societies' decisions to incorporate Union laws, standards and norms and undertake a process of 'Europeanisation'.[17] Others have argued that the EU's influence is also felt more globally through a 'Brussels effect' of EU regulations being taken up by governments, international organisations and companies around the world – and that this has become the most significant foundation of the Union's power and influence.[18] The EU is sometimes referred to as a 'regulatory superpower'.

In its use of these types of action, the EU has been memorably likened to a kind of neo-mediaeval empire that lacks a singular locus of sovereignty yet reproduces itself as it pursues its interests across other territories.[19] Critical theorists have long seen this external governance not so much as a benign project based on universal values and genuine help for other states to develop and reform, but more as a strategy to exert hegemony over other countries, against their own free will and context-specific models of governance. Post-structuralist critics see the EU's replication of its internal model as a means of imposing a form of 'governmentality' on other states – a very securitised form of surreptitious control over the Union's periphery on the basis of rules rather than brute power.[20]

An outside-in framework for the new normal

While these traditional approaches continue to offer essential insights, the broad arc of EU external action over time invites a reworked analytical lens. The analytical debates and approaches that have long dominated the study of EU external action – about internal coordination, distinctive EU identities and the spread of EU rules – continue to be important. However, they do not fully capture changes afoot in the current era. They need to be complemented – not replaced – by an alternative prism on EU external action. This book employs a conceptual framework that seeks to move the study of EU external action with the ethos of current policy imperatives. This framework reflects the way that global affairs have shifted, how EU policies have begun to adjust in response and how these emerging trends raise questions that are not fully at the forefront of the traditional approaches outlined above.

The framework is not a theory but more modestly presents a different way of approaching EU external action. It is a template that examines a different set of questions from those traditionally investigated. These are questions that home in on the external challenges, internationally important events, crises and exogenous trends that have increasingly crowded in on the EU and set its foreign-policy agenda. For shorthand it might be referred to as an outside-in conceptual framework, as it takes its lead from externally generated tests and imperatives. The framework does not directly contradict the traditional approaches above; it represents a shift in emphasis in what analytical work on EU external action must most importantly uncover and explain. Many studies have examined other countries' perceptions of the EU, but this is not the sense in which 'outside-in' is meant here.[21]

The framework's starting point is to unpack the principal *external challenges* facing the EU. Each thematic and geographical chapter that follows begins by outlining these challenges and explaining why they present novel and heightened tests for EU external action. The framework's core focus is on the EU's specific responses to these new kinds of external challenges. Instead of limiting itself to the EU's complex institutional trees it foregrounds the larger forest of shifting global trends and their ramifications for European interests.[22] In an effort to complement traditional approaches' focus on the processes of EU policy-making, the outside-in conceptual framework pays primary attention to whether EU foreign policy is becoming better attuned to global changes and emerging challenges.

Of course, the EU has always responded to external events and the international sphere has always presented difficult and evolving challenges. The EU has often been criticised for being too reactive to crises, rather than acting to pre-empt these. However, the conceptual framework used here proceeds from the assumption that external factors have become a more significant causal driver of EU policies. They have become more taxing, more numerous and, in many cases, more existential to European countries. As pointed out in Chapter 2, the 2016 EU Global Strategy claimed that EU security policy has become vital to the very survival of the European project itself.[23] Standard security threats have been compounded by so-called ontological insecurity that menaces European identities in the profoundest sense.[24]

This calls for something of an inversion in the traditional analytical approach to EU external action: instead of working outwards from *sui generis* internal EU dynamics, rather working inwards from the Union's external challenges. A number of analysts have acknowledged that the widening array of strategic challenges raises questions over the erstwhile imbalance towards 'inside-out' approaches.[25] Often the focus on complex internal dynamics between member states and the turf battles between different parts of the Union's institutional machinery has left articles on EU external action strikingly bereft of any coverage of emerging geopolitical factors.[26] Those writing from an institutionalist perspective have also argued for work able to explain how rooted institutional processes might facilitate externally driven change.[27]

The book's chapters show that a wide range of outside-in challenges have become more consequential in influencing EU external action and that they have triggered policy change in contrasting ways. One level of change is structural: there is no longer quite such a singular, all-embracing international order that safeguards European interests. The international order has fragmented into different sub-orders with unsettled and fractious dynamics. Alongside this the EU has lost relative weight in many domains, from hard security through to economic issues. A second level of predicament comes from more specific but cross-cutting thematic challenges – economic nationalism, migration, climate and energy constraints, recrudescent authoritarianism. And at a third level are individual crises like the ongoing conflicts across the Middle East and Russian actions in Ukraine. The chapters that follow unpack these three different levels of externally generated change, from the overarching structural shifts in international order, to cross-cutting themes and then through to conjunctural country and regional crises.

The outside-in conceptual framework highlights how these external challenges have driven both greater unity and, in some areas, more national self-help strategies. It situates the evolution of these long-present twin dynamics – *convergence and divergence* – more centrally within the changed external environment. Many writers argue that changes to the international system have increasingly pulled European governments in different directions and left the EU a less united, self-enclosed foreign policy system.[28] EU external action has become increasingly 'politicised' as technocratic policy rooted in consensual, internal norms has given way to higher-profile, sharper contestation over security imperatives.[29] Prominent theorists point to a general drift back towards intergovernmental dynamics, with member states pushing their own initiatives and preferences at the European level in a way that strains unity.[30] In the last several years, the importance has grown of small subsets of member states pursuing separate aims outside the channels of EU coordination.[31]

However, others detect more convergent trends: precisely because the international order is changing shape and power is shifting to non-Western powers a stronger motive has developed for deeper coordination on external action.[32] Some argue that while member states have taken hold of some external issues, the External Action Service has gradually developed autonomy to advance more united policies.[33] The new normal of international politics is both pulling European governments together and driving them part. Some of the main anchors of European unity are slipping away while others actually become weightier. The conceptual framework deployed through the book adds precision by highlighting where intra-European unity has deepened and where, in contrast, discrepancies and nationally separate policies have become more significant.

As it charts EU responses to emergent challenges, the conceptual framework focuses on uncovering how the Union no longer functions as quite such a *distinctive power*. It moves beyond uncritical assumptions that the EU's own integration project gives it robust enough soft power to further core foreign and security-policy interests. As the integration model has suffered internally during the last decade, it no longer has such an exalted or venerated appeal outside Europe. Functional approaches may exist in a small number of areas like trade, certain technical

regulations and enlargement, but very different and more strategic modes of operation have increasingly appeared in other dimensions of EU external action.[34] The
book's thematic and geographical chapters shed light on how the EU has come to
pursue geopolitical action of a more standard kind. For a long time, there was an
aversion to the power calculations of geopolitics among both EU policy-makers and
analysts of EU external action; many observers have increasingly recognised this as
a weakness that needs correcting.[35]

Many aspects of internal EU politics and the much-debated populist surge in
recent years have sat uneasily with the bloc's traditionally liberal foreign policy
identity.[36] Against this backdrop, the outside-in conceptual framework avoids
studying the EU as a qualitatively superior form of superpower in the making. It
offers a careful examination of what remains distinctive about actual EU policies
and what in its external action has become more normalised. It highlights an
emerging relationship between liberal norms and EU geopolitics that is varied
across different crises and thematic challenges; it helps understand how such
norms have become instrumentalised rather than seen as an intrinsic part of EU
external identities.

Flowing from this, the outside-in conceptual framework explores the EU's adop-
tion of a more *protective* approach towards its immediate interests. The ethos has
become one of protecting internal European security and stability as opposed to
the EU remoulding conditions outside its borders with a view to longer-term and
more diffuse benefits. It moves at least partly beyond the criterion of EU transformative power – the notion that the EU is able to fundamentally remodel other
countries and societies as the leading edge of its external influence. The supposedly
quintessential EU aversion to power politics rubs uneasily with the rise of a more
tightly securitised external agenda, again requiring analytical perspectives that
pay more attention to the way the Union's external action has sought to protect
direct, material interests.[37]

Traditional approaches have commonly assessed fairly generic EU identities and
values more than the Union's concrete deployment of power resources to protect
its interests in immediate ways.[38] The book seeks to correct this by focusing on
what it terms 'protective security'. It situates this concern with protection within
big-picture debates about the kinds of geopolitical dynamics that have become
more prominent in contemporary international relations.[39] The outside-in conceptual framework homes in on explaining how the EU has responded to external challenges and how it has begun to fashion an approach towards geopolitics tailored to
protecting specific interests. This reworks the traditional exploration of 'interests
versus values' as it rather compares immediate protective interests with more diffuse longer-range interests; the framework uncovers how the EU's priorities have
tilted towards the former.

As part of all these shifts, the outside-in framework also approaches the question of EU *influence* in a different manner. It takes on board the fact that the Union's
impact has come to assume more measured and modest proportions. This is not to
dismiss the EU's importance or to suggest that its main policies have uniformly
failed. Rather it is to recognise that a conceptually updated lens is needed to evaluate the EU's effectiveness as an international actor. Prominent writers have

suggested that in the future the EU's impact will need to be measured simply as one set of influences among many in global affairs, devoid of any particularly special power or transformational potential.[40]

The EU's long present concern has been with exerting the leverage of a major power – and, most recently, with measuring its sources of influence against those of the US and China, and, to some extent, Russia. Yet measuring impact and effectiveness in this sense has become more complex, in a world in which the whole nature of power has changed in important ways. Simply reaching a common EU position on a given topic may no longer be quite as consequential as it was assumed to be in the past.[41] Moreover, the EU may continue to shape events in the rest of the world, but will also be increasingly shaped by other powers' more assertive and active foreign policies. All this calls for a reshaped framework for measuring its influence as an international actor.

Box 3.1 An outside-in conceptual framework

Five analytical concerns:

External challenges – a stronger driver of EU external action.

Different levels of external driver	Overarching structural shifts
	Cross-cutting thematic challenges: economic nationalism, migration, climate change, energy constraints, authoritarianism
	Specific crises – Syria, Libya, Ukraine and others.

Unity–diversity dynamics – how external challenges have driven new areas of unity, but also divergence.

Distinctive power identities – how the EU has moved to adopt less distinctive forms of external action.

Protective dynamics – how EU external action has centred in on a more protective form of security and interest calculation.

EU influence – how the degree and form of EU influence over international issues have changed.

Conclusion

In sum, the outside-in framework incorporates five strands of analytical focus: external challenges; external drivers of unity and difference; loss of EU distinctiveness; protective security calculations; and reshaped measures of EU power. Box 3.1 offers a schematic snapshot of the framework, as an accessible reference point for the way that the book's chapters are framed. In a very general sense, the outside-in conceptual framework chimes with and seeks to advance some of the overarching concerns that have emerged in the study of EU external action in recent years.

Marrying traditional approaches with this updated framework defines the contemporary analytical challenges for studies of EU external action. Experts have called for greater methodological pluralism, embracing a combination of realist, rationalist, constructivist, intergovernmental, geopolitical and other dynamics that are all germane in different ways to EU foreign and security policy – and they have insisted that such composite approaches must look beyond the EU's *sui generis* features and the longstanding tendency to think that focusing on these suffices for an analysis of European external action.[42] Moving beyond a focus on EU policy-making processes and rules is necessary to develop mid-range explanations of the Union's evolving role in international security.[43] The book takes up these injunctions and explores in detail their policy and analytical implications.

PART II
THEMES

4 Navigating the Reshaped International Order

Moving on to the EU's thematic challenges, this chapter examines the Union's approach to global order. It shows the EU's enduring commitment to the liberal international order, while also highlighting its shift towards a more selective and flexible support of multilateral norms. The post-war liberal order has faced threats both from non-Western powers and changes in US foreign policy. The EU has come to position and present itself as the main champion and upholder of the liberal international order. At the same time, in recent years the EU's own record on upholding this order has been far from perfect. During the 2010s the EU became a more selective and instrumental liberal-multilateralist. This was seen in the Union's evolving policies towards the United States, China and other rising powers. The outside-in conceptual framework helps identify and evaluate these core policy changes. It shows that beneath the standard EU narrative about the pivotal importance of defending multilateralism, European views on the future of global order have remoulded themselves to a dynamic of protective self-interest.

The challenges

In its most all-embracing external challenge, the EU has had to adjust to a reshaped global order. What analysts commonly term the 'liberal international order' that Western powers designed and oversaw after the Second World War has long been the structural bedrock of EU foreign policy. The foundations of this order have been weakening for a significant number of years. While definitions differ, the liberal international order is generally taken to refer to the prominent influence of multilateral institutions and norms; open markets and trade liberalisation; cooperative approaches to security; and support for human rights and democratic values. Governments around the world have increasingly questioned and defied these norms.

The prevalent view among experts is that the liberal international order has gradually given way to a system based far more on self-help geopolitical power, with non-Western powers attaching priority to relative power gains over multilateral rules.[1] Non-Western powers have increasingly had the confidence and leverage to resist Western norms and policies. Many countries' actions have begun to undermine international law in multiple policy areas. In particular, China has used its rising power to challenge many of the long-established norms of global order and in many sectors set up its own initiatives outside existing multilateral institutions. Its Belt and Road Initiative has become a vast network exerting powerful influence over scores of countries crucial to European strategic interests – see Figure 4.1. Some experts insist that China has fashioned a diplomacy that rejects the whole

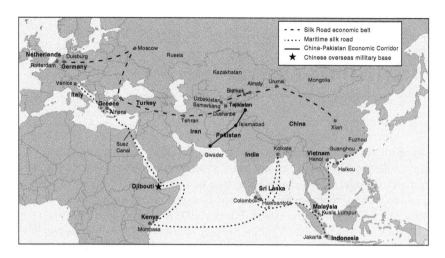

Figure 4.1 China's Belt and Road Initiative
Source: www.gisreportsonline.com

concept of universal rules and that the West has been forced to adapt to China's notion of global order far more than the other way round.[2] Some insist that an interregnum between the Western-run liberal order and a successor order is now dominated by fierce self-help state strategies, as powers jostle for geopolitical advantage in setting new terms for the future global system.[3]

An increasingly common argument is that Western governments must focus more on protecting their own immediate interests and projecting the power capable of achieving this end.[4] Global trends push Western governments towards 'thinner' multilateral commitments that include only the most basic of rules.[5] What the West frames as liberal 'solidarism', others have increasingly seen as the coercive enforcement of Western, including European, self-interest – and this pushback has progressively weakened globally accepted principles of order.[6] Such dynamics have become especially significant in relation to the new geopolitical structures spanning the Eurasian land mass, as Russia, Turkey, India, China and others have all sought greater control over this vitally important area.[7]

The threat to liberal international order intensified dramatically as President Trump revamped the US's international position after 2016. While there were doubts about the US's commitment to multilateralism under previous administrations, Trump's assault on international order was of a different order. After 2016 the US administration stepped away from or rejected important international agreements. To the extent that the US had for decades underpinned the liberal order, this was deeply problematic for EU powers. After elections at the end of 2020 President-elect Joe Biden promised more constructive international engagement, although doubts remained over many elements of the US's commitment to multilateral rules. More broadly, the COVID-19 pandemic shook the foundations of global order as it drew power further away from a chaotic and retrenched US, sharpened US–China rivalry and prompted many other states to turn fearfully inwards.[8]

Other readings of changes to global order have been more nuanced. Some experts contend that rising powers have not existentially threatened the liberal world order, but rather sought more influence in running the institutions that make up this order. Some argue that the end of Western hegemony opens the way to a more balanced global order that allows a wider range of powers to co-shape multilateralism.[9] A more varied order is taking shape, mixing liberal and illiberal elements. Moreover the very nature of order is changing as power has shifted away not just from Western states, but from states per se towards other actors.[10] The new order has become more polycentric, drawing dynamism from increased social empowerment and interconnections.[11] State-based international relations has given way to multi-actor world politics.[12]

Defending liberal order

For many years, the EU has been strongly invested in the liberal international order and many of its core approaches to security have been heavily dependent upon it. The EU underpinned liberal order as part of its own core, founding identity. The EU was prominent in its support for many of the key advances of the multilateral architecture, including the Nuclear Non-proliferation Treaty, the Human Rights Council and the International Criminal Court, and provided about half the UN's budget. From an early stage, European governments saw support for multilateral organisations as a natural extension of the same principles that informed the EU integration project itself.[13]

The 2003 European Security Strategy declared the principle of 'effective multi-lateralism' to be the guiding tenet of EU foreign policy. During the 2010s, the EU gradually improved its coordination in international organisations.[14] At the same time, less positive elements of EU multilateralism emerged in this period. European states reduced their contributions to UN peacekeeping missions and sought to put a brake on UN reform proposals that would reduce the EU's overall weight and presence in different parts of the UN machinery. The Eurozone crisis also placed an enormous strain on international financial institutions.

As the 2010s progressed and the changes in global order accelerated, the EU reinforced its formal commitments to multilateralism. The Union adopted relatively tough measures in response to Russia's annexation of Crimea and incursions into eastern Ukraine in 2014. Chapter 12 covers this matter in detail; it suffices to note here that the EU forswore full partnership with Russia due to order-related tensions. It did not completely break off engagement with Russia and towards the end of the decade some member states – France and Germany in particular – explored ways of renewing strategic dialogue with Russia. However, in broad terms the EU's worries over the state of rules-based order led it into a Russia strategy based at least in part on more assertive containment.

The EU increased its funding to some UN bodies as it came out of the Eurozone crisis.[15] The 2016 Global Strategy stated that: 'The EU will promote a rules-based global order with multilateralism as its key principle and the United Nations at its core.'[16] At the end of her term as High Representative in 2019, Federica Mogherini insisted that the EU's support for multilateralism was now stronger than ever before. She listed as evidence the bloc's support for climate change negotiations, an agreement on Iran's nuclear capabilities, beefed-up treaties on arms control, a stronger World Trade Organisation, the 2030 agenda for sustainable development and cooperation with regional bodies.[17] Mogherini claimed: 'we are by our very nature a cooperative partner'.[18] The EU's New Strategic Agenda agreed in 2019 promised a stronger commitment to 'rules-based international order'.[19]

This positioning has been integral not only at the EU level but also with regard to member states' policies. The defence of global order has been a particularly prominent element of German foreign policy. In 2018, Germany launched a new Alliance for Multilateralism. This gathered medium-sized powers in defence of the international order. German foreign minister Heiko Maas explained that this was 'an association of states convinced of the benefits of multilateralism, who believe in international cooperation and the rule of law'.[20] France joined the effort and in 2019 the Alliance for Multilateralism launched at the UN as a joint Franco-German initiative, with around 50 states initially signed up and a stated aim of defending and extending multilateral arrangements.[21]

The COVID-19 pandemic led EU leaders to call for stronger global governance.[22] European leaders backed globally coordinated recovery plans through the G7 and the G20 and supported UN and World Bank emergency plans in the poorest developing countries. They advocated stronger global governance in relation to pandemic management, including enhanced powers for the World Health Organisation. Indeed, EU leaders shifted to stress the health, climate and social elements of multilateralism more than the economic aspects of global order. Germany convened the UN Security Council to discuss a 'security and pandemics' initiative and mobilised the new Alliance for Multilateralism for emergency coordination.[23] The European Commission coordinated an international pledging conference in an attempt to lead a multilateral response to the pandemic and then funded the international Covax facility for vaccine development. It also launched a new strategy to boost multilateral cooperation against Covid-related disinformation.[24]

Qualified multilateralist

Notwithstanding all these commitments, from the late 2000s the EU began to shift towards a less purist vision of multilateralism. It began to seek more concrete and immediate results from international cooperation, as opposed to the diffuse and generic benefits of a global system based on predictable and constraining rules.[25] European leaders insisted that this shift was not about undercutting multilateralism but finding ways of ensuring it delivered.[26] While other powers' attacks on global order in some ways made the EU more determined to defend multilateralism, the new context also gave European perspectives on order a more protective feel and tone.

For all its familiar language on rules-based order, the 2016 Global Strategy was framed around a far thinner form of liberal order. The strategy's central concept of 'principled pragmatism' seemed to portend harder-edged EU external action less concerned with the well-being of the global system. In line with this, the notion of 'strategic autonomy' gained prominence, mainly as a prompt to defence and security capacities separate from multilateral operations. Diplomats talked of a shift from 'effective multilateralism' to 'post-multilateralist' notions of order. Taking office as High Representative, Josep Borrell listed 'realism' as his top guiding strategic principle.[27] By 2020 the EU's promise to be more 'geopolitical' sowed uncertainty over its commitment to multilateral order; the new discourse certainly implied a tilt towards more visceral power politics. Borrell explained the emerging aim was 'to act multilaterally if we can, autonomously if we must'.[28]

Member-state politicians have also adapted their discourse. While promoting notions of multilateral alliance, Heiko Maas stressed that the EU needed a sharper 'geopolitical identity'.[29] German Chancellor Angela Merkel argued that the EU needed to 'reposition itself' strategically to protect its interests.[30] In a widely cited speech in 2019, Dutch prime minister Mark Rutte argued: 'The EU needs a reality check; power is not a dirty word. Realpolitik must be an essential part of Europe's foreign policy toolkit. Because if we only preach the merits of principles and shy away from exercising power in the geopolitical arena, our continent may always be right, but it will seldom be relevant.'[31] Also in 2019, President Macron insisted that the EU 'needs to become sovereign once again and to rediscover a form of realpolitik ... We need to equip ourselves with the grammar of today, which is a grammar of power and sovereignty.'[32]

The EU's new tone internationally was also related to its own internal difficulties.[33] The populist surge that has dominated politics in many member states has had an impact on external strategies: the EU's internal illiberal drift has bred a primary concern with 'ontological security' that sits uneasily with the Union's claim to be last defender of the liberal international order.[34] Those turning to vote for illiberal populists have also become more hostile to the open global liberal order.[35] National governments have increasingly seen international order questions through such 'national lenses' and in terms of carefully calibrated cost–benefit political calculations.[36]

In many areas, EU support to the UN has diminished or become more conditional. Other chapters in the book show this in detail with regard to trade, energy and human rights policies; other examples can be more briefly mentioned here. Figure 4.2 shows the downward trend in European governments' share of the UN

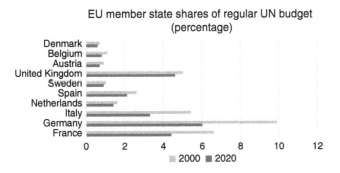

Figure 4.2 European commitments to UN budget
Source: United Nations

operating budget. Each year since 2015 EU states have contributed only 5–7 per cent of the troops deployed in UN peacekeeping missions; Ireland launched an initiative in 2018 with five other small member states to try to reverse the decline in such commitments.[37] European aid has drifted apart from the multilateral norms underpinning the Sustainable Development Goals towards more security-oriented funding.[38] Nine EU countries – Central and Eastern European states, plus Austria and Italy – did not support a 2019 UN Migration Pact.[39] While the EU has supported UN reform, with France and the UK backing changes to the UN Security Council, European governments have also sought to hang on to their own over-representation. Other countries were highly critical when EU governments insisted in 2019 that Christine Lagarde's successor as IMF director-general was another European; Bulgarian Kristalina Georgieva was eventually appointed. Other powers have increasingly seen such stances as a distortion of genuine liberal order.[40]

The EU has looked for ways around the impasse that many multilateral institutions have suffered in recent years. At the end of the 2010s, the EU staked out a 'variable geometry multilateralism' under which it would support different coalitions on different issues – a 'smart multilateralism' based on a new balance between 'flexibility and inclusivity'.[41] It has supported an increasing number of these kinds of plurilateral arrangements in sectors like health, arms control, internet governance and trade as a pragmatic and fluid way of keeping international cooperation afloat.[42] The EU advanced cyber-security norms through minilateral groupings with the US and others, causing some friction with China, Russia, India and Brazil who tried to introduce new multilateral rules at the United Nations.[43] President Macron launched an initiative on internet trust and safety with around 50 governments; France developed this separate from established multilateral organisations, then placed its operational management under UN structures. Macron argued that the EU needed far more of these 'alliances of convenience, alliances that are tactical … subject-dependent'.[44] Fitting this kind of model, in 2020 the UK proposed a 'D10' initiative that aimed to have ten democracies – the G7 plus Australia, India and South Korea – combine to push back against Chinese digital technology.[45]

While calling for stronger multilateralism in response to the COVID-19 pandemic, in practice EU member states foregrounded nationally preferential responses. Few elements of their emergency plans were coordinated at the European, let alone global level. The EU and member states professed solidarity with other countries but declined to increase external aid, in contrast to the huge hike in internal resources that was forthcoming to mitigate the pandemic's impact. Macron insisted that the pandemic forced a 'rethink of multilateralism' and called for an approach that combined 'more health multilateralism, more political multilateralism' with more national sovereignty and strategic autonomy.[46] In a new strategy for multilateralism introduced in early 2021, the EU promised a more 'interests-based approach' to liberal order. If 'strategic autonomy' was first conceived in relation to the EU undertaking its own defence and security missions, it has gradually been raised to the level of a wider guiding principle for COVID-era EU external action[47]. EU states adopted a protective stance as the pandemic opened an era of competitive 'biopolitics'. Box 4.1 details EU responses to the pandemic.

Box 4.1 External dimensions of COVID-19

As European leaders called for strengthened global governance and international cooperation in the COVID-19 emergency, so the EU released several layers of support related to the pandemic. European governments and the Commission offered support for G20, World Bank and IMF coordination to help economic recovery on a global level, with the aim of strengthening multilateral action on this priority. They likewise supported the UN's call for a global ceasefire in conflicts around the world.

In an example of functional minilateralism seeking to circumvent US–China rivalry, France, Germany, Italy and the UK teamed up with Brazil, Canada, Indonesia, Mexico, Morocco, Peru, Korea, Singapore and Turkey in a 13-state group to deepen international COVID-19 coordination.

The Commission put together an initial 15.6 billion-euro aid package. This comprised 500 million euros for immediate emergency relief, 3 billion to strengthen health systems in hard-hit countries and 12 billion to mitigate the economic impact across the developing world. The EU then offered another 3 billion euros of loans for macro-economic assistance to countries in its neighbourhood, with most of this going to Ukraine, Tunisia and several Balkan states.

Most member states redirected their bilateral aid towards emergency support for the pandemic – including a French contribution of over 1 billion euros.[48] Emergency aid was coordinated under a 'Team Europe' single framework made up of Commission, member states, European Bank for Reconstruction and Development and European Investment Bank resources.

In May 2020, the Commission hosted a pledging conference that raised 7.5 billion euros, mainly aimed at spurring the development of a vaccine. European pledges included 1.5 billion euros from France, 500 million from Germany, 450 million from the UK, 200 million from the Netherlands, 125 million from Spain and smaller amounts under 100 million from Denmark, Italy, Finland and Sweden.[49] Over the second half of 2020, the Commission released several tranches of support to the multilateral Covax facility, eventually totalling 500 million euros.

Notwithstanding all this, the EU response also illustrated the limits to multilateral and global governance commitments. The emergency aid consisted almost entirely of resources repurposed from other programmes, not new funds. The Commission's 1 billion-euro package announced at the May pledging conference was money 're-prioritised' from other aid funds; the same was true for most member state commitments too. With the exception of the UK, Germany and Sweden, European contributions to the WHO remained relatively low and few stepped forward with significant pledges to the World Food Programme's emergency campaign.[50]

The US dilemma

The EU's support for the liberal international order was forged in the shadow of the US's underwriting of that order. The EU provided a secondary support to the US's ostensibly lead sponsorship of the post-war international liberal order. This equation began to fray from the mid-2000s. The US veered towards more unilateral actions in a number of spheres during the administration of George W. Bush. From 2008, Barack Obama's presidency saw only partial correction of the Bush years in this respect. The EU saw Obama's administration as very selectively multilateral, while the Obama team believed they often failed to obtain sufficient European support for key order-related challenges. On some such challenges the EU provided back-up support to the US, on others it opposed US outlooks, while on many it mapped a subtly different concept of international order from that of the US. The transatlantic dynamic became one of competitive cooperation.[51]

Tensions deepened during the late 2010s. While not all order-related transatlantic differences originated with President Trump, his presidency fundamentally changed the EU strategic calculus. The risk was of the US becoming a zero-sum competitor to European powers in strategic affairs. European governments grappled with the question of whether the US was moving from being an anchoring security-protector to a security problem. US ambivalence over multilateralism galvanised the EU to move up a gear in its own commitments to international order. The EU increasingly insisted it was now the primary defender of the beleaguered liberal order partly because of the shift in US foreign policy; this refrain became a mainstay of much European geostrategic discourse. The EU's commitments to deepen defence coordination (covered in Chapter 7) and to uphold the international agreement on Iran's nuclear programme (examined in Chapter 11) were both driven in large measure by the US's changed strategic trajectory.

Unsurprisingly perhaps, member states' readings of the US dilemma were far from identical. For some in the EU, this was a watershed change that required the bloc to move apart from the US as the latter ceased to be a fully committed ally. Many European governments rhetorically stressed that they no longer saw the US as a reliable partner or guarantor of the liberal order. Others held back from taking a confrontational approach too far. Central and Eastern European states benefitted from the US's new $7 billion European Deterrence Initiative; from their perspective, the US did not seem to be such a fast-retreating global ally. During his time in government in 2018 and 2019, Lega party leader Mateo Salvini expressly sought to position Italy as the US's 'closest partner' in Europe, insisting he saw world order challenges in the same way as President Trump.[52] Dutch prime minister Marc Rutte argued that the EU should harness Trump's disruptive style to push reforms to global institutions necessary for the Union's own interests.[53] Some states' desire to bandwagon on US policies was stronger than their commitment to develop a fully autonomous foreign policy capable of challenging the US.[54]

The French position in this debate was intriguing. President Macron initially tried to build constructive cooperation with Trump. Security and counter-terrorist coordination between France and the United States deepened and on issues like North Korea and Iran the French government shared many of the US's concerns.

Yet an increasingly frustrated Macron then became the most vocal advocate of more autonomy from the US. In what became one of the most dissected statements of recent years, in November 2019 Macron derided NATO as 'brain-dead'.[55] Germany and other member states responded testily that strategic partnership with the US continued to be a necessary fulcrum of European security. Brexit added a further complication: the UK has on some issues veered towards a more transactional rapprochement with the US, undercutting EU order-maintenance goals, yet on many big strategic questions has remained closer to EU than US positions.

The EU has increasingly mixed elements of the two approaches – balancing and bandwagoning. It sought to hedge on whether Trump's 2016–2020 term was an anomaly or the start of a long-term trend. The EU countered Trump with both its own more directly transactional diplomacy and a more rules-based playbook – an uneasy balance of strategic logics.[56] Joe Biden's election victory in November 2020 opened the prospect of a return to more cooperative transatlantic relations and the EU quickly offered a new 'EU-US Agenda for Global Change' oriented towards defence of the liberal international order. Still, tensions and uncertainties remained at this stage. Increasingly, the EU has tried to confront the US on some issues while maintaining a core framework of cooperation. Member states have differed over the feasibility of the EU being able to shore up the liberal order without clear US leadership. The evolution in US policy has been a catalyst for the EU's reinforced commitment to liberal order but also helps explain its more selective and instrumental approach to multilateral norms.

China as rival-partner

If the EU has had to work hard to adjust to changes in US policies, it has faced an equally thorny challenge in relation to China. Since the 1990s, the EU's stated aim was to include China more fully within networks of international cooperation to bolster support for the global order. In practice, the EU and member state governments focused more on their commercial relations with China than on order-related strategic considerations. The EU slowly and belatedly began to redress this imbalance as by the 2010s China's centrality became even more evident not just to economic interests but to the whole shape and redefinition of international politics. The EU has gradually developed a tighter and more highly prioritised focus on order-maintenance considerations in its relations with China. Other chapters of this book deal specifically with the trade, climate-change and human rights elements of the EU–China relationship; here it is germane to note the EU's overarching approach to China as it relates to international order.

The EU signed a trade and cooperation agreement with China in 1985. After the Chinese regime cracked down against student democracy protestors in Tiananmen Square in 1989, the EU imposed sanctions. In the early 1990s, it removed all critical measures, with the exception of an arms embargo. After this the EU's strategy was one of broadly positive engagement. As the 1990s and 2000s unfolded, the Union introduced a large of number of initiatives to promote trade and investment and business links with China. It raised the level and regularity of dialogue; annual

EU–China summits began in 1998. The EU supported China's accession into the WTO in 2001, agreeing terms for this more readily and quickly than did the United States. While this step was motivated in large measure by trade interests, the EU also justified it as reinforcing China's stake in multilateral rules. In 1996, the EU launched its flagship diplomatic initiative for Asia, the so-called ASEM (Asia–Europe Meeting) process. This grouped China together with other Asian powers, again with the intent of enticing the Chinese regime into regional cooperation programmes. In 2003 the EU offered one of its select, flagship Strategic Partnerships with China.

Talks on a new EU–China Partnership and Cooperation Agreement started in 2007, but did not advance far because of differences over market access, human rights and the EU's refusal to lift its arms embargo. The EU instead offered high-level strategic and commercial dialogues, and these developed some momentum as the EU diluted its preconditions on deeper cooperation with China.[57] In the early 2010s, many member states focused on their need for Chinese funding to help mitigate the Eurozone debt crisis. China did not confront the EU as directly as Russia did; it clearly took advantage of the Union's successive crises for its own benefit but cooperated on shoring up the basic economic elements of order during the financial crisis.

In 2013 an EU–China 2020 Strategic Agenda for Cooperation set out goals for deepening the relationship and in the years that followed the EU added many sector dialogues with China, including on security issues. In addition to leaders' summits, European and Chinese foreign affairs ministers met more regularly. On some order-related issues the EU and China began to align their positions – the Iran nuclear deal, anti-piracy and multilateral peacekeeping operations being cases in point.[58] Most European governments supported China's Asian Infrastructure Investment Bank initiative and managed to get Beijing to bring this at least partially into line with multilateral development norms. The EU engaged China in more systematic dialogue about how the two actors might cooperate on regional order issues in places like Africa.[59] Table 4.1 shows the evolution over time of the various EU–China accords.

Table 4.1 Key EU–China agreements and milestones

	1985 Trade and Cooperation Agreement
	1996 ASEM, includes China
	2003 EU Strategic Partnership with China
	2007 Talks on new Partnership and Cooperation agreement – not concluded
	2013 EU–China 2020 Strategic Agenda
	2016 EU–China Strategy
	2019 EU–China Strategic Outlook
	2020 Comprehensive Agreement on Investment

Some European messaging on China has gradually hardened, albeit inconsistently. In March 2019, the EU published what was widely seen as a landmark document in which it labelled China a 'systemic rival' and criticised its increasing tendency to undercut global rules. It noted that while on some order-related issues China was 'a cooperation partner with whom the EU has closely aligned objectives' the Union needed to focus more assertively on the fact that its 'engagement in favour of multilateralism is sometimes selective'.[60] The following week, Federica Mogherini described China in more positive terms as a 'comprehensive strategic partner' and held an EU–China Strategic Dialogue.[61] In April 2019, the EU and China then held a leaders' summit, at which some European leaders adopted a tougher position on order-related norms. President Macron said after this summit: 'The period of European naivety is over.'[62] Macron, Angela Merkel and Jean-Claude Juncker then combined forces at a meeting with President Xi in Paris, reinforcing the pressure for China to work with Europe to defend global order.

The reorientation of Germany's position was especially significant. In the 2010s Germany pursued deeper and more positive engagement with China than other member states, setting up more than 80 bilateral strands of cooperation with Beijing. Yet even Germany has begun to express deep concern about Chinese attacks on multilateral norms. The UK seemed to move in the opposite direction, promoting what it called a Golden Era in British–Chinese relations and in 2015 signing a Global Comprehensive Strategic Partnership. Its focus was narrowly on commercial gain, neither fully taking advantage of China's interest in strengthening some areas of the global order – like on climate change and non-proliferation – nor pushing back in those areas where China was trying to undermine multilateral norms.[63] China's so-called '16 plus 1' trade and investment initiative with Central and Eastern European states compounded divisions between these countries and those member states wanting a more robust China strategy; this became the 17-plus-1 forum when Greece joined in 2019 and China apparently upgraded its importance when President Xi attended its 2020 annual meeting.

European strategy increasingly had to factor in the shifting nature of the US's China policy under President Trump. In a remarkable turn, on some occasions the EU seemed to align with China against the United States. In 2018, when President Trump criticised the multilateral order at several summits, EU and Chinese responses were similar. On other occasions, the EU seemed to ride the coattails of Trump's more belligerent approach to China. The Dutch government, for example, argued that the EU should do more to take advantage of the US's newly toughened pressure on China.[64] President Macron initially tried to convince Trump to join forces against China, before drifting to a position of seeking more autonomy from both.[65] The EU has sought to ride two horses. It has eschewed the talk of 'decoupling' from China that has grown in some US policy circles and has sometimes focused on encouraging China to play a more prominent role in upholding global rules as a counterbalance to the drift in US policy. At other times, the Union has backed up the US's efforts to bear down on China's threat to multilateral rules. When the US secretary of state Mike Pompeo called for an 'alliance of democracies' to coordinate policies towards China, EU states were not enthusiastic; however, the External Action Service and US State Department then launched a regular dialogue process in October 2020 better to coordinate positions on China.

As the COVID-19 pandemic intensified geopolitical tensions between the United States and China, this arguably became the EU's most defining strategic question. The Union became even more exasperated with the Trump administration as it rejected efforts to spur multilateral health cooperation. Yet events related to the COVID-19 pandemic also hardened some European perspectives on China. China was heavy-handed in its anti-Western messaging over the virus and in its use of disinformation. Perhaps the sharpest European adjustment came from the UK undertaking a far-reaching reappraisal of its cooperation with China. Still, the EU and China cooperated on shoring up the WHO and on the Covax facility in the face of Trump's hostility.[66] While Josep Borrell called for a more 'robust' and 'less naïve' approach towards China, he also insisted that the EU must not be forced to 'choose sides' in the US–China rivalry.[67] At the end of 2020, the EU and China concluded a Comprehensive Agreement on Investment they had been negotiating for seven years. Biden's election victory generated relief but also some internal EU differences over how much importance should be given to rebuilding transatlantic relations; most European leaders concurred that the Union still needed to craft strategic autonomy from both the US and China, as a structural imperative that transcended the difficulties of the Trump years.

Cooperation with other powers

As the task of upholding the liberal order has become more onerous, the EU has intensified its efforts to build strategic partnerships with non-Western, rising powers. In the early 2000s the EU signed a number of so-called strategic partnerships with other powers across the world – Brazil, Canada, Japan, India, Mexico, South Africa and South Korea, in addition to China and the US. These strategic partnerships went under different names and were extremely varied in ambition and content. Yet in their inception the EU seemed to be acknowledging that it needed to do a lot more to defend international order and in particular that it needed a more targeted and tailored set of alliances to do so.[68]

These strategic partnerships in practice remained focused on bilateral relations and were devoid of meaningful cooperation on order-related challenges; most of them fell into de facto abeyance.[69] Under the ASEM process, the EU developed a number of fairly uncontroversial strands of cooperation with Asian rising powers on issues such as connectivity, but cooperation did not advance on order-related strategic issues.[70] Acknowledging it had made negligible progress on such cooperation with non-Western powers, as the 2010s progressed the EU pursued an upgraded series of global partnerships with a smaller number of countries more clearly linked to its concern with protecting the liberal international order.

The gear-change in EU cooperation was especially significant with Japan. In 2018, the EU and Japan concluded a free trade accord and added to this a Strategic Partnership Agreement whose aims were expressly targeted at preserving a rules-based international system. The EU has upgraded cooperation with Japan more in recent years than in many previous decades, now seeing the country as a bulwark against Chinese and other threats to rules-based order. The EU–Japan trade agreement was the first to include formalised and joint commitments to uphold the Paris climate agreement, reflecting a stronger desire to use trade accords to shore up liberal order more broadly. Cooperation between the EU and Japan on defending digital rights – implicitly with Chinese interference in mind – was one of the first fruits of the new accord. While the signing of the accord was strategically important, there was some feeling on both sides that the substantive follow-up was modest.

The EU and India signed a strategic partnership in 2004, but this delivered few foreign policy results. In late 2018, the EU agreed a new India strategy. This committed the two sides to enhanced dialogue on global issues and deeper coordination to underpin rules-based global order. The strategy promised EU cooperation to increase India's strategic engagement in regions like the Middle East and Africa. It committed to a more regular and upgraded Strategic Dialogue, multi-level coordination on foreign policy issues, new links between Europol and Indian law enforcement institutions, and joint initiatives on peacekeeping. It proposed new military-to-military ties and a joint 'platform' on counter-terrorism and threat assessment.[71] In early 2019, EU military representatives for the first time visited Delhi to talk to Indian officials about defence and maritime security cooperation. The Indian navy started a coordination exercise with the EU's Operation Atalanta off the coast of Somalia.

The EU has deepened and expanded several other partnerships across Asia. The EU–South Korea partnership has become more extensive and strategic. An EU–Indonesia Security and Defence Partnership has slowly gained momentum. The EU–ASEAN relationship was upgraded to a Strategic Partnership in 2020. The EU also developed its alternative to China's Belt and Road Initiative. It sold this to Asian partners as a rules-based framework that offered protection against crude Chinese power strategies, although it was a modest effort when set alongside the amount of funding flowing through China's initiative and the 140-plus states signed up to it.[72] Member states have formed their own bilateral partnerships across Asia as well. France introduced a new 'Indo-Pacific strategy' in 2018 that promised deeper cooperation in particular with Australia and India as a counterweight to US–China rivalry. Germany established bilateral, strategic partnerships with Vietnam and Indonesia, moving beyond its traditional partners in the region. In 2016, the UK signed a trilateral security agreement with Japan and the US.

Maritime security has become a central feature of new EU partnerships in Asia. In the last decade the EU has upgraded programmes on maritime security with Japan and ASEAN states with a view to getting China to accept navigation rules through the South China Sea. In 2018, the EU agreed a new Maritime Security Strategy and promised to support Japan's Free and Open Indo-Pacific concept. France and the UK have launched bilateral initiatives with Japan and India on maritime security; in 2020, Germany deployed a frigate to the Indian Ocean and the UK was set to send its new aircraft carrier to the region on its maiden voyage. Still, Asian states have seen EU powers as cautious in confronting China's actions and reluctant to provide firm military support. Several member states – Hungary, Greece and Croatia – have blocked EU criticism of Chinese actions in the South China Sea.[73] Despite their coordinated 'freedom of navigation' sailings through the

South China Sea, France and the UK have stepped back from any overt challenge to China.[74] EU policy has been an uneasy mix of rules-based injunctions, measures to balance against Chinese power and acquiescence to Beijing's rising influence over maritime issues.[75]

The EU has also made efforts beyond Asia. In a new format grouping EU and African Union foreign affairs ministers, in 2019 Federica Mogherini insisted that the EU was changing tack to work with African states as partners to strengthen global order and security, and not primarily as development partners.[76] In March 2020, the EU launched a new strategy for Africa that promised a policy aimed at EU–African strategic 'collective action' over multilateralism.[77] The May 2019 new EU–Central Asia strategy was much more strategic than the previous 2007 strategy, more focused on the region as a Eurasian crossroads and more committed to 'Eurasian connectivity'.[78] Taken together these partnerships illustrate the EU's shift to a more targeted approach: if previously the Union focused on strengthening general rules-based principles at the global level, it has increasingly turned to bilateral strategic accords with individual partners or regional sub-groups.[79] The COVID-19 pandemic, and the US–China tensions it stoked, prompted the EU further in this direction, with a raft of promises to prioritise relations with middle-powers.

Themes and analysis

Resonating strongly with the outside-in conceptual framework, EU external action has in recent years sought to deal more systematically with the pressing challenge of maintaining global order. An outside-in perspective draws attention to structural shifts in global politics and how these have altered the basic foundations of EU external action since the 2000s. A lot of EU rhetoric in recent years has proclaimed a stronger commitment to upholding the rules, institutions and principles of liberal international order. This objective has assumed a higher prominence in European external action as other powers have increasingly questioned and menaced elements of the liberal order. With this order already having shifted shape, the EU has had to engage with systemic level re-ordering to a greater extent than in previous decades.

While the EU has remained a positive and vital pillar of the international liberal order, it has also inched towards a more carefully rationalised and varied support for global norms. Its harder-edged external action has been tailored towards a more proximate defence of European interests. EU external action has increasingly aimed at an international order that is more tangibly protective of core European strategic interests. The emergence of a new global order – or fragmented sub-orders within the international system – has both driven EU member states together and placed new strains on their cooperation. In many ways it has reinforced the importance of defending liberal, cooperative security principles. In other ways, it has encouraged European governments to engage in a degree of strategic hedging: no longer able to rely on the principles of liberal order, they have sought more direct and expedient back-ups in defence of their vital interests. The narrative of the EU being uniquely committed to the liberal order is partially true, but it is also in part a story the Union tells to and about itself that distorts what is a far messier and more eclectic reality.

The delicate balance in EU positioning resonates with suggestions that a hybrid mix of analytical perspectives is relevant. The Union's uneasy combination of strategic logics is reflective of the emerging international order itself – with some liberal principles proving resilient, while self-help realpolitik becomes more evident in other areas. Diplomats and many observers have certainly supported these trends as an overdue change in line with the realities of a reconfigured international order. The EU has sought to preserve the benefits of multilateralism where feasible, while adjusting to the dynamics of competitive power politics where these have intensified. This is a mix of longstanding principles with a more pragmatic 'turn to strategy' to protect immediate interests.[80] EU external action has adapted but without the US's hard power take on the decline of Western power.[81]

The EU has in recent years combined expedient bilateral relations, plurilateral approaches and its more traditional multilateralism. It has sometimes made these different levels of action compatible with each other, while sometimes prioritising interests that cut across order-related aims.[82] Member states have supported and indeed pressed for upgraded EU initiatives, but have also advanced their own national policies separate from these. The weight of parallel national member-state policies has increased towards the US, China and across Asia. While in some respects concerned with enhancing common EU support for the liberal international order, German and French national policies have played an increasingly prominent and separate role in the kind of order-based strategic hedging that has come to define overall European external action. This denotes a more multi-actor and multi-level approach to global order challenges.

Core to order-related challenges has been the complex and shifting triangular relationship between the US, China and European Union. Transatlantic relations have been strained by a structural divergence that goes beyond the very obvious challenges related specifically to President Trump's term in office. This is because shifts in global order have affected the EU and US in different ways: as a superpower the US has sought more power-based manoeuvrability to defend its interests and its understanding of international order, while the EU has sought a mix of power-based and rules-based protection of its interests.[83] The EU has come late to thinking about the order-related aspects of China's rise, but it has begun to take these on board, just as it seeks a degree of 'soft balancing' against the US too. The EU's engagement with China has increased to safeguard specific interests, while many in the Union have lost faith in the prospects of enveloping China within rules of diffuse reciprocity.[84]

The EU has had to respond to rising tensions in the US–China relationship, now probably the most determinant arbiter of global order. While this has reduced the Union's manoeuvrability, on some issues the EU has learnt to play China and the US off against each other – a strategy based not on liberal rules but on more Machiavellian self-protection. Many EU statements have presented the Union as bridge-builder between the US and China.[85] Still, there is a hinterland of transatlantic cooperation far deeper than anything in the Union's relations with China.

The transatlantic community has simultaneously fractured but has also on some issues bonded against China and other challenger powers. It might be most accurate to say that the EU's relations with both the US and China have become more modular, working with these powers on a case-by-case basis but increasingly standing back from unconditional across-the-board engagement with both. While Biden's election victory in November 2020 clearly opened the prospect of deeper and smoother transatlantic cooperation, this complex triangular diplomacy looks set to remain as a powerful shaper of EU external action.

While showing a more circumspect caution towards the United States and China, EU external action has focused on more strategic engagement with middle-sized powers. Middle powers – including European states and many non-Western rising economies – have sought a recast, pragmatic and negotiated form of multi-lateralism to protect against both Chinese and US disregard for global rules.[86] While member states have favoured different tactics towards China and the US, they have concurred on the need to build this wider set of global alliances – and have agreed that this effort needs to be taken a lot further than it has progressed to date. The new normal of global politics is not all about threats, but also about partners' new capacities to work with the EU on order maintenance. Indeed, EU governments have not exhibited such existential fear and negativity about ongoing global re-ordering as the US. Many accounts tend to leave an impression that all the strategic cards have fallen into non-Western hands; yet the EU has also been able to widen its global networks and alliances as other powers look to it for support as much as it seeks order-preservation support from others.

It is less clear that the EU has been sufficiently open to qualitative change of the global order. The Union has tended to imply that the old liberal order can be salvaged simply through more effort on its part. This ignores the deep structural flaws that beset the current international system and the need for a different *kind* of rules-based order. The EU line has routinely suggested that threats to liberal order come entirely from other powers and the bloc has done little to address the ways in which European actions themselves contribute to the imbalances and fragility of that order. The EU has often been clear-headed in detecting the power politics lurking behind US approaches to liberal order, while failing to admit that its own policies include at least a softer version of the same dynamics.[87] While EU politicians have insisted sovereignty is a defunct concept when they explain the need for integration in Europe, confusingly they have come to press for the concept of 'European sovereignty' to be given *greater* weight when the EU interacts with the world.[88]

European states have edged towards a more state-oriented order as opposed to an order based around cosmopolitan rights. Arguably, the EU has been concerned with a rules-based order that foregrounds self-preservation and stability more than genuinely liberal norms.[89] Certainly, other powers have not seen the EU's understanding of global order as particularly principled or balanced. The standard European refrains about the liberal EU helping drag other powers away from their presumed global illiberalism often paint a demeaning and simplistic picture of the rest of the world. What the EU presents as a principled defence of multilateral norms, other powers see as European governments focusing more tightly on their own autonomy, power and narrow self-interest.[90] If the EU has spun a narrative that it is the 'good multilateralist', to many around the world European powers can seem like an obstacle rather than fillip to a fairer and co-shaped rules-based order.

Concluding summary

External challenges. The ongoing restructuring of international power balances and the parlous state of global order have prompted significant adjustments in EU external action since the mid-2010s. This exogenous shift has become a more potent variable in explaining EU external action.

Unity–diversity dynamics. Issues related to global order command significant EU unity, while member states follow their own nuances around a central pillar of common principles. Common EU and national actions have intensified in parallel with each other. Member state initiatives aimed at adjusting to global re-ordering have become a more prominent part of overall EU external action.

Distinctive power identities. The EU's commitment to liberal international order has in some ways become more distinctive as some other powers have stepped back from defending that order. Yet European powers have also moved towards a more instrumental approach to global norms, in line with other countries around the world.

Protective dynamics. The EU's overarching approach to global order exhibits the kind of protective logic central to the outside-in conceptual framework. While the EU still endeavours and aspires proactively to shape the international system, it has increasingly complemented this outward-looking agenda with a more immediate defence of its own interests against externally driven order change.

EU influence. Without EU commitments to international rules, norms and institutions the global order would have struggled to withstand the threats that have assailed it in recent years. Yet the EU has not been able fully to revive the health of liberal international order; rather, it should be seen as one among many actors contributing to more tailored, conditional and varied forms of multilateralism.

5 Europe and the Rise of Protective Security

Moving down from the overarching international order, this chapter examines some of the more specific strategic issues that have in recent years gained prominence in EU external action: defence, counter-terrorism, migration and cyber-security. These issues are grouped together in this chapter both because the EU has come to see them as priority issues and because its response to each of them reveals a common and increasingly prominent 'protective' approach to security. Protective security includes but extends well beyond the traditional area of defence policy and has become a broad-ranging leitmotif of EU external action. It encapsulates the search for direct protection, rather than an aim to transform other states and societies as an indirect way of defusing possible risks to European security. Although the EU has still in places aspired to be a transformative power, the core elements of its security strategies have veered towards *protective power*.

At their September 2016 summit, European leaders expressly agreed that 'protection' should be the EU's guiding principle.[1] After several years of neglect, European commitments to defence have since then become stronger. In a similar vein, the priority that many EU governments attached to limiting inward flows of migrants and refugees drove notable changes in the Union's foreign policies from 2016. In response to a wave of attacks in the late 2010s, EU counter-terrorist cooperation deepened and became a pre-eminent pillar of the bloc's external action. And protection against cyberattacks has dramatically risen in importance on the EU's external agenda. The chapter assesses the achievements and downsides of this protective security and explains how – in line with the book's outside-in conceptual framework – it has inverted some of the formerly defining dynamics of EU external action.

The challenges

Developments in a number of areas have raised heightened security challenges for the EU and its member states. While many of these conditioned EU external action from its earliest years, they have intensified appreciably and aggravated a sense of vulnerability in the last several years. A first concern relates to the traditional area of *military* strength. Other powers have beefed up their military capabilities relative to the European Union and the West in general. Over the decade 2009–2019 global military spending increased by 5.4 per cent. China's military spend almost doubled over this decade. Russian military expenditure rose dramatically up to 2016 before plateauing. Over the decade as a whole, global defence spending rose but fell in Europe.[2] Russia's military build-up bred the most proximate concerns;

after intervening in Crimea and eastern Ukraine, Russia intimated threats to several EU member states – covered in Chapter 12.

Migration has been a second area of growing concern. Migratory pressure has long been an EU policy concern, but in the mid-2010s it became perhaps the highest-profile of all issues. In 2015, more than 1 million refugees and migrants came into Europe, mainly from Syria, Iraq and Afghanistan, and high numbers continued to arrive throughout 2016 and 2017. The crisis overwhelmed the EU's so-called Dublin asylum system, under which refugees were supposed to register in the member state where they first arrived. Border control became a priority for many European citizens.[3] While the inflow of refugees eased from 2017, the crisis was not solved. Tens of thousands of people were still trapped in Greece. Migrants moved towards central Mediterranean routes into Italy and then into Spain, moving progressively westwards, and the number of deaths in the Mediterranean remained shockingly high. Arrivals surged again in 2019 and 2020. In September 2020, a fire in a Lesbos refugee camp reignited migration debates and revealed deplorable conditions in the camps. Whether migration really presented such a serious 'crisis' as governments insisted was contested but it was clear that the issue increasingly infused EU foreign policy calculations.

Terrorism has been a further challenge. Attacks in the US in 2011, Madrid in 2004 and London in 2005 made counter-terrorism (CT) a priority European concern. In the latter half of the 2010s the foreign policy dimension of counter-terrorism became more prominent as successive attacks shook Paris, Brussels, Nice, Berlin, London, Stockholm and Manchester, amongst other cities. Radicals linked to Islamic State (IS) were responsible for these attacks and the organisation regularly threatened a wave of further violence. Fears intensified of a so-called 'third generation' of terrorism, with IS morphing into a more decentralised grouping focused on attacking Europe.[4] At the end of the decade, Europol warned of increasingly active jihadist groups within member states and the resurgence of radical groups in the Middle East, Sahel and Africa.[5] Attacks in France and Austria at the end of 2020 kept this issue at the very top of the EU's internal and external policy agendas.

Cyber-security has been a final area of fast-emerging priority. The number of cyberattacks against critical infrastructure spiralled in the late 2010s. Many of these attacks came from external sources and carried foreign policy implications. By the end of the decade, over 80 per cent of organisations in the EU had experienced some kind of cyberattack; nearly half of attacks globally had been aimed at EU member states. The prominence of state-sponsored attacks has become especially notable, as governments 'weaponise' offensive cyber capabilities.[6] Most state-backed attacks have come from Russia and China, although over 30 other countries were also implicated. Cyberattacks and misinformation operations have expanded from critical infrastructure to electoral processes; as several elections in EU countries were subject to cyberattacks, these now seemed a threat to the very integrity of European democracy. Digital attacks spiked further during the COVID-19 emergency.[7] More broadly, the strategic misuse of embryonic Artificial Intelligence crept onto the international agenda by the late 2010s.[8]

Defence upgraded

Defence has gone from being the most neglected area of EU external action to an area of the highest priority. For many years, proposals for deeper defence cooperation failed to gain momentum. After proposals for a European Defence Community failed in the 1950s, this area of policy was largely absent from EU integration for many years. As a modest degree of cooperation got underway in the 1990s it was around broader 'security' goals rather than 'defence' in the strict sense; that is, it was based on targets for out-of-area expeditionary capabilities that would strengthen European involvement in peacekeeping and stabilisation missions. This was the core essence of the then newly created Common Security and Defence Policy (CSDP).

Under this rubric, the EU conducted its first military operation in 2003 in Macedonia. In what was perhaps the point of peak ambition for external intervention, in 2008 the EU committed to being able to conduct two major stabilisation and reconstruction operations at the same time, two rapid-response operations using EU Battlegroups, and maritime and air surveillance missions. In practice, the Union had not still used any of the Battlegroups by the end of the 2010s. Over the early 2010s, CSDP missions were regularly deployed, although they were mostly small-scale and had limited impact on European geo-strategy.[9]

The policy balance shifted during the latter 2010s and even reversed, as the focus increasingly shifted to defending Europe itself. The Lisbon treaty committed the EU to the 'progressive framing of a common defence policy that might lead to a common defence'. It also introduced a 'mutual assistance' clause. As external threats intensified, European governments were concerned to boost defence capabilities after a decade between 2005 and 2015 in which overall EU defence expenditure decreased by over 10 per cent. In a much-cited intervention, US defence secretary Robert Gates warned in 2011 that if EU states did not increase defence spending then US commitments to NATO and to European security would begin to wane.[10] Russian actions in Eastern Europe were a further catalyst for deeper EU defence cooperation, as was the need to cut out wasteful duplication in military spending as the Eurozone economic crisis hit hard. The momentum behind defence policy was reinforced when President Trump took office and cast further doubt on the US's commitment to defending Europe.

Leaders discussed defence cooperation at a summit in December 2013, for the first time since 2008. At the end of 2012, member states agreed on a new Code of Conduct for Pooling and Sharing military capabilities and widened the European Defence Agency's mandate. A European Commission Task Force on Defence Industries and Markets devised ways of removing barriers to cooperation among defence firms. The aim of achieving 'strategic autonomy' now drove high-profile capability-strengthening initiatives. This was generally taken to indicate a commitment to developing capabilities separate from NATO that would enable Europe to defend itself without the United States to a greater degree than in the past. A common EU-wide defence planning or CARD (Coordinated Annual Review on Defence) process began in 2019.

From 2017, the EU developed its PESCO (Permanent Structured Cooperation) process designed to spur cooperation between member states on enhanced defence capabilities. By 2020, the EU had launched 47 different PESCO projects to enhance the EU's critical defence capabilities. Notable examples included projects for a Euro-drone and new Tiger helicopter. A European Defence Fund (EDF) started work in 2018. Its initial budget of 500 million euros rose to 1.8 billion euros per year; the EDF was then allocated 7 billion euros under the 2021–2027 multiannual financial framework. All this was guided by a Capability Development Plan to make sure that projects were all linked to a common strategic logic. The External Action Service's deputy secretary general claimed all this was 'the most ambitious and comprehensive multilateral cooperation mechanism for the development of defence capability ever conceived'.[11]

Alongside the EU-level advances, member states agreed a host of new cooperative initiatives. The UK and France signed their landmark Lancaster House agreement in 2011 to deepen defence cooperation. Smaller groupings of Nordic states, the Benelux group (Belgium, the Netherlands, and Luxembourg) and the Visegrad group (the Czech Republic, Hungary, Poland, and Slovakia) similarly deepened such cooperation. The 2010 Ghent framework gave a coordinating umbrella for these various pooling and sharing initiatives. France, Germany and Spain began cooperation on a new FCAS (Future Combat Air System) fighter jet project. The 2019 Aachen treaty was perhaps most notable for France and Germany agreeing a mutual defence clause beyond NATO's Article 5.

At the end of 2018, a momentum of new ambition in defence led President Macron to call for 'a real European army'. Merkel, and the Spanish prime minister Pedro Sanchez, supported his call. Merkel referred to the Aachen treaty as a 'contribution to the emergence of a European army'. In February 2020, President Macron offered other EU member states dialogue over the use of France's nuclear capability, in an effort to provide more robust European protection against outside threats. In 2020 the incoming EU leadership created a new Commissioner for defence and a new Directorate-General for Defence Industry and Space. In July 2020 the EU began preparing a 'Strategic Compass' to pinpoint additional defence needs.

Most European defence budgets started to increase again from around 2016. In 2019, EU defence spending was 289 billion dollars, for the first time exceeding the 280 billion reached before the economic crisis hit in 2008. German defence spending increased from around 30 billion euros in 2014 to 48 billion euros in 2019, now not far behind the UK (54 billion) and France (52 billion). Central and Eastern European states also boosted spending, while Spain increased the size of its military spend in 2017–2018 for the first time in many years. In a precise reversal of trends in previous years, in 2018 military spending as a share of GDP fell in all regions except the EU, where it increased 1.8 per cent.[12] At the end of 2020 the UK agreed 16 billion pounds of extra military spending up to 2024, by far its biggest injection of funds since the Cold War, while Sweden also announced a particularly significant hike in its defence budget.

Notwithstanding this turnaround, defence commitments remained subject to limitations. Some experts doubted that the projects supported under PESCO and the EDF were of a type that would give the Union far-reaching defence autonomy from the US.[13] As of 2019 only a handful of EU states – Greece, the UK, Estonia, Latvia, Lithuania and Poland – met the NATO stipulation that military spending should be at least 2 per cent of GDP, even if most others had plans to move towards this target. As a whole, EU states were still around 100 billion euros short of meeting the 2 per cent target. The US's 650 billion-euro military budget was still two and a half times greater than all EU member states' budgets put together.[14] Box 5.1 outlines the potentially serious impact of the UK's departure. In 2019, Germany reduced its planned increases in military spending, falling back from the 2 per cent target again. In the same year, Spain, Italy, Cyprus, Latvia, Austria and Luxembourg also cut their defence budgets. In 2020, the economic impact of COVID-19 put downward pressure on defence budgets; the Dutch government, for instance, admitted that this would prevent it from meeting the 2 per cent target.[15] Figures 5.1 and 5.2 detail European defence spending.

The turn towards military cooperation has been overwhelmingly about standard, protective defence; the European appetite to intervene in conflicts around the world has abated. The number and frequency of CSDP deployments tailed off during the 2010s.[16] Later chapters will show in detail the EU's reluctance to intervene

---

Box 5.1 Brexit and EU defence

With the UK's exit, the EU has lost about a fifth of its military capabilities. After the 2016 referendum, the UK regularly made positive commitments that it would participate in EU defence arrangements. A new EU–NATO cooperation agreement was signed in 2018 in part to address this issue of UK involvement. However, into 2020 the institutional processes for UK–EU security cooperation had still not been resolved; defence and foreign policy were not included in the EU-UK Brexit accord signed at the end of 2020. Several options were discussed, such as giving the UK a seat in the Political and Security Committee in return for it adopting EU decisions, but ultimately both sides recoiled from these.[19] Most in the EU were reluctant to offer anything beyond standard third-country rules that would invite the UK to sign up to agreed EU missions. The UK rejected such a passive, rule-taking status.

The Dutch, Eastern European states and some Nordic states were keen to involve the UK as deeply as possible; Spain, Belgium and others were less enthusiastic. The UK for its part remained unclear about how far it wished to participate in PESCO or the European Defence Agency. It was keen to demonstrate commitment to defence cooperation, although in many initiatives outside the EU framework. It launched a programme with Sweden and Italy to develop a new stealth fighter aircraft, the Tempest – this competing with the Franco-German-Spanish FCAS project. Franco-British defence cooperation remained key; the two countries renewed their vows to deepen this cooperation and the UK upgraded its deployments to French-led operations in the Sahel in 2020. Yet France seemed to prefer deepening this cooperation bilaterally rather than through formal UK participation in EU initiatives.

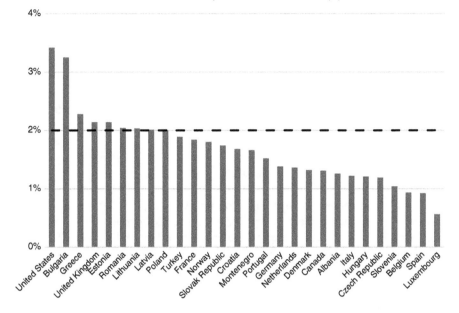

Figure 5.1 NATO defence spending, military spend per % GDP, 2019

Source: NATO (2019) https://www.nato.int/nato_static_fl2014/assets/pdf/pdf_2019_11/20191129_
pr-2019-123-en.pdf

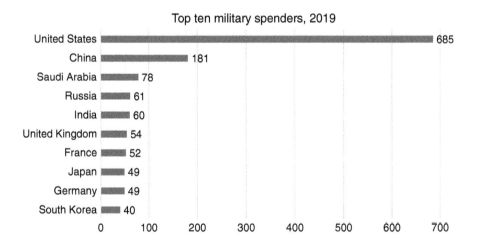

Figure 5.2 Top ten military spenders, 2019

Source: NATO (2019) https://www.nato.int/nato_static_fl2014/assets/pdf/pdf_2019_11/20191129_
pr-2019-123-en.pdf

in fully committed military operations in Syria, Libya and Ukraine. French-led operations have been significant in the Sahel since the mid-2010s, but the EU has generally moved to support African-led missions and kept its own CSDP missions at a modest scale and limited mainly to training and civilian technical assistance.[17] In 2018, President Macron proposed a separate European Intervention Initiative (EII) outside the framework of the EU; 14 member states had signed up to this by late-2020, but as yet it has remained unused. Noted defence experts concur that the EU has shifted towards classical defence and raised the threshold for deploying military assets outside the Union.[18]

Migration and external action

This book is not concerned with migration policy per se; most of this is, in strict terms, internal rather than external policy as it concerns the conditions under which people from third countries might be allowed to arrive and stay in EU states. However, this is also an issue where internal and external issues of security overlap and where this link has become an increasingly powerful driver of EU external relations. This is the very specific part of the migration agenda relevant to this book: the way in which concerns over migration have conditioned the EU's external action.

Borders. A common argument among policy-makers has been that the EU needs to gain control of its borders if it is to protect itself effectively.[20] A prioritisation of border control began in the mid-2000s. In 2005, the border-management Frontex agency had a budget of 5 million euros; by 2008 this had risen to 70 million euros. The body set up rapid intervention teams to patrol the EU's borders and negotiated with third countries for them to take back their citizens when these were caught. Several member states' navies commenced patrols in the Mediterranean. The mid-2010s refugee surge spurred further advances in integration in border control. EU leaders insisted that if the fundamental norms of openness, cooperation and free movement were to be retained within Europe, the EU required stronger and more common efforts to control its common external frontier. Figure 5.3 shows the surge and how this evolved.

The EU upgraded Frontex into a fully-fledged European Border and Coastguard Agency. In late 2018, the Commission announced plans to beef up the new agency to 10,000 border guards by 2027. Member states supported the extra protection, although some, like Spain and Italy, baulked at the sovereignty ramifications of having other states involved in controlling their national borders; this led to some tightening of the emergency conditions under which EU border control powers would kick-in. From mid-2016, the EU released several tranches of emergency aid to southern and eastern member states, the bulk of which was spent on strengthening border fences.[21] The 2021–2027 budget tripled funds related to asylum, migration and border management compared to the 2014–2020 period, to well over 20 billion euros. The Commission published a New Pact on Migration and Asylum in September 2020 that committed further funds for border controls.[22]

The migration crisis led to some Europeanisation of maritime patrols as the EU took over Italy's national mission in the Mediterranean, with a tripling of funding

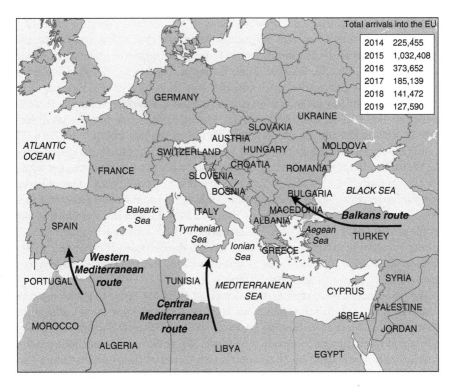

Total arrivals into the EU	
2014	225,455
2015	1,032,408
2016	373,652
2017	185,139
2018	141,472
2019	127,590

Figure 5.3 Refugee and migration inflows
Source: UNHCR (2019) and Migration.iom.int

in 2016. Operations Sophia and Triton in the Mediterranean were gradually beefed up to provide more extensive patrols. NATO also deployed a Maritime Group to cut lines of trafficking and smuggling. Debate ensued between member states over rescue missions, with several objecting that these were acting as a pull factor and wanting patrols to focus on surveillance more exclusively. In 2019 the new Italian coalition government between the far-right Lega and the Five Star Movement insisted that Operation Sophia cease to deploy rescue ships. President Macron scathingly berated Italy's hard-line anti-immigration actions, causing a major diplomatic spat; yet he similarly refused to allow rescue ships to dock in French ports. After the Lega left government, in 2020 the Austrian government took the lead in blocking any restart to rescue operations; Operation Sophia was then transformed into a mission to enforce an arms embargo on Libya.

Aid for migration compacts. The refugee surge spurred the Commission and member states into increasing aid flows to source countries. Some of this increase was for general development purposes, on the assumption that better economic development would stem migration flows. The largest share of it, however, was for beefing up other states' border controls and equipping third countries to stop people leaving for Europe. The EU pushed policies against human trafficking, presenting such trafficking and general migratory flows as a conjoined threat to security. It pressed third countries to sign 'migration compacts' that reinforced the foreign policy dimension of the migration issue. Under a first round of these with Jordan, Lebanon, Niger, Nigeria, Senegal, Mali, Ethiopia, Tunisia and Libya, EU aid was used explicitly to dissuade refugees and migrants from travelling to Europe.

The scale of funding for migration control purposes was reflected in the fact that countries like Turkey, Iraq, Afghanistan, Morocco, Ethiopia, Somalia and Syria were all among the top 10 recipients of EU aid in the late 2010s.[23] In 2016, EU member states promised an extra 200 million euros for multilateral agencies like the World Food Programme and the UN Refugee Agency to manage refugees within the Middle East. The EU's Madad Trust Fund was set up specifically to provide support for Syrian refugees in countries like Jordan and Lebanon. By 2020, this fund stood at over 2 billion euros, with contributions from 21 member states. Most high profile was the EU's awarding of 6 billion euros to the Turkish government in 2016 to keep refugees in camps inside Turkey. In 2020 the EU ceded another 485 million euros in an attempt to sustain this migration accord after the Turkish government again began to push refugees into European states.

The EU launched a separate Emergency Trust Fund for Africa to stem migration from North and sub-Saharan Africa. Table 5.1 and Figure 5.4 show the allocations from the Fund. Most of its funding focused on border controls and migration management in the recipient countries.[24] As much of a 'governance' tranche in practice paid for 'border stations', by 2020 around two-thirds of the Fund's 4 billion-euro allocation had been spent on border control projects.[25] Funds went to increasing the capacities of border and police forces even where this entailed cooperation with militia groups.[26] Through other sources, the EU pumped funds into the Libyan coastguard to intercept and turn back migrants embarked for Europe. Spain pushed for and won 140 million euros more EU aid for Morocco for migration controls in 2018 and at the end of 2019 the EU allocated a further 389 million euros to Morocco, 101 million of which was for border control technology.[27] In 2020 the new Spanish government offered migration control support to the Algerian regime, despite this regime having just stolen elections in the face of popular protests.

Repatriation. The EU also began to tie external cooperation more tightly to readmission, partner countries receiving aid only if they agreed to take back migrants from Europe. In late 2016, the Commission claimed that the EU had got third countries to take back more migrants over the summer months of 2016 than in many previous years combined.[28] In the same month, the EU unveiled plans to

Table 5.1 EU Emergency Trust Fund for Africa

	2018 top recipients, million Eur
Somalia	195
Libya	124
Ethiopia	99
Morocco	54
Sudan	52

Source: European Commission (2018) https://ec.europa.eu/trustfundforafrica/index_en

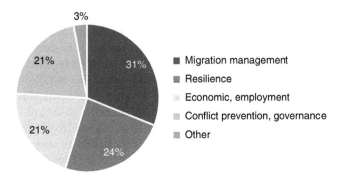

EU Emergency Trust Fund for Africa
Breakdown by theme

- Migration management
- Resilience
- Economic, employment
- Conflict prevention, governance
- Other

Figure 5.4 EU Emergency Trust Fund for Africa, top recipients, euros millions, 2018
Source: European Commission (2018)

repatriate Afghan asylum seekers in return for a new aid package to Afghanistan. In 2019, High Representative Federica Mogherini declared readmission-linked aid a success because it had got 'tens of thousands' of Africans to return home.[29] Germany introduced tough measures to speed readmissions in North Africa.[30] In 2019 and 2020, the Spanish government adopted a more restrictive policy, accepting fewer refugees, deporting increasing numbers of arrivals and pressing Morocco into an agreement under which it would take back migrants rescued in the Mediterranean.[31] A majority of member state governments have pushed for the EU to refuse trade accords with countries not accepting repatriations. European development NGOs strongly criticised the EU for forcing readmissions on third countries and challenged forced repatriations in the courts.[32] The September 2020 New Pact on Migration and Asylum included a new express process for returning arrivals and a provision to allow member states to pay for deportations rather than accept a quota of new arrivals.[33]

Counter-terrorism

Cooperation on counter-terrorism developed slowly until the 2000s. The EU agreed three packages of CT measures, in 1999, 2004 and 2009. As terror attacks hit the US on 11 September 2001, then Madrid in 2004, London in 2005 and a range of other places, so the EU's 'Freedom, security and justice' pillar placed progressively greater stress on core CT coordination and capacities. A 2005 Counter-Terrorism Strategy introduced a raft of commitments to enhance cooperation in surveillance of suspects and intelligence sharing, tighten law enforcement provisions and invest in security technology. It strengthened Europol's remit, although this still did not cover law enforcement or core counter-terrorism work. Member states introduced a large number of new domestic anti-terror laws. From the mid-2000s European governments detained increasing numbers of suspects. They also began to invest heavily in preventive counter-radicalisation initiatives, both within and beyond European borders.

While these measures were overwhelmingly about internal security, from 2008 the EU also began meetings to coordinate external dimensions of CT work as well. From the early 2010s the EU developed CT cooperation with other governments around the world, supporting them in increasingly tough and often lethal operations against radical groups, in countries like Pakistan. This entailed a rising portion of EU external funds going to initiatives related to counter-terrorism. In 2010 the Commission-managed Stability Instrument created a stream of funding specifically for CT cooperation. The EU began at this stage to insert clauses into its third-country agreements requiring partner governments to cooperate with the EU on counter-terrorism. It added a large number of international groups to its list of proscribed terrorist organisations. The EU's pressure for cooperation on counter-terrorism and migration control were now routinely combined, leaving the impression that these were treated as parts of the same problem. From 2017 the External Action Service appointed CT experts to delegations around the world.

EU terrorism legislation in 2016 included an expansive definition of terrorism. The wave of attacks from 2015 led governments to tighten measures domestically. After the Paris attacks, the French government imposed a state of emergency, tightened terror laws and reinstated security checks at the country's borders. In 2017 President Macron made these temporary emergency measures permanent. The Investigatory Powers Act passed into law in the UK in November 2016 dramatically extended the British government's powers of surveillance. After three attacks in the UK in the first half of 2017, the Conservative government increased its counter-terrorism spending to more than 2 billion pounds a year.[34] In June 2017 France and the UK agreed new counter-terrorism cooperation, especially to clamp down on online radicalism.

Such measures spilled over into a battery of new CT measures and commitments within EU external action. The French government invoked the Lisbon treaty's mutual assistance clause after the Paris attacks in November 2015 specifically to prompt the EU to engage in counter-terrorist actions outside the Union.[35] Counter-terrorism was the centrepiece of a 2015 European Agenda for Security.[36] The Global Strategy promised a particularly notable upgrading of CT work, including through information-sharing between member states, monitoring and counter-radicalisation dialogues.[37] By 2017 the EU had introduced six implementation packages to take forward the Agenda for Security, and appointed a commissioner to oversee a new concept of Security Union, designed to catalyse security coordination.[38] In 2019 the EU extended its list of countries deemed to have inadequate financial controls on terrorist groups.

Cooperation between internal security forces intensified and the EU's Internal Security Fund increased to 3.8 billion euros for 2014–2020.[39] Europol opened a European Counter Terrorism Centre in 2016. This dispatched experts into refugee arrival camps to stop jihadis slipping into Europe as asylum seekers. Governments deepened cooperation between police forces and judiciaries through Europol and Eurojust. Europol oversaw a reinforced intelligence-sharing arrangement. Again, all these primarily internal measures incrementally gained external components. In 2016, the French and German foreign ministers called for a fusion of internal and external CT policies.[40] The Commission departments, DG Home and DG Justice, gained more of a hold on external funding and drove an increased use of external funds for counter-terrorism purposes.[41] A new European Peace Facility was created in part to boost external CT support.

The Sahel saw perhaps the most dramatic increase in European CT engagements. France beefed up its counter-terrorist deployments across Sahel countries. Its Opération Barkhane deployed just under 5000 troops for CT operations in Mali and counted on support from a number of member states. The French airforce carried out air attacks in Chad against terrorist-linked rebel forces. The CSDP missions that deployed from the mid-2010s across Mali, Niger and Somalia focused on CT cooperation with government forces rather than classical peacekeeping or state-building.[42] CSDP missions become a form of extended border protection against both terrorism and migration; the lines blurred between CSDP and Frontex, Europol and Eurojust.[43] In 2020, the French government moved to upgrade Barkhane with a parallel Operation Takuba, more tightly focused on CT cooperation with regimes across the Sahel and drawing in increased member state contributions. European CT programmes continued in Mali even after a military coup in August 2020. Terrorist attacks in France and Austria in late 2020 led member state governments to promise a major upgrade to both border control and external CT cooperation, while French operations moved up a gear in the Sahel and killed several jihadist leaders there.

Cyber-security

A new dimension of protective security emerged from the mid-2010s: the need to mitigate the risks of cyberattacks. As the EU put in place a large number of initiatives in the realm of cyber-security and disinformation, so these issues became part of the bloc's external agenda. Cyber-security became a priority element in EU relations with third countries and very often a source of major tension with those partners. Dozens of new EU strategies and legislative proposals were introduced in the latter half of the 2010s. An initial EU Cyber-security Strategy in 2013 was designed mainly to draw together the large number of fragmented areas of cyber-security work in the EU and relate these more tightly to foreign policy. A Cyber-security Emergency Response Team initiative was one of the largest projects funded under PECSO, while a European Cyber-security Research and Competence Centre also gained influence.

In 2017 the EU introduced a Cyber Diplomacy Toolbox. The issue was ostensibly mainstreamed into core defence policy through a 2014 Cyber Defence Policy Framework; this was updated and significantly expanded in 2018. Overall EU spending on cyber-security increased exponentially, running into the billions by the end of the 2010s.[44] The EU Agency for Network Information Security (ENISA) morphed into a more institutionalised Cyber-Security Agency, gaining powers and resources. In 2019, its budget doubled from around 10 to over 20 million euros a year. The Union agreed a framework for a Joint EU Diplomatic Response to Malicious Cyber Activities. By 2019, cyber-security accounted for half the workload of the Security Union.[45] The EU introduced cyber-security dialogues into all its main strategic partnerships and in 2018 the High Representative convened a Global Tech Panel to examine the geostrategic implications of digital technology.

In parallel with these core cyber-security initiatives, in 2015 the External Action Service set up a small unit called Stratcom to counter Russian disinformation in the countries of Eastern Europe. This worked to counter and correct Russian disinformation and spread good news stories about the EU. As the salience of this agenda increased, in 2018 the EU decided to expand the operation, increasing its budget from 1.1 million in 2018 to 5 million in 2019, and also extending such work to the Balkans and southern Mediterranean.

A combination of cyber-security, fake news and social media issues has gradually fused into a nexus of so-called 'hybrid threats'. The EU set up a European Centre of Excellence for Countering Hybrid Threats. In 2018 the EU agreed an Action Plan against Disinformation, set up a 24/7 Rapid Alert System for member states to notify of foreign disinformation campaigns and got the major online platforms to sign a Code of Conduct to cooperate on tackling disinformation. G7 leaders agreed to the so-called Charlevoix Commitment on Defending Democracy from Foreign Threats, to take concerted action to respond to outside threats to democratic elections. In December 2020, the High Representative presented a new EU Cybersecurity Strategy that promised a comprehensive series of policy upgrades.

The concern with cyberattacks inside the EU led the Union to allocate funds for digital security initiatives in third countries as a way of boosting their cyber-resilience. Under the Instrument contributing to Stability and Peace the EU funded an increasing number of cyber-security projects in other countries. While cyber-funding has been aimed mainly at boosting cyber-security capabilities within the Union, the external component has begun to expand.[46] Most of an updated Security Union Strategy for 2020–2025 was again given over to cyber issues; it promised further upgrades to hybrid-threat capacities and more external funding for third countries' cyber capacities, and also called for a mutual assistance mechanism against external digital attacks.[47] In what was potentially the most direct ramification for wider foreign policy, the EU adopted a new sanctions regime against third-country nationals and entities found guilty of cyberattacks; in July 2020, the first measures were imposed against Russian, Chinese and North Korean hackers. The UK's security and defence review in 2020 also redirected resources into a new National Cyber Force and the British government acknowledged it had begun using offensive cyber capabilities to attack, for example, the financial assets of Russian officials.

Notwithstanding all these new initiatives, the European approach to cyber infringements has been cautious. The EU collectively, and member states individually, have begun a large number of cyber-dialogues with third countries, but these have resulted in few concrete policy measures. The EU's Cyber Diplomacy Toolbox espoused the need for common norms but has generally not led to robust responses when states breach such norms.[48] Cyber-dialogues have done little to attenuate the growing threat from Russia and China.[49] As early as 2015 the Commission proposed tighter controls on European companies' export of digital surveillance equipment; a significant number of member states were not supportive and agreement on a 'Recast dual-use regulation' was reached only in late 2020 by when it was clear that the EU had been remiss in allowing the flow of digital technology to hostile regimes.[50] There have been several incidents of the EU apparently holding back from criticising hacking and disinformation incidents from Russia and China to avoid political tensions, in particular related to the COVID-19 crisis.[51]

The EU has more recently begun to take on board the possible foreign-policy dimensions of the broader and longer-term development of Artificial Intelligence. The Commission established a High-Level Expert Group on Artificial Intelligence, tasked with mapping possible EU approaches to the social, economic, political and international impact of AI. This delivered a report on ethical guidelines for trustworthy AI in April 2019 and another in June 2019 suggesting a possible governance framework. The EU also launched a Joint European Disruptive Initiative to consider the future role of AI in European military technologies. By 2019, 15 member states had their own national AI strategies. These initiatives were relatively speculative and at an early stage of development but signalled that the security aspects of AI were gradually coming to the fore in EU foreign-policy debates.

Themes and analysis

The different dimensions of external policies covered in this chapter directly reflect the ethos of 'protective security' at the heart of the book's core conceptual framework. They are linked together in this chapter because they are elements of policy that show how far the EU has felt obliged to shift the basic orientation of its relationship with the outside world. If EU external action was traditionally seen as mainly a matter of the bloc acting in and on other societies with transformative intent, today some of its principal developments have been about blocking risks from the outside. The outside-in perspective trains our eye to the cluster of challenges crowding in on European countries as very direct policy imperatives – or at least, to the fact that policy-makers judge these issues to be of the utmost importance.

Most of these issues were part of the EU external agenda for many years even prior to the 2000s and the subject of some cooperative initiatives – this being the case in relation to defence, migration and counter-terrorism. Yet their development and importance intensified from the mid-2010s. The 'protection' narrative became key to the very core credibility of EU external action, as governments sought to reassure their citizens that the Union would and could help assuage the growing concerns over external threats.[52] These elements of EU policies have in common a prime focus on internal protection; yet this internal focus has brought with it important implications for the bloc's external action.

Many common EU-level initiatives have been forthcoming in these areas, yet they are policy domains in which member states' separate national strategies have also played an increasingly prominent role. Protective security has tilted the centre of gravity in EU external action towards national governments to at least a degree.

The chapter shows how in each area of protective security governments have pressed hard for more robust EU action while also developing stronger national initiatives. Member states have positioned themselves at different places on a spectrum running from harder through to more moderate security stances, but they have all beefed up national protective actions. Protective security is an area where national governments have (re-)engaged as drivers of policy decisions, generating both a degree of renationalisation and a more instrumental use of EU initiatives.

For some, the new prioritisation of military defence has been too little, for others misdirected. PESCO has remained process-heavy security: a lot of new process for so far relatively modest gains in actual capability. European states have not freed themselves from the need for US military power to provide credible deterrence. Yet the advances in defence capacities have put to rest the notion of a purely 'civilian power Europe'. The increases in funding for military capacities have outstripped most areas of external action since 2016. From being the poor relation of European security, defence became the most dynamic area of new cooperation. Speeches given by senior figures have regularly celebrated the battery of new defence-related initiatives as the most notable success in EU external action. This focus is clearly on protection: as defence cooperation has advanced, the general European willingness to intervene in conflicts has diminished not grown.

On migration and terrorism, the EU increasingly moved towards what has been termed 'bordering power' in the 2010s.[53] The border control priority was a reversal of previous EU narratives centred on dissolving the role of borders around the European borderlands. Polls and surveys regularly suggested that European citizens wanted the EU to play a more effective role in tightening borders and restricting access for outsiders; in this sense, a combination of internal and external pressures has pushed this element of protective security to the top of the EU agenda.[54] The much-mentioned 'fusing' of internal and external agendas has taken the form of interior and migration ministries and directorates wielding more influence over external action.[55] EU migration and asylum measures have increasingly cemented a 'deterrence' logic to security.[56] The EU points out that it has done enough through its migration-management funding to prevent dramatic collapse and instability in countries like Jordan, Lebanon and Turkey. Yet, in its efforts to stem flows the EU has shored up the very authoritarian regimes that drive migration and foment the criminal networks that menace European security. It is doubtful that the focus on 'hard bordering' has replenished the EU's sense of security or unity.[57]

Counter-terrorism developments after 2015 were a breakthrough after many years of limited progress in this area. In its external dimension, the CT agenda had the effective aim of bringing Arab and African regimes into a common security complex.[58] Some experts, however, question how much protection this has provided. One former security coordinator noted that many of the upgrades have been about internal processes, rather than more strategic output.[59] The very nature of modern terrorism means that intelligence operations still struggle to pre-empt attacks.[60] EU operations have struggled to infiltrate or get a strong hold on jihadist groups operating outside the Union. The EU has been training and offering capacity building to the very same regimes and security forces responsible for stoking instability and radicalism.[61] Again, it must be doubtful that this offers European citizens a robust form of protection.

Cyber-security is the newest of the different strands of protective security and the development of external EU policies in this area is still relatively embryonic. Yet it has also been the fastest emerging of the issues. The impact of cyber-security and wider disinformation concerns on a range of EU external action has become notable. While the EU has, in recent years, introduced an impressive number of new initiatives, agencies, action plans and funding streams relating to cyber-security and other digital issues, it has largely eschewed highly confrontational cyber-diplomacy. As the Union has slowly moved towards a less hesitant approach, this issue is set to gain importance in EU external action. One risk is that it becomes rather too easy for the EU to paint disinformation and other cyber problems as issues coming mainly from external powers when they equally reflect problems within European states' own information spaces and political systems.

The EU has upgraded all these areas of protective security with the aim of cushioning itself against external risks and more or less maintaining its own status quo, as opposed to its erstwhile more ambitious external aims of improving the world beyond Europe. EU policy-makers have generally cast the beguiling concept of 'strategic autonomy' as being about self-reliant inoculation against external vagaries.[62] While the Global Strategy talked in standard terms of the EU being a benign 'security provider', in reality it has become more of a 'security defender'. The issues linked together in this chapter show how EU relations with the external world have come to be dominated by a concern for immediate protection rather than the more diffuse benefits of helping to transform other societies. Today much EU policy is about the protection not projection of power.

While all security is about protection in some form, the emerging tenor of this protective security is different because it has inverted the basic philosophy of EU external action: instead of the EU trying to blend its own norms and internal politics outwards into the world, the Union has come to view security as being about *breaking* the transmission belts between the outside world and its own internal politics. This shift in strategic rationale has not been absolute; other chapters show that the EU's commitment to liberal transformative power has not completely evaporated. Yet the redirection has been significant and has gone beyond a few individual policy tweaks. This is perhaps the essential spine of what the outside-in conceptual framework points towards and helps assess.

Some writers were arguing even in the early 2000s that in order to preserve the spirit of Kantian idealism internally, the EU needed a more Hobbesian toughness externally.[63] In the years after 2015, the EU moved to implement this logic as perhaps the central pillar of its basic approach to external action. It is this very narrative of protection that has helped to drive deeper institutional cooperation within the EU. Convergence has occurred, but not around especially liberal notions of external action, as was widely assumed would be the natural direction of travel in such convergence.[64] Questioning an often unspoken assumption in analyses of EU external action, the rise of protective security shows that 'more Europe' does not necessarily equate to better or more effective policy.

Concluding summary

External challenges. In very palpable ways the EU has upgraded and adjusted key policies in the areas of defence, migration, counter-terrorism and cyber-security directly in response to outside challenges. The chapter shows the strong impact on EU external action of what diplomats have judged to be serious new strategic risks that have come to assail the EU from beyond its borders.

Unity–diversity. There has been notable unity between member states and EU institutions over the need for stronger protective-security policies. At the same time, more nationally-based actions have proliferated in these areas of policy. Migration is the policy area that has caused the deepest rifts between member states, although all member states have supported the general 'bordering' logic to EU security.

Distinctive power. The policy developments outlined in this chapter are those that have perhaps most clearly moved in a direction that is at odds with the EU's supposedly distinctive, liberal approaches to international relations.

Protective security. This chapter has grouped together those elements of EU external action that most directly constitute the EU's protective turn. Protective security is the common logic that has increasingly run through such core areas of policy as defence, migration, counter-terrorism and cyber issues.

EU Influence. Proponents of the turn to protective security insist these policy developments have given EU states a greater degree of control against external threats and challenges, although it remains unclear how far this is really the case. The EU's inward turn has conversely been to the detriment of the bloc's external, cooperation-oriented influences in a number of areas.

6 Geo-Economic Europe

In recent years, the EU and its member states have become more geo-economic in the way they act internationally. Geo-economic strategies are understood here as those that prioritise relative economic power and often entail foreign policy instruments being deployed in the service of economic interests. Geo-economics contrasts with geopolitics, which is more concerned with the wider dimensions of strategic rivalry and can entail economic instruments being used in the service of other foreign policy goals.[1] The EU's geo-economic turn is reflected in the remoulding of EU trade policies and member states' pursuit of commercial diplomacy. This chapter examines the EU's longstanding international economic identity and charts the rise during the 2010s of a European 'soft mercantilism' as member states have confronted sharper economic challenges, both externally and internally. It shows how this adjustment has been especially notable with regard to the geo-economics of technology. The chapter distinguishes member states' and EU institutions' differing approaches to geo-economics and examines whether the geo-economic turn is fully compatible with the EU's supposed broader global vision. The analysis shows how the relationship between commercial diplomacy and strategic interests has become a crucial question for EU external action.

The challenges

The economic elements of changes in global order have been especially profound in recent years. The EU's economic challenges have deepened due to a combination of external changes and internal crisis. Internal austerity during the 2010s increased the need for external trade promotion. The EU's share of global trade and investment decreased, while the Eurozone crisis left the Union more clearly in need of external markets and funds. At the end of the decade, the EU was still the largest exporter of goods in the world, slightly ahead of China, and the largest services exporter, ahead of the US.[2] However, its share of global trade and investment has been declining for some years. The EU's share of global exports was over 20 per cent until the early 2000s; in 2017, it was 15.8 per cent. In 2008, half of global FDI came from EU; in 2018, this figure was under a third. China's investment into Europe rose dramatically up to 2016. In 2016, EU investment outflows dipped below those of other major powers – although the Union still had the largest stock of overseas investment.[3] Figures 6.1, 6.2 and 6.3 chart the evolution of EU external trade and investment.

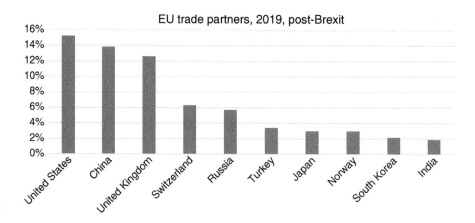

Figure 6.1 EU trade partners post-Brexit, 2019
Source: European Commission (2019a)

While the EU's global economic weight remained significant, its trade interests were squeezed by the rise of other powers. In parallel to the decline in EU relative weight, another 2010s trend was the rise of protectionism and something of a turn against globalism in many parts of the world. Trade tensions worsened between the US and China. Under President Trump, the US recoiled from the free trade agenda and regularly threatened tariffs on multiple actors, including the EU. China hardened many of its trade practices, which other countries had complained were unfair. The world seemed to spiral towards zero-sum global geo-economics: a

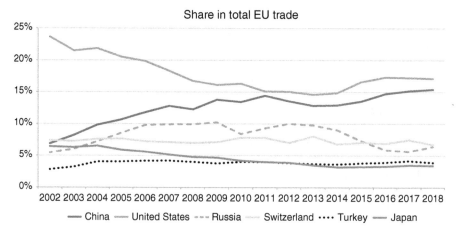

Figure 6.2 EU trade partners, 2002–2018
Source: World Economic Forum (2019)

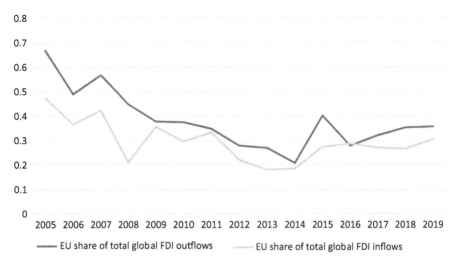

Figure 6.3 EU share of foreign direct investment
Source: OECD

situation in which political control over resources was deemed more important than global rules.[4] In 2020, the COVID-19 pandemic introduced additional geo-economic dilemmas as the emergency revealed EU member states' vulnerabilities to global supply chains, especially in relation to medical equipment; debates ensued over what many saw as the need for greater economic autonomy in the post-virus recovery phase.

Rising powers have come to navigate the global economic system with apparently greater success than many European economies. This has provided EU states with new commercial opportunities, while also dramatically altering the politics of global trade. In the space of a relatively short period of time, debates switched around dramatically: for a long time, a widespread concern was that Western states were pushing globalisation to advance solely their own interests; yet now developing economies seemed to be doing a lot better from the global economy and Western countries were those often pushing back against globalism. The EU wielded extensive power over trade for several decades and was a prominent influence in the way that global trading rules developed, in large part based around the EU's regulatory power. Other powers have come more strongly to challenge such regulations and norms, while the EU's economic weight and its own economic health have suffered setbacks.

The geo-economics of technology has emerged in recent years as an issue of priority concern. Technology has generated poles of wealth in a few places, with an oligopolistic concentration of wealth generating sharper divisions between, but also within countries. Governments have behaved in a more zero-sum way to generate or protect themselves against such technological clusters. The original ideas of web openness have given way to a political battle over what type of Internet prevails – one for confrontational political use (as in the Chinese vision), one for commercial dominance (as in the US) or one for geopolitical disruption (as in Russia). The foreign policy crossover is that governments have increasingly pushed technology and the Internet in certain directions linked to strategic interests.[5]

Control over digital technologies has become an issue of not only economic prosperity but also political power. At the end of the 2010s, the EU accounted for less than 2 per cent of the global share of artificial intelligence (AI) technology, with China and the US dominating this sector. Europe had no companies in the top 20 information technology firms in the world. The Union struggled to establish itself in the marrying of AI, data and military capacities, the so-called 'disruptive technology' set to revolutionise armed forces. It was a long way behind China and US in battery cell production, behind Japan and the US in AI patents and behind all main competitors in research spending on digital and other enabling technologies.[6] Many experts fear that digital dependency has come to undercut de facto European sovereignty, turning the EU from regulatory power to technology vassal.[7]

The result of all this is that geo-economic dynamics are an increasingly important shaper of EU external action. Geo-economics involves the strategic deployment of resources to advance economic interests. It entails the use of statecraft for economic ends; a focus on relative economic gain and power; a concern with gaining control of resources; the enmeshing of state and business sectors; and the high importance attached to economic relative to other forms of security.[8] Classifications of economic diplomacy can be seen as falling on a continuum: at one end, states' full control over economic tools to further a comprehensive concept of national power; at the other end, looser forms of state backing for their own companies' external actions.[9] A range of such approaches has become prevalent within overall EU external action.

Towards strategic trade policy

For a long time, the EU acted as an important catalyst of global free trade. In the years through to the early 2000s, the EU's efforts to liberalise trade within Europe extended into the international sphere. The EU was a driving force behind the main multilateral trade accords. It played a significant role in negotiating successive multilateral trade liberalisation packages during the 1980s and 1990s. It was a key architect and sponsor of the World Trade Organisation (WTO), when this was set up as a permanent body to oversee, cement and advance multilateral trade in 1995. In the 1990s the EU played a major role in expanding the global trade agenda to include issues such as investment, services and intellectual property rights, based on its own single market programme. While member states often flouted liberal rules to protect their own domestic markets, the general trend in EU trade policies was in favour of more liberalisation.

The EU was then instrumental in further widening the scope of global trade deals into new areas of market opening – so-called 'behind-the-border' issues, like ensuring competition policy or technical regulations become less of an obstacle to international trade. The fact that trade was the area of external relations where competence was most highly centralised at the EU level helped the Commission become a strong negotiator on behalf of member states. It is unlikely that the globalised economy would have developed in the way that it did without these powers and the 'trading state' role of the European Union.

The EU used the WTO frequently to open cases against the US for breaking trade rules. In 2007, the Commission fined Microsoft a hefty 600 million dollars for infringing competition rules, in a landmark case that many cited as the clearest example of both the EU's economic power and its upholding of multilateral trade rules. Moreover, as the EU played a prominent role in opening global trade and setting the technical norms under which this occurred, so many countries around the world moved to adopt EU regulatory standards – including large economies like China. The EU pushed for a new round of WTO talks ostensibly adjusted to take on board developmental aims, in what came to be known as the Doha trade round.

The EU's early trade agreements were mostly asymmetrical: the EU was willing to open its markets without requiring developing or industrialising economies to remove protective barriers to the same extent. In 1996, the EU stopped negotiating bilateral trade deals as it feared that these were undermining efforts to advance trade liberalisation at the multilateral level. Bilateral deals had a tendency to mix commercial and political issues, and the EU was ostensibly keen to move beyond this situation in order to embed objective trade rules at the global level.

From the late 2000s, some of the longstanding tenets of the EU's trade policy began to change. The bloc reacted to the emergence of new geo-economic challenges by striking what it saw as a more carefully balanced position on international economic policies. The EU remained broadly supportive of open trade, but adopted a more varied and qualified approach to this. For a while, during the worst of the European financial and Eurozone crisis, some new EU measures pushed in an overtly protectionist direction. The WTO secretariat noted that from around 2007, the EU was one of the heaviest users of new export subsidies that sat uneasily with multilateral commitments.[10] Fears of a repeat of 1930s wholesale protectionism were not borne out, however, and as the EU gradually clawed itself out of the Eurozone crisis some of its focus returned to shoring up the global trading system.

As threats to open trade accumulated around the world in the late 2010s, the EU sought a middle position. Its aim was to counter and limit the prospective rise of protectionism, while also taming the increasingly evident downsides of globalisation and simultaneously pushing back against other powers' increasing commercial assertiveness. The Union remained a broadly liberal economic actor but shifted towards what many policy-makers labelled a more *strategic* trade policy. This was the crux of President Macron's often-stated push for 'European economic sovereignty'. DG Trade director-general Sabine Weyand explained the EU's emerging approach in late 2019: 'Trade policy does not just follow economic logic but becomes part of a whole arsenal of instruments we are able to deploy, because that's what partners like China and the US are doing.'[11]

Five trends towards strategic geo-economics

The shift towards a more strategic approach to international economic issues has been evident in a number of specific EU policy trends:

Bilateral trade deals

The first notable trend has been the proliferation of bilateral trade deals. In 2006, the EU dropped its policy of not signing bilateral accords, in a key policy redefinition that stressed the 'strategic' reasons for this change of stance.[12] The EU's fear was that it was getting left behind as emerging economies signed a large number of free trade deals between themselves, while the Union excluded itself from this new race for market shares. Since then the EU has pursued an increasing number of free trade agreements on either a bilateral or an interregional basis. In fact, the EU has in recent years put in place more preferential trade agreements than any other power.

Notable trade deals (free trade agreements or less ambitious accords) have been concluded, in approximate order, with South Korea, Central America, Peru, Colombia, Canada, Singapore, Japan, Mexico, Mercosur and Vietnam. Significantly, most of these trade deals were accompanied by commitments to foreign policy cooperation and the EU commonly presented them as a platform for political and not merely commercial engagement. Into the 2020s, further free trade talks remained open and were progressing at varying speeds with Australia, New Zealand, Chile, ASEAN, Indonesia and the Philippines, amongst others. Talks were either formally suspended or de facto on hold with India, Malaysia, Myanmar and Thailand, amongst others.

In addition, the EU devised a specific type of Deep and Comprehensive Free Trade Area for countries in its immediate neighbourhood. It concluded such agreements with Georgia, Moldova and Ukraine in 2014, and opened talks with Morocco and Tunisia. In African, Caribbean and Pacific (ACP) states from the early 2000s the EU introduced Economic Partnership Agreements that obliged developing states to open their economies alongside EU market liberalisation. Many ACP states signed such agreements, although into the 2020s many were still resisting; as of 2020 talks were either 'paused' or still not opened with 16 African countries.[13] These states were concerned that the EPAs were so strongly oriented to European commercial advantage that poorer developing economies would suffer badly – a fear that economic models corroborated.[14] Table 6.1 shows the EU's recent free trade agreements across the world. Boxes 6.1 and 6.2 outline the geo-economic tenor of trade talks between the EU and post-Brexit UK and the US, respectively.

Table 6.1 EU free trade agreements

Signed FTAs	FTA talks opened
South Korea 2011	Malaysia: talks on hold since 2012
Georgia, Ukraine, Moldova DCFTAs 2014	Morocco: DCFTA talks from 2013
Canada 2017	India: talks on hold since 2013
Japan 2018	Thailand: talks on hold since 2014
Singapore 2018	Myanmar: talks from 2014
Vietnam 2019	Philippines: talks from 2015
Mercosur 2019	Tunisia: DCFTA talks from 2015
	Indonesia: talks from 2016
	ASEAN: talks from 2017
	Chile: talks from 2017
	Australia: talks from 2018
	New Zealand: talks from 2018

Box 6.1 Brexit and geo-economics

The UK's exit from the EU had important geo-economic considerations and involved notable elements of strategic trade policy. Brexit had a profoundly geo-economic effect on both the EU and UK. This was evident in the EU-UK free trade deal agreed in December 2020, as well as in the impact on both actors' global trade policies.

The EU took a particularly strategic approach to trade negotiations with the UK. It refused to offer the UK a standard free trade deal and made British access to European markets contingent on the UK aligning with a wide range of EU laws. The approach was not so much about positive-sum open trade as mutual calculations of relative power, and about the EU seeking to solidify its own institutional robustness in the face of a UK that was now an external challenge.

In terms of wider global trade policies, Brexit generated a mix of cooperation and heightened competition. In some senses, there continued to be strong cooperation and a basic convergence of views on trade. The UK and the EU moved to work together as allies in shoring up the WTO. At the same time, the UK was set to become more of a commercial competitor in pursuit of its own global trading deals.[35] Brexit took away from the EU one of the actors most doubtful about taking strategic trade policy too far.

For many UK politicians, Brexit was an opportunity to extend Britain's global trade links. Prime Minister Boris Johnson insisted that the UK would move away from the EU's increasing tendency to use tariffs 'like cudgels in debates on foreign policy'.[36] Yet Brexit also prompted the UK into a flurry of commercial diplomacy of its own. A difficult issue in EU–UK trade talks was the Conservative government's insistence on being able to use state aid to build up national technological and other capabilities against international competition.

In sum, Brexit both reflected the salience of geo-economic thinking and further reinforced both actors' geo-economic turn. Brexit increased the geo-economic imperative for an internationally straitened UK, while also acting as a further ratchet in the EU's more strategic approach to trade policy.

Box 6.2 EU–US trade talks

Trade talks between the EU and US have become highly political and one of the most emblematic cases of the thorny relationship between commercial and strategic objectives.

The EU and US launched negotiations for a Transatlantic Trade and Investment Partnership (TTIP) in 2013. They promised the world's largest ever free trade area, covering over a third of global trade. After a long history of calls for transatlantic free trade, the two sides finally agreed to open talks at this moment in part due to the collapse of the Doha round of multilateral negotiations. With tariff levels already low, much of the focus was to be on reducing non-tariff barriers and on technical alignment. Given the fraught international context, the two sides presented TTIP has also having a strategic dimension – a platform for broader transatlantic unity against rising powers.

The talks ended in failure in 2016. This was largely due to President Trump's sceptical position, although major differences between the two sides had already emerged before he took office, especially on health and environmental standards. Tensions then deepened after the US imposed tariffs on EU steel and aluminium and the EU imposed extensive counter-measures. These measures seemed to help bring the US back to the table: after two years of stasis, in July 2018 the two sides agreed to prepare new talks. They insisted that technical preparations made progress, although there was no breakthrough sufficient formally to launch new negotiations before the US elections in November 2020.

Indeed, EU–US trade relations suffered a further series of tit-for-tat restrictive measures. In 2019 the WTO ruled that EU subsidies to Airbus were illegal, allowing the US to impose tariffs on a range of European goods; in October 2020 the WTO ruled similarly against US subsidies to Boeing and the EU moved to impose tariffs on a range of US goods.

The TTIP talks became emblematic not only of transatlantic tensions but of wider popular reactions against free trade. They became the most controversial and contested trade talks the EU has ever overseen. Despite the Commission claiming that the agreement would add 120 billion dollars to the European economy and create several million jobs, many protests erupted against the negotiations. A proposed Investors-State Dispute Settlement mechanism was especially controversial, as this would allow companies to bring actions directly against host governments; the EU diluted this after the proposal unleashed fierce opposition. Beyond the content of the proposed accord, there were also concerns about the lack of transparency in the talks – although after criticism the Commission released many negotiating documents. A European Citizens' Initiative collected more than 3 million signatures against an EU–US free trade area. Criticism centred on the fear that technical alignment with the US would undermine the EU's social model, rights and standards.

At the end of 2020 there was hope that under the incoming Biden presidency the two sides might overcome their differences. Yet, both sides still faced domestic pressures against a free trade deal, cutting across the strategic benefits of closer transatlantic unity.

Less focus on multilateral trade liberalisation

As its focus on signing new bilateral deals intensified, so the EU's efforts to defend and improve multilateral trading rules weakened to a degree. Experts noted that from the late 2000s, the EU became less active and outspoken in pushing for free trade in multilateral forums.[15] Indeed, rising and developing economies took an increasing number of WTO cases against the EU for infringing multilateral rules from the late 2000s.[16] Trade experts observed that the bilateral deals the EU brought forward after dropping its moratorium in 2006 were mainly about negotiating access to specific sectors of Asian markets and in doing so detracted from efforts to extend balanced rules-based trade liberalisation within the WTO.[17]

The EU insisted that as it developed its new trade deals it worked hard to ensure that these were compatible with multilateral trading rules and would help reignite support for the WTO. The bloc generally claimed its new bilateral deals were 'WTO-plus' in that they went beyond existing commitments and opened the path towards new provisions at the multilateral level.[18] The EU has insisted it has still worked as a priority to uphold and, where possible, advance multilateral rules in the WTO. Much EU activity in the WTO recently has been aimed specifically at Chinese discriminatory practices, the Union becoming much more assertively instrumental in the way it uses this multilateral route.[19] Curiously, it then set up a joint working group with China to protect the WTO from President Trump's policies.

However, policy-makers admit that bilateral deals have invariably contained elements that cut across multilateral trade norms. DG Trade officials have worried that the EU tilted too far to making expedient deals with China and other powers and that this has diminished the commitment to multilateral advances. In the Doha multilateral trade round – which ground to a halt over the 2010s – the EU declined to offer significant moves on agriculture to help unlock other areas like investment, services, and intellectual property. While the EU argued it simply tried to keep some degree of post-Doha trade liberalisation moving forward, the Union was itself partly (not primarily) to blame for Doha's failure.[20] Arguably, many deals have been about shoring up political support more than they have rested on solid economic foundations.[21]

In June 2018 EU governments charged the Commission with devising a strategy for modernising the WTO. The Commission produced a series of far-reaching ideas, including tougher measures against trade-distorting subsidies and state-owned enterprises; fewer exemptions for developing states; and more scope for plurilateral deals within the WTO.[22] These proposals were closely aligned to the EU's own immediate interests and also mirrored US concerns with China's status in the WTO. Later the focus switched to the more basic task of keeping the WTO functioning as the US refused to renew members of the body's appeal body; in early 2020, the EU agreed an alternative dispute mechanism with other powers to deal with sector-specific issues. The EU has both sought to keep the WTO working effectively and turned its attention to other ways of pursuing its commercial interests.

Soft protection

A third development is that the EU has become more concerned with protecting some areas of its internal market from outside economic competition. It would be an exaggeration to claim that the Union has become a protectionist power, but it has resorted increasingly to a subtle or covert forms of market protection. During the years of the Eurozone crisis, the EU became one of the most frequent users of new trade restrictions in the G20.[23] The WTO had to issue several hundred disciplinary measures against EU member states after 2009.[24] The EU introduced more discriminatory trade measures than any other region or country during these years.[25] Newer forms of behind-the-border restrictions rose faster in Europe than in any other region.[26]

In the aftermath of this Eurozone crisis, the EU has resorted to softer, indirect restrictions. The Commission's 2015 *Trade for All* policy document promised that the Union would deploy regulatory norms to protect consumers from many types of imports.[27] Some writers argue that the EU has become more assertive in pushing its own technical regulations as part of its strategic approach to trade.[28] In response, other powers complain that the EU has wielded such regulations in effect as a form of soft protection to hinder access to certain market sectors and have increasingly resisted them.[29] The Commission moved to widen its use of anti-dumping penalties against markets with significant government intervention. Pressure from citizen protests and parliaments (national and the European Parliament) have also ensured that soft-protection safeguards have found their way into most EU bilateral accords, especially those with Korea, Canada and Japan.[30]

Tougher market access conditions

Fourth, the EU has become more willing to use access to its own market as a negotiating tool. To some extent this was always the case, but it has become a more systematically used tactic. Beginning after 2010, EU trade strategy promised a more aggressive use of market access as a bargaining tool and more 'balanced trade agreements'.[31] In October 2012, the Commission presented formal proposals for 'reciprocity' in public contract rules through an International Procurement Instrument.[32] Years later these were revised and won broad political support in late 2020, the initiative unblocked after a change in Germany's position. In the last few years, President Macron has pushed especially hard to ensure that Europe's commercial partners open their markets in reciprocal fashion to the Union's market-opening moves. In 2020 a new Commission white paper aimed to tighten market access for non-EU companies benefitting from subsidies from their governments, with these companies' activities being subject to an 'EU interest test.'[33]

If part of this dynamic has been about purely commercial interests, part of it has been about the link between trade and other areas of EU external action. The EU has increasingly used market access as leverage over third countries' climate and development policies. This reflects a genuine interest in pushing progress on these areas of policy, while also dovetailing with the tougher and more strategic approach to opening European markets. In the latest phase of this trend, in 2020 the French and Dutch governments devised proposals to tighten labour standards and environmental preconditions in EU trade agreements. The EU has removed Generalised System of Preferences (GSP) access from middle-income states and pressed them for more reciprocal arrangements. A 2012 regulation reduced the scope of the GSP scheme so that the number of states eligible for the scheme fell from 177 to 71 by the start of 2020, with the share of EU imports benefitting from its preferential access provisions falling from 6.1 per cent in 2013 to 3.8 per cent in 2018.[34]

Investment screening

In a more specific development, since the mid-2010s efforts have taken shape to limit investments coming into some sectors of the European economy. Around a dozen member states introduced national 'screening' processes, of differing toughness. A key factor behind these was that by 2017 Chinese investment flows into the EU were seven times larger than EU investment into China. After the EU tightened measures, the dramatic annual rises in Chinese investment into Europe flattened off after 2017. Following a 2017 French–German–Italian joint letter, in 2018 the Commission proposed a common EU screening mechanism. Member states consented in 2019 and the instrument became operational in October 2020.[37] France has pushed most strongly for rigorous controls on inward investment. Germany shifted position from being sceptical to supportive as Chinese investment in the country increased and moved into sensitive sectors. Germany used its new national rules to block Chinese and other investments for the first time in 2018. The German government set up a new investment fund to be used to prevent takeovers, especially from China, by the state stepping in to buy companies targeted by foreign buyers in key sectors.[38]

Southern and eastern European states have pushed for less onerous screening criteria and to keep the mechanism non-binding, anxious not to choke off much-needed inward investment. Some states were still keen to attract more Chinese investment. By 2020, 13 member states had signed some kind of deal with China formally endorsing the Belt and Road Initiative. In 2019, the UK accepted a bid from Chinese company Jingye for British Steel and President Xi visited Athens and Rome to cement a raft of new investment deals. The EU-level mechanism was significant, but was essentially about loosely coordinating national processes. France and some other member states floated the idea of giving the High Representative powers to overrule investment deals on security grounds; however, this idea did not win widespread support. While President Macron berated southern and eastern European countries for accepting so much Chinese investment into sensitive sectors, he concluded a deal to expand French nuclear plants and technology in China.

Nevertheless, the COVID-19 crisis reinforced the focus on investment screening. The EU trade commissioner pushed to accelerate and beef up the new screening mechanism to prevent the kind of asset sell-offs seen in the Eurozone crisis occurring in the pandemic.[39] European governments' national investment controls tightened as China sought to snap up assets on the back of the COVID-19 crisis. Arguably, this played a role in the EU and China concluding their Comprehensive Agreement on Investment in December 2020, improving some market access conditions for European companies in the Chinese market. The UK introduced a National Security and Investment Bill in 2020 that was accelerated and extended due to COVID-19 and the British government blocked a number of hostile Chinese takeover bids in the emergency.

EU support for European champions in international markets

Overlapping with the move towards investment screening, the French and German governments led a push to dilute EU anti-merger rules to make it easier for the EU to build and actively support European champions to compete internationally and, in particular, defend against Chinese state-backed companies. Promises of a new industrial policy have become ubiquitous in EU debates in recent years, an apparent U-turn from the 1990s and early 2000s. This became a major issue in early 2019 in the context of a planned merger between Alstrom and Siemens, which the French government said was needed to compete with Chinese train-makers. After the EU's competition commissioner Margrethe Vestager blocked the merger, France and Germany pushed for a wholesale loosening of competition rules; this again included suggestions that the High Representative be able to use security arguments to overrule competition barriers on mergers between EU companies.[40] Most other member states supported France and Germany to some degree, although some feared the new controls were a ploy to favour big German and French companies over their own national firms.

In late 2019, the Commission proposed a 100 billion-euro fund to foster European champions. The new Commission president, Ursula Von der Leyen, quickly took up the theme of industrial policy to protect and foster EU companies. The Commission approved several instances of state aid from 2018 for pan-European consortia in sectors like battery cell manufacturing and microelectronics, waiving state aid rules expressly to build European champions. When the EU presented the European Green Deal in December 2019, the US and other powers complained that it seemed to indicate that subsidy rules would be relaxed for renewable projects inside the EU in a way that contravened WTO rules.[41] German foreign minister, Heiko Maas stated that the priority was now to support local producers and reduce external dependencies in 'energy, IT, food, logistics, raw materials and rare earths'.[42]

Into 2020, France and Germany, with support from Italy and others, pressed Vestager increasingly hard to move ahead with the relaxation of competition rules; the Commission, backed by Sweden and other liberal trading states, pushed back against any major revamp. The COVID-19 emergency also had an impact on this area of policy. The virus deepened concerns about the EU's dependency on global supply chains for medical equipment and more broadly. President Macron argued that France and other EU states needed to bring manufacturing and medical production 'back home' from China and elsewhere.[43] The Commission's Covid Recovery

Instrument included a clause on using new funds to support EU champions against takeovers. Spain, Sweden and some other states warned that the EU should not move too far towards import-substitution policies and that COVID-19 did not itself delegitimise the benefits of economic openness.

Commercial diplomacy and foreign investment

A final trend has been towards a stronger and more systemic use of commercial diplomacy. The practice of commercial or economic diplomacy refers to governments actively supporting their own national companies in their pursuit of investment contracts: it is diplomacy deployed specifically for commercial gain. While European governments have long engaged in such commercial diplomacy, in the last decade it has become a far more prominent element of their external economic relations. Nearly all member states introduced new strategies of commercial diplomacy in the 2010s. Geo-economic factors have become more prominent in relations between member states themselves, and this has reinforced the prominence of these often highly competitive factors internationally as well.[44]

Germany consolidated itself as Europe's most successful purveyor of national economic diplomacy and archetype of the 'trading state'.[45] France had long been active in commercial diplomacy and intensified its efforts under the administration of President Hollande. The British government produced a white paper on commercial diplomacy in 2011 that brought in new export finance products and political backing for UK companies seeking large-scale contracts.[46] In Spain, Marca España (Trademark Spain) was an effort to capture big commercial deals; while this morphed into España Global more focused on the country's political image, the government that took office in January 2020 made 'economic diplomacy' its express priority and appointed a trade bureaucrat as foreign minister.[47] Italy introduced an upgraded commercial diplomacy strategy in 2020 to help its firms overcome the COVID-19 crisis.[48] The Netherlands put in place a new commercial diplomacy strategy in 2012 and Prime Minister Mark Rutte named economic diplomacy as his government's top international priority.[49]

Member states have pursued slightly different types of commercial diplomacy. German state bodies plan for a strategic concept of economic competitiveness; the French government tends to a narrower diplomatic backing of national champions to secure contracts in global markets; the UK, the Netherlands and the Nordic countries have become more geo-economic but are slightly more reluctant for state strategies to cut across multilateral rules overtly.[50] While member states have increasingly competed with each other through these new commercial strategies, some policy changes have occurred at the EU level too. The EU's 2018 India strategy called for a systematic and upgraded policy of European Economic Diplomacy in the country.[51] The EU has made a particular effort to expand a European Economic Diplomacy network across fast-growing Africa as the continent offers new and untapped investment opportunities.[52] President Macron took the EU trade commissioner and German representatives with him on a 2019 trip to Beijing, in addition to French business leaders.[53] Linked to these common commercial efforts, the

EU has also promoted a wider international role for the Euro (Box 6.3). Still, the rise of commercial diplomacy has in general increased the salience of competitive national-level external economic policies.

The geo-economics of technology

While developing a more strategic trade policy, EU institutions and member states were slow to react to the gathering geo-economic rivalries over the control of digital technologies. Realising it was getting dangerously left behind by the US and China, and indeed some other powers too, the Union began to move towards a more geo-economic, strategic approach to digital technologies in the late 2010s. While advocating international openness and coordination, the EU has begun to think more in terms of technological autonomy than before, reflecting a growing concern to protect both its economic and political interests. Whether the Union has yet developed a fully strategic perspective on the geo-economic of technology is still debatable.

It is in the areas of digital privacy and data regulation that the EU has wielded most power in recent years, as countries around the world have felt obliged to take on some of the Union's standards and rules on these elements of the tech sector. The General Data Protection Regulation (GDPR) had a particularly significant international influence in this sense. Many other powers have accused the EU of using the GDPR as a protectionist tool and several have raised the issue in the WTO against the Union. The EU has increasingly pushed to get rules formally enshrined in the EU to ensure that trade deals do not undermine digital privacy or safeguards on how companies use data. Taking office at the end of 2019, the new Commission made a priority of tightening restrictive measures against US tech giants.[54]

Nearly all member states have launched their own AI development strategies, with France in particular investing heavily to catch up with China and the US through a 1.5 billion-euro fund created in 2018. These strategies have focused on strengthening research capacities, improving conditions for AI start-ups, venture capital, and help for European companies to extend their international presence. The Commission has made available a fund for research and development in new technologies that count on the participation of several member states.

In February 2019, the Commissioner for Security Union, Julian King, warned that the EU urgently needed to move beyond its customary regulatory approach and begin directly to address the security implications of digital geo-economic trends.[55] In November 2019, Angela Merkel made her most forceful and explicit call for the EU to develop a policy for 'digital sovereignty' and to regain control over data from US tech giants, backing plans for a European cloud computing initiative, Gaia-X.[56] Into 2020 this line was more prominent in German thinking, with Merkel stressing explicitly that the EU must work to have its own chip, battery cell and other advanced technology producers and not rely on global trade for these.[57]

In early 2020, the Commission published a new strategy for digital issues more generally and a white paper on AI. It explicitly set the aim of 'reducing dependency on other parts of the globe' in the digital and AI sectors. It set a targeted investment of 20 billion euros per year for AI development and 6 billion euros per year for an EU cloud initiative. It promised a tougher use of competition rules and a new alliance – a Global Digital Cooperation Strategy – with countries on trustworthy and open data use. The AI strategy talked of firms needing to develop AI based on EU data, not data generated in other countries.[58]

One high-profile debate was over whether Chinese company Huawei's participation in 5G contracts was a security risk. Estonia, Poland and Romania wanted to ban Huawei's access to 5G auctions.[59] Hungary was at the other end of the spectrum, being one of the first states to award 5G to Huawei. After drawn-out debates, most members decided to allow Huawei to participate but only in non-core elements of 5G, in what became a relatively common European position. Reflecting this, the Commission published guidelines for common EU-level assessments to keep suppliers deemed a security risk out of sensitive areas, while leaving member states to make their own decisions on these companies' access to other parts of the 5G network. However, in 2020 a number of states began to toughen their positions on Huawei, as a result of COVID-19-related tensions with China and growing pressure from the US. The French government introduced a de facto ban on Huawei, saying it would not renew licences for operators using its 5G equipment. The Swedish government followed suit. In late 2020 Germany less decisively introduced a 'trustworthiness' test that might make it more difficult for the Chinese company to win 5G contracts.[60] Shifting even further than most EU states, the British government explicitly required all Huawei equipment to be phased out.

Despite the quest for more digital autonomy, the EU and member states have held back from a fully political-strategic approach to technology. The EU has been reluctant to define AI as an issue of zero-sum geo-economics in quite such the explicit way that China and US have favoured. European governments have tended

Box 6.3 The Euro's international role

In the 2010s, the Juncker Commission made a priority commitment to strengthening the international role of the euro. It linked this aim explicitly to the change in US foreign policy that made European governments feel more vulnerable to the dollar's global predominance. Ursula Von der Leyen reinforced this commitment in her first interventions as new Commission president in late 2019 and High Representative Josep Borrell included it as one of his core foreign policy priorities.

Far from growing steadily since the currency's creation, the euro's international presence peaked quickly and has seemed to be on a long-term trend in a downward direction – the opposite of what was initially predicted. The euro's share of global reserves and foreign exchange transactions hit a high of 30 per cent in 2005; it then declined year on year down to a low of 18 per cent in 2017; after that it increased modestly back to 20 per cent by 2019. While this makes the euro the world's second most used currency, it is far behind the dollar – which still accounts for over 50 per cent of reserves and foreign exchange transactions. The dollar's international influence if anything strengthened during and as a result of the post-2008 economic crisis, as dollar lending was key to containing financial collapse in this period. There are still relatively few attractive euro-denominated assets and EU capital markets remain fragmented.[62]

In recent years, the Commission has actively promoted greater use of the euro in cross-border invoicing and energy trade – for example, reaching an accord with Russia to move oil and gas trade from dollars to euros. It has brought in the European Central Bank to work on these goals, opening the bank to a more geo-economic role. The ECB's more relaxed monetary policy of recent years has fed into a geo-economic strategy to lower the value of the euro as a means of boosting exports. The EU's novel trading mechanism agreed for Iran was seen as an embryonic experiment for how the EU might circumvent dollar-trade. In December 2018, the Commission published a paper – *Towards a stronger international role for the euro* – with plans with give incentives to third countries to use euros in payment clearing houses and in debt transactions.

France and the Commission, in particular, have pushed a stronger global role for the euro, seeing this as part of a wider geo-economic agenda of strengthening the EU's economic independence. Despite the many new initiatives, however, the EU has eschewed a fully committed effort to make the euro a global currency and vehicle for European power in the same way that China is now doing with the renminbi and the US has long done with the dollar. The ECB lacks the Federal Reserve's powers to pursue such an international policy. Germany has been particularly reluctant unequivocally to back such a geopolitical strategy for fear of its possible monetary policy implications.

to see AI as something to regulate and contain rather than an opportunity for outward power extension. Most EU activity has still been about regulation, not an overtly confrontational geo-economics of technology. European efforts to develop AI in the military sphere have remained relatively limited. The Commission's AI Strategy has focused mainly on using regulations to make sure technological development is limited to conform to ethical norms and values. EU regulations and data protection have had significant global influence, but this has arguably diverted the Union from grappling with the raw power struggles for control of technology markets globally.[61]

Themes and analysis

The outside-in conceptual framework sheds light on the notable geo-economic turn within EU external action. The EU has fought to retain market power and its wider economic interests, while also taking advantage of more positive opportunities that have opened up as other economies have grown. Foreign economic policy has been the core of EU external action for many years. Increasingly, however, the prominence of this area of EU external action has become more marked due to challenges of a profoundly geo-economic nature. The EU's international economic manoeuvrability has been truncated by the bloc's internal economic weaknesses, by domestic unease with globalisation and by international pressures. COVID-19 responses have had a profoundly geo-economic dimension too.

Geo-economic trends have forced the EU to adjust its approach to external economic relations. International rivalry has not only become more acute but also seeped into the economic domain too; this has partially, although not entirely, diluted the EU's conviction that win–win economic and commercial cooperation work to contain zero-sum geopolitical rivalry. This core pillar of liberal internationalism has become shakier in a more fractious global environment. While the EU has in recent years presented itself as defender of the liberal order and rules-based economic globalism, under the surface policy-makers have looked increasingly hard at whether these tenets serve the Union's proximate interests.

The rising salience of geo-economics has contributed to a new balance between EU-level and national external policies. Curiously, while trade has remained the most strongly Europeanised area of EU external action, commercial diplomacy is one of the policy areas where national action has developed most strongly. Member states have come increasingly to frame geo-economic strategies against each other as well as powers beyond Europe. This has been a response to global structural shifts, but also internal challenges – a clear spillover from domestic crises to EU external action. The EU's 'twenty-first century trade politics' have become a matter of navigating domestic challenges and adjusting to sharper external imperatives at the same time.[63] The Eurozone crisis was one factor that pushed member state governments to seek greater sway over external economic policies in order to inject these with more geo-economic calculations and wrest influence from the traditionally liberal European Commission.[64]

Influence has run both ways: geo-economic goals have brought member states' national policies centre stage; in turn, the influence of member states' concern with relative economic strength has compounded geo-economic dynamics. In geo-economics – as in other policy areas covered though the book – a certain renationalisation and Europeanisation of external action have developed together rather than being mutually exclusive of each other. This combination has been especially evident in the increasingly crucial field of technology geo-economics: the battle for control over digital resources has catalysed common EU initiatives on some questions, while on other issues raising the primacy of national preferences and decisions.

The EU as a whole has sought to contain other powers' protectionism, but has become moderately more mercantile itself. It has moved to be more assertive in seeking commercial opportunities and opening new markets, but it has also talked more about limiting elements of economic globalism. This delicate balance means the EU has increasingly presented itself as defender of open markets against rising protectionism, while also promising to defend European citizens against those same open markets. Experts have defined the EU's approach as a policy increasingly designed to 'shape markets' through 'strategic liberalisation'.[65] They note that the EU has gradually homed in on traditional commercial interests and shifted away from its erstwhile aim to use trade power as a platform for spreading the Union's more political norms.[66] A greater degree of commercial realism has crept into the EU's tactical choices of when to pursue bilateral trade deals or multilateral rules.[67] Policy-makers insist this shift has been only partial; but it has nonetheless been a significant change.

The EU has often claimed its approach seeks 'fair' and 'balanced' trade; yet, to other countries around the world, the Union's notion of 'taming globalisation' has looked heavily skewed to its own immediate material interests. The EU's core, basic stance in the global political economy has shifted away from 'cooperative interdependence' towards 'competitive interdependence' – a focus on its own market shares and competitiveness rather than an economic order of generic, milieu benefit.[68] The line between balanced reciprocal market opening and power-related soft-protectionism has become a blurred one in practice. The digital sovereignty push, in particular, has cut across the free trade agenda, adding to tensions in transatlantic trade talks. The COVID-19 emergency brought the EU narrative of economic autonomy further to the foreground. Policy-makers have insisted that this does not portend out-and-out protectionism and that the aim is to reduce EU vulnerabilities by crafting a wider diversity of negotiated supply deals; reflecting this, the somewhat puzzling term of 'open autonomy' has taken root in Brussels. Yet, this has become a highly contested question within the EU institutions and member states.

The relationship between the EU's geo-economic and geopolitical interests is a difficult and complex one. Some dynamics point to the EU using trade policy for broader foreign policy positioning and for specific aims like pushing other countries to make cuts in carbon emissions. Yet the inverse dynamic has become more pre-eminent: the EU deploying its broadest political power to further its relative economic positioning. The EU has come to use trade in a political means to shore up its relative economic power – more than it has used trade as a tool for political aims or normative-liberal change within other countries.[69] While other countries have taken up many EU economic regulations in most cases this has not given the EU more influence over them on political and security issues. European market-access decisions for tech companies have not been tied systematically to overall security aims.[70]

The EU and member states have increasingly deployed political and diplomatic resources to further immediate commercial interests. It is less clear that they have a clear notion of using economic statecraft to boost the broader parameters of EU global power. One severe criticism is that the EU has increasingly put short-term 'profit-making' above long-term strategic deliberation.[71] Sceptics say the EU still struggles to wean itself away from a 'shopkeepers' mentality' of using power for immediate commercial gain rather than foregoing such gain for influence over the wider contours of global politics.[72] This might be a harsh assessment, but the EU itself seems aware it has only just started on what will be a long path of geo-economic adjustment.

Concluding summary

External challenges. In the economic domain, outside-in pressures and global market shifts have become primary drivers of EU policy changes. An inside-out dynamic also remains important, as the EU's internal challenges during the 2010s had a powerful impact on the bloc's external geo-economics.

Unity–diversity. In many areas of external economic relations, the EU has acted as an effectively united single bloc; at the same time, member state governments have increasingly pursued their own commercial initiatives. Unity in core strategic trade policy has co-existed with competitive national approaches to the wider elements of geo-economics.

Distinctive power. Many elements of EU external economic relations have retained their distinctive nature; the EU institutions and member states have, sought to sharpen the Union's unique regulatory power for geo-economic interests. Alongside this, more standard forms of commercial diplomacy have taken root within EU external action.

Protective dynamics. The protective logic has perhaps not extended so far in the economic sphere as in many other elements of EU external action; the Union has remained a relatively open economic power. Yet its increasingly strategic approach to trade, commercial interests and digital technology has entailed more of a balance between protective and outward-looking dynamics than previously existed.

EU influence. European influence in trade and wider geo-economic rivalry has remained significant and the EU's more strategic approach to geo-economics has in some ways even strengthened it in recent years. Yet the gain in geo-economic influence has not necessarily had a positive impact on the EU's sway over wider geopolitics.

7 Enlargement and Its Limits

For many years, the topic of enlargement has held a prominent place in EU external action. Enlargement is the mechanism that has given the EU its strongest claim to distinctiveness as an international power. The EU has been able to extend its own domestic space, a process outside the normal foreign policy toolbox. Towards the end of the 2010s it seemed that the EU's enlargement-based foreign policy might have reached its limit. The chapter examines how this situation arose and assesses the implications. While the prospects of further enlargement into the Balkans have just about remained on track, the EU is struggling to achieve its aims in this region. Turkey has in de facto terms fallen even more clearly outside the enlargement paradigm, both changing and reducing EU influence over this strategically important country. An outside-in conceptual framework helps capture the way that enlargement has run out of steam as the EU's most distinctive external strategy and also what this portends for the nature and effectiveness of European power. Doubts over future enlargement have undercut EU influence, while encouraging the EU to think and act in more traditionally strategic ways in Turkey, the Balkans and elsewhere.

The challenges

One foreign policy challenge is very specific to the European Union: the EU has come to face increasingly difficult questions about the future of enlargement. Enlargement has been the EU's most influential tool of foreign policy, as offering to bring in other states has given the Union unparalleled leverage over those countries wanting to join. The dilemma that emerged during the 2010s was whether the EU was willing and able to retain the promise of accession as part of its foreign policy arsenal. It made promises to Turkey and the Balkan states that they could become members of the EU and needed to decide whether it was willing to follow through on those promises. And it faced the question of whether to admit any other states beyond those already in entry negotiations.

As an international organisation and not a state, the EU has been able set the terms for other countries to join its ranks: its most effective foreign policy has been turning external into internal policy. The Union has been able to persuade outside states to incorporate EU laws and norms in a way that fundamentally changes their political and economic systems and turns these countries into strategic allies and indeed additional assets for its global influence. This has long been celebrated and analytically dissected as the most quintessential of EU external approaches. It produced what was for many years the main bulk of conceptual work on EU external action: namely, assessment of the conditions under which non-EU governments chose to remodel their countries around EU rules and regulations.[1] Table 7.1 shows how enlargement extended to southern and eastern Europe in the wake of democratic transitions.

Table 7.1 Post-democratisation accessions

	Date of accession to EU
Greece	1981
Spain	1986
Portugal	1986
Estonia	2004
Lithuania	2004
Latvia	2004
Poland	2004
Slovakia	2004
Czech Republic	2004
Hungary	2004
Slovenia	2004
Bulgaria	2007
Romania	2007
Croatia	2013

The strategic power derived from enlargement was first seen in southern Europe. Greece, Portugal and Spain joined the then European Communities in the 1980s after, in contrasting ways, making the transition from authoritarianism to democracy. The offer to join the European club helped anchor these three countries' reform processes and many believed it was pivotal in the precarious moments when their transitions could easily have unwound. Analysts from these countries have exhaustively debated how relevant the EU factor was in these transitions. Some argue that the accession process was the primary explanatory variable and that democratic transition may not have succeeded without the European factor. Others insist the transitions were domestically driven, with accession playing a vital but more secondary role in anchoring political reforms once these had been agreed by alliances between different political actors within each state.[2] Either way, as a foreign policy tool enlargement clearly succeeded in enhancing the Union's own weight, size and power; widening the realm of Europe's stability-preserving security community; and cementing the loyalties and capabilities of important strategic allies.

The enlargement process then played an even more epoch-defining and geopolitical role in the east. This was a reaction to the structural change of the Cold War's conclusion and it served to extend the reach of liberal order. Prior to the momentous events of 1989, there was little European democracy-support policy as such towards the countries of eastern Europe; German policy, in particular, was to aid and stabilise East Germany and other Soviet satellites, rather than push proactively for democratic resistance. Democratic policy instruments kicked in mainly when central and eastern European states were freed of Soviet tutelage and declared their aspiration to join the European Union. Over a decade later, ten new members were admitted in 2004 – including Cyprus and Malta, in addition to eastern states – with Romania and Bulgaria joining in 2007. The EU set strict entry conditions, the so-called Copenhagen criteria that became a kind of template for the Union's commitment to democratic and market reforms. By this stage the *acquis* was more extensive than it had been at the time of the southern European enlargement, so the process of alignment for eastern European states was even more onerous and influential. While candidate states had already made a basic choice in favour of democracy quite separate from the accession process, EU conditions certainly pushed elites that held back transitions to unblock reforms – Slovakia being a prime example of this happening.[3]

The process went through many ups and downs, and the Union changed strategy several times as it debated whether to let all post-Soviet states in together or in stages depending on their relative degrees of reform. Some member state governments expressed doubts about the whole enterprise – France being a prominent case. The Commission rolled out an extensive aid programme to help reforms in the applicant countries. Some criticised the Union for holding out too long and being too strict in its pre-entry conditionality; others thought it threw away its leverage too cheaply and that this later explained the illiberal backlash witnessed in central and eastern Europe – as shown in Figure 7.1. Some saw eastern enlargement as a stirring ideational project of re-uniting Europe; others argued that the more ambivalent member states reluctantly and rather less nobly found it difficult to block the process after the EU had made so many promises to the candidates.[4] Beyond such contrasting interpretations, most saw – and still see – the eastern enlargement as the EU's most game-changing foreign policy success story. In hindsight, it might be said to represent the high point of EU external influence and ambition.

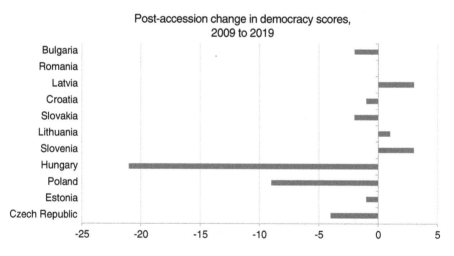

Figure 7.1 Post-accession change in democracy scores 2009 to 2019
Source: Freedom House (2020)

In sum, through enlargement in both southern and eastern Europe, the EU gained additional international heft, a wider circle of strategic allies and the power to transform political and economic systems. Enlargement seemed so successful that it gained influence even in states to which the EU had not offered membership. In a growing number of countries, the EU sought to mimic the accession process without its end product. The Union sought to influence third countries' internal and external behaviour by having them incorporate swathes of EU laws, standards, regulations and norms. As we will see in later chapters, from the early 2000s the EU sought in this way to extend modified versions of the accession dynamic to the Arab states of the southern Mediterranean and more countries of the former Soviet bloc in the east. This generated a whole lexicon of 'approximation' and 'harmonisation' at the heart of EU external action. It became the core pillar of the Union's claim to be a fundamentally different kind of international actor, one that seemed capable of remodelling whole societies not by military might but by surreptitious bureaucratic fiat.

If this was the EU's most distinctive strength it also became something of a double-edged sword. Difficult, long and often tense debates led Iceland, Norway and Switzerland to reject the enlargement model. The attempts to replicate the accession model to the EU's south and east met with limited success. To the south it failed utterly and indeed was even counter-productive as Arab states resented being treated as EU satellites expected to conform to European models and norms (although some aspects of the model proved relevant to post-2011 Tunisia). To the east it gained some traction in places like Ukraine and Georgia, but met with firm resistance elsewhere. Moreover, the EU often seemed reluctant or unable to think outside the enlargement or harmonisation paradigm. The EU's mind-set remained one of seeking to domesticate foreign policy, even in countries where geopolitical factors were increasingly prevalent and clearly militated against such technocratic approximation.

As the 2010s progressed, the whole logic of successive enlargement seemed to run aground. The EU Global Strategy insisted that enlargement was the Union's 'irreplaceable tool' for foreign policy aims.[5] In practice, however, the prospects for further enlargement looked increasingly slim. In the most explicit recognition of this, in 2014 Jean-Claude Juncker declared that there would be no further enlargement during his term as Commission president. Several member states became openly hostile to further EU expansion and committed to holding referendums before any future enlargement. Debates over the Union's finite absorption capacity gained currency, with the economic crisis compounding a new defensiveness.

The prospect of enlargement reaching a limit was challenging in two different contexts. First, in those states already granted an accession promise: the candidate countries of the Balkans and Turkey are examined below. The development of broad relevance here was that as several Balkan states inched nearer to accession, in 2020 the EU redefined the whole methodology of enlargement in a way that added new political uncertainty, to the extent that it added hurdles in the move from accession negotiations to actual membership. Second, in those states seeking a so-called membership perspective for the future. Chapter 11 will show that as

Ukraine, Georgia and Moldova pushed harder to be considered as candidates, so the EU became more reluctant to grant them this status. While the prospect of the Union expanding into North Africa was always remote, by the late 2010s it was a complete non-issue. If member states were apparently reluctant to allow more states in, it also seemed that there were anyway few states now committed to the democratic reforms needed to meet the entry criteria.

Against this uncertain backdrop, debates (re-)emerged in the 2010s about flexible or differentiated forms of integration involving a kind of graduated membership – outside states participating in a select number of EU policies without full accession as such. Some governments insisted this might give the EU more leverage over these states and a better platform from which to deal with their security challenges. Such ideas were not new, but governments have given them more serious consideration in recent years. If the EU were to move in this direction, the relationship between the Union and its periphery would change fundamentally and have profound implications for the nature of European external action. While enthusiasts have pushed such a blurring of EU borders, the Union has not yet moved towards a fully flexible or graduated model of third-country inclusion.

The Balkans

The violence that erupted in the aftermath of Yugoslavia's break-up at the end of the Cold War became one of the principal international challenges of the 1990s. It represented an early test for the EU's new Common Foreign and Security Policy to demonstrate strategic independence from the United States. EU member states led a battery of mediation efforts but failed to exert sufficient leverage to halt conflict. They took different positions on which of the new Balkan states should be recognised, when and under which conditions – and these differences fanned the flames of violence. In the most serious conflict in Bosnia and Herzegovina, member states were broadly united but showed different levels of sympathy with the warring Serb, Croat and Muslim communities. After talking tough, the EU declined to intervene militarily. Only when the US led NATO airstrikes and then took control of peace talks did the conflict wind down and, even then, lower-level tensions persisted. The whole sobering and salutary experience did much to galvanise efforts to improve EU external action in subsequent years.

The EU started to play a more significant role after hostilities ceased and the Dayton peace accord was signed in 1995. The EU moved to offer so-called Stabilisation and Association Agreements with Balkan states. Between 2000 and 2020, the Balkan states received over 20 billion euros of European aid. Aid to candidate countries from the Instrument for Pre-Accession was higher than funding amounts anywhere else in the world; Turkey and Serbia appeared first and second on the list of highest EU aid recipients from the early 2000s. In 2000 the EU agreed that all Balkan states should be given an accession perspective and made this a firm and formal promise in 2003. However, the process then moved slowly and at some points seemed to stall completely. Croatia joined the EU in 2013 but no other Balkan state was admitted. Only Montenegro and Serbia even began

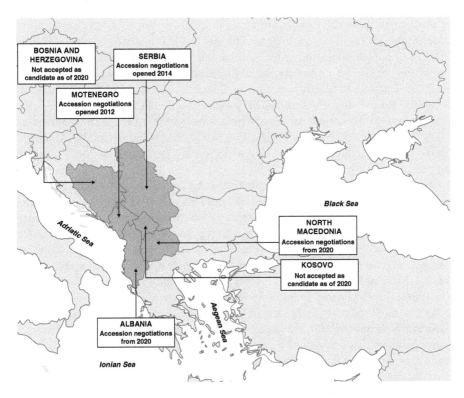

Figure 7.2 Balkans accession, state of play as of 2020

accession negotiations, in 2012 and 2014 respectively, and they faltered in their progress towards meeting the EU's entry criteria.[6] Figure 7.2 shows the state of candidate applications in the Balkans.

The EU undertook significant diplomatic interventions in the Balkans. The EU intervened to stem tensions in Macedonia in 2001, and again mediated an agreement between rival parties in 2016 after tensions reappeared. In 2006, the Union played a central role in negotiating Montenegro's independence from Serbia. In 2014, the German government promoted what came to be known as the Berlin process, which sought to improve relations between the different Balkan states. Yet, alongside these multiple initiatives, the accession process seemed to run out of steam. The Berlin process encapsulated a very practical focus on improving connections between the different Balkan countries and a conflict-mediation approach; this was different to the focus on accession and seemed to take the priority away from enlargement for a number of years.

A particular difficulty was the ongoing tension between Serbia and Kosovo. Several member states participated in NATO's 1999 military intervention against Serbia's attacks on Kosovars. After 2008, 23 member states then recognised Kosovo as an independent state. EU pressure and good offices produced an agreement between the two governments in 2013 – routinely cited as one of the bloc's main success stories in foreign relations. This EU-mediated process stalled in 2018. Serbia refused to recognise Kosovo and maintained parallel institutional structures for the Serb minority there. EU leverage was undercut by a lack of EU unity on Kosovo's status; Cyprus, Greece, Romania, Slovakia and Spain refused to recognise Kosovo and undermined EU pressure on Serbia to normalise relations. The five states not recognising Kosovo have remained reluctant to see it move forward in pre-accession cooperation. Kosovo complained bitterly that the EU moved ahead much faster in accession talks with Serbia when the latter had been the aggressor in the conflict.

Kosovo also stepped back from the EU process in part because some European leaders and officials appeared to support the idea of a land swap to unblock the impasse between the two states – Serbia in effect being granted Serb-majority areas in Kosovo in return for peace and recognition. High Representative Federica Mogherini said she was open to the idea; her successor Josep Borrell did likewise. Several member states, and especially Germany, feared the idea would revive border disputes across the region.[7] After the EU-led process lost momentum, the US stepped in to play a stronger role in mediation between the two sides. While talks resumed under the EU's lead in July 2020, severe problems remained. The Kosovan government still complained the EU was biased against it, with both Borrell and his new envoy to the conflict, former Slovak foreign minister Miroslav Lajčák, coming from states refusing to recognise Kosovo. After his party regained a parliamentary majority in June 2020, hard-line Serbian president Aleksandar Vučić insisted he would forgo EU membership rather than recognise Kosovo. The leverage of accession appeared modest on both sides of the conflict.

The EU's challenge in Bosnia and Herzegovina (BiH) has been that the 1995 Dayton peace accord shared out power between the three warring ethnic communities in a way that militated against BiH functioning as a unitary state. For many years the EU sought to help and press community leaders into building stronger and more singular state capacities as a step towards joining the Union. EU interventions in Bosnia were often heavy-handed, with its representative there having the ability to fire swathes of local officials and judges. From 2006, the Union took a step back from doing this and intervened less directly. The EU position was to press for a new constitution and unitary political system to move away at least partially from the Dayton power-sharing framework. From 2008, the EU held up its Stabilisation and Association Agreement with BiH as it pressed in particular for the creation of a single, national police force. In 2015 the EU effectively abandoned this attempt and agreed to move forward with the agreement after limited reforms that kept security issues divided out between the country's different factions. After this, the EU focused on cooperation with BiH in the absence of far-reaching political reform and with peace in the state still extremely fragile.[8]

A number of Common Security and Defence Policy (CSDP) missions have also taken place in the Balkans: two in Bosnia, three in Macedonia and one in Kosovo. These have been mainly about policing and law enforcement and have been framed as part of the accession process. Althea has been the longest-running CSDP mission. It started work in BiH in 2004 and was still running into 2020, assisting with disarmament, demining and security sector reform. In Kosovo the still-ongoing EULEX rule-of-law mission has been the largest CSDP mission ever, with over 2000 staff for most of its duration. While these missions have helped stabilisation, they have not resolved the region's rule-of-law problems. The EU defined EULEX as 'status-neutral' and Kosovan politicians believe this has increasingly held back pre-accession state-building preparations.[9]

The EU's priorities have since the mid-2010s moved onto issues separate from the accession process. Many member state governments have come to see the Balkans through the prism of migration challenges – that is, as a key bulwark against the kind of large-scale inflows of people seen in and after 2016. The focus has been on shoring up strong security-states in the region rather than pressing democratic reform processes or progress on other accession preconditions.[10] An increasing share of EU funding in the Balkan states has gone to control migration and the EU has expanded Frontex operations into the region. The EU has come to see the Balkan states as necessary parts of the chain controlling migration routes. This has given Balkan states leverage but has also led the EU to treat them as buffers as much as candidates.

With accession preparations suffering atrophy and instability returning to the Balkans, in 2018 the Commission devised a strategy to revive EU engagement, built around six 'flagship initiatives' of sectoral cooperation. However, it was careful not to make any firm promises on membership, talking only of 'a possible 2025 perspective'. Twenty-three years on from the Dayton peace deal, the document stressed that all states in the region still had a long way to go to meet EU criteria – on political and economic reform, and in resolving outstanding border and territorial disputes. It repeated the injunction that Serbia and Kosovo would need to sign a binding peace agreement before being allowed into the Union. It also called for member states to increase funding to and support to the region, to allow Balkan countries to participate in more internal EU meetings and initiatives, and to back deeper cooperation with them on security and migration. The Commission tied all this together in an Action Plan in Support of the Transformation of the Western Balkans.[11]

Yet political trends in the Balkans added complications. The region increasingly slid into a soft authoritarianism, with hyper-majoritarian governments, rising patronage and tighter media restrictions. Freedom House democracy scores declined in the Balkans during the 2010s. Democracy's retreat was especially far-reaching in Serbia. From 2018 the EU's pressure on democratic backsliding in the Western Balkans has increased, as it worked up procedures to reduce pre-accession aid where democratic recession occurred. Dynamics of both cause and effect have been at play: some member states have used this as an additional reason for not moving ahead with accession; in turn, many in the Balkans have cited the apparently endless delay in accession as one reason why democracy has become so precarious. Protestors that took to the streets against creeping authoritarianism across the Balkans from 2018 felt they did not win fulsome EU backing. Amid political turmoil, in 2019 the EU stipulated another 14 'key priorities' that BiH would need to fulfil prior to accession talks. The Hungarian government of Viktor Orban was an increasingly disruptive and nefarious impediment to EU support for democratic voices in the Balkans.

Something of a crunch point came right at the end of the decade. The new 2018 EU strategy coincided with a breakthrough when the governments in Athens and Skopje agreed that the 'Former Yugoslav Republic of Macedonia' would be called North Macedonia. This agreement on the country's name removed the obstacle that for nearly two decades had held up its accession perspectives. This presented a positive opportunity to break a core piece of the Balkans logjam. In May 2019 the Commission's yearly progress reports recommended that the EU open accession talks with North Macedonia and Albania. Thirteen member states led by Italy, Poland and Austria pushed for a positive decision.[12] However, matters reached a crisis point in October 2019, when France formally vetoed the opening of talks with North Macedonia, and France, Denmark and Netherlands blocked talks with Albania. President Macron argued that the EU needed to deepen internally first and that the Union should not risk importing crime and instability from the Balkans.

Macron's decision awoke fears in other EU governments that the Balkans would be tempted into the hands of Russian and Turkish influences. EU officials despaired that the decisions undid twenty years of work in the Balkans. Macron then called for a half-way membership status that would include Balkan states in some EU policies without being given full membership rights. He cast wider doubt on the whole logic of enlargement, insisting that the EU needed to 'examine the consistency of an approach that amounts to saying: "the heart of our foreign policy is enlargement". That would mean Europe thinks of its influence only in terms of access.'[13] France also forwarded ideas to make entry criteria more onerous. Austria, the Czech Republic, Italy, Poland, Slovakia and Slovenia joined forces to insist that such changes should not become a pretext for delaying the opening of talks with Balkan states.[14] Many also felt some states were overstating the rise in Russian influence in the Balkans as a pretext for not moving forward decisively with accession.[15]

The Commission adopted French demands that entry preconditions be made more stringent and member states be more easily able to halt accession talks in the future.[16] Reassured, the French government lifted its veto in March 2020. While the EU agreed to open entry negotiations formally with North Macedonia and Albania it gave no commitment on when these talks would actually start. It was also not clear what the revised enlargement methodology would mean for other Balkan states. A virtual EU–Balkans summit in May 2020 conspicuously omitted any commitments to accession talks proceeding and reverted to a looser reference to the region's 'European perspective'. The Commission's October 2020 progress report on the region was generally upbeat but still made no firm commitment on opening talks with North Macedonia and Albania.[17] At this stage, Bulgaria introduced further demands related to historical legacy issues in North Macedonia. Deep uncertainty remained over whether the EU would actually one day extend to the Balkans region as a whole.

Turkey

As accession momentum faltered in the Balkans, in Turkey it stalled even more dramatically. The EU's relations with Turkey have gone through several phases, with sharp tensions accumulating between the two as the 2010s unfolded. From being one of the most impressive instances of deep-seated EU influence, Turkey became perhaps the most sobering emblem of thwarted European power.

To accession and back

The EU and Turkey signed an Association Agreement in 1963. Their relationship made limited progress after that and many tensions arose, including over Turkey's 1974 intervention in Cyprus. The EU froze the agreement after a military coup in Turkey in 1980. Turkey applied for membership in 1987; the EU rejected the bid. A customs union entered into force in 1996. In 1997, the EU excluded Turkey from its impending round of enlargement. After government positions changed in both Greece and Germany, in 1999 the EU reversed its position and accepted Turkey's candidacy. Turkey reformed over 50 laws in eight Harmonisation Packages, five of which came after the Islamist AKP won elections in 2002. After the Commission concluded that Turkey had made progress on entry preconditions, in late 2004 EU leaders agreed to open accession talks; these talks began officially in October 2005. The EU allocated Turkey a significant increase in funding to help prepare the country for accession; dedicated pre-accession funds began in 2002 and were raised to around 5 billion euros for the 2007 to 2013 period.[18] Figure 7.3 shows how the EU distributed pre-accession funds between Turkey and the Balkans for 2014–2020.

After this high point, relations gradually deteriorated and the accession dynamic evaporated. Unlike with other candidates, the EU soon started intimating that Turkey might be subject to long post-entry transition periods and not be treated as a full member for a long time. After Cyprus rejected a UN peace plan for the divided island, Turkey hardened its stance on not accepting ships flying the Cypriot flag or aircraft from Cyprus; the EU in turn cited this as a reason for suspending negotiations in eight 'chapters' or policy areas. New leaders in Germany (Angela Merkel) and France (Nicolas Sarkozy) became openly sceptical towards Turkish accession. Merkel advocated the alternative of a 'privileged partnership'. Sarkozy blocked the opening of new negotiating chapters. In 2009, Cyprus additionally blocked a further raft of chapter negotiations.

Political trends in Turkey became a complicating factor. From around 2009 Turkey's democratic reform process slowed, then ceased, before reversing into a clearly authoritarian direction. The EU was critical of the Turkish government's repressive crackdown against the Gezi Park protests in 2013. Turkey moved further away from meeting the EU's entry preconditions. In 2012 the EU launched the so-called Positive Agenda in an attempt to keep a degree of constructive momentum in its relationship with Turkey. This foresaw deeper cooperation on specific issues

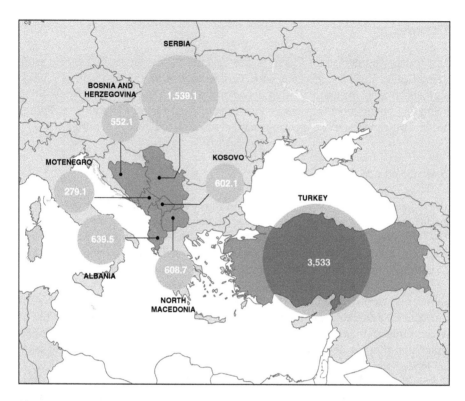

Figure 7.3 Pre-accession funding to Turkey and the Balkans 2014–2020
Source: Youngs (2020)

like counter-terrorism and energy. In 2013, the EU and Turkey signed a visa liberalisation and re-admission agreement and, in 2015 the two sides agreed to upgrade
their customs union. These new proposals for cooperation were all more or less
de-linked from the accession process.

The migration trade-off

Through a joint action plan agreed in late 2015, the focus shifted to migration and
refugee flows. In return for agreeing to take back refugees and migrants crossing
illegally from Turkey into Greece, the Turkish government won from the EU
commitments to move forward the accession process and visa liberalisation. The
EU also pledged an aid package of 3 billion euros, with another 3 billion euros
possible as a second tranche specifically to help Turkey deal with the refugees. The
EU would accept one legal refugee for each illegal returnee taken back by Turkey.

Despite the commitment to unlock the accession process and visa agreement, in
practice member states showed little appetite for either step, opening only two
negotiating chapters in the years that followed. The EU justified this in part with

reference to President Recep Tayyip Erdoğan's markedly authoritarian drift. After a failed coup attempt in July 2016, the government introduced a state of emergency, overturned the freedom of assembly, restricted civic freedoms and initiated a purge from state bodies of those alleged to have links with the Gulenist movement, which the regime accused of being behind the coup. After somewhat half-heartedly backing Erdoğan against the coup plotters, the EU responded to the post-coup autocratic trends in critical fashion.

In the 2018 Varieties of Democracy ranking of global democracy Turkey's democracy score suffered a bigger decline than any other country in the world, while Freedom House downgraded Turkey from 'Partly Free' to 'Not Free'.[19] In 2017, Erdoğan manipulated a referendum to authorise a more centralised presidential system. The government renewed security-force incursions into Kurdish areas. It closed thousands of NGOs and arrested hundreds of journalists. It replaced elected mayors with government appointees. The government brought spurious judicial cases against members of the Republican Peoples' Party, the largest opposition party.

EU reactions walked a fine line. On the one hand, the EU needed continued cooperation from Erdoğan on migration and security issues. On the other hand, Turkey's authoritarian drift strengthened many member states' reluctance to move the accession process forward. While the EU needed Turkey's support in the battle against Islamic State, the country's own internal fragility now represented a major strategic concern for European governments and it could hardly be defined as a reliable strategic partner.[20] While the EU was reluctant to suspend the accession process formally, most member states now showed little appetite for pushing it forward in practice.

German–Turkish relations became particularly abrasive after Turkey detained a German journalist and other German citizens and the Merkel government offered asylum to Turkish military officers implicated in the coup. Germany hinted at possible aid reductions after the Turkish government arrested a group of human rights activists that included Amnesty International's country director. In the 2017 German election campaign, the opposition Social Democratic Party called for accession talks to be indefinitely ended and Chancellor Merkel called for these negotiations to be suspended. As relations worsened, Germany threatened to remove its troops stationed at a NATO base in Turkey. Germany and others vetoed the previously agreed updating of the customs union.

While German–Turkish relations attracted particular attention, most other member states also turned against the very principle of Turkey one day joining the EU. President Macron advocated taking accession off the table. The Austrian government wanted a freeze to entry talks. The Dutch government joined with Merkel to call for cuts in EU aid to Turkey; a row erupted when the Dutch authorities refused a Turkish minister entry to the consulate and Erdoğan called them 'Nazi remnants'. Many governments seemed opposed to Turkish membership now regardless of whether or not Turkey returned to a more democratic path. Their use of democratic and other conditionality almost seemed designed to make sure Turkish accession never happened.

An era of critical measures

Turkey's pre-accession aid allocations were around 650 million euros each year for the 2014–2020 period; from 2018, the EU started holding back some of each year's allocation, so that the amounts Turkey actually received went down from over 600 million euros a year up to 2017, to 387 million in 2018, only 248 million euros in 2019 and fell ever further, to 168 million, in 2020 (as shown in Figure 7.4). While the EU cut pre-accession funds, it further increased aid to help refugees in Turkey – half of this aid coming from member states. The bulk of EU aid was now no longer about preparing Turkey for accession.[21] In 2018, the EU released the 3 billion-euro second tranche of support under the migration control deal with Turkey. This did not go directly into the government's budget but was disbursed through local civil society implementing agencies.

EU support for Turkish civil society organisations increased, in an attempt to counter-balance government repression. Moreover, the EU moved from engaging with CSOs mainly as partners in accession preparations to viewing civil society as key to offsetting Turkey's authoritarianism. If for many years the EU had supported a rather apolitical type of civil society initiative structured around its own harmonisation agenda, this began to change, in part because of the need to defend core rights in Turkey and in part because the accession process stalled. The European Commission took over management of civil society programmes from the Turkish authorities.[22] An innovative new Sivil Düşün programme was able to channel funds to civic organisations not formally registered.[23] The Commission adjusted its priorities, focusing on rights-protection more than standard approximation-based institution-building and twinning programmes - noting that Turkey's alignment with EU laws and regulations largely ground to a halt even on technical issues separate from pre-accession processes.[24]

The cuts in pre-accession aid were a compromise between those governments that wanted a formal suspension of entry talks and those reluctant to adopt any

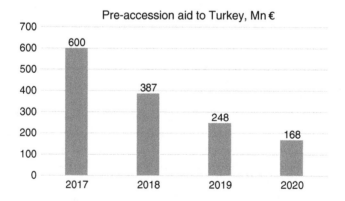

Figure 7.4 Pre-accession aid to Turkey, euros million

Source: Youngs and Zihnioğlu (2021)

critical measures against Turkey. The European Parliament pushed for the aid cuts to be larger than the Commission initially proposed. Aid became highly strategic: the de facto paralysis of accession and the cuts in pre-accession aid did not impede the 6 billion-euro migration aid package or a 485 million-euro follow-on to this agreed in 2020. Even those states most critical of Turkey's human rights record saw these funds as strategically necessary. While the EU did not formally suspend the accession process, in 2018 the European Council declared the process in effect to be in abeyance.

Strategic rupture

In late 2019, relations between the EU and Turkey became even more strained following Turkey's cross-border military operations into northeast Syria. Nearly all member states were critical of this invasion, which undercut years of EU efforts cooperating with Kurdish forces. President Erdoğan justified the invasion on the grounds that a safe zone was needed to house the 3.6 million refugees currently in Turkey. The situation reached a crisis point in March 2020: frustrated by European governments' refusal to help Turkey in its attempts to repel Syrian regime attacks in Idlib, Erdoğan effectively pulled out of the 2016 migration accord. He opened Turkey's borders and began pushing refugees towards EU territory. Some member states halted arms exports to Turkey; others blocked an EU-wide arms embargo. France's line was toughest, as it even questioned whether Turkey should now be in NATO.[25]

In short order, a number of other sources of conflict also arose. Turkey began drilling for gas in contested waters off Cyprus and sent warships as protection. The EU deemed the drilling illegal. In 2019, it drew up targeted sanctions against individuals involved in the gas drilling, cancelled association council meetings with Turkey and suspended talks on an air transport agreement.[26] During the course of 2020 the EU gradually expanded the scope of measures targeted at Turkish officials, although it put back consideration of any wider sanctions. France, Greece, Italy and Cyprus pushed for an especially tough response, while others like Germany sought to get Greece and Turkey to negotiate and to preserve cooperation on migration. In a dramatic ratchet, France deployed frigates and other military assets, and French and Turkish warships almost came to blows. France, Italy, Greece and Cyprus began military exercises in the area. Then, Turkey's military support for Azerbaijan in the autumn 2020 flare-up in its conflict with Armenia over Nagorno-Karabakh added yet another area of discord. With tensions multiplying, in November 2020 President Erdoğan called for a boycott of French goods in response to President Macron's clampdown against Islamist groups after terrorist attacks in France.

By this stage, relations stood at a new low. The EU and Turkey accused each other of failing to respect their side of the refugee agreement. Turkey berated the EU for not meeting its promises to accelerate visa liberalisation, a new customs union and accession talks, as well as for having offered legal resettlement only to a paltry 25,000 refugees stranded in Turkey. The EU insisted that Turkey had moved further away from the reform requirements it needed to meet before the EU could offer these steps. EU conditionality and restrictive measures did little to pull Turkey away from its confrontational and autocratic path. The relationship was increasingly focused on conflict containment, not preparations for Turkey's accession. Internal authoritarianism combined with a range of strategic tensions to make any hope of Turkish accession now look fanciful.

Themes and analysis

In the period between the late 1980s and early 2000s, the process of enlargement fuelled much upbeat optimism about the EU's growing influence beyond its borders. In recent years, this *sui generis* model of external action has faltered – and may even have reached its endpoint. In southern and eastern Europe, the EU's influence over democratic transitions was perhaps not as strong or primary as many claimed; as in all processes of change, external influences in these regions worked to the extent they moulded themselves around the domestic drivers of democratisation. Yet enlargement certainly helped countries transform their internal structures and brought into the Union new allies that added power to the EU's external presence. It was enlargement more than anything else that made the EU different and extended its influence into the nitty-gritty detail of countries' economic and political systems in a way that the US or other powers could not match.

In the Balkans, the EU helped quell conflict and contributed to the region's relative calm during the 2010s. The Union has kept enlargement formally on track and some of the relatively small states from the region have retained the possibility to make it into the Union eventually. Even if this happens, however, it will have taken an inordinately long time – so long that the EU will have contributed as much to the region's continued fragility as to its stabilisation. The EU's pull factor in the region has not completely disappeared but has certainly weakened. The EU has had continuously to strike a balance, trying to retain the momentum of the accession process in order to keep peace in the region, while also pressing for democratic reforms that governments have been reluctant fully to implement.

Balkan politicians have seen the EU's appetite for enlargement evaporate; fearing the Union has increasingly been bluffing on its accession promises, regional elites have had less incentive to undertake reforms. Notwithstanding their rhetorical commitments to bringing Balkan states into the Union, France and Germany, along with some other member states, have lost the conviction that there is an overwhelming strategic rationale for enlargement in this region. Their doubts have moved beyond those focused on the practical problems of making enlargement work effectively to a questioning of its whole strategic justification. Within the candidate countries, in turn, dynamics have moved beyond careful cost–benefit analyses of 'compliance' to a more geopolitical resistance to EU strictures. Arguably, the high-point of EU leverage has passed as the Union has kept states in the waiting room so long it has begun to lose credibility and influence.[27]

In line with one of the strands of the book's conceptual framework, this represents a particularly notable example of transformative power giving way to more protective security. Over the last decade priorities have shifted from accession preparations to conflict mediation and containment. For a long time, the formal EU line was that the enlargement process was itself the best form of conflict resolution in the Balkans. Critics often argued that the Union erred in making this assumption: partly due to the pre-accession frame, EU policies have helped manage and regulate conflict dynamics but not addressed their roots.[28] The EU has moved to attach greater importance to diplomatic initiatives aimed at maintaining stability; these have typically still been framed as part of the enlargement process, but the pre-accession ambition has receded. The Union has wielded much stabilising influence but has not succeeded in giving stability deep and secure roots or in encouraging Balkan states towards a firm commitment to democratic values.

The Balkans and Turkish cases are very different but also encapsulate some similar accession-related dynamics. With Turkey, the accession process has ruptured in an even more dramatic and clear-cut fashion. Far from concluding accession talks successfully, the EU and Turkey have become strikingly hostile to each other. Analysts now talk of Turkey undergoing a deep-rooted process of de-Europeanisation[29] – the very opposite of what the offer of membership was supposed to generate. The EU's conditionality and membership perspective played an important role in incentivising political and economic reforms in Turkey during the early 2000s. They were not strong enough to lock-in these reforms, however, or to prevent the country's subsequent authoritarian restoration.

Unsurprisingly, the EU and Turkey have traded accusations over who is most to blame for their drifting apart. Many in Turkey would feel the EU delayed progress in accession talks so egregiously that it lost any ability to prevent the country's backlash. Many in the EU would argue that it was Erdoğan's anti-democratic backlash that was most responsible for the delays in accession negotiations. Either way, as they each adopted harder-edged actions against each other both the EU and Turkey suffered: into the 2020s, the EU suffered payback for not following through on its accession promise to Turkey, while Turkey paid a price for its confrontational hostility towards the EU.

Beyond these chicken-and-egg debates, many on both sides were probably never entirely comfortable with the prospect of Turkish membership even before relations deteriorated most precipitously in the late 2010s. Many might see Turkey's failure to become an EU member less as a surprising policy failure than as something that was never likely to happen anyway. To an even greater extent than in the Balkans, the EU has changed approach to prioritise protective security over transformative power through these adjusted approaches; failure of the accession process has not been a failure of all EU foreign policy aims. Nevertheless, it is striking how far and how quickly the EU has gone from being an aspirational reference point to the 'othered' adversary for many in Turkey.

While undoubtedly having lost momentum, further accession has not been formally discounted. Yet, both in the Balkans and even more so in the case of Turkey, into the 2020s the accession processes have remained open partially out of inertia. The Union has lost interest in moving forward with further enlargement, but has not formally ended the process either. One positive reading is that the pre-accession processes prompted helpful reforms in many states, even though the enlargement momentum began to dissipate. The less charitable take is that the EU should not have made promises it was not certain it could see through to completion, and that the Union's strategic relations with Turkey and some Balkan states have become frostier and more tense than they would have been if membership had never been offered.

In this area of policy, a combination of the outside-in framework, more traditional analytical approaches and internal EU dynamics is needed to explain recent policy shifts. Outside-in challenges have combined with internal doubts to explain the evolution of EU policy. Member states have increasingly cited domestic factors as a reason for their coolness to further enlargement. In the 2000s policy-makers and analysts came to acknowledge that long-held assumptions that there was a binary divide between widening and deepening were simplistic; yet President Macron regressed to precisely this reasoning that internal EU reform imperatives militated against further enlargement. In addition, however, external explanatory factors have played a role due to political and strategic trends in the candidate countries themselves. Externally driven challenges have increased the need for pragmatic and transactional cooperation with the candidate countries on migration and security issues.

The accession template means traditional analytical approaches to EU external action are still highly relevant in the Balkans and Turkey. Yet even here the Union has moved to widen cooperation and fashion strategic cooperation with its partners outside these standard frameworks. A more transactional set of relationships has taken shape, structured less around preparing for membership and more around shared interests on specific policies. This is more obviously the case with Turkey than with the Balkans, but it applies in both cases. EU external action in these cases has increasingly gone beyond the enlargement paradigm. Still, the EU has struggled to offer forms of new policy cooperation sufficient to retain its influence in Turkey and the Balkans. As accession has stalled, the EU's strategic interests have looked less protected in these areas, not better guaranteed. In both cases, de-democratisation has gone hand in hand with resurgent nationalism and more combative geostrategic stances towards the EU.

The faltering process of enlargement offers a particularly vivid example of the Union's change in security logics and its drift towards becoming a less unique international actor. If the EU's accession-related conditionality and pre-accession funding worked as an element of transformative power in southern and eastern Europe, it has exerted far less leverage in Turkey and the Balkans. The EU has increasingly come to prioritise support for protective bulwarks around its borders, against the aim of expanding its own, norm-based security community. The aspiration to a normatively constructed shared community-of-fate has endured with the Balkan candidates and more tenuously with Turkey, but as a driver of day-to-day, immediate policy decisions this has been increasingly eclipsed by more carefully rationalised, strategic calculation. The unwinding of the enlargement dynamic is one factor that contributes to the EU becoming a more standard or less distinctive foreign policy actor.

Integral to this is the role of member states. European governments have come to play a more influential role in decision-making over accession. While accession is still a policy area driven by archetypal Europeanisation dynamics, national governments have gradually taken closer watch of the process. A number of these governments have been the primary players in putting the brakes on enlargement to existing candidate countries and in questioning the process's wider strategic value. Not only have there been very evident differences between member states over whether further enlargement should go ahead and if so under what conditions; in addition, several governments have developed more nationally based strategies in Turkey and the Balkans as they search for strategic engagement outside the accession framework. In this area of policy, renationalisation and Europeanisation have sat uneasily alongside each other.

The enlargement atrophy is not just about the Balkans and Turkey, the current candidates. The EU has refused to offer an accession perspective to any other states that have not already been given one. As we will see later, this has incurred strategic costs. It was perhaps always the case that the Union would eventually have to draw a limit to its own geography and that this would inevitably prejudice relations with those left out. Yet the process of doing this has certainly been messily expedient and more costly than necessary. The EU has taken its offers of cooperation with many states to the east and perhaps one or two to the south almost as far as it can without offering full membership. As a general foreign policy tool the EU is increasingly less able to replicate the spirit of enlargement without actual membership offers.

Concluding summary

External challenges. The way that enlargement stuttered during the 2010s was mainly the result of internally-driven factors, although even here outside-in factors related to political developments in and around candidate countries have also begun to weigh more heavily.

Unity–diversity. While enlargement is one of the most Europeanised areas of EU external action, as it has approached decisive crunch points so member state governments have exerted more influence over the process. With governments' diverging strategic views moving to the foreground, enlargement has been subject to some of the re-nationalisation dynamics evident in other policy areas.

Distinctive power. If enlargement has been the EU's most distinctive foreign policy tool, its loss of momentum has left the EU looking like a less qualitatively different international power. The EU has increasingly looked for more traditional forms of engagement with candidate states outside the distinctive accession paradigm.

Protective dynamics. The stalling of enlargement reflects – and indeed is a key part of – the EU's turn to protective security. Many member state governments have placed more of an onus on keeping aspirant neighbouring states at bay as protective buffers than on including them as partners in cooperative security.

EU influence. The changes in this area of EU external action have involved a clear loss in EU influence – especially over Turkey, although in parts of the Balkans too. The EU has struggled to find non-accession forms of engagement that afford it significant power and influence.

8 Climate Change and Energy Policy

Over a period of many years the EU has moved to incorporate climate policy goals and energy security at the heart of its external action. This chapter examines how the EU has approached the imperative of tackling climate change and how its more traditional security-of-supply aims have evolved – examining these two tightly entwined policy areas together and in relation to each other. These have become increasingly important issues and the EU has faced the urgent need to put in place effective and united external climate and energy strategies. The EU created an Energy Union in 2015 that promised radically to strengthen the foreign policy dimensions of both energy and climate issues. The chapter examines the EU's increasing support for low-carbon energy transition globally, new climate security initiatives and the creation of new energy partnerships around the world. In accordance with the outside-in conceptual framework, the chapter highlights how exogenuous challenges have driven significant adjustments to EU external action that include new approaches to climate geopolitics and energy geo-economics, along with elements of more protective security. It stresses that the EU has begun to grapple with the strategic elements of new global energy scenarios but has not implemented a fully developed strategy for the wider geopolitical impacts of climate change – a challenge that may come to dwarf all other international dilemmas in future years.

The challenges

The most high-profile challenge in this area has been that of meeting international *climate change targets*. While most elements of Europe's low-carbon transition are about domestic policy and lie outside the scope of this book, many key elements have become central to EU external action. One imperative has been for EU states to meet their own climate change commitments; another has been for the Union to ensure more far-reaching progress on climate issues at the international level. After many years of relatively modest multilateral advances, a major global climate deal was signed in Paris in 2015. Under this accord, 195 countries agreed goals to limit global temperature rises to below 2 degrees Celsius and to pursue efforts to keep the rise to 1.5 degrees; they then forwarded national pledges to reduce emissions.

Into the 2020s implementation has been modest and current national pledges would still push temperatures up 4 degrees by 2100 over pre-industrial levels.[1] At the end of 2018, the Intergovernmental Panel on Climate Change (IPCC) released an influential report whose updated scientific evidence suggested a much higher level of global ambition would be needed to meet the Paris targets.[2] An additional challenge came from the Trump administration's refusal to abide by the Paris commitments. Developed countries have pushed other countries to increase their emission-reduction ambitions. Developing countries have pressed rich countries to take on more of the burden and deliver on a 100 billion-dollar target for climate financing – the funds designed to help less developed states meet their climate targets. For all these commitments and regular multilateral negotiations, global warming has remained on course to breach crucial tipping points if governments fail to take more radical action. A global summit in Madrid at the end of 2019 – the 25th regular meeting of the so-called committee of the parties (COP) – failed to agree to upgraded commitments.

Climate change has begun to generate heightened *security* challenges. So-called climate security has already emerged as a major challenge and is set to pose increasingly acute difficulties in the future. Climate change has aggravated instability and conflict dynamics as different communities seek access to ever-more finite resources. It has begun to increase the number of migrants fleeing from the states hardest hit by global warming. It increasingly puts global supply chains at risk and could seriously threaten international trade flows. Such strains could weaken the whole framework of multilateral institutions and lead to a far more zero-sum security panorama.[3] This is a complex issue and there remain uncertainties over exactly how climate change triggers conflict and global tensions; climate change's impact is dependent on very locally specific conditions. Yet there is widespread agreement that climate change has already begun to have a profound impact on security. By 2020 experts were pointing out that even if states met their current emissions targets, these security consequences will be far-reaching and long-lasting.[4] Scientific experts argued that COVID-19 was in part related to climate stresses and an example of the kind of global event set to become more prevalent in the future.[5]

More generally, climate change and energy transitions have begun to have repercussions for international power balances. As fossil-fuel suppliers lose power, other countries will gain influence as exporters of power generated by renewables and the minerals that have become crucial to new battery technologies. With the EU housing few of the critical minerals like lithium, cobalt and magnesium and rare earths needed in renewables technology, new patters of dependencies lie ahead. China holds the largest deposits of these minerals; they are also heavily present in states subject to conflict and fragility and could be the focus of further security problems, becoming 'green conflict minerals'.[6] Alliances have begun to shift; groups have formed of states heavily involved in producing solar energy and geothermal energy. The politics of trade in renewables have become a major international issue.[7] Debates have arisen over what these scenarios might entail for foreign policy strategies. Some writers have argued that governments need to protect themselves from climate-related geopolitical uncertainties by adopting a 'lifeboat' strategy of self-preservation, others insist that deeper multilateral cooperation becomes more imperative.[8] Table 8.1 and Figure 8.1 show countries' climate vulnerabilities and attendant security risks.

In addition to climate change, the EU has faced the traditional challenge of securing *oil and gas supplies*. The EU has for a long time been the region most highly dependent on oil and gas imports. As EU states' own oil and gas production has decreased, so the Union's dependency on hydrocarbon imports has increased. The

Table 8.1 Countries most affected by climate change, 1998–2008

1. Puerto Rico
2. Honduras
3. Myanmar
4. Haiti
5. Philippines
6. Nicaragua
7. Bangladesh
8. Pakistan
9. Vietnam
10. Dominica
11. Nepal
12. Dominican Republic
13. Thailand
14. Guatemala
15. India
16. El Salvador
17. Madagascar
18. France
19. Cambodia
20. Fiji

Source: Germanwatch (2019)

EU imported 58 per cent of its energy needs in 2018, up from 56 per cent in 2000.[9] Russia has remained the EU's largest supplier of oil and gas, even though it accounted for a lower share of EU imports into the 2020s than it did in the early 2000s. Figures 8.2 and 8.3 show the main sources of EU oil and gas. Access to oil and gas supplies has become more uncertain. Russia's assertive foreign policy actions in the last decade have intensified the need for energy diversification; it has remained the sole supplier to a handful of member states. With the Middle East holding over 50 per cent of global hydrocarbon reserves, severe geopolitical instability in this region compounded energy supply uncertainties during the 2010s.

Notwithstanding these tightening constraints, in some senses the EU's security-of-supply challenges have eased somewhat in the last several years. EU oil and gas consumption has decreased; energy requirements have begun to ease compared with the past and may have peaked in 2019.[10] Global gas production has increased since the mid-2010s, even to the point of over-supply. There has been downward

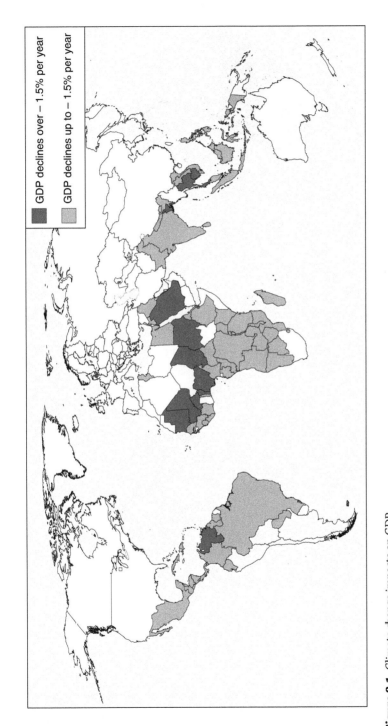

Figure 8.1 Climate change impacts on GDP

Source: Adapted from Pretis et al. (2018)

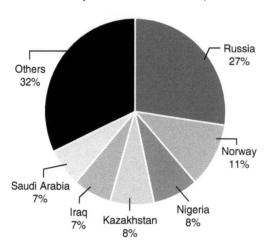

Figure 8.2 EU oil imports, 2018
Source: Eurostat database

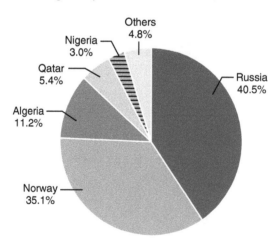

Figure 8.3 EU gas imports, 2018
Source: Eurostat database

pressure on prices in an era of ample global supply and oil price rivalries between Saudi Arabia, Russia and the US. Oil prices collapsed dramatically as the COVID-19 virus spread across the world, with geopolitical repercussions. The increase in US oil production has been of particular importance, as has the wider importance of shale gas supplies in many countries around the world. The falling costs of renewable technologies like wind and solar power have further deflated hydrocarbon prices.

Climate change and EU external action

Climate change has come increasingly to occupy a prominent place on the EU's policy agenda at multiple different levels. Most of the climate change agenda is about energy transition at the domestic level and is beyond this book's remit. Yet the international dimension of climate change is relevant as it has established itself as a core element of EU external action. Indeed, it has been widely argued for many years that the EU has done more than any other actor to strengthen international commitments to limit climate change. Analysts have often pointed out that the EU's internal climate policy commitments drove it into a proactive role internationally. The EU's international climate diplomacy has been one of the most dynamic, forward-looking and successful aspects of the Union's global presence. Certainly, the EU's role in relation to climate change has in some senses become more notable than in other areas of energy policy.

The EU has incrementally increased its own targets for reducing emissions. In 2008, the EU committed to cutting carbon emissions (from a 1990 baseline) by 20 per cent by the end of 2020 and it has been on target to achieve this. As part of the Paris agreement, the EU then committed to a 40 per cent emission reduction by 2030. In 2018, the Commission called for a net-zero emissions target for 2050; in March 2020, this was enshrined in a new EU Climate Law. At the national level, the UK was the first to enshrine the net-zero commitment in legislation; Finland committed to being carbon neutral by 2035. Having made more progress on cutting carbon emissions than other regions, the EU has been able to exert significant influence in multilateral negotiations. The EU has been more willing to sign up to ambitious targets to mitigate climate change than other powers and has more broadly influenced the direction of global debates.

At the global level, the EU supported some early policy moves, such as the creation of the multilateral IPCC in 1988. The EU's lead role in multilateral climate diplomacy emerged in earnest in the 2000s when it played a defining part in designing and then pushing through the seminal Kyoto Protocol, which was ratified in 2005. The EU acted in the face of US opposition to this treaty and cajoled other powers to come on board. The Union's decision to offer Russia WTO entry in return for its signing up to Kyoto was an especially significant move – although perhaps one with questionable value from a wider strategic perspective. The Commission and member states found effective ways to coordinate despite the complex division of policy competences between different institutional levels and directorate-generals.[11]

At a summit in Copenhagen in 2009 the EU suffered a serious setback: it failed to broker agreement on what kind of emissions commitments should follow on from the Kyoto accord and other powers expressly excluded the Union from their negotiations. While this episode was for some time cited as a sign of EU failure, the Union recovered and in the following years played an important role in negotiations that led up to the 2015 Paris agreement. The EU was the main advocate of the binding accord and engaged with other powers to win their support. It was a leader in the 'high ambition coalition' in Paris and had some success in pushing China, India and for a time the United States to accept tougher emissions targets for the post-2015 period. Since 2015 the EU has been active in building momentum behind the Paris commitments. In 2017, it began working with China and Canada in a minilateral sub-group – the so-called ministerial on climate action – designed to deal with the consequences of the US's withdrawal from the Paris agreement.[12]

In 2005 the EU introduced its Emissions Trading Scheme (ETS), which introduced carbon pricing as a means to push producers towards renewable sources. The ETS had an external dimension to the extent that the EU sought to get third countries to adopt the scheme. It has not had a great deal of success in this. Member states diluted the ETS to the point that it failed to have an immediately dramatic impact on carbon emission levels. Emission allowances were so generous that carbon surpluses accumulated in the years of economic crisis. EU states have ended up buying a great deal of 'dirty' energy from third countries, without this counting towards their domestic targets for clean energy usage. The EU gradually tightened the ETS during the 2010s, especially through a major reform in 2018, and the scheme has begun to have more of an impact. Still, it has not become a leading edge of EU external energy policies in the way that many policy-makers initially hoped would be the case.[13]

The aspect of European policy that has grown most dramatically is that of external climate funds. Since the late 2000s, the EU has intensified its support for third countries' energy transitions and climate adaptation. So-called climate finance has become one of the fastest-growing dimensions of EU external policy. This type of funding began in 2008 when the EU allocated a modest 300 million euros to a Global Climate Change Alliance to help developing countries increase their use of renewable energy sources. In 2009 the EU committed 7.2 billion euros to its first formalised package of climate funding. Since then the EU's climate financing has grown dramatically, and totalled 21.7 billion euros in 2018. The EU has provided nearly half the global total of such climate financing.[14]

The Multi-Annual Financial Framework for 2021–2027 stipulated that a minimum of 30 per cent of all EU funding would be spent on climate issues and energy transitions. At the broader global level, in 2019 EU states committed to increase their contributions to the UN Green Climate Fund to help developing states with energy transition; France, Germany and the UK all doubled their pledges. The Commission and member states committed to covering the decrease in US funds for key climate financing funds. By the end of the 2010s, the European Investment Bank and European Bank for Reconstruction and Development were allocating between a third and a half of their external lending to green finance. Germany announced an especially significant increase in its climate funding to 4 billion euros in 2020.

Alongside this funding the EU has developed a more geo-economic strand to its policies in the form of climate-related trade conditionality. This has aimed at pressing other countries to raise their climate targets but also to protect the EU's own immediate economic interests. So-called 'green clauses' have become a more prominent part of the Union's trade agreements and one of the most tangible ways in which the climate change priority has begun to infuse other areas of EU external action. In late 2010s EU–ASEAN talks, the Union insisted on a cap on biofuel exports from Indonesia and Malaysia as long as these countries continued to undertake mass deforestation in their palm oil production. As of late 2020, France, Ireland, Germany and others were holding back from ratifying the EU–Mercosur free trade agreement in response to President Bolsonaro's harmful actions in the Amazon, although some other member states wanted to push forward with the accord. Developing countries have angrily protested that this 'green protectionism' has become a pretext for defending European commercial interests. The EU has certainly become more geo-economically assertive in trying to neuter other states' competitive advantages and position itself economically in the changed global energy landscape.

The EU has likewise moved towards making not only trade but also some aid conditional on developing countries' efforts to reduce carbon emissions. This has become controversial: developing countries have increasingly complained that the Union has imposed climate objectives and projects that are not their priority, cutting across the EU's ostensible commitment to local ownership in aid and drawing money away from poverty-relief projects. Local groups have accused the EU of 'eco-colonialism' and of undermining their traditional livelihoods.[15] Developing states have also criticised the EU for refusing to relax intellectual property restrictions on renewables technology to help its uptake across the world, accusing the Union of prioritising its own commercial gains from renewables technology ahead of climate goals. European governments have often insisted that EU-supported renewables projects in third countries be used to increase energy supplies into Europe rather than increase the energy resilience of the source countries. Morocco resisted the large bio-thermal, Desertec project for this reason.[16]

The Commission's 'European Green Deal' published in December 2019 wrapped these various strands of external policy into a more concerted strategy. It proposed an upgraded 'green deal diplomacy' across the world with more focus on supporting energy transition in other regions and promised to build 'green alliances' through its foreign policy instruments. In what promised to be one of the EU's most consequential external actions, the deal also mentioned a possible carbon border tax; this would in effect charge non-green energy production in other countries and potentially have a major impact on the global trading system.[17] European leaders insisted these commitments represented a major upgrade to its international climate action. This was infused with elements of tougher mercantile and protective power. The Green Deal promised to use the EU's broader international power more purposively for climate goals, while also using climate measures more tightly to protect its own vital interests. The pursuit of 'green industrial strategy' and desire to create European renewables champions have certainly become increasingly powerful drivers of the mercantilism outlined in Chapter 6.

In some ways, the COVID-19 pandemic risked displacing climate issues from the top of the international agenda and pushed government to redirect external funding towards the health emergency as a top priority. In other ways, however, the pandemic revealed what damage a major global, transboundary threat could leave in its wake. Calls for a different economic model based on less extensive global supply chains indirectly reinforced the need for climate action. The EU and most member states individually promised to upgrade their climate action as a result of the pandemic. France and the Netherlands launched proposals further to toughen climate conditionality in EU trade accords. Signals that post-COVID funding would be more oriented towards renewables technology helped push carbon-credit prices up strongly later in 2020. At the end of 2020, leaders agreed to a more ambitious target of reducing carbon emissions by 55 per cent by 2030.

For over a decade EU leaders and policy-makers have insisted that ambitious policies to limit climate change and support energy transitions are not only necessary in their own right but are also beneficial for wider geo-strategic reasons. The EU has attached a broad strategic logic to its support for energy transitions at the global level and sought to position itself to leverage international political influence from this.[18] These elements have, in particular, become increasingly central to the Union's strategic and geo-economic approaches to China outlined in previous chapters. European policy-makers apparently calculate that pressing for decarbonisation around the world could offer at least partial disentanglement from the fraught geopolitics of oil and gas supplies. Commissioner Miguel Arias Cañete said in early 2018: 'energy transition … remains our answer to the geopolitical uncertainties we are facing.'[19]

Climate security

Beyond the EU's standard climate action and its lead role in the international politics of energy transition is a wider agenda of climate security. Climate security is about a whole series of ways in which climate change has become more integral to core foreign and security policy: it is an agenda that ostensibly goes well beyond EU leadership on emissions targets or its investment in energy transition across the world. Climate security refers to external action needing to change in specific ways to deal with the risks generated by climate change.

The EU was one of the first organisations to identify climate change as a security issue in this way. In 2008 it published an influential paper framing climate change as a 'threat multiplier' that needed to be placed at the heart of EU security policy. Climate change was becoming a core security issue as it led to intensified conflict over resources; more and costly humanitarian operations; new disputes over land and maritime borders; increased environmental migration; more state fragility, accompanied by radicalisation; more pressure for nuclear energy, with problems for non-proliferation; and tensions between north and south, and also between rising powers and least developed countries.[20]

The EU set up a steering group on climate change and international security, and through a large number of events and training sessions generated a hub of diplomats working on this issue.[21] In a 2008 revision of the European Security Strategy, climate change was identified as a core strategic and not merely environmental challenge. In March 2010, a European Council summit was for the first time devoted to the strategic challenge of climate change and energy issues.[22] In July 2011, the EU agreed new council conclusions on 'climate diplomacy', after the UK and

Germany combined to push the External Action Service to begin engaging in more tangible and systematic fashion on the foreign policy dimensions of climate change. The new climate diplomacy strategy promised identifiable action on the security strand of EU policy.[23] In 2012, the EU devised a new Arctic strategy that promised commitment to managing the strategic fall-out of climate impacts on the region.[24]

In 2013, the foreign affairs council adopted conclusions on climate diplomacy and security, together with a new External Action Service reflection paper, supposedly providing a new high-level political impetus. These made a number of operational commitments, including a mainstreaming of climate security into all external dialogues and an annual review of progress made in injecting foreign and security policy parameters into climate change strategies.[25] Over the early 2010s most member states introduced their own climate security strategies and oversaw a similar range of events, research, scenario planning and regional dialogues. Denmark, Germany, Sweden and the UK developed particularly notable national strategies.[26]

European militaries engaged early and strongly with the climate security agenda. In the late 2000s the UK had a rear admiral serving as its envoy for climate security. The British, Spanish and Swedish militaries undertook early exercises in assessing how climate threats would require military capabilities to be reconfigured. Nordic militaries adjusted to face likely threats in the Arctic. Militaries adapted for more regular deployment in response to extreme weather events; Spain, for example, created a widely admired Military Emergency Unit. Militaries also beefed up their resources and plans for defending home territories against extreme weather, reflecting a 'renewed interest in national civil defence capacity'.[27] Armed forces became greener, looking at ways of using more renewable energy sources.

In February 2018, the European Council committed to doing more on all aspects of climate security, promising to 'further mainstream the nexus between climate change and security in policy dialogue, conflict prevention, development and humanitarian action and disaster risk strategies'. In June 2018, on the tenth anniversary of the 2008 'threat multiplier' paper, the EU promised more of a security-led role in climate issues, in particular through a new early-warning mechanism and the High Representative beginning to play a role in this area.[28] The European Commission's key *A clean planet for all* document talked of the EU 'anticipating and preparing for the geopolitical and geo-economic shifts inherent in the low carbon transition, such as new and changed dependencies ... as well as the management of climate-security risks'.[29]

Council conclusions in 2019 reiterated the commitment to tackling climate change as an 'existential' issue of international security.[30] The 2019 implementation report of the Global Strategy insisted that the 'climate–security nexus' was one of areas where a 'joined-up' approach had advanced most effectively between different parts of the EU and claimed that 'climate action has become an integral part of our work on conflict prevention and sustainable security'.[31] Germany launched an effort to get the UN Security Council to deal with climate issues in fragile states and for UN peacekeeping to build in a climate angle. The UK announced a significant increase in funding for 'climate crises' overseas. EU defence ministers discussed climate change for the first time in August 2019 and the December 2019 European Green Deal promised further action on climate security.[32] The EU appointed an ambassador-at-large for the Arctic in 2017 as climate-change effects have begun to intensify geopolitical manoeuvring there.

Despite all these commitments and activities, however, the EU has in practice remained at a preliminary stage in climate security. While the challenge of climate security could be of existential importance, it has not been tangible or immediate enough to trigger wide-ranging, firm EU action. Short-term crises have crowded climate security from the EU's highest foreign policy priorities. European initiatives have remained at a level of awareness-raising, generic dialogues and building scenarios for the strategic impact that climate change is likely to have. It is harder to see where the issue has prompted concrete EU engagement.

Climate security stresses have not prompted the EU to intervene in conflicts. While EU planners have begun to assess climate factors as part of conflict management scenario-building, governments have not seen armed interventions as being a central part of this agenda.[33] EU leaders have often pointed to the climate stresses behind the Syrian conflict; yet the EU's position in this conflict has been strikingly hands-off. There has been little sign of committed EU diplomatic engagement in the key flashpoints of climate stress – like the tension between Ethiopia and Egypt over the Nile, or in the Mekong delta. The European Parliament has criticised the EU's lack of preparedness to deal with climate-related conflict.[34] The EU's Civil Protection Mechanism was reformed at the end of 2018, in part around climate risks, but with a narrow mandate of providing equipment for climate-related disasters like storms and forest fires. The EU has gained little practical, on-the-ground traction in the Arctic, not least because Russia has refused to let it into the Arctic Council. The main fruit of Germany's efforts in the UN Security Council was the commissioning of more foresight work, not concrete climate-security intervention.

Climate security has put pressure on governments to turn armed forces inwards to deal with domestic floods and storms; in consequence, the danger has emerged of climate change actually weakening the focus on foreign policy engagements.[35] There are traces here of the protective perspective on security prominent in other areas of EU external action. Governments have used climate-security concerns to justify a certain fusion of CSDP missions with border-control assets within Frontex and more widely. In the wider sense of how geopolitical alliances need to shift, climate issues have been far more mainstreamed within US than European military planning.[36]

While the EU has increased its climate funding in developing countries this has had a relatively weak security read-over. Most climate funding has gone to fairly generic energy transition initiatives devoid of any direct security relevance. Through such funding the EU has prioritised a very indirect and developmental approach towards climate security. Indeed, it has often seemed that the EU has reduced climate security mainly to a justification for more climate funding. In practice, European climate funding has in places financed the very governments and other actors responsible for fomenting instability. Using development funds to support deforestation programmes and the like may be desirable but it is doubtful they contribute directly towards security strategy.[37]

The 2018 council conclusions stressed that the EU still needed to change its security policy in light of climate change, but were mainly about the Paris accord and climate finance, not saying anything about tangible changes to EU security approaches in particular countries.[38] The European Court of Auditors concluded in 2017 that the EU and member states remain unprepared for the security impact of climate change.[39] The Union has responded ad hoc to extreme weather events, but has exhibited little urgency in developing a foreign policy framework to ensure that the generic background risks of climate change produce more specific security responses.[40] Over a decade on from the 2008 'threat multiplier' report, much European activity in this field was still aimed at gathering data and carrying out foresight exercises.

The EU's basic conceptualisation of climate security has remained relatively narrow. The Union has understood international climate politics as being largely about the issue of reducing carbon emissions; it has focused less on how the wider range of climate impacts requires far-reaching or systemic change to the EU's geo-economic, military, developmental, migration and other policies. Yet carbon emissions are one symptom of climate change alongside a multiplicity of deeper, root causes driving climate insecurity. Even if all emissions targets were met, global temperatures would continue rising for some time along with attendant insecurity; the EU has leant on these targets almost as a security strategy by default. Flowing from this, it has tended to define climate instability as being 'out there' beyond Europe's borders rather than acknowledging the way that the EU's own economic models and external policies add to that instability.

The EU still has to address the climate-related challenges to its broader set of international alliances.[41] Although the Commission published several documents in the 2010s on the importance of critical minerals, European states have only just begun to seek partnerships with the African, Latin American and Asian countries that have materials like cobalt and lithium that will be key sources of power in the post-carbon era. Germany, for instance, has concluded access deals on such materials in Central Asia. Yet the EU has still to devise an overarching approach to this issue. The US headed a ten-country Energy Resource Governance Initiative designed to shift alliances to access minerals needed for non-carbon technologies; the EU had no equivalent and no European country joined the US initiative. Promising to correct this inaction, in September 2020 the Commission published a strategy for an industry alliance to reduce EU dependency on critical rare-earths, framing this as part of the wider post-Covid aim of bringing more production back onshore, especially from China. While Europe does not house vast amounts of these critical minerals, the Commission has begun to refer to an aim of greater self-sufficiency in some of them, like lithium.[42] The UK launched a similar initiative with its Five-Eyes intelligence-sharing partners (the US, Canada, Australia and New Zealand).[43] This is set to be a thorny question for future EU external action; European countries will need access to these materials but rare-mineral dependencies could become just as constraining as current oil and gas dependencies.

While the EU insists that climate security is of unmatched importance, in reality it has pursued other policy aims in ways that undermine climate security aims.

Migration might be a necessary climate adaptation strategy – people moving out of climate-stressed locations – but the EU has focused on closing off migration routes. In any given third country, the EU typically operates a handful of projects on decarbonisation, but then works with them to expand trade that relies on the very economic model causing climate stresses. Simply pushing other states through trade and regulatory conditionality to follow EU templates for cutting emissions has actually stirred up hostility and local tensions in third countries. In sum, while the EU has become more engaged in the nexus between climate change and security, most of its actions in this field have been about putting sticking plasters on a problem whose geostrategic amplifiers continue to accelerate.

Security of energy supplies

If issues related to climate change have become a progressively more prominent part of the EU's external action, European approaches towards oil and gas supplies have been more varied. Moreover, rather than energy security and climate security working together, they have increasingly cut across each other in EU external action. The more conventional dimension of energy security has long been one of the EU's Achilles' heels. Member states have traditionally pursued their own interests in securing oil and gas supplies, and this has undermined other EU foreign policy objectives. From the early years of European integration, the EU lacked a common external energy policy. In the 2010s the EU moved to fill this missing piece of the energy policy jigsaw. It honed a focus on the external dimensions of energy security, even if it did not create a single, united energy policy.[44]

In the early 2000s the EU focused on completing its internal energy market and assumed such market-led rules would give the Union international leverage too. However, in the early 2010s the EU found itself in a particularly vulnerable position in terms of its energy supplies. Even as internal energy market integration advanced, member states' different internal energy mixes and their contrasting views on international energy markets led them to different positions on geostrategic questions relating to energy supplies. This was one of the policy areas in which national governments' actions remained most prominent and internal differences most significant. Some thought markets would suffice to provide adequate energy supplies, others believed deals had to be negotiated with key suppliers – and that these should be pursued as a priority area of EU foreign and security policy.[45]

Member state governments were forced to rethink in particular after a 2009 gas dispute between Russia and Ukraine that made real the prospect of energy supplies being cut off for political reasons. This crisis strengthened the EU's determination to diversify its energy supplies and pushed energy geopolitics to the top of the foreign policy agenda. Many member state governments also took it to show that a market-led approach to energy needed to be supplemented with more political actions. The dispute suggested that the costs of EU disunity in the field of energy security could be extremely serious. This was a watershed moment in the long history of attempts to develop a united EU external energy strategy.

The EU then played a prominent role in relation to the so-called Nabucco and South Stream pipeline projects. The Commission gave political support to the Nabucco project that was planned as an alternative to supplies coming from Russia. However, this project collapsed as the supplier states backing it concluded that EU commitments to the supplies were not fully guaranteed. The Russian-backed South Stream pipeline was a route for Russian supplies into South East Europe that would circumvent Ukraine. Some member states were keen to benefit from this project; others were resolutely opposed to it. The Commission used competition law against the six EU member states that signed up to this project, on the grounds that they were helping Russian provider Gazprom maintain anti-competitive practices. In response, President Putin announced Russia would no longer pursue South Stream, citing EU opposition as the reason for this apparently momentous decision. This became one of the most celebrated examples of internal EU market rules having an external geopolitical impact.

In 2014 the Commission produced an Energy Security Strategy and in 2015 the EU agreed the broader and more developed Energy Union.[46] The Energy Union promised that the EU would 'use all its foreign policy instruments to establish strategic energy partnerships with increasingly important producing and transit countries'.[47] The EU launched a concept of Energy Diplomacy, to mobilise foreign policy instruments behind energy interests. The driving force behind the EU's new initiatives was to diversify energy supplies and, in particular, reduce dependence on Russia. Despite this, most member states retained cooperation with Russia on gas supplies. By the end of the 2010s, Russia was still the largest source of EU gas imports. Bulgaria, Greece and Hungary began to receive Russian supplies through the Turkstream pipeline that opened in early 2020, bringing gas under the Black Sea. The high-profile saga of Germany's support for the Nordstream pipeline supplying Russian gas is covered in Box 8.1. Still, a broad consensus has taken shape around the importance of developing a wider range of energy relationships.

During the 2010s, the EU signed a significant number of new external energy partnerships. As of 2020, the EU had 18 energy dialogues with individual countries, 29 memorandums of understanding and declarations on energy cooperation, and 7 regional initiatives covering the Eastern Partnership, Union for the Mediterranean, Africa, the Gulf Cooperation Council, ASEAN and the Caspian area, along with the Energy Community Treaty. This extensive range of initiatives showed that the EU had moved away from simply seeking to export its energy governance laws and instead adopted a strategy of energy diplomacy, pursuing politically negotiated energy deals with third-country supplier states.[48] There was a flavour here in the energy sector of the geo-economic dynamics becoming more widely prevalent in the EU's external relations (as covered in Chapter 6).

As a replacement to the Nabucco project, the Commission became a strong supporter of the various components of the so-called Southern Gas Corridor – as shown in Figure 8.4, this is made up of source links through the Southern Caucasus from Azerbaijan (and potentially under the Caspian Sea from Turkmenistan too), the Trans-Anatolian pipeline across Turkey and then the Trans-Adriatic pipeline bringing supplies into southern Italy. The middle section through Turkey opened

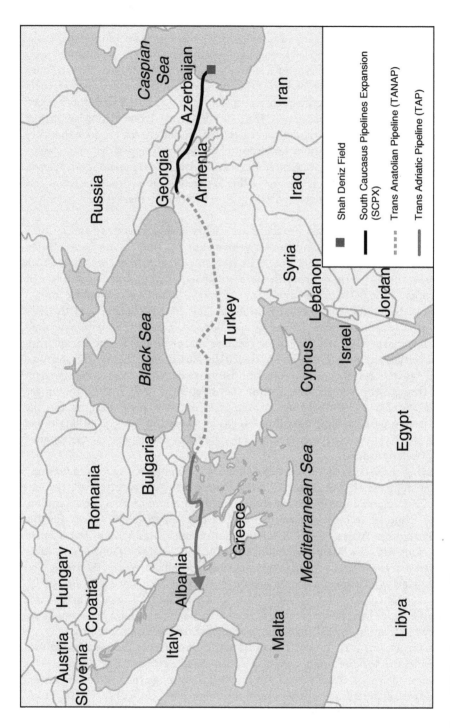

Figure 8.4 Southern gas corridor

in 2018, as Azerbaijan's extensive Shah Deniz II field began producing. While the Nabucco line would have rested heavily on applying EU regulations, arrangements for the Southern Gas Corridor have been based more on geopolitical deals than EU energy market rules. The Southern Corridor has made Caspian supplies more important; Azerbaijan has provided a modest share of overall EU gas imports, but has been of significance for Italy, Greece and Bulgaria.

The European Bank for Reconstruction and Development invested 500 million euros into the Trans-Anatolian pipeline. In 2018, the European Investment Bank lent another 1.5 billion euros, in one of its largest-ever energy-related operations. The Commission pushed for the Southern Gas Corridor's capacity to be doubled by the end of the 2020s. The EU has supported the project despite doubts over whether this is fully justified on pure market grounds, demonstrating its geopolitical foundations. The EU negotiated a strategic cooperation agreement with Azerbaijan to advance energy cooperation – detailed in Chapter 11 – and signed energy partnerships with Kazakhstan in 2006, Turkmenistan in 2008 and Uzbekistan in 2011. The EU offered support to the Turkmen government to link Turkmenistan's gas into the Southern Gas Corridor. Still, the capacity of the Southern Gas Corridor remained below that of Russian-supplied pipelines into Europe.[49]

Energy cooperation has also deepened to the south. In 2014, the EU agreed to develop Euro-Mediterranean energy platforms to promote market integration. In the Middle East and North Africa region the EU has moved away from pushing states to converge around the Union's own market and regulatory structures; the three Platforms resembled traditional security-of-supply arrangements.[50] The Union for the Mediterranean (UfM) has funded an increasing number of projects to boost production capacity in the southern Mediterranean and increase exports into Europe. The EU agreed an energy partnership with Algeria in 2013; after years of stalemate in their relations, in 2017 the EU and Algeria signed an accord and a set of 'partnership priorities'. European Investment Bank funds supported the Medgaz pipeline between Algeria and Spain. Spain concluded its own bilateral ten-year supply deal with Algeria in October 2020.

The EU signed a similar memorandum with Egypt in 2018, promising assistance for the country's oil and gas sector and the development of an Energy Hub. This accord was one of several actions prompted by the discovery of gas in the East Mediterranean. France, Italy, Greece and Cyprus formed the East Mediterranean Gas Forum in 2019, along with Israel, Jordan, Palestine and Egypt, to work up plans to export gas from fields near Cyprus. The EU deployed the European Fund for Strategic Investments to support the construction of new LNG terminals to boost imports from Egypt. The Commission has also supported preparations for pipeline capacity to help bring East Mediterranean gas into EU member states. In what became one of the most geopolitical areas of energy policy, Turkey and the Libyan government reached a deal on maritime issues that sought to block this planned East Med gas pipeline. The previous chapter already detailed how several EU states confronted in Turkey in 2019 and 2020 to defend this element of external energy-security strategy, as this fused with other Turkey-related strategic concerns.

The Commission has gained modest powers to assess the compatibility of member states' bilateral energy agreements with EU rules. Rules introduced in 2012 required member states to share information on the energy deals they intend to sign with third countries. The Commission was tasked with offering advice on each agreement's compatibility with EU energy goals. These rules were tightened in 2017. The European Court of Justice effectively ruled in 2019 that member states should no longer make energy-infrastructure decisions without considering other member states' interests: prompted by a Polish challenge, it overturned the German regulator's decision to let Gazprom use the so-called Opal onshore continuation of Nordstream on the grounds it did not meet the criterion of solidarity with other states.[51] A balance has been struck on this much-debated and sensitive issue. European governments have not been willing to give the Commission powers to vet energy contracts concluded by member states with third countries – national energy deals have not been replaced by single EU energy contrasts with third countries. Yet member states have sought a framework for managing the most serious of disputes over external energy relations.[52]

While the EU has gradually and incompletely put in place a more political and common security-of-supply strategy, the energy panorama has changed significantly. The external, outside-in challenges of traditional energy security have been serious, given the more adversarial geopolitical stances adopted by key oil and gas suppliers in recent years. Yet as the EU's energy transition has gathered pace so oil and gas supplies have lost some of their centrality to foreign policy challenges. This, combined with high levels of global gas production and supplies, mean that alternative pipeline routes have lost some of their visceral importance; Chapters 10 and 11 show how other security concerns have in recent years taken precedence over energy security to both the south and east. Geopolitical problems have made it more difficult for the EU to diversify its supplies away from Russia to the Middle East and North Africa. At the same time, deeper internal coordination – including through an EU Gas Directive – has helped to reduce external vulnerabilities.

Flowing from this is the question of how EU energy security and climate policies relate to each other. The EU has seen apparently mundane measures of energy transition and efficiency at the domestic level as a way to ease the thorny geostrategic dilemmas associated with oil and gas supplies. The Commission's *A clean planet for all* strategy document claimed that if the EU met all its commitments related to internal energy transition, its dependence on external energy supplies would fall from 55 per cent in 2018 to 20 per cent in 2050.[53] Reflecting this, some member states and EU institutions have expressed doubts over whether new pipeline projects remain necessary and over their incompatibility with climate goals.[54] While the EU has initiatives to help oil and gas producers move away from hydrocarbon dependency, it then invariably works in deeper partnership with them to expand those same energy supplies.[55] By the end of the 2010s, the EU already had an incoming pipeline capacity well in excess of what its hydrocarbons consumption must be to meet its 2050 emission targets. In short, the EU's ramping up of energy security policies has come to sit uneasily with climate change commitments.

Box 8.1 Nordstream

The Nordstream pipeline, which directly connects Russia with German markets, started pumping in November 2011. The follow-on Nordstream 2 project has become a highly geopolitical issue and has occasioned serious disagreements within the EU institutions and between member states. Germany's decision to proceed with a second pipeline directly from Russia engendered considerable anger, with many member states furious that its decision undermined years of EU efforts to tighten pressure on Russia.

In its 2017 revision of the EU Gas Directive, the Commission sought explicitly to extend competition rules to pipelines coming into Europe as a means of clarifying that these rules would be applied to Nordstream 2. This has become a key battle line drawn in external energy policy. The Commission effectively wanted a legal mandate to negotiate a framework with Russia that obliged Gazprom to accept stringent conditions under which it would be able to export additional gas into Europe. In effect, the Commission revised the Gas Directive in an effort to gain a legal mandate that would allow it to stop or least limit Nordstream 2.

Several Eastern European states have supported the Commission in its bid to use this kind of regulatory focus against Nordstream 2. Conversely, other members have sought to fend off the Commission's bid for more power in this domain. The legal services of the Council argued the Commission was acting beyond its competences. Denmark and Sweden called in a joint letter for more EU powers to curtail the pipeline project, against Germany's claim that it had the national powers to proceed without EU interference. Russia took the EU to the WTO dispute settlement body; the EU was also subject to a case under the Energy Charter Treaty.

In 2017, the Danish government stipulated that it would separate market and geopolitical factors in assessing Nordstream 2, giving itself the scope to oppose the pipeline for wider foreign policy reasons separate from energy interests. While no other member state has proceeded as far as Denmark in formalising such a security-oriented process, the influence of wider geopolitical considerations has become stronger. Even German politicians acknowledged that the project should not be separated from wider EU concerns over Russian foreign policy actions and insisted that Russia not bypass Ukraine and thus deprive that country of vital revenues.

Uncertainties began to mount. In 2019, the Commission, member states and the European Parliament agreed on a compromise, under which Nordstream 2 could proceed but subject to tougher transparency standards and shared usage rules potentially increasing the influence of EU legal norms over Russia. The project was delayed in 2019 as it waited for environmental clearance from the Danish government. The impact of the above-mentioned Opal decision added dilemmas over the management of supply capacity coming into Germany. In 2019, the US imposed sanctions on companies directly involved in building the pipeline and construction work largely ceased. In 2020, the US moved to penalise those facilitating the project in any way; even the EU member states hostile to the pipeline were unhappy at the US's use of extra-territorial measures. After the poisoning of Russian opposition leader, Alexei Navalny in summer 2020, German politicians from across the spectrum raised questions about the pipeline, although Chancellor Merkel insisted she would not cancel it.[56] By late 2020, EU states were buying amounts of Russian gas well below the pipeline capacity that already existed. A map of Nordstream is shown in Figure 8.5.

Figure 8.5 Nordstream pipelines

Source: www.gisreportsonline.com

Themes and analysis

Climate change is arguably the most existential, long-term outside-in challenge facing Europe. The EU has undoubtedly played an important role in pushing forward global commitments to limit the effects of climate change. The Union has often been guilty of overly idealising its international leadership on climate change. Its own record on cutting emissions and hastening low-carbon energy transition has been far from perfect. Yet this is a policy arena in which the EU has undoubtedly been influential and where it counts for a great deal at the international level. Interestingly, the EU's influence has been strongest as a negotiator and agenda-shaper, rather than through the Union being able to externalise its own climate initiatives to other countries. Of course, the sobering reality is that despite the EU's international achievements in spurring more global coordination, this is still an area of policy where failure hangs in the air: governments have not reacted fast enough or radically enough to prevent climate change wreaking serious damage, within and beyond Europe itself.

The EU began to address the more specific area of *climate security* as one of its flagship priorities more than a decade ago and did much to galvanise the international attention given to this challenge. Yet EU and member state policies in this area have remained fairly low-profile. Despite the Union producing and supporting scores of climate security scenario exercises and discussions on this question, EU policies in particular countries have not changed in a significant or tangible manner as a result of climate security concerns. While militaries' engagement with this issue led to some concern that EU climate action could become overly securitised, to date the EU has pursued a relatively soft, development-funding-led approach to climate security.

An emerging imbalance is that the EU equates climate security with pushing other powers to cut carbon emissions while doing little to address the bigger geopolitical ramifications. The EU's external budget for climate action is sizeable, but has remained well below what is necessary to deal fully with the strategic magnitude of this challenge. Focused on its own emission targets the EU has begun to push for access to the critical minerals needed for low-carbon battery and other technology, even though mining for these could wreak even more serious environmental damage. Relating all this back to the outside-in framework, the EU's approach to climate geopolitics resonates with the concept of protective security, and the Union has arguably prioritised its own relative power within energy-transition scenarios more than a distinctively liberal, comprehensive approach to climate change.[57]

While climate-related issues have become more prominent in the mix of EU external policies, the outside-in challenges of *energy security* have evolved in more varied ways. To some degree, the EU has stepped up its focus on securing oil and gas supplies from a wider range of countries. In doing so, it has shifted from an external policy that relied mainly on a market-based approach to one with notable geo-economic elements. The 'geo-economic Europe' outlined elsewhere in the book has become especially evident in the energy sector. The energy partnerships the Union signed during the 2010s brought negotiated mercantilism to the fore rather than being led overwhelmingly by a rules-based, regulatory approach.[58] At the same time, however, traditional security-of-supply challenges have become slightly less determinant for EU external action. While the EU has usually been criticised for focusing too exclusively on short-term hydrocarbon supplies to the detriment of other goals, by the 2020s this was no longer quite so clearly the case.

Despite remaining differences between member states and within different parts of the EU institutional structure, there has been a degree of convergence in external energy policies in the last several years. This is reflected in the EU's intricate balancing of climate policies, security of supply and other external objectives. National governments have played an important and, in some areas, increasing role in external energy and climate policies. The chapter highlights how governments have prioritised their distinctive interests and positions in response to external challenges. Yet it also shows areas of deeper cooperation. While many actors have a role in EU energy policy and eschew any single vision or voice, they have pulled in broadly similar directions.[59] Some analysts detect a 'lite' form of collective securitisation here: strategic concerns have pushed member states towards more coordination on external energy questions, even if national governments have remained wary over increasing EU-level powers.[60] Speaking to one strand of the book's outside-in framework, the heightened salience of energy and climate-related geopolitics has both galvanised and fragmented EU external action.

Taken together, the international elements of climate change and energy security have had far-reaching but contrasting effects on the overarching contours of EU external action. In some ways the EU has deepened its commitment to distinctive public-good focused action in the field of climate change and rules-based cooperation related to climate security. Yet, in some ways these challenges have also tempted the EU to turn inwards, with energy transition seen as a means of reducing the need for complicated external engagements. Notwithstanding repeated commitments to multilateral cooperation on climate issues, elements of the EU's climate security policies have shown traces of a lifeboat-style, protective-security approach. In the area of energy supply security the EU has, if anything, turned towards a more old-style geopolitics – notably, one not entirely consistent with the Union's own climate aims. The EU's climate and energy policies have taken shape as an uneasy combination of these contrasting dynamics.

Concluding summary

External challenges. The geopolitical impact of climate change is perhaps the most obvious and dramatic example of an emerging exogenous challenge driving far-reaching changes in EU external action – although critics insist it has not yet prompted sufficient change. The impact of internal EU energy-market changes has remained significant but has been less primary in recent years.

Unity–diversity. Broad unity on the foreign policy dimensions of climate change has strengthened, but alongside persistent differences related to states' energy mixes and specific gas pipeline projects. Energy and climate policies have become more clearly multi-level, involving an increasingly complex mix of national and EU-level actors and influences.

Distinctive power. The emerging approach to climate security involves several distinctive EU approaches but is overlain with a layer of more traditional geopolitical and geo-economic action. The same is true of strategy towards security-of-supply that has increasingly balanced distinctive regulatory cooperation with more strategic balancing and alliance-building.

Protective dynamics. Mainstream climate diplomacy and climate funding have been among the EU's most outward-looking policies in recent years. On climate security, the EU nominally commits to outward engagement and rules-based cooperation, but in practice elements of more autarchic protection have crept into the Union's policy mix. While the EU has sought deeper global energy partnerships, it has also created more protective resilience against traditional security-of-supply challenges.

EU influence. Unlike many other areas covered in the book that show a weakening of EU influence, in global climate politics European leverage remains paramount and, if anything, has increased. The EU has remained in the difficult position of being demandeur for oil and gas supplies, but modest moves towards lowering its external dependency have slightly widened its foreign policy manoeuvrability.

9 Democracy and Human Rights

The EU has habitually claimed that democracy and human rights are such fundamentally core elements of its own identity that they sit naturally at the heart of its external action. The EU has long insisted that no other international actor has shown such strong commitment to supporting human rights and democracy around the world. This chapter outlines the extensive range of policy instruments and resources that the EU has mobilised to support human rights and democratic values internationally. Deploying strands of the outside-in conceptual framework, it also explains why democracy support has become more difficult and charts how EU institutions and most member states have become less ambitious in this policy sphere in recent years. While the EU may still favour a more democratic world – for both strategic and ideational reasons – its support for democracy and human rights has been increasingly passive and low-key. A detailed look at the tactics the EU deploys in support of human rights and democracy casts doubt on the still-widespread assumption that these are foundational pillars of European external action. The EU has done much to encourage human rights and democratic reform around the world, but also much that has undermined these values.

The challenges

The EU's commitment to advance democratic norms has had to contend with an increasingly unpropitious global context. Democracy looked increasingly to be on the back foot as the 2010s progressed. The general direction of travel was towards more authoritarian forms of government, albeit with mixed trends as some states undertook democratising reforms. Different indices reported similar global dynamics. The Economist Intelligence Unit's Democracy Index saw democracy flatlining after the 2000s and up to 2016, after which its global aggregate scores declined; its 2020 index recorded the worst overall global democracy score since the index started in 2006.[1] Freedom House's 2020 Freedom in the World report returned the 14th consecutive year of decline in the global level of democracy, with twice as many states registering a worsening democracy score as those improving.[2] The influential Varieties of Democracy index noted a process of 'autocratisation' beginning from around 2016; in 2020 this survey reported another surge in authoritarianism, with non-democratic regimes now the majority of states in the world for the first time since 2001.[3]

All three of these indices uncovered a rise in pro-democratic protests across the world in the late 2010s as citizens pushed back against government repression. Many democratic indicators declined over the whole decade, especially related to trust in parties and government, as well as civil liberties, while citizens' political participation in protests and other direct action increased.[4] The slide away from democracy has in most cases been gradual and undramatic. Governments have typically centralised power in incremental fashion. Democracy has been threatened not by dramatic coups overturning democratic constitutional order, but by governments themselves chipping away at democratic quality. The trend cuts across different types of regime: there has been democratic deterioration in consolidated democracies, reversals or stagnation in hybrid regimes (that combine elements of democracy and autocracy) and more intense repression in non-democratic regimes.[5]

Many regimes have become assertive in seeking to neuter or block external support for democracy and human rights. Over 100 governments (including many in the European Union) have in recent years imposed some kind of restrictions on independent civil society, ranging from outright violent attacks on opposition activists through to harsh new NGO laws and on to more covert forms of intimidation. Many have clamped down hard against pro-democracy protests and their intimidation of journalists is also on the rise.[6] Even actors in principle keen to receive democracy support funding have pushed back against donors and insisted that local actors be given more complete ownership over such policies.[7] Many regimes have used digital surveillance technology to great effect in their clampdowns against democratic opposition and civil society figures and in their control over electoral processes.

Meanwhile, the US's commitment to democracy support has waned. President Obama was committed to human rights and democracy but relatively cautious in this area of policy. President Trump's transactional approach to foreign policy and celebration of many dictators around the world soon became a hallmark of his presidency. Thanks to Congress, the level of US democracy aid remained relatively high, and there were some elements of US policy that remained broadly favourable to democracy support. Yet the general direction of US foreign policy risked leaving the EU more alone in upholding human rights and democratic norms – at least in some countries. A further complicating factor came from challenges to liberal democracy from within the EU's own ranks, especially from governments in Hungary and Poland, but from some other states too. Some member states were always ambivalent about democracy support, but some of them have come more fundamentally to question such liberal universalism.

Taken together, these challenges have raised some profound and searching questions about human rights and democracy support. International support for democracy and human rights has faced stiffer resistance than in the early 2000s. The danger has become greater today of outside support being counter-productive in certain contexts, with democracy promotion efforts causing regimes bent on the centralisation of power to clampdown far more than in the past. Yet large-scale protests around the world have suggested that citizens still seek more democracy and open forms of government; the last several years have witnessed an unprecedented increase in revolts – successively in Venezuela, Chile, Algeria, Sudan, Lebanon, Zimbabwe, Ethiopia, Korea, Hong Kong, Belarus and many others. Both the demand for and the obstacles to democracy have become stronger.

Early priorities

The treaties that govern the EU institutions mention democracy as both a founding value and a principle of external action. The Union began to develop a policy of international support for democracy in the mid-1990s. From this point, the EU insisted that all third-country partners sign a so-called essential elements clause committing them to respect democratic norms and human rights standards. In the 1990s and early 2000s, democracy spread globally, and the Union offered assistance to the many governments that committed themselves to political reform. As explained in Chapter 7, the enlargement process was in this period the main focus of EU efforts to encourage reform, but this also gave a certain momentum to the Union's more global efforts to support human rights and democracy.

Significantly, the EU began to put in place democracy and human rights policies mainly under the rubric of its development policy. Outside the enlargement process, the Union began to incorporate funding for political projects through the various strands of its development budgets – rather than through the prism of high-level security strategy, as was more apparent in the United States. On some occasions the EU held back its development aid where government infringed democratic norms or human rights. It removed Generalised System of Preferences (GSP) trade preferences from Belarus (2007), Burma/Myanmar (1997) and Sri Lanka (2010) for these countries' failure to ratify labour rights conventions.

Still, in many countries the EU's diplomatic, financial and commercial pressure was limited. In the 2000s the EU offered various forms of cooperation agreements to a large number of states around the world, most of whom were autocratic. The EU imposed sanctions on Zimbabwe in 2002 but began to remove these after President Robert Mugabe agreed to a government of national unity in 2008. In general, the focus was on providing positive assistance to governments and civil society to build democratic institutions, whether in Russia and the post-communist bloc, post-conflict scenarios in the Balkans, the Arab states that had signed up to human rights cooperation under the Euro-Mediterranean Partnership in 1995 or the many African states that launched national conventions for political change in the 1990s and early 2000s.

In an effort to maintain momentum in its democracy and human rights policies, in 2009 governments agreed a set of Council Conclusions that reiterated the commitment to these elements of external action. In 2012, the EU agreed a Strategic Framework and Action Plan on Human Rights and Democracy, with a 36-point action plan. EU development cooperation became more political in its stated aims, with the European Commission's Agenda for Change placing support for democracy and human rights at the heart of development aid.[8] Democracy support was also formally built into an array of external policy frameworks, like the EU Consensus on Development and the European Neighbourhood Policy. From 2016 EU delegations were obliged to report on Commission and member state initiatives in support of democracy and human rights in their respective countries.[9]

While most observers interpreted the 2016 Global Strategy as a relatively realpolitik document, it did at least formally confirm EU support for human rights and democratic norms around the world: EU foreign policy would aim to foster 'resilient states' based on a conviction that 'a resilient society featuring democracy, trust in institutions, and sustainable development lies at the heart of a resilient state'. Through its Democracy Support and Election Coordination Group, the European Parliament increased its work from 2014, mainly in the form of election observation and exchanges with other parliaments. In October 2019, European governments issued Council Conclusions with an upgraded commitment to democracy support.[10] In March 2020, the Commission published an updated Action Plan for Human Rights and Democracy promising inter alia to provide more funding for new types of democracy activism and digital technologies; make security policies comply better with human rights norms; and focus more on human rights in multilateral forums.[11]

Several member states updated and strengthened their national commitment to democracy and human rights in these years. Denmark, Finland, the UK and Germany published democracy and human rights strategy documents. In late 2011, the Dutch Foreign Ministry produced an updated human rights strategy that talked of wielding more rights-based sanctions and of political criteria guiding the reduction of aid recipients. The Swedish government's 2018–2022 development aid strategy stressed that increased support for political reform was the key to development and gender aims; in 2019 Sweden launched a 'Drive for Democracy'. Central and Eastern European states became committed players in this sphere, at least until their own politics shifted in an illiberal direction. Traditionally seen as a sceptic on democracy support, the French government presented a new human rights strategy at the end of 2018 and embedded 'governance units' within its embassies around the world.

Critical engagement

The EU has constantly grappled with the use of critical pressure and sanctions in support of human rights and democracy. The Union has not been averse to using sanctions; it had more than 40 sets of restrictive measures in place at the end of the 2010s.[12] These have commonly been linked to wider United Nations sanctions and related to security concerns, as, for example, in Afghanistan, Iran, Mali, Russia, Somalia, South Sudan, Syria and Yemen. These security sanctions often in practice punish human rights abusers, even if a concern with human rights was not the main reason why they were imposed. After several years of internal debate, at the end of 2020 the EU agreed a new sanctions regime specifically targeted at individuals guilty of human rights abuses. This was a potentially significant change, even if it came nearly a decade after the US's similar Magnitsky Act. The EU used the new provisions for the first time against Russian officials implicated in the detention of opposition leader, Alexei Navalny. The UK introduced its own human rights sanctions regime and in June 2020 imposed measures against Russian, Saudi Arabian, Burmese and North Korean officials involved in killings.[13]

Overall, the EU has used its own autonomous sanctions in relation to human rights and democracy in only a small number of cases, as shown in Table 9.1.

Alongside sanctions, the EU has often sought leverage over human rights and democracy by holding back or removing aid and trade agreements. One country where the EU has combined these different forms of pressure over many years is Burma/Myanmar. The EU imposed one of its most extensive range of sanctions for many years against the military junta in Myanmar. When the military initiated the tentative beginnings of a reform process in 2011, the EU gradually removed sanctions and included the country in its GSP scheme in 2013. As the regime then backtracked on reform commitments and perpetrated abuses against the Rohingya minority, the EU reinstated targeted sanctions. It decided not to remove GSP trade preferences but decreased many areas of cooperation. When the military reassumed direct control in early 2021, the EU moved to extend its list of restrictive measures against members of the Myanmar regime.

Diverse cases show the EU's approach of holding back aid and trade provisions in response to concerns over democracy and human rights. It has delayed macroeconomic aid to Ukraine due to a lack of progress on anti-corruption reforms and to Moldova after the government annulled 2018 mayoral elections in Chisinau that were won by an opposition activist – Chapter 11 provides more detail on these Eastern European examples. As detailed in Chapter 7, the EU has since 2018 held back portions of pre-accession aid to increasingly autocratic Turkey. The EU also cut aid to Honduras after a coup in 2009 and to Tanzania in 2018 in response to negative political developments.

These examples show that the EU has, in some cases, exerted pressure on democracy-related issues. In general, however, the EU has preferred to avoid strongly punitive policies. As Table 9.1 makes clear, the EU's human rights and democracy sanctions have nearly always taken the form of asset freezes and travel bans targeted at a small number of regime officials, rather than more sweeping measures. After President Maduro effectively suspended Venezuela's parliament in 2017, the EU targeted financial sanctions against just 18 individuals, with another batch of names added in 2020. Its focus was mainly on trying to encourage a

Table 9.1 EU autonomous human rights and democracy sanctions

Belarus	Measures on regime officials from 2004. Removed in 2016 (from all but four individuals). New measures in 2020
Burundi	Measures on regime officials for undermining democracy, from 2015
China	Arms embargo, from 1989 Tiananmen Square repression
DRC	Measures on regime officials involved in human rights abuses, from 2016
Guinea	Measures on regime officials for human rights abuses, from 2009
Iran	Measures on regime officials for human rights abuses, from 2011
Myanmar	Extensive sanctions from 1996; lifted 2013, except arms embargo; new measures on regime officials for human rights abuses from 2018
Nicaragua	Measures on regime officials for human rights abuses, from 2019
Venezuela	Measures on regime officials for human rights abuses and democratic infringements, from 2017
Zimbabwe	Restrictive measures from 2002, lifted from 2013

Source: EU sanctions map. www.sanctionsmap.eu/#/main

power-sharing accord between Maduro and the opposition. Spain continued to provide aid and sell arms to Venezuela well into the late 2010s; the US threatened measures against Spain for these links with the regime.[14] The EU put the onus on humanitarian support as the situation inside the country became so bad. The Union did not recognise elections in December 2020 as being free and fair and extended sanctions to more members of the regime, although it also stepped back from such clear support for opposition leader Juan Guaidó.

The democracy and human rights clause included in external agreements has only been activated in sub-Saharan Africa and only used to freeze aid not trade relations. There are some examples of the EU reducing funds to countries suffering incremental autocratic trends – like Burundi and South Africa – but the numbers do not suggest a systematic policy in this regard. In 2020 the EU removed GSP trade preferences from Cambodia after its autocratic regime dissolved the main opposition party. However, the EU has declined to remove GSP trade preferences from countries like Pakistan and the Philippines where human rights have clearly worsened; it insists that the scheme's dialogue-based monitoring mechanisms have sufficed to improve recipients' labour standards.[15] Many believed the EU moved too quickly to remove sanctions on the Burmese regime after 2011 because European states were keen mainly to displace Chinese influence, even though democratic momentum was still extremely modest – as soon became apparent.

While the EU offered support to the Arab spring revolts that began in 2001, it then adopted a hands-off approach as Middle Eastern and North African governments pushed back against democracy. The EU normalised its relations with Egypt despite the regime there becoming more authoritarian than it was before the 2011 revolution; from 2017 the European Commission and several member states increased funding to President al-Sisi's highly repressive government. The EU removed most sanctions against Iran due to an agreement on nuclear issues, even though the country's human rights record and general level of political repression have worsened in recent years – the EU only imposed targeted measures on a small number of Iranian nationals implicated in the killing of dissidents on European soil.[16] Chapter 10 examines the Middle East region in greater detail.

The EU has also rewarded governments that either have not reformed or have become more repressive. The vast majority of European external funds in recent years have gone to authoritarian or semi-authoritarian regimes.[17] All the 26 countries eligible for the EU Emergency Trust Fund for Africa were autocracies, except the two 'flawed democracies' of Tunisia and Ghana (Box 9.1 details EU policies in key African states).[18] The EU signed a new Political Dialogue and Cooperation Agreement with Cuba in November 2017, and increased aid as human rights conditions worsened on the island after this. While several leadership changes did not result in meaningful political openings in Central Asia, the EU offered new-generation trade and cooperation agreements to Kazakhstan, Kyrgyzstan and Uzbekistan.[19] Many EU governments pushed for and secured Russia's full readmission to the Council of Europe assembly in 2019. While Thailand's 2019 elections were widely condemned as unfair and further deepened the military's grip on power, in 2020 the EU pushed to restart talks on a free trade agreement with the Thai junta. The EU ratified a free trade agreement with Vietnam in 2019 and tripled

Box 9.1 Development aid and democracy in Africa

The EU has influence in Africa due to the highly structured and far-reaching nature of its development aid and trade partnerships. Cases from Africa show how the EU has often applied pressure for democracy and human rights but that it has done so cautiously, while attaching priority to other policy aims. The frequency of democratic sanctions in Africa decreased during the 2010s. One factor in Africa has been China's rising importance, which has emboldened states to ignore EU pressure and encouraged the Union into a softer stance.[28]

The EU froze much of its development aid to Uganda in 2013, but then resumed it in 2018, despite President Museveni removing term and age limits in 2017 and cracking down with lethal force when protests erupted against his clinging to power. A similar logic of deepening EU cooperation was seen in Angola, prior to long-time autocratic leader President dos Santos being forced out of office by domestic pressures. The EU supported the democratic breakthrough in Burkina Faso when protestors pushed President Compaoré from office in 2014; but it had a supportive relationship with the regime before this happened and the French government even offered to fly the discredited leader to safety.

The EU increased aid in the immediate aftermath of stolen elections in Kenya with a 4.5 billion-euro aid envelope.[29] In recent years, France has ramped up financial and counter-terrorist military support to the autocratic President Deby in Chad.[30] After the EU suspended funding to the Burundi government in 2015, France broke ranks and resumed financial cooperation there despite the lack of improvements on human rights and democracy.[31] European aid to Ivory Coast continued after the incumbent President Ouattara won an unconstitutional third term in November 2020.

In the late 2000s, the EU rewarded Rwanda with increased aid, even as democracy indicators were getting worse. The EU and most bilateral donors suspended aid in 2012 in relation to Rwanda's military incursions into the Democratic Republic of the Congo (DRC). In the mid-2010s, European aid flows to Rwanda increased once more; in 2015 only Belgium and the Commission withheld funding in response to the deteriorating human rights situation.[32] In 2020, President Kagame introduced provisions enabling him to retain power until 2034; the EU continued to increase funding levels and deepen economic ties. European policy was distorted by an old divide, France's support for the previous Hutu regime made it cooler towards Tutsi Kagame than the UK, which sensed an opportunity to displace French influence in backing him.

In Ethiopia, the EU held back some aid temporarily in 2005 after stolen elections unleashed violence; but donors soon resumed funding. The EU awarded the Ethiopian government 500 million euros of additional aid through a new Strategic Engagement partnership after the regime took all seats in parliamentary elections in 2015 and clamped down more harshly against civil society. The EU did not change its approach when long-time ruler Meles Zenawi died. After protests forced a change of government, the EU upgraded cooperation with the reformist President Abiy.[33] When Abiy's government launched military attacks on rebel opposition strongholds in the Tigray region in late 2020, the EU criticised the use of force and held back some direct budgetary support but was reluctant to cut off its core aid and security cooperation.

In the DRC, the EU cut support to members of the government involved in human rights violations in the run up to elections in 2018 and it pushed President Joseph Kabila hard from 2016 each time he delayed elections. Yet the 2018 elections were not free and fair, as Kabila struck a deal with the winning candidate that gave him influence from behind the scenes. Despite not being allowed to observe the elections and expressing doubts over their legitimacy, the EU implicitly accepted the outcome and continued with its aid projects and trade preferences for the DRC.

In Zimbabwe, the EU diluted sanctions even as Robert Mugabe retained control into the 2010s. When the Zimbabwean military forced Mugabe out of power in 2017, the EU moved to upgrade cooperation and remove remaining sanctions. The military controlled the first post-Mugabe elections in 2018 and democratic breakthrough remained elusive. Opposition figures criticised the UK, and to a lesser extent the EU delegation, for being too close to the new government and rushing to get access to resources in Zimbabwe.

its aid to the country between 2016 and 2020 – despite the country's deepening authoritarianism.[20]

The EU has largely turned a blind eye to deepening repression and authoritarianism in China over the last decade. The EU–China human rights dialogue ground to a halt. There was no European response to China's tightening control of Tibet.[21] Most member states would not unequivocally congratulate Taiwan's pro-independence president after her electoral victory in 2020 for fear of China's response. When in 2020 the US imposed Magnitsky sanctions on Chinese officials linked to 're-education' camps of Uighurs in Xinxiang, EU states pointedly declined to do so. The EU has got tougher on China's economic and technology policies but not on its human rights abuses. Most European action has come from non-governmental actors or local politicians: Swedish city governments cut links with China and a Swedish NGO awarded a prize to a Chinese dissident, while the mayor of Prague spoke out against repression in Tibet and began a twinning partnership with Taipei. When the mayor then teamed up with the president of the Czech senate to lead a 90-strong delegation to Taipei in September 2020, other member states did not unite in favour of offering Taiwan more support.[22]

The EU did little to react to the smothering of democratic freedoms in Hong Kong, declining to offer concrete backing for protestors that took to the streets there in 2014 and again in 2019 and 2020. While the US passed a Hong Kong Human Rights Freedom Act, European states appealed for dialogue between the protestors and the China-backed administration. When China's new security law effectively ended Hong Kong's autonomy in 2020 the EU declined unequivocally to condemn the move.[23] Of member states, only Sweden was willing to contemplate any kind of critical measures against China.[24] Against the deteriorating political backdrop, the EU's willingness to sign a Comprehensive Agreement on Investment with China at the end of 2020 risked doing serious damage to the credibility of its human rights and democracy commitments – in the same week that this accord was signed, authorities imprisoned 53 pro-democracy opposition figures in Hong Kong. The UK's tone was now more critical and it moved to offer Hong Kong citizens a fast-track to British citizenship.

Beyond particular country policies, more general or cross-cutting limitations have also been apparent. Despite an EU code of conduct on arms sales, member states have increased the export of military equipment to authoritarian regimes.[25] The EU has also made limited headway against online repression. Its 2011 No Disconnect Strategy – aimed at confronting regimes guilty of online harassment against opposition reformers – effectively ground to a halt by 2016 as the High Representative was not keen on taking it forward. As mentioned in Chapter 5, for many years member states delayed Commission proposals to restrict the export of invasive digital surveillance equipment from EU states to repressive regimes; they agreed to a diluted 'dual-use' regulation only in late 2020. Western companies have supplied most of the surveillance technology used by authoritarian regimes around the world.[26] While supporting the new human rights sanctions regime, at the end of 2020 member states baulked at the idea of allowing sanctions to be imposed on the basis of a qualified majority rather than unanimity.

In 2020, the COVID-19 emergency additionally drew the EU's policy focus away from democracy and human rights issues. The need to help global efforts to contain the pandemic took precedence and led the EU to work in alliance with many authoritarian regimes on the health emergency. Borrell pushed the EU to help prop up authoritarian governments in Iran, Venezuela and Syria to head off possible instability in the health crisis.[27] The EU stressed that emergency measures that regimes around the world introduced to deal with the pandemic should not be used as a pretext for extended authoritarianism. Yet the priority was at this stage clearly on dealing with the pandemic – and, of course, member states themselves introduced restrictions on democratic rights in order to deal with the pandemic.

Democracy and human rights funding

Given the limited use of sanctions and other punitive measures, in most places the EU's funding for democracy and human rights projects has been the most concrete element of its nominally transformative power. The Commission and several member states have become relatively large-scale donors to initiatives designed to support democratic reforms and human rights improvements around the world. From relatively small beginnings in the early 1990s, this area of aid activity has become a core element of EU external action.

The budget specifically dedicated to democracy and human rights funding, the European Instrument for Democracy and Human Rights (EIDHR), amounted to 160 million euros a year from 2014 to 2020 – around 2 per cent of the Commission's total aid budget.[34] In this period, the EIDHR began financing projects on strengthening multi-party systems, parliaments and a large-scale Media4Democracy project on media freedom. Over several decades the EU has deployed 8 to 10 Election Observation Missions (EOMs) a year; it has sent an increasing number of Electoral Follow-up Missions designed to make sure that EOM recommendations are implemented and that election missions feed into long-term democracy support. From 2020, EOMs expanded their remit to monitor online interference in elections.

The EU's focus on civil society support has intensified. EU delegations in 107 countries agreed civil society roadmaps for 2014–2017; 56 of these were renewed for 2018–2020. The Commission's Supporting Democracy initiative provided 5 million euros for experts to work with civil society actors in the latter half of the 2010s. In 2018 the EU ran a CivicTech4Democracy initiative and launched a new 5 million-euro call to support civic activism through digital technologies. The EU has also increasingly used funds from mainstream development budgets for initiatives related to democracy.[35] Additionally, it has funded human rights projects under its hugely increased humanitarian relief budgets, especially in the Middle East and Sahel regions.

Through its multiple financial instruments, the EU has moved to increase democracy assistance where new opportunities have arisen in recent years: notable examples include Tunisia, Fiji, Myanmar, Ukraine and Armenia. At a donor conference in June 2020 several donors committed new funds to help Sudan's shaky democratic transition a year after protests drove an authoritarian regime from power: the Commission promised 312 million euros, the UK 166 million, Germany 150 million and France 100 million. The EU has continued to fund some civil society actors even in extremely repressive countries like Azerbaijan, Belarus, Egypt and Zimbabwe – and even to a very limited degree in Russia.[36] However, it has shied away from offering funding support for pro-democracy mass protests; in large-scale revolts, EU statements have nearly always called for restraint and dialogue.

Much European development aid labelled as democracy-related has traditionally been relatively technical in nature as it has focused on state institutions. Most EU political aid has aimed at better technical governance standards through functional cooperation on EU laws, economic development and social-service delivery. Around two-thirds of EU development aid for 'good governance' has gone to governments and state institutions.[37] Whether these approaches actually help democratisation is difficult to prove. The EU's large number of governance programmes can include elements that genuinely help human rights and democracy, but they commonly help non-democratic regimes operate more effectively.[38] The EU has been running functionalist-governance initiatives on a large scale for two decades or more in countries whose record on democracy and human rights has got worse not better.

Recent studies show recipients of significant EU aid have in general not made progress in wrestling with corruption.[39]

In recent years more of the EU's funding has gone directly to protecting activists from state repression. EU democracy support has shifted towards pushing back against attacks on civil society, disinformation and interference with electoral integrity. The EIDHR's Emergency Fund for human rights defenders has channelled funds at speed when defenders face a moment of acute risk. The EU has funded a Human Rights Defenders Protection Mechanism, known as Protectdefenders.eu. Under this, a consortium of 12 international NGOs has provided emergency grants to move activists abroad or give them legal support. By 2020, Protectdefenders.eu had provided over a thousand emergency grants, training for 5,000 human rights defenders at risk and given some kind of other support to over 10,000 activists.[40] Box 9.2 notes the additional support for civil society activists that has come from a separate organisation, the European Endowment for Democracy.

In addition to European Commission funds, a handful of member states have allocated meaningful amounts of funding for democracy and human rights. Germany launched a Marshall Plan with Africa in the late 2010s that promised increased support for 'Democracy, rule of law, and human rights'.[41] Sweden has long been the most generous funder of democracy in proportional terms, with this area of policy accounting for around 20 per cent of its total aid, worth 580 million euros in 2018.[42] Denmark has been the other highest-level funder in proportional terms.[43] In the latter half of the 2010s, the Dutch coalition government significantly increased the budget for the Netherlands Human Rights Fund. The UK has

---

Box 9.2 European Endowment for Democracy

In 2013, a novel addition to European democracy funding began work: the European Endowment for Democracy. The EED functions outside the formal EU institutional structures, although it is funded by the Commission and member states. The EED follows 'an unconventional approach to democracy support' designed to fund democratic activists that do not receive help from other donors. It has flexible administrative rules that make it easier to support small, informal or non-registered organisations or even individuals. It tends to fund new types of activism rather than large formal NGOs, including civic initiatives that can be confrontational towards regimes. It has confidentiality provisions to give recipients some protection from state repression.

By the end of the decade the EED had funded over a thousand projects, worth more than 50 million euros. 23 member states had contributed funds. Initially it worked only in European Neighbourhood Policy states, but in the latter part of the decade expanded to Russia, Turkey and the Balkans. The EED's budget is still relatively small, at under 20 million euros a year, but the organisation has established a high profile within European democracy support.[48] Perhaps reflecting this, the Russian government moved to expel it in 2020.

provided large amounts of governance funding; this has mostly gone to building basic institutional capacities in conflict states rather for helping states undergoing democratic transition.[44] A new UK strategy published in 2019 promised more focus on democracy and support in moments of democratic breakthrough.[45] The OECD has ranked Germany second, the UK third, Sweden fourth, the Netherlands fifth and Denmark tenth largest donors worldwide for a broader category of 'Governance' aid, with their political aid amounts increasing over the 2010s.[46]

Still, funds for democracy and human rights have been modest relative to other areas of EU spending. Different definitions mean exact figures are hard to compile, but on a fairly expansive notion of democracy and human rights aid this category has amounted to 1–2 billion euros a year. This is a small fraction of the EU military spend of over well over 200 billion euros a year. While the EU claims to have incorporated support for human rights and democracy into its much larger funds for migration and counter-terrorism initiatives, project details suggest this claim is unconvincing; European projects have even trained security and border forces to use invasive surveillance equipment.[47] The EIDHR has been the smallest of all EU funding instruments. Only a handful of member states have devoted meaningful amounts of their external aid to human rights and democracy. The EU's new 2021–2027 budget includes a modest increase in human rights and democracy funds, but member states insisted these funds be reduced from the Commission's initial proposal and used for other purposes, especially in the wake of the COVID-19 pandemic. Box 9.3 outlines the shift away from democracy funding in conflict interventions.

Box 9.3 Democracy and conflict

The EU and some member states have made a particular commitment to support democracy in conflict scenarios. The EU put democracy and human rights funding at the heart of its comprehensive approach to conflict resolution. In 2018 it added a Civilian Compact to the CSDP to focus on the rule of law and human rights. In 2019 the External Action Service created a 75-person Directorate for an Integrated Approach to Security and Peace. A 2019 Atrocity Prevention Toolkit committed to human rights work in violent contexts.[49]

The EU has set up civilian response teams to engage in issues such as rule of law training. It rolled out a number of so-called state-building contracts – in Ukraine, Mali, South Sudan and other places – linked to the EU's upgraded commitment to fragile states. The conflict-related Instrument contributing to Peace and Stability (IcSP) has funded work on political parties in Colombia, electoral violence in Kenya and constitutional reform in Sudan.[50]

Yet overall EU conflict interventions have become less ambitious. By the late 2010s they were mainly about crisis management and containing insurgencies. After disappointing experiences in the Balkans, Afghanistan and Iraq, the EU's conflict policies have moved away from democracy support.[51] The largest share of EU Trust Fund money in Africa has gone to security-sector projects; civilian deployments have been modest, with only France having more than 20 personnel committed to civilian CSDP missions across the whole of Africa between 2010 and 2019.[52] While France intervened in Mali in 2013 to restore democracy, French-led operations in the Sahel have focused mainly on support for security forces against radical groups. In 2020, France sent an additional 600 troops to the Sahel under an upgraded Takuba mission that promised the region's largely non-democratic regimes more direct security support. Protests erupted in several states against this French support for autocratic rulers and eventually led to a military coup in Mali in August 2020; even after this, European funding and security support continued.

CSDP missions have increasingly focused on training and advisory functions. Deployments have increased of military personnel to the three security-training CSDP missions in Mali, Central Africa Republic and Somalia; as of 2019 the largest contingents to these came from Spain (313 personnel), Germany (147) and Italy (135).[53] One of the first PESCO projects was for a Centre of Excellence for EU Training Missions. However welcome this security training, it has little bearing on underlying political structures in conflict states.

From the late 2000s, operations in Afghanistan were about containing a new Taliban insurgency, while reform-oriented programmes like the EU police mission were wound down. The EU and member states provided a quarter of all international support to Afghanistan after 2011, including a new 5 billion-euro injection in 2016. The UK, Commission and Germany were the largest donors to institution-building efforts. Yet like the US, the EU prioritised security support to President Hamid Karzai to combat the Taliban, even when he undercut democracy.[54] This failed, and in 2020 the US and EU states reduced their force deployments on the back of a power-sharing deal that, nearly two decades after the post-2011 military intervention, brought the Taliban back into government.

The EU has focused on cautious mediation and moved away from its initial aims to press far-reaching political reforms as a means of reducing wars and violence. It has worked to an increasingly narrow understanding of security in conflicts, moving away from far-reaching engagement in local politics.[55] The EU has sought influence over fragile societies but without taking responsibility for redressing conflict drivers.[56]

Themes and analysis

Democracy and human rights support has been a daunting enterprise in light of the outside-in challenges of what has become a markedly more illiberal age. It is significant that the EU has retained its commitment to support liberal rights and political reforms in such unfavourable circumstances, even if it is equally relevant that these aims have slipped down its list of foreign-policy priorities. In the reshaped global order, international support for democracy must be measured by modest metrics. Actors like the EU and its member states can rarely hope to guide wholesale transformation anymore; more prosaically they have helped small islands of activism and modest steps of political improvement where possible. The paradox is that the EU has become more tactically sophisticated in its democracy support even as expectations in what it can achieve have lowered. In line with the outside-in conceptual framework, the external conditioners of EU policies have become more determinant in this policy area.

The predictable point to be made is that the EU's tilt towards a security-first agenda has undercut its support for human rights and democracy. This has indeed been the case in many instances. It might be said that the EU has stepped back from strongly-committed democracy and human rights support in part due to adverse political trends across the world, in part out of political judgement. Yet, overall the picture has also been more varied than this. In some instances, geostrategy has catalysed democracy support. While the EU has desisted from pressuring authoritarian regimes with which it has sought deeper security and migration cooperation, it has rarely opposed democratic breakthroughs if and when such regimes do collapse. It has in recent years been more agnostic about regime types than either firmly committed to or against democratisation.

Much criticism in recent years holds the line that the EU must step back from being overly zealous in its support for democracy and liberal rights in proper adjustment to the zeitgeist of zero-sum realpolitik. A standard critique is that the EU must stop 'preaching and lecturing' about democracy and human rights. Much academic work has taken the EU to task for being too assertive and rigid in its democracy-building in a way that unfairly ignores other countries' different values.[57] Yet it is many years now since the Union could justifiably be accused of *overdoing* its focus on democracy and human rights. The EU's approach to democracy and human rights has become increasingly cautious, mild and indirect. EU approaches have remained rooted in a mix of elite negotiations and functionalist governance programmes rather than overtly political efforts to build countervailing checks on autocratic regimes. Far from imposing draconian conditionality, the vast bulk of EU aid has gone to non- or weakly democratic states. In fact, a sceptical spin on the aid figures would be that the EU has been the biggest funder of authoritarian governments in the world.

The EU and member states have struggled to respond to the global trend of *gradual* autocratisation. In response to the increasingly common trend of incremental declines in democratic quality, as opposed to dramatic military coups, the EU has normally opted for increasing its engagement in the hope of persuading governments to reverse direction. The Union has been left partnering with semi-autocratic governments at the moment when democratic protests have managed to dislodge these regimes from power – leaving many activists with the impression that the EU has been a barrier to rather than enabler of democratic transition. In an era of popular revolts, the EU has stuck rather discordantly to its preferred template of smooth and non-contentious political change. The EU has tended to point to its large numbers of democracy and human rights projects without indicating how these relate to the specific political challenges present in recipient states or to overarching EU external actions.[58]

A common claim is that the EU has helped democratisation in other countries through a sheer density of policy, economic and social linkages and regulatory convergence.[59] Yet the evidence of recent years weighs against these traditional claims.

Echoing a broader point from the book's conceptual framework, it might be doubted whether it now makes sense to assume that distinctive EU governance templates and policy linkages can really be counted as European 'democracy support'. These approaches tend to aim at modest advances in human rights or governance norms, not systemic political change. While critics often charge the EU with supporting a minimal or illiberal democracy,[60] the EU has more often tilted towards the opposite policy of supporting liberal reforms within autocracies. A related charge often heard is that the EU imposes a narrow concept of political rights without social rights; again, this received wisdom has become more questionable given that EU spending on social development projects has far exceeded what it spends on democracy.

Moreover, whether support for democracy and human rights has really been a *distinctive and common* European policy priority is debatable. The standard line has for a long time been that these normative principles sit at the heart of EU foreign policy in part because they are so vital to the Union's own internal identity. These are core values that have commanded firm support from member states, as they have been so integral to the whole project of European integration. The murky trends of European illiberalism and realpolitik of recent years have cast shadows over such habitual reasoning. Only around six to eight member states have invested meaningful levels of resources in democracy and human rights work; the rest have been uninterested or sceptical.

A related common assumption is that member states have typically pushed these sensitive issues of human rights and democracy onto the External Action Service and the Commission to keep their own bilateral interests unaffected. Yet, in recent years these EU-level actors have certainly not been the most committed actors in this area of policy. Not one of the four High Representatives to date has been willing to play lead role in democracy and human rights. A small core of member states has developed the most assertive initiatives in favour of human rights and democracy as a way of getting round the insipidness of EU-level positions. In a complex relationship between EU-level and national-level initiatives, it would be most accurate to say that a select group of member states have worked with select parts of the EU institutional machinery to develop democracy and human rights policies often against the reluctance of other member states and some other Brussels-based actors.

Moreover, as said, EU and member state policies have become more varied, firmly backing democracy in some instances and authoritarian stability in others. It is difficult to account for this inconsistency by reference to a supposedly distinctive EU liberal idealism. Overall, it might be concluded that EU policies may have made some semi-democratic states slightly more democratic but have also contributed to shoring up some autocratic regimes. EU democracy policies have become much more varied across different countries, either because their domestic politics are so different or because the EU's own interests vary. While some correlations show higher levels of democracy aid have had a broadly positive impact on reform, a common finding is that the impact of these initiatives has varied depending on each national context.[61] The EU's democratic ambivalence has been both cause and effect: it is one among many factors that helps explain the world's democratic regression during the 2010s; at the same time, it has been a response to that regression, as the Union has reacted to a less democratic world not by reinvigorating its commitment to democracy but by hedging its bets.

A final observation: while these are all themes that look somewhat inwards to the EU's own strength of commitment and policy approaches, the big-picture challenge is how the Union can adjust its democracy and human rights support to the contours of a post-Western world. The EU has not moved far in the direction of coordinating these kinds of policies with other democratic powers. Countries like Brazil, Chile, South Africa, South Korea, Indonesia and India have come to invest resources in democracy and governance programmes abroad – even though several of these countries have themselves moved in a decidedly illiberal direction in recent years. The democracy-support elements of the EU's strategic partnerships with other states have remained negligible, unlike their security and trade dimensions. Most member states have been lukewarm towards cooperation on global human rights with non-Western democracies, for fear this would further complicate relations with Russia and China. If not corrected, this neglect of wider democratic partnerships is likely to prove a damaging shortfall in EU external action in the future.

Concluding summary

External challenges. The challenging environment that besets global democracy has made EU democracy support more difficult and has led some member states and EU institutional actors to downgrade their efforts to uphold human rights and democratic norms.

Unity–diversity. Deeper divisions have taken root inside the EU over democracy and human rights strategy. A handful of member state governments, alongside some parts of the EU institutions, have developed their own strategies for democracy and human rights support, while other member states have increasingly stepped back from such commitment.

Distinctive power. To the extent the democracy and human rights support has been a signature element of EU liberal power, the loss of momentum behind this area of external action has left the EU a less distinctive power. The EU's tactics in democracy and human rights support have also moved away from a reliance on distinctive EU institutional instruments.

Protective dynamics. The EU and some member states still dedicate significant resources to shaping external political trends rather than simply protecting against them. However, the generally more tepid approach to international democracy and human rights norms is consonant with the EU's general turn to protective security.

EU influence. Internal and external factors have merged to weaken the EU's influence over political trends in countries around the world, even though the Union's role has remained strong in shaping political reform in some countries in its immediate neighbourhood.

PART III
GEOGRAPHICAL CHALLENGES

10 Geopolitical Shifts in the Middle East and North Africa

The themes central to the outside-in conceptual framework have crystallised in particularly potent and intricate ways in the Middle East and North Africa (MENA) region. This region has presented the EU with some of its thorniest strategic challenges and these resonate strongly with the cross-cutting thematic issues covered in the previous chapters. Over the last decade, the EU's influence in the MENA region has weakened in the shadow of complex and divisive political trends within the region. The EU failed fully to grasp the Arab spring's fleeting moment of positive opportunity. It has been progressively marginalised from the Syrian and Libyan conflicts, while maintaining a more consequential role in relation to the stand-off between Iran, the US and other powers in the region. As turbulence has increased and other powers have become more assertively engaged, the EU's priorities have shifted to the management of refugee and migration flows, along with the challenge posed by Islamic State and other radical groups. The bloc's previously comprehensive approaches to security in the southern Mediterranean have given way to a shallower, more ad hoc, protective and transactional European engagement with Arab partners. The chapter shows how the book's conceptual themes of externally-driven policy adjustment, protective security, multilayered EU external action and diminished European influence play out in one specific region.

The challenges

In the last decade, inter-state and intra-state conflicts have shaken the foundations of the Middle Eastern order. Sectarian antagonism has intensified and the rivalry between Iran and Saudi Arabia has been one of the fiercest in global politics. A complex mosaic of tensions has also deepened amongst Sunni states. Divisions between Turkey and Qatar, on the one hand, and Egypt, Saudi Arabia and the United Arab Emirates, on the other hand, have taken shape in particular around differing positions towards the role of the Muslim Brotherhood across the region. US power in the region declined in the aftermath of the 2003 Iraq invasion. Russia has filled some of the vacuum and has returned as a power of note in the MENA region. The regional order has become increasingly unsettled, uncertain and fractious.[1]

Democracy has remained largely absent from the region. After the region-wide protests of the Arab spring in 2011 and 2012, some regimes were forced from office and others promised liberalising reforms. Gradually, however, authoritarianism reasserted itself. Only Tunisia has retained some degree of genuinely democratic politics, and even here transition faltered into the 2020s. Authoritarian resilience, turbo-charged identity politics, an evolution of religious identities, economic inequality and standard power competition have all fed off and overlapped with each other. Nationalism has deepened, often as the by-product of authoritarian regimes' tactics for maintaining themselves in power. This has pulled the region away from support for deeper interdependence with other regions; the MENA is less integrated into the global economy and has weaker regional institutions than any other region. Contentious politics have remained vibrant: protests in 2019 in Algeria deposed President Bouteflikka but led to elections controlled by regime insiders, while parallel protests in Lebanon, Iraq and Iran indicated an unmet desire for change. The COVID-19 pandemic interrupted protests and empowered authoritarian regimes, but also intensified many underlying popular grievances and drivers of instability in the region.

Wars have raged in Syria and Libya, while the Arab–Israeli conflict has drifted further away from a peace settlement. The Assad regime gained the upper hand in Syria's conflict, with Russian and Iranian support.[2] Islamic State took root in the chaos of this war; in 2019 it seemed to have been defeated, but then recovered in pockets of Iraq and Syria. Meanwhile, Libya's civil war worsened and drew in Russian and Turkish operatives on different sides of this conflict. Perhaps most worryingly, US–Iranian tensions mounted towards the end of the decade. A US drone strike in Baghdad in January 2020 killed talismanic Iranian general Qasam Soleimani, the commander who had built up and run networks of Shia military forces in Yemen, Lebanon, Syria and Iraq. Iran retaliated with missile attacks on a US base in Iraq and moved to restart its nuclear programme. In late 2020, divisions deepened after the United Arab Emirates and Bahrain signed a peace treaty to normalise relations with Israel; a feud on this between the UAE and Turkey became a core axis of tension and many Arab states sought to push back against what they saw as Turkey's belligerent interventionism across the region.

Shifting frames in EU–Mediterranean relations

The EU's main focus has been on one part of the MENA region: the Mediterranean. After years of relatively low-level relations during the Cold War, the EU devised an innovative new framework for Euro-Mediterranean cooperation in 1995. While in previous decades the EU had sought to build a Euro-Arab Dialogue, it now formulated its policy around a subset of states in the Maghreb and Mashreq, and the new policy was christened the Euro-Mediterranean Partnership (EMP) – shown in Figure 10.1. This was one of the EU's most distinctive foreign policy initiatives. It was designed around the concepts of cooperative security, joint decision-making and region building, and was significant for including Israel alongside Arab states. Its centrepiece was the commitment to work towards a Euro-Mediterranean free trade area and deep economic integration between the two regions. The EMP kickstarted initiatives in just about every major policy sector, bringing together businesses, unions, energy experts, youth groups, artists, parliamentarians, NGOs, municipalities and many others across the Mediterranean Sea.

Figure 10.1 EU–Mediterranean Partnership members

In practice, several factors limited cooperation and integration. Progress on trade liberalisation was limited in practice and economic ties across the Mediterranean did not expand. In the political sphere, Arab regimes signed up to cooperation on human rights and democracy, but then resisted any reform on these issues. Security cooperation was held back as the 1994 Oslo peace accords between Israel and the Palestinian Authority broke down; indeed, it was the resurfacing of tensions over this question that became the main obstacle to cooperation and integration in all the different policy sectors of the EMP.

After the terrorist attacks of 11 September 2001 in New York and Washington, DC, and those later in Madrid and London, counter-terrorism and security came to dominate Euro-Mediterranean relations. The EU began a strand of de-radicalisation initiatives under the EMP, while member states stepped up their bilateral, direct security cooperation with Arab regimes. The EMP changed into a more functional framework for such issues and drifted away from being concerned with building a common, integrated Euro-Mediterranean region. In some ways, this brought European states closer to Arab governments – the latter having long advocated a tighter bearing down on terrorism and radical Islamist groups. This came at a cost, however, in terms of a diminished concern with human rights and underlying economic integration between the two regions. Rhetorically, EU leaders insisted the 9/11 attacks showed it was more important than ever to encourage Arab states to introduce political reforms and to open up their economies to speed development and undercut the causes of radicalisation. In practice, the EU made little effort to follow through on such rhetoric.

At this stage the European Neighbourhood Policy was introduced, as a means of offering more tailored individual action plans in each partner state. The EU moved to place greater stress on its bilateral relations with each southern Mediterranean state. Yet, after a burst of policy activity following 9/11, by the late 2000s the EU's focus on the Mediterranean was fading somewhat. Terrorism appeared to have been contained and other powers around the world offered more promising market opportunities. In 2008, the French government pushed the creation of a new institution, the Union for the Mediterranean (UfM). In tense internal debate, Germany insisted that this be linked to the EMP and all EU states included. The new UfM institution started work, focusing on relatively apolitical areas of cooperation. It marked another step towards policies based around pragmatic, low-politics projects.

Mixed responses to the Arab spring

Against this backdrop, the EU was caught off-guard by the Arab spring – as indeed were other powers and international organisations. As large-scale protests in Tunisia and Egypt overturned autocratic regimes and uprisings spread across the region, European governments scrambled to catch up with events. After initially offering to help protect the Tunisian regime, President Sarkozy made a firm commitment: 'We must support the emergence of democracy in Arab countries with all our might...Stability can no longer be the alpha and omega of French diplomacy.'[3] The UK government declared that supporting Arab citizens' pressure for 'legitimate institutions' would be key to future stability in the region.[4]

The EU offered additional aid of around 1 billion euros to the region; the prospect of visa liberalisation; a new Civil Society Facility to help reformers; new European Investment Bank and European Bank for Reconstruction and Development operations worth over 3 billion euros in the southern Mediterranean; and talks on deep and comprehensive free trade areas (DCFTAs). It also stressed that it would be stricter in its use of democracy-related conditionality in the future.[5] Conversely, the Union moved away from insisting that partners harmonise with whole swathes of EU legislation, leaving Arab states to choose their own level of alignment with EU norms.

The larger member states coordinated additional loans worth several billion euros through what became the G8 Transition Fund. Member states mandated the Council of Europe's Venice Commission to begin a series of initiatives on rule of law reform in the Arab region. The European Commission then devised a new programme called Spring that offered 350 million euros tied to the implementation of political reforms.[6] The EU named a special representative for the Arab spring – Spanish diplomat Bernadino León – who launched a series of reform task forces. In parallel to these EU initiatives, Germany launched its own Transformation Partnership, the UK an Arab Partnership Fund and Spain a Masar programme to help Arab civil society, while the Danish government beefed up its already existing Arab Partnership Initiative and the Dutch government extended its Matra reform programme from eastern Europe to the Arab region. Overall, these EU responses compared favourably in scale and breadth with the US's reaction to the Arab spring.[7]

However, despite all these policy upgrades, the EU's overall response to the Arab spring was less than fulsome. If the 1989 revolutions in eastern Europe undermined the EU's communist rivals, the Arab revolts of 2011 undermined its nominal allies. The EU's ambivalence about the impact of political change solidi-fied as regimes pushed back against reform – Table 10.1 shows how by the end of the 2010s there was little democracy present in the region. The Union modestly upgraded its range of standard policy instruments but did not qualitatively change its strategy or its modalities of cooperation in the region.[8] The additional 1 billion euros was not much when divided across all southern Neighbourhood recipients. Bilateral aid flows did not expand dramatically; indeed, French, Spanish and Italian aid to the region fell after 2012. Most civil society funds still went to the most formal and well-established NGOs, many of which had some kind of understanding with their respective regimes, and not to the newer social

Table 10.1 Middle East and North Africa political regimes

Country	Regime type
Israel	Flawed democracy
Tunisia	Flawed democracy
Morocco	Hybrid regime
Lebanon	Hybrid regime
Algeria	Hybrid regime
Jordan	Authoritarian
Kuwait	Authoritarian
Palestine	Authoritarian
Iraq	Authoritarian
Qatar	Authoritarian
Egypt	Authoritarian
Oman	Authoritarian
United Arab Emirates	Authoritarian
Sudan	Authoritarian
Bahrain	Authoritarian
Iran	Authoritarian
Libya	Authoritarian
Yemen	Authoritarian
Saudi Arabia	Authoritarian
Syria	Authoritarian

Source: Economist Intelligence Unit (2020)

movements that led the Arab revolts after 2011. Divisions between northern and southern EU states remained and even widened, the latter urging more strategic realism.[9]

As regime repression increased in nearly all states, the EU declined to use strong conditionality. It offered increased aid to governments in Morocco, Algeria and Jordan that by 2014 or 2015 were clearly not reforming, but resisting meaningful change.[10] EU, French and Spanish leaders routinely praised the Moroccan government for its reform programme, and the country remained the largest EMP aid recipient, even though its democracy indicators worsened. While the EU allocated aid increases to Tunisia, its offer of a Privileged Partnership was little incentive as the Union had already offered this to the ousted autocratic regime.[11] Beyond the Mediterranean, Germany, the UK, France and Spain increased arms sales across the Gulf and declined meaningfully to support democratic activists, even as regime repression became more brutal in this most autocratic part of the region.

Economic relations across the Mediterranean remained limited.[12] The EU offered to negotiate DCFTAs with four states – Egypt, Jordan, Morocco and Tunisia – but by 2020 none of these had been signed. While the EU offered some Arab states greater inclusion in Union policies, regimes in the southern Mediterranean became less willing to sign up to the bloc's rules and norms. Indeed, the Commission itself recognised that the EU's traditional method of trying to export governance rules and regulations was increasingly problematic.[13] Morocco suspended its association councils with the EU between 2015 and 2019 because the European Court of Justice ruled that new fisheries and agricultural agreements could not apply to the contested Western Saharan region. The UfM did not engage in work related to the Arab spring but stuck doggedly to an apolitical programme of technical projects.

Era of containment

By the late 2010s, the momentum of the Arab spring had evaporated and the EU's relations with the southern Mediterranean and wider MENA region gradually reverted to more traditional security concerns.[14] While the EU persevered with many of its initiatives aimed at economic cooperation, civil society linkages and political reform, it was obliged to adapt to a more challenging strategic environment. The rising influence of Russia and China in the MENA, Gulf powers' more active regional diplomacy, Turkey's more assertive foreign policy interventions and the US's retreat combined as external changes that narrowed EU manoeuvrability. The EU sought policy tools to contain and mitigate the dynamics of instability and fragmentation that now characterised the wider Middle East region.

In perhaps the clearest case of protective security, the EU's attention turned to migration and refugee flows triggered, in particular, by war in Syria. Chapter 6 covered the EU's general policy response to the surge in migration after 2016; these overarching changes also had specific ramifications for EU relations with MENA states. Even before the 2016 surge, the Commission moved to beef up Frontex, put more money into border controls and exert more pressure for Arab states to sign readmission clauses.[15] After 2016 the share of ENP resources going into controlling migration became significantly greater, clearly eclipsing other priorities. The EU redirected much new funding for this purpose towards Turkey, the Sahel and sub-Saharan Arica. It gave both Jordan and Lebanon aid packages worth several hundred million euros in return for them hosting Syrian refugees; regimes in these countries used the refugee surge as a bargaining chip to win money from EU, helping them entrench their power.[16] As a result of this new migration- and security-related funding, the share of EU aid going to the MENA region rose from 18 per cent in 2013 to 26 per cent in 2018.[17] Table 10.2 shows the main EU aid flows to different countries in the region.

In Tunisia, the EU responded to democratic reform through the first use of its so-called 'umbrella funds' and trebled macro-financial assistance.[18] The Union also gradually shifted its funding to new training for Tunisian border guards and exchanges between Europol and Tunisian security forces; the Commission and several member states separately launched initiatives to strengthen Tunisia's security forces from 2015 after terrorist attacks in the country. The EU was reluctant to back protests against the stalling of democratisation; Tunisian democrats berated the EU for its increasingly security-led approach.[19] Similarly, in Egypt, the EU unblocked sectoral aid from 2017 and funded projects to stem migration flows. The Egyptian regime not merely slid back into autocracy but was directly implicated in the murder of an Italian student, Giulio Regeni and brazenly detained Egyptians based in Europe. Still, Italy authorised the sale of warships to Egypt. After terrorist attacks in France and Austria, at the end of 2020 Council president Charles Michel travelled to Cairo to link Egypt into the EU's new counter-terrorism strategy and President Macron granted President al- Sisi a state visit in order to deepen security cooperation.

Spain pushed for border control assistance to Morocco and diluted any criticism of the regime; several organisations even took the Spanish government to court, alleging that its significant increase in support to the Moroccan security services to stop migration was illegal.[20] The EU stood back from Algeria's pro-democracy protests in 2019 and continued security cooperation with the military leaders that kept themselves in control after heavily manipulated elections. The Spanish government openly positioned itself as a strong supporter of the new Algerian government and expressly offered it backing against the continuing unrest. Prime Minister Pedro Sanchez visited Algeria in October 2020 to agree an energy deal and

Table 10.2 EU aid to MENA states

European Commission 2018, aid recipients	Aid, $ mln	EC Recipient in world
Morocco	546	3rd
Syria	462	4th
Tunisia	455	5th
Egypt	322	9th
West Bank and Gaza Strip	296	10th

Source: OECD

cooperation on migrant returns and counter-terrorism despite the regime's ongoing repression and refusal to open up to political reform.[21]

In Lebanon, the EU increased cooperation during the 2010s and was reluctant to push for reform to the country's interdenominational power-sharing system. France and other EU donors began to apply a degree of governance conditionality after a 2018 conference raised new aid, but they were not particularly supportive of pro-reform protests in 2019 that ushered in a Hezbollah-led government. After the tragic explosion in Beirut's port in August 2020, President Macron took the lead in pushing more strongly for reforms. As factional leaders blocked reform, France and EU powers offered humanitarian aid but pulled back from releasing a larger package of macro-economic assistance. While pressing for reform, EU governments remained wary of Hezbollah, the force that would be likely to gain from a shift to non-sectarian, majoritarian democracy. Macron's personal involvement and strictures on the need for reform won support, but also stirred echoes of anti-colonial resentment. Lebanese civil society leaders criticised Macron for promoting pro-Western figures to head key government posts without qualitative change to the country's systemic failings.[22]

Reflecting a core theme of the book's conceptual framework, the EU shifted away from *sui generis* policies predicated on partners' approximation to the Union's rules and claimed that this helped unlock more standard security coordination. The Union began a wave of security training and capacity building under a new Security Sector Reform strategy for the southern Mediterranean.[23] The EU replaced ENP action plans with 'partnership priorities' that moved away from regulatory harmonisation and the ambitious notions of an integrated Euro-Mediterranean security community towards more pragmatic cooperation with individual Arab states.[24] The EU's multiple dialogues with religious leaders and groups across the region have reverted from focusing on these actors' political potential back to a concern with containing Islam's perceived security risk. Spain and others have also pushed to make the UfM more of a security initiative. European policy in the region has become as much about member states' national diplomacy and security initiatives as Brussels-centred policy instruments.

Syria's war and failed insurgency

These themes of diluted distinctive EU influences have been even more painfully pre-eminent in Syria. When the Syrian war erupted in 2011, the EU was trying to entice the Assad regime into an association agreement. As President Assad cracked down on protests, the EU suspended aid and talks on the new agreement. In the early days of the conflict, the EU line was to call for dialogue and work with Assad to introduce reforms capable of placating the opposition. As the regime's attacks became more violent, the EU imposed sanctions, declared that Assad had to step down and started to offer capacity-building help to opposition forces. The EU backed mediation efforts during 2012 and 2013 by the Arab League and then the United Nations and consented to plans that would keep the regime in power in at least some measure as a quid pro quo for peace and power-sharing mechanisms. As these talks failed to progress, however, its line against the regime hardened. The Union gradually expanded its sanctions; those member states initially reluctant to tighten punitive measures accepted these after Assad refused to compromise in international talks.[25]

As the conflict spiralled, European support to opposition forces increased. France was the most forward-leaning in offering opposition forces formal recognition and funding, although some criticised it for favouring Paris-based Syrian intellectuals with little political experience inside the country. The EU sponsored several meetings of Syrian opposition groups with the aim of fostering greater unity and coordination among them. However, European governments refused to arm the opposition and ruled out any broader military intervention, although several EU governments did aid Kurdish peshmerga forces for operations against Islamic State. After the Assad regime used chemical weapons, killing over a thousand people in a Damascus suburb in August 2013, the UK, France and Denmark joined with the US in threatening a military response. However, the UK parliament blocked British involvement and this dissuaded the US and French governments from proceeding. In 2018, France and the UK did join the United States in limited airstrikes after Assad's repeat use of chemical weapons.

By now the European priority was to contain Islamic State. Five member states – Belgium, Denmark, France, the Netherlands and the UK – undertook airstrikes as part of the international coalition against Islamic State. The European contribution was relatively modest; the number of airstrikes undertaken by these five states was a small fraction of those carried out by the United States. Yet the political shift was significant, as the EU now shared with the Assad regime and Russia the aim of pushing back against Islamic State's precipitous rise. While the actions against Islamic State were not necessarily incompatible with the declared goal of pushing for Assad to leave office, European governments were now anxious to avoid even more of an institutional vacuum that would further empower the jihadist group.

Away from high-level international diplomacy, the European Commission funded aid projects within opposition-held areas worth several hundred million euros that sought to enhance governance capacities and strengthen civil society organisations. The aim was to build firmer foundations for a political settlement over the longer term and to create well-governed semi-autonomous areas.[26] The UK provided particularly significant additional bilateral funding to help run local councils in opposition areas.[27] The French, German, Swedish, Dutch and Finnish governments also ran a handful of projects each to help effective governance and service delivery in areas run by the opposition. Yet these efforts did not help opposition areas withstand the regime's military onslaughts in 2017 and 2018. Where the regime did not win back control, radical jihadist groups became the dominant force within local councils – leading most European donors to cease their programmes.[28]

With the regime having largely won the war by 2019, the EU faced another series of strategic choices. Even with the opposition decimated, the EU line was that reconstruction aid and the removal of its sanctions against Syria would depend on the Assad regime agreeing to an inclusive political process. The EU aim was to retain at least some autonomous areas outside the regime's full control. The goal was now to maintain some pressure on Assad while also cajoling opposition forces to work within parameters set by the regime. As 2019 progressed, differences began to appear between member states. The Italian government, in particular, expressed a desire to re-establish diplomatic relations with Syria, and the Czech foreign minister visited Damascus. There were increasingly intense debates within the EU about whether accommodation with the Assad regime was now inevitable.

As the regime gained ground, the Commission and member states increased their humanitarian relief, in part to head off another wave of refugees. By 2020, the EU had spent 16 billion euros on such emergency aid related to the Syria conflict. This aid was about containing spillover from the conflict not trying to solve the conflict itself. Indeed, much humanitarian aid was channelled through the Syrian regime, apparently empowering this with more resources. At the EU-sponsored donors' meeting on Syria in March 2019, Federica Mogherini's focus was on rejecting military involvement and on the EU playing a primarily humanitarian role.[29] Mogherini tried at this stage to set the EU mainly as mediator between all the main factions and outside players.[30] Yet the EU was increasingly excluded from international diplomatic efforts. Russia was now the dominant external power; its military assistance to the Assad regime had proven to be a game-changer when opposition forces were moving on Damascus. Arrangements to protect the northern Idlib province were agreed by Russia and Turkey, with little European involvement. In 2019, Russian, Turkish and Iranian leaders met to plan the future of Syria, without European input. Figure 10.2 shows the conflict's standing at this point.

In 2019 the international coalition together with Kurdish forces made gains against Islamic State – indeed, by the middle of the year it looked like IS had been defeated. While this was an important strategic gain for European governments, it also benefitted the Assad regime. Although it was not back in control of all Syrian territory, the regime no longer faced any danger of being defeated. The withdrawal of US troops

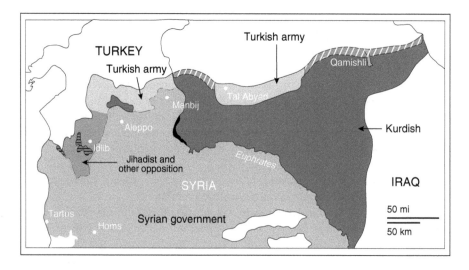

Figure 10.2 Syria conflict, as of 2020

Source: Liveuamap.com

then allowed Turkey to attack the very Kurdish forces that EU donors had been supporting. Member states rejected the notion that European troops might replace the departing US forces. When Germany's defence minister proposed that EU troops help police a 'security zone' other governments and the German cabinet rejected the idea. Turkey undertook military action against Syrian and Russian attacks on Idlib and was so angered at the lack of EU support that it moved to re-open its borders and push refugees into Europe. If the EU prudently kept itself out of the Syrian quagmire, in so doing it allowed other powers to set terms increasingly prejudicial to European aims.

Libya

Conflict has been as enduring in Libya as in Syria, and the EU's stabilisation efforts apparently just as powerless. While Libya chose not to join the EMP, in the early 2000s European governments sought and achieved some modest rapprochement with the country as Colonel Qaddafi relinquished chemical weapons and became less antagonistic towards Europe. When Qaddafi reacted with lethal brutality against pro-democracy protestors in 2011, the EU suspended talks on a new framework agreement with Libya, imposed an arms embargo and incrementally tightened sanctions against the regime. When the regime threatened to bomb protestors, the UK and France moved to set up a no-fly zone. The Italian government had been most committed to building a new rapprochement with Qaddafi and was the slowest to accept these measures, but it eventually did so.

Major differences between member states then emerged over military action. The UK and France pushed for military intervention, while the German government openly opposed them. Germany abstained in the vote on UN Resolution 1973, which authorised military action in Libya. While the UK and France pushed most strongly for a military attack, in the action that followed most strikes used US missiles. Of EU states only the UK, France, Denmark and Belgium participated in hitting targets. Germany and other states accused the UK and France of straying beyond the UN resolution's remit to protect civilians. France recognised the rebels' National Transitional Council without consulting other EU member states. French and British special forces provided on-the-ground support to the anti-regime rebels. A combination of airstrikes, persistent mobilisations within Libya, practical support for the rebels and internal fractures within the regime eventually sufficed to force Qaddafi from power.

After Qaddafi's exit, EU states promised they would increase support and not abandon Libya, learning lessons from previous interventions. The Commission allocated 70 million euros for humanitarian relief, 30 million for immediate stabilisation and 50 million for longer-term development projects. Several programmes supported capacity building for state institutions and the EU provided vocational training to 200,000 militia members to help with their disarmament. The UK provided a quickly injected 15 million pounds and a beefed-up team of so-called stabilisation advisors.[31] All this support was modest, however, compared to the strains that Libya was now under, as rival militia fought one other and radical groups gained ground. Learning lessons from Iraq, the international community did not try to disband regime security forces and sought to engage members of the Qaddafi inner circle. Yet these former regime members increasingly sought to regain a hold on power. There was no consideration of any kind of EU stabilisation force that might have contained militia forces.

Moderates won elections in 2012, and yet violence intensified rather than abating – leading to criticisms that outside powers had made the familiar mistake of pushing for elections too quickly. Increasingly, European support focused on measures aimed at security imperatives. Italy prioritised funding for high-tech border management and surveillance equipment. In 2013 an EU Border Assistance Mission likewise deployed a team of experts in border management. The EU presence soon became highly controversial as the border mission was found to be channelling funds to militia forces to help control refugee flows through Libya. The EU found itself on the receiving end of increasingly tough criticism from the United Nations for worsening the crisis and being complicit in the inhuman conditions in Libyan refugee detention centres.[32]

After a complex series of political manoeuvrings, in 2014 the country divided into competing factions and violent conflict spread. Islamist militants took Tripoli; forces led by General Haftar formed a separate administration in the eastern city of Tobruk. Recriminations followed that EU governments had not been attentive enough in bearing down on the Islamists and had even allowed funds to go to their militia.[33] Libya's renewed violence now became a theatre for broader regional geopolitics. Qatar and Turkey were favourable to the Muslim Brotherhood-linked administration in Tripoli, while Egypt and the UAE intervened to support Haftar with weapons. Most EU states criticised Haftar's military actions but mainly sought to mediate between the two administrations.

European states supported a UN peace deal in late 2015 based around a so-called Government of National Accord (GNA). The EU leant hard on the different actors to sign the unity accord by making future cooperation conditional upon this. The deal soon collapsed, widening differences between member states. Italy and others insisted that the priority was to support the unity government. In contrast, France sought to work with Haftar despite his refusal to join the GNA. The renegade general cooperated on the ground with several European governments to push back against Islamic State. France saw Haftar as an ally against radical groups in the Sahel. French-supplied Javelin missiles were discovered in Haftar's arsenal, despite an arms embargo imposed as far back as 2011.

For Italy, stemming migration was key and this required broader stability and a strong GNA. Much funding went through Italy's bilateral accord with the GNA, signed in 2017 and extended in 2020. The EU formally backed the GNA, but did not provide sufficient support to help it work in practice; over 80 per cent of EU funds to Libya were now for migration control.[34] The EU's deployment through the Border Mission essentially sought to outsource migration management to Libyan bodies. Three civil society networks took the Union to court on the grounds that this approach entailed funds going to violent militia forces.[35] By 2020, the EU had dispersed a relatively limited 100 million euros for capacity-building projects and, unlike in Syria, did not develop a strategy to build local governance structures. The UK and US wanted to intensify efforts to build state institutions without Haftar's involvement; France insisted he had to be included in international support plans.[36]

In April 2019, Haftar began an assault on the GNA in Tripoli that would last into 2020. Despite formally recognising the GNA as the legitimate government, the EU did relatively little to help protect it. France was still reluctant to be too critical of Haftar, diluting an EU statement suggesting he pull his troops back.[37] When EU states pushed for a ceasefire rather than unambiguously siding with the GNA, the French government went a step further and insisted this be based around new lines on the ground that would allow Haftar to keep the territory he had gained.

Germany hosted talks in Berlin in January 2020 to revive peace plans, but these talks failed to achieve a breakthrough. In early 2020, the conflict intensified as Russian mercenaries deployed in support of Haftar and Turkey intervened to back the GNA. Figure 10.3 captures this phase in the conflict. The EU did not step

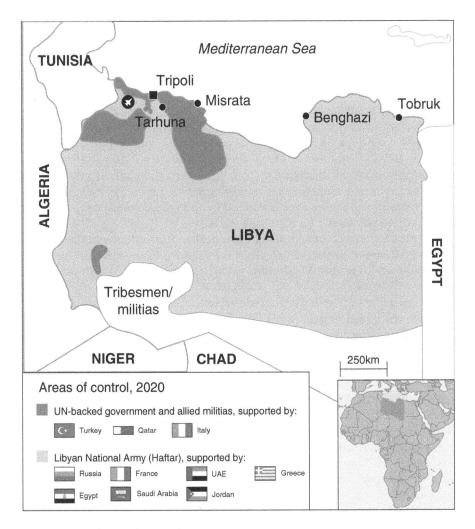

Figure 10.3 Libya conflict, as of 2020

Source: Liveuamap.com

forward to provide any operational support to Turkey or the GNA. Indeed, President Macron remonstrated that he would 'not tolerate the role that Turkey is playing in Libya' and French hostility intensified when Turkey signed a deal with the Libyan government aimed at scuppering EU states' plans for East Mediterranean gas exploration.[38] The EU launched a naval mission, Operation Irini, with the modest mandate of policing the arms embargo; some member states did not participate as they feared the mission actually undercut the GNA's ability to defend itself. While EU states watched from the sidelines, Turkey's intervention was enough to force Haftar into a retreat and ceasefire. There was internal debate over a possible EU mission to monitor the ceasefire, although with the situation still unstable this remained speculative.[39] Indeed, as part of the ceasefire terms Haftar pushed for a reduction in EU security and border-control funding going through the GNA. As in Syria, European influence looked increasingly defensive and directed at a limited form of conflict containment.

Iran and regional rivalries

A particularly significant part of the EU's wider Middle Eastern strategy was its engagement with Iran on the latter's nuclear programme. As commented in Chapter 4, the EU saw its commitment to the so-called Joint Comprehensive Plan of Action (JCPOA), signed in 2015 and designed to limit Iran's nuclear activities, as important not only for this issue in itself but also as a symbolic flagship for the Union's broader adherence to multilateral security strategies. By 2020 the JCPOA was in jeopardy and the tensions centred on Iran and the United States had by this point become a flashpoint for regional instability.

After the 1979 revolution, which brought a theocratic regime to power, EU relations with Iran were distant, although not as strained as those of the United States. The EU responded to the 1997 electoral victory of reformist Mohamed Khatami by changing its 'critical dialogue' into a 'comprehensive dialogue' and explored new areas of cooperation. Explicitly countering President Bush's 'axis of evil' denomination after the terrorist attacks of 11 September 2001, the EU opened negotiations for a trade and investment agreement with Iran in 2002.

This turned out to be the high point in EU–Iran relations. In 2002, evidence emerged that Iran was developing a nuclear programme. European diplomacy now focused on trying to contain this. France, Germany and the UK coordinated to present Iran with a quid pro quo: help in developing a civilian nuclear programme and further trade provisions in return for Iran giving access to International Atomic Energy Agency (IAEA) inspectors. In 2004, the three EU states signed an agreement with Iran on this basis. As talks unfolded, the High Representative also joined the innovative format, bringing in a wider EU dimension. However, in 2005 Khatami lost elections to hard-liner Mahmoud Ahmadinejad, who restarted Iran's programme of uranium enrichment. The EU imposed several rounds of sanctions in the late 2000s; by 2012 these had expanded incrementally to be more severe than anywhere else in the world. Several years of acrimonious talks over technical details were unproductive; by the early 2010s Iran was only a few months from being able to make a nuclear weapon, should it so choose.

The EU had to wait for changes in both the US and Iran to return to a rapprochement. The breakthrough came between Presidents Obama and Rouhani after 2013. The US now played a lead role, adopting the basic contours of a policy the EU had been pursuing for a decade. The Union was midwife to a series of historic new contacts between the US and Iran. The US, France, Germany, the UK, the EU, China and Russia signed the JCPOA in 2015. Iran would limit its uranium enrichment below a specified threshold, and in return Western governments would remove sanctions. The big three EU member states continued to play an important diplomatic role, now in tight concert with the High Representative's office. These ad hoc arrangements seemed to work; the IAEA reported that Iran largely abided by its commitment to limit enrichment in the years after 2015. The EU's concern was not just with non-proliferation rules; on the back of the JCPOA it began a programme of energy cooperation with Iran and aimed to entice Iranian gas supplies into the Southern Gas Corridor project.

President Trump withdrew the US from the accord in 2018 and re-imposed sanctions on Iran. The EU, and especially the French government, tried to mediate a revamped deal to address US concerns over Iran's expanding regional actions. Once this effort failed, the EU's challenge was to counteract the US's secondary sanctions on European companies doing business in Iran. EU states set up a bartering-based 'special-purpose vehicle' called Instex that would allow trade to continue with Iran by avoiding cross-border financial transactions. The EU also offered Iran 50 million euros of economic cooperation funds in 2018. The Trump administration's line was that European states were ignoring Iran's regional expansionism and especially its increased involvement in Syria's war in support of the Assad regime. The EU's retort was that it would abide by the IAEA's judgement that the nuclear deal was still essentially intact.

Iran was frustrated that EU support did not provide meaningful compensation for the effect of US sanctions. Instex was difficult to make work in part due to US financial actions, was not operational until well into 2019 and covered a limited range of essential goods. By the time it was set up, European companies had largely pulled out of Iran, concerned that they would lose business in the US market. EU–Iran trade dried up, with European exports falling by 90 per cent between 2018 and 2020. In May 2019, Iran announced it would intensify its uranium enrichment beyond the limits stipulated in the JCPOA.[40] Iranian proxies undertook multiple attacks on oil infrastructure and shipping in the Gulf and regime security forces shot dead several hundred pro-democracy protestors on the streets of Tehran at the end of 2019. EU governments respond only rhetorically to these events, as they were so keen to retain engagement. Even when the regime was implicated in targeting Iranian opposition leaders in France and Denmark, European reactions were tepid and did not extend beyond restrictive measures on a few officials.

A curious chain of events unfolded involving the UK. The British navy detained an Iranian ship in Gibraltar on the grounds that it was taking oil to Syria in contravention of EU sanctions. Iran retaliated by detaining two UK flagged ships in the

Gulf. Many suspected the UK had naively walked into a trap set by the US administration that was keen to ratchet up international actions against Iran. Keen not to become entangled with US military escorts, the UK government called for European coordination to protect shipping in the Gulf. When other EU states were not keen, the UK joined a US-led naval force; Germany declined to do so. Later in 2020 a small French-led maritime mission began to protect European shipping in the Persian Gulf.

After the US killed General Soleimeni in January 2020, the EU tried to salvage its various strands of engagement with Iran and the anti-IS operations of the 3000 European troops still in Iraq. The EU's priority was to persuade an angry Iranian regime not to pull out of the JCPOA. As Rouhani revealed that Iran was moving to a higher level of enrichment, EU states felt obliged to trigger the JCPOA's dispute resolution mechanism but did not re-impose sanctions. For some months, the EU persuaded Iran to continue allowing IAEA inspectors. However, in June 2020 Iran blocked these. Still, in a complex set of procedural UN debates, European states pushed back against US pressure for sanctions to be re-imposed. The first Instex payment was made to cover EU medical supplies to Iran as the coronavirus struck hard. The harsh impact of COVID-19 also led EU leaders and officials to push for a sizeable injection of aid into Iran and for emergency IMF support; this widened the gap with US policy that turned even further in the direction of 'maximum pressure' during the pandemic.

In these years, European governments held to a broadly common line, although there were sharper internal debates about whether the EU was failing to wield influence because it had been too accommodating towards Iran or insufficiently generous in the incentives it had offered. While France and the UK shared many US concerns and in a notable move Germany outlawed Hezbollah in early 2020, Iran's confrontational actions across the region have in broad terms made EU powers more intent on maintaining engagement and the nuclear accord. Iran and its proxies have gained regional influence rather than losing it. The EU did not dilute its engagement in response to internal and external Iranian violence as keeping the nuclear accord was its key goal, yet neither did it offer Iran a long-term vision capable of the Union more positive leverage towards this end. By late 2020, European governments' hope was that the new Biden administration would return to the JCPOA and help unlock cooperation with Iran.

These shifting considerations with Iran have had an impact on other elements of the EU's MENA strategy. While the US's Middle East Strategic Alliance was framed explicitly as an attempt to support Sunni Arab regimes against Iran, European positions sought a balance. Parallel to the engagement with Iran, in 2019 the EU held its first ever summit with the Arab League, in an effort to enhance its regional role. It engaged Iran in dialogue over the regional implications of the Yemen conflict, trying to facilitate diplomatic links between Iran and Sunni regimes. Still, France and the UK pressed hard to counterbalance Iran's regional role through engagement with Arab Gulf states.[41] In Bahrain, Britain opened its first permanent naval base in the region in forty years and the UK and France assisted Saudi-led attacks in Yemen that were aimed at limiting Iranian influence. After the Saudi regime carried out the brutal murder of journalist Jamal Khashoggi in 2018, European states split: several (Denmark, Finland, Germany) imposed limited sanctions but France and the UK maintained strategic cooperation.[42] France established its own strategic partnership with the UAE in 2020, based on a shared concern with containing Turkish influence.

In its aim to balance its engagement with Iran and Saudi Arabia, the EU now struggled to maintain smooth relations with both these key powers and even more so to act as bridge-builder between them. The JCPOA deal with Iran has widened differences between Gulf states, one cause among several of the Saudi-led blockade and diplomatic isolation of Qatar, and this has undermined the EU's nominal goal of supporting regional cooperation. While High Representative Josep Borrell called ritually for a 'regional solution', the EU did not get Arab states to support its engagement with Iran nor did it leverage Iran into a more cooperative stance towards Arab powers. As the US disengaged and regional tension intensified, the EU struggled to link together different parts of the region into a single strategy (The additional spill-over problems of this for the Israel-Palestinian conflict are summarised in Box 10.1).[43]

Box 10.1 The Israeli-Palestinian conflict

The Israeli-Palestinian conflict has lost its central place in EU policy in the Middle East. Ever since the 1994 Oslo peace agreement, the EU's main role has been to fund the building of Palestinian institutions. The Commission and member states have for nearly thirty years been by far the largest donors to the Palestinian Authority. The Occupied Palestinian Territories administration has for many years received well over a billion euros a year from EU donors, making it one of the largest per capita aid recipients in the world. EU funding has included a long-running mission training Palestinian security forces.

The Union has helped build a quasi-state institutional structure, ready for Palestinian independence. Yet the EU has struggled to leverage this support for any decisive breakthrough in the peace process. From the mid-2010s, this peace process gradually unravelled and the Israeli government refused to move forward with Palestinian sovereignty.

The EU's influence over Israeli actions was minimal in this context. The EU moved to take some modest critical measures, excluding Israel from a number of the Union's funding schemes and removing trade preferences from goods made in illegal Israeli settlements. However, many (especially eastern European) member states recoiled from exerting stronger pressure on Israel. Still, when the EU began to label settlement products in 2015, Israel excluded the EU from peace talks and the EU-Israel association council did not meet after 2016. Israel challenged the settlement labelling and it was only in

November 2019 that the European Court of Justice ruled that products from settlements must be labelled as such.

Within the Occupied Palestinian Territories, the EU supported an institutional structure that could not fulfil the functions of a state because of the Israeli occupation. Moreover, the EU aligned itself with one part of a divided Palestine, refusing after elections in 2006 to have contact with the Hamas administration in the Gaza Strip and favouring its rival Fatah in the West Bank. The EU promised backing for several attempts at Palestinian unity and supported technical projects aimed to bring the West Bank and Gaza judicial and economic systems back into sync with each other. It rolled out half a billion euros in reconstruction aid in Gaza after Israeli bombing raids in 2014. However, the divide between the West Bank and Gaza remained a major impediment to Palestinian statehood.

With the peace process blocked, the EU struggled to find an alternative approach. Sweden formally recognised Palestine as an independent state, without waiting for an agreed settlement. Some other member states debated this option, but none took the same step. France suggested another peace initiative in 2017, but Israel refused to engage with it.

The US presented a new peace plan in early 2020. This proposed such a limited form of Palestinian sovereignty and on such reduced territory that it amounted to de facto Israeli control of the West Bank and did not meet the minimum attributes of statehood. Palestinians would have no control of their own borders, no capital in East Jerusalem, no right of return for refugees and no right to challenge Israel in the International Criminal Court. EU leaders condemned the plan.[44] As the US withdrew support to the Palestinians, the EU stepped up its support to compensate. Yet, the EU refrained from taking any concrete actions to advance an alternative route forward. Member states did not move towards unilateral recognition of Palestinian statehood, which now became more important for Palestinian leaders as they broke off cooperation with both Israel and the US.

When the Israeli government announced plans to move ahead with a de facto annexation of parts of the West Bank in May 2020, little EU action followed. The High Representative and national governments made statements opposing the annexation and threatening 'consequences.' Yet several member states including Austria, Germany, Italy, the Czech Republic and Hungary insisted that cooperation with Israel continue; UK criticism was also muted.[45] As the Palestinian Authority withdrew from all peace agreements, the UAE and Bahrain decided to normalise relations with Israel. The EU welcomed and supported this normalisation, despite it undercutting Palestinians' quest for statehood. This dramatic inflexion point raised fundamental doubts about what have been the core aspects of EU peace-process policies over three decades.

Themes and analysis

Challenges in the MENA region encapsulate in particularly intense form the trends in EU external action that the outside-in conceptual framework helps uncover. In the last several years, other powers have pursued assertive diplomatic policies and the EU has lost much geostrategic weight in this region. The prospect of deep integration and a meaningful 'community of values' being developed between Europe and MENA states has all but evaporated. In response to geopolitical trends and power shifts in the MENA region, this erstwhile EU aspiration has given way to more limited, less distinctive and transactional strategy. The EU's strategic vision towards the Arab world has narrowed.

Power dynamics in the MENA have essentially overridden the notion of the EU sitting at the heart of a pan-regional, hub-and-spokes Euro-Mediterranean process of Europeanisation and norms alignment.[46] Such a perspective has become so incongruent it feels like the geo-strategy of a distant, bygone age. Notwithstanding a commitment to address the root causes of security risks related to the MENA region, in practice EU initiatives backing modernising reforms have progressively withered. The Global Strategy expressly promised that the EU would not accept authoritarian retrenchment after the Arab spring. Yet this is exactly what the EU has done. In 2019, Federica Mogherini insisted that the EU was still working harder for Arab democratic reform than another actor, 'and more so than ever before'.[47] The evidence suggested otherwise.

There has been some unity around the changed EU approach, although nuanced differences between member states, remain in different parts of the MENA region. Whether unity is in this case particularly to be welcomed is debatable. It is doubtful that burgeoning security cooperation with autocratic regimes has bought EU countries deep stability, while it certainly has damaged the bloc's standing with actors other than governments. The focus on migration has made the politics of EU-Mediterranean relations more fractious and undercut years of initiatives aimed at building a more genuinely shared security culture.

In the late 2010s, the nuclear deal with Iran was the lynchpin of the EU's evolving and wider MENA strategy. As this dissolved, so the Union's wider geopolitical approach has struggled to retain traction. Unlike the US administration, the EU believed that Iran could be enticed into a benign regional role. Clearly this has not happened, as rivalries have deepened and fear over Iran's rising influence has even driven Israel and Arab states into new strategic alignment. The EU powers have tried to chart a middle course, and in particular to build bridges between Iran and Saudi Arabia. Yet they have lacked the leverage to succeed in this. Despite confronting the Trump administration on its bellicose policy towards Iran, the EU has had neither the strategy nor power to counteract the divisive drift in US policy.

In Syria, the EU sought to exert leverage over an inclusive transition without providing the means to make this a likely outcome. In 2019 Mogherini insisted the EU had been successful as an impartial mediator and in helping peace.[48] It was difficult see how events on the ground gave any credence at all to her claims. The EU's local capacity-building efforts reflected state-of-the-art thinking in conflict studies and seemed to take on board the lessons of previous conflicts.[49] Yet these initiatives did not work in Syria. The Commission and national donors tried to create the conditions for peace from the ground up, but this did not give them strong influence at the diplomatic level.

In Libya, the dynamics were in some sense the opposite of those in Syria: apparently successful intervention dislodged a regime and opened the way for stabilisation efforts. Yet the Union also failed here due to its internal differences, conflicting aims and lack of deep commitment. The long-lasting Syrian and Libyan conflicts became microcosms of European disempowerment and stand-back protective security. While most in the EU felt the Union was right in eschewing direct involvement, this allowed Russia and Turkey to undertake actions whose consequences were borne by Europe. In these two theatres, the EU has paid the strategic price for reneging on its accession promises to Turkey – the latter now more clearly a rival than partner. The EU has also been unable to influence the US's erratic fluctuations in these conflicts.

All these geopolitical adjustments entailed a shift in the internal dynamics of EU external action – one picked up by the conceptual framework in other chapters in the book. The role of member state governments within the overall mix of EU external action has evolved significantly. EU external action has become more eclectic in the region, balancing national diplomatic tools with Commission-based funding and functional instruments. Several member states have increasingly pursued national policy initiatives in the region, while others have remained relatively unengaged. In some instances, national and EU-level actions have pulled in the same direction and been complementary. This was true on some political reform issues for a short time after the Arab spring and in the innovative format used in relations with Iran – with the three largest member states leading diplomacy, with wider EU buy-in.[50] Yet on most issues the EU has struggled to make these more mixed dynamics work.[51]

In sum, the EU has responded in flexible and even expedient fashion to the fluidity and specificity of domestic developments within different parts of the Middle East. The vast majority of policy-makers and analysts have seen this as a welcome and overdue adjustment. Yet, increasingly, the EU risks being neither one thing nor the other: it has drifted away from offering the Arab world very much of a genuinely people-centred, liberal power, yet has not been able to compete with the geopolitical power of the US, Russia or regional players like Turkey and Saudi Arabia. While European strategists have tried to combine the best elements of liberal and realist power, in the MENA region the EU's influence has weakened on both metrics.

Concluding summary

External challenges. The MENA region has presented several layers of challenge that have played a prominent role in reshaping EU external action. This is an area where outside-in dynamics have become an especially strong driver of EU policy adjustment in recent years.

Unity–diversity. Member states and EU institutions have largely agreed on the move towards containment-based policy in the MENA. However, internal EU divisions over Libya have been profound, while divides on tactical choices towards Syria, terrorism, human rights and engagement with Iran have also widened.

Distinctive power. The quintessential EU governance-based foreign-policy toolbox has lost relevance in the MENA region. National governments' diplomacy has gained in prominence. In the MENA region, the EU's drift away from being a distinctive international power has been telling in recent years.

Protective dynamics. The dynamics of protective security have pulled the EU back from deep engagement in conflicts in the MENA region. Beyond conflicts, the EU's ambitions have lowered to a progressively tighter focus on containment, as efforts to reshape the region's governance and geopolitics have foundered.

EU influence. The EU's loss of influence over the conflicts in Libya and Syria has been especially sobering. Across the MENA region, European external action has become more of a dependent than independent variable: it has been re-shaped by events across the region more than it has shaped politics and security in the Arab states and Iran.

11 War in Ukraine and the Russia Challenge in Eastern Europe

The outside-in conceptual approach is highly relevant to the visceral and taxing geopolitics the EU has faced to its east. Since 2014 the EU has grappled with ongoing war in Ukraine and a series of broader concerns flowing from Russian actions. The EU has rethought its approach and modified its policies towards Russia in significant ways in response to events in Crimea and Donbas. It has played a more influential role in Ukraine's conflict than in the Middle East and has been at least partially successful in containing the war between Ukrainian forces and separatists backed by Russia. The EU has run its largest ever support programme to help strengthen Ukraine and sought a geopolitical response to Russian attempts to unsettle the European security order. Geopolitical concerns have also prompted the EU to adjust its policies towards other states in the region. To the east, traditional policy and analytical approaches to EU external action have retained greater relevance than elsewhere; yet the shifts in European policies also reflect the more protective, geopolitical and less institutionalised strategies that the book has uncovered in other areas of policy. While this mix has given the EU a significant degree of influence, it has not done enough to allay the strategic risks that lie to the east.

The challenges

Tensions between the EU and Russia grew on a range of international issues as the 2000s proceeded. A Russian incursion into Georgia in 2008 was one serious flashpoint, while general EU and Russia positions on the wider global order also diverged markedly. A far more dramatic crisis then unfolded from the mid-2010s. In 2013 Russia began a concerted effort to scupper EU policies in the states of the Eastern Partnership (EaP) – Armenia, Azerbaijan, Belarus, Georgia, Moldova and Ukraine, as shown in Figure 11.1. It imposed punitive economic measures against several EaP states as they prepared to sign association agreements with the European Union. In September 2013 Armenia pulled out of its EU agreement to join Russia's embryonic Eurasian Economic Union. This was followed by Russia's success in pushing President Viktor Yanukovich to announce that Ukraine would also reject its EU accord. When Yanukovich was pushed from power by a popular uprising, Russia moved swiftly to annex Crimea.

Russia then militarily supported separatist rebels across eastern Ukraine. While Moscow formally denied any officially sanctioned involvement, many of the rebel

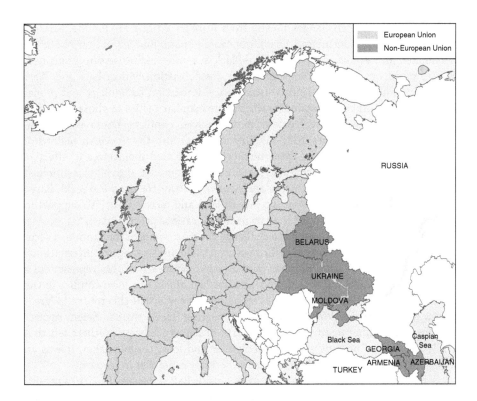

Figure 11.1 The Eastern Partnership (until Brexit)

fighters were Russian and Russia moved tens of thousands of troops to its border with Ukraine. Ukraine's armed forces could not prevent the Russian-backed separatist forces winning territorial gains. President Putin talked of Russian claims to a far greater swathe of what he called 'Novorossiya'. An international investigation found that the missile that brought down a Malaysian Airlines flight over eastern Ukraine in July 2014, killing 298 people, was fired from separatist-controlled territory. Russian troops became more openly involved in the fighting and separatists gradually consolidated their hold over two areas in the Donbas region, around Luhansk and Donetsk.

In September 2014, the so-called Minsk accord proposed peace based on far-reaching autonomy or self-government for the rebel-held areas. Yet the fighting worsened. A second Minsk accord was signed in 2015, with France and Germany central players from among EU states. Since then, the conflict has been somewhat contained. Fighting has continued at a relatively low level, with periodic flare-ups. An uneasy stalemate took root: Ukrainian troops were unable to retake the occupied territories, but nor could Russian-backed forces push the frontline further into Ukraine. The Minsk deal more or less held, yet without its core conditions being fulfilled: Russia did not return control of Ukraine's borders to the Kiev government, while the latter stalled on self-government for the two occupied territories. By the end of 2020, over 13,000 people had been killed in the fighting.

Broader strategic challenges flowed from Russian actions in Ukraine. Russian fighter planes made incursions into European air space. Russia's military build-up accelerated and its naval activity in the Black Sea and Mediterranean intensified. Russia rolled out a new toolbox of covert destabilisation within East and West European states, through criminal networks, information technology and propaganda tools. In other EaP states Russia pursued similar tactics to those it used in Ukraine, extending its involvement in unresolved conflicts across the region. Following on from Russia's 2008 military incursion into the Georgian regions of Abkhazia and South Ossetia, these territories committed themselves to effective integration into Russian security forces. A very different set of dynamics unfolded when the conflict between Armenia and Azerbaijan over Nagorno-Karabakh flared up in late 2020; Azerbaijan won swathes of land and received Turkish support in doing so, before Russia stepped in to oversee a precarious peace deal.

Many Russian actions seemed to challenge the core tenets of the European security order. Russia's annexation of Crimea clearly violated a range of international laws and treaties.[1] A large number of analysts concurred that this represented a systemic geopolitical watershed, and was not just about one local conflict in the south and east of Ukraine.[2] The Russian perspective was that this return to 'great power rivalry' was the West's fault for not treating Russia with sufficient respect and for encroaching upon Russia's interests in Eastern Europe.[3] Others felt that while Russia had become an effective spoiler and local troublemaker, it was an exaggeration to think the whole European security order was in jeopardy.[4]

Geopolitical shifts affected developments inside EaP states too. In 2014 a pro-EU government took power in Ukraine and incoming president Petro Poroshenko committed to economic and political reform. His government signed laws that strengthened judicial independence, tightened parliamentary control of the security forces and regulated party funding to reduce oligarchs' influence. Yet presidential power gradually increased, the government blocked high-level anti-corruption cases and political parties remained the personal projects of different oligarchs. Critics charged Poroshenko with using the security situation in the east as a pretext for delaying reforms.[5] Popular frustration gave comedian Volodymyr Zelenksy a landslide electoral victory in 2019. He adopted a somewhat populist style of politics, but one that initially unblocked several areas of EU-linked reforms. Over the 2010s, turbulent popular mobilisations also had significant political effects in Armenia, Belarus, Georgia and Moldova, posing further challenges for EU external action.

Russia and semi-containment

In the early 2000s, the EU made repeated attempts to deepen and improve relations with Russia, through successive proposals for 'common spaces' of alignment, a Strategic Partnership, a Partnership and Cooperation Agreement, a Modernisation Partnership and even, somewhat improbably, for Russia to be part of the European Neighbourhood Policy. Despite such efforts, relations gradually soured. Then Russia's annexation of Crimea, its involvement in the Donbas conflict and actions elsewhere in the region reshaped the EU's relations with Moscow.

They were also a key consideration that propelled EU states to strengthen their defensive, protective security.

Sanctions

The EU applied sanctions against Russia as a core part of its response to both Crimea's annexation and Russia's involvement in fostering violence in eastern Ukraine. This was a major change in strategic orientation, as in the years prior to the crisis in 2014 the EU had sought engagement and cooperation with Russia. In the early 2000s, France in particular had tightened strategic relations with Russia as a counterweight to shifts in global power.[6] Baltic states had warned that Moscow might not reciprocate the quest for positive partnership.[7] After 2014, the change in direction of German–Russian relations was especially noteworthy and Chancellor Angela Merkel's support for the sanctions was influential.[8] Eastern European and some other member states called for a move from détente with Russia back to Cold War deterrence.[9]

The EU applied sanctions on Russia in stages. It immediately suspended talks on visa liberalisation and a new partnership and cooperation agreement. It then quickly imposed asset freezes and visa bans on members of the Russian government involved in the Crimea annexation, stopped military cooperation and introduced an arms embargo. It then moved incrementally to a broader range of economic sanctions. Western governments reduced the G8 to the G7, meeting without Russia. The Commission, European Investment Bank and European Bank for Reconstruction and Development suspended aid projects in Russia. By 2020 the sanctions had been widened and tightened several times, while Russia imposed its own sanctions on EU products.

The EU imposed sanctions against opposition from large companies and banks. Against initial signs to the contrary, France cancelled the sale of two warships to Russia and the UK accepted measures affecting the financial sector. From 2012 to 2018 EU exports to Russia dropped by a third.[10] Each time the sanctions came up for their six-monthly renewal, a number of member states suggested it was time to dilute or remove them, but the majority view was that they should continue in force. Governments in Greece, Italy and Hungary pressed to remove sanctions at moments when the conflict in Ukraine was less intense. Each time conditions worsened again on the ground, the case for keeping the sanctions strengthened again. When the relatively dovish High Representative, Federica Mogherini brought forward ideas for restarting cooperation with Russia, most member states rebuffed her. Even technical-level contacts dried up between EU and Russian officials.[11] In 2020 a number of member states suggested the EU should remove the sanctions to help Russia fight the COVID-19 pandemic; for the moment, however, they remained in place. Separately, the EU imposed measures against individual Russian officials under its chemical weapons sanctions regime after attacks on a former intelligence operative and his daughter in the UK town of Salisbury and in 2020 after the poisoning of opposition leader Alexei Navalny. Figure 11.2 shows that sanctions have had a significant impact on EU–Russia trade.

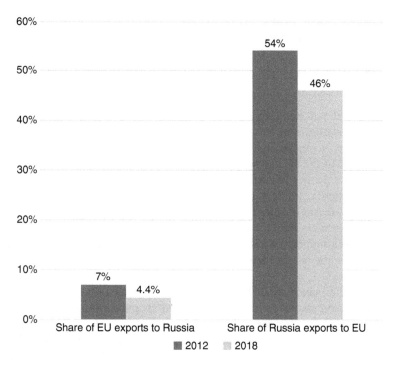

Figure 11.2 EU–Russia trade
Source: European Commission

Defensive security

European governments also reinforced defence measures, including through NATO. They stepped up surveillance flights over Baltic states, with new NATO Baltic Air Policing mission scrambling on a regular basis. NATO beefed up border defences, for instance in Romania. The US launched a $1 billion US European Reassurance Initiative. Romania and Poland led an initiative for NATO eastern-flank states to deepen military cooperation amongst themselves. The increase in German deployments in the east was especially notable, while the UK deployed weapons systems to Poland. NATO's Response Force was expanded from 13,000 to 25,000 troops and a 5000-strong Very High Readiness Task Force was created to be deployable within 48 hours. NATO deployed Battlegroups in the three Baltic states and Poland. It also increased training and capacity building for Ukrainian armed forces.[12] Russian actions in Ukraine were not the only reason behind the general increase in European defence budgets – outlined in Chapter 5 – but they were one major factor.

Cold engagement

Overall, the EU fashioned a kind of 'cold engagement' with Russia. The EU did not break off relations completely and its approach was not entirely punitive. The relationship with Moscow became more distant and based more on functional necessity than any ethos of trusting partnership. This entailed efforts to lower hostilities. EU sanctions excluded the all-important energy sector and many areas of European investment in Russia prospered. The EU offered a series of dialogues with Russian officials to explore ways of helping EaP states develop positive trade relations with both the Union and Russia.[13] The EU offered new cooperation with the Eurasian Economic Union. European leaders rejected any kind of military deployment within Ukraine itself. Germany and other states opposed calls for permanent bases in Eastern Europe. Many European politicians were unsupportive of the Ukraine's decision to drop its non-aligned status and reinforced their opposition of extending NATO membership further into Eastern Europe (even though NATO's official position was still favourable to Georgian and Ukrainian membership).

Many national governments were reluctant to be overly confrontational towards Russia. Cypriot, French, German, Greek, Hungarian, Italian, Slovakian and Spanish politicians and senior EU figures regularly called for dialogue with Moscow to temper geopolitical tensions. As German foreign minister and then president, Frank-Walter Steinmeier was an especially influential advocate of such engagement. Commission president Jean-Claude Juncker insisted obliquely that, 'The EU cannot let its relations with Russia be dictated by the US', implying a preference for continued cooperation with Moscow.[14] Several European leaders and governments encouraged the OSCE to launch discussions over a new security arrangement to include Russia, in what became the so-called 'Helsinki plus 40' initiative.[15] Germany pushed for the OSCE to launch a Structured Dialogue in 2016 to build consultations with Russia on a range of security challenges.[16] In 2019 France and Germany successfully pushed for Russia to be allowed back into the Council of Europe assembly, after its voting rights were suspended in 2014.

In 2019, President Macron called for a new effort to rebuild strategic relations with Russia. He invited President Putin for dialogue just before the G7 in France in August 2019 and said he wanted to include Russia in 'new security architecture for Europe that runs from Lisbon to Vladivostock'.[17] He called for relations with Russia to be 're-visited' and for a new initiative based on 'trust and security'.[18] Having stirred up considerable unease from many other member states and EaP partners, Macron then seemed to pull back, saying there could be no far-reaching change for many years, given Russia's current stances.[19] When President Trump suggested inviting Putin to a G7 summit set for autumn 2020, no European state was supportive of the idea. The detention of opposition leader Alexei Navalny hardened member state views and when the High Representative went to Russia in early 2021 in search of strategic dialogue, the Russian foreign minister dismissed the EU as an 'unreliable partner'. Most efforts to reach out to Moscow were unproductive and into the 2020s cold engagement remained the guiding tenet in EU relations with Russia.

Conflict management in Ukraine

Alongside the general change in its Russia policy, the EU grappled in more specific ways with Russian actions inside Ukraine. The EU was unequivocal in its criticism of Russia's annexation of Crimea; in Donbas its main focus was on reaching a mediated settlement. As conflict spread in eastern Ukraine, France and Germany emerged as the lead players, these two states meeting with Russian and Ukrainian officials in what became known as the Normandy format. Influenced by France and Germany, the EU called for restraint from both separatists and Ukrainian troops – despite most observers seeing the war as an external invasion of Ukraine's sovereign territory.[20] Germany opposed references to Russia having 'invaded' eastern Ukraine. Several EU states sought to discourage President Poroshenko from ramping up military operations against the separatists. Those supporting even-handed mediation noted that Russia showed no signs of seeking to annex the separatist territories as it had done with Crimea.

The Minsk peace accord was based on a ceasefire in return for moves towards autonomy in the occupied territories of eastern Ukraine. Under the second Minsk accord in 2015, separatists won additional territory and promises of more far-reaching autonomy for rebel-held areas. Several member states, including the Polish and Baltic governments, accused France and Germany of acting against EU positions in agreeing to this. The High Representative's role on the Donbas issue was negligible and this weighed against a common EU line. European leaders pressed the Poroshenko government to get a grip on volunteer battalions still fighting and to respect the ceasefire against the tide of Ukrainian domestic opinion. Protests in Kiev strongly criticised European governments for preventing Ukraine from defending its territorial rights. The EU did not support Ukraine's request in 2016 for a military border mission based on the model of the Union's mission in Georgia.

France, Germany and the EU ambassador in Kiev pushed the Ukrainian government to accelerate moves towards some form of autonomy for the separatist-held territories. The Ukrainian government was reluctant to do so before it regained full control over its territorial borders and accused the EU of putting Ukraine's territorial integrity at risk. Some other member states complained that Germany in particular seemed to be backing Russia's view of the peace accords, with the separatists gaining autonomy before Ukraine's interests had been fully secured. Lithuania's foreign minister criticised those in the EU who seemed to be pushing Ukraine harder than they were pushing Russia to comply with the Minsk accord.[21]

Most member states refused to provide weapons to Ukrainian security forces. Only a small number of Baltic and Eastern European states provided modest amounts of military equipment. A Lithuanian–Polish–Ukrainian armed unit was set up. UK, Polish, Romanian, Bulgarian and Lithuanian militaries offered training for Ukrainian troops and non-lethal equipment. In 2018, the US and Canada began supplying Ukraine with significant amounts of lethal military hardware; EU states generally refused to do so. From 2017, European influence was somewhat displaced by the US's re-engagement. The US special representative Kurt Volker played a lead role in reviving peace talks, sidelining the largely invisible Federica Mogherini.

In 2018, the EU supported proposals for a UN peacekeeping force, even though Ukraine feared this would in effect legitimise and freeze separatist control over the two occupied territories. This proposal did not move forward because of differences between the US and Russia about where exactly it should be deployed and with what mandate. In November 2018, Russia moved to tighten control of the Kerch Strait in violation of international law and took a number of Ukrainian sailors captive in the Azov Sea. The EU again called for 'de-escalation from both sides'. In fact, it pushed hardest on President Poroshenko to refrain from declaring martial law in response to the incident; only six months later did the EU implement a modest tightening of its sanctions against Russia in a belated effort to contain its push into the Azov Sea.

The Minsk process continued to look fragile and the conflict became more deadly at the frontline during 2018 and 2019. On the fifth anniversary of the Crimea annexation, Ukraine's foreign minister penned a joint letter with 10 EU foreign ministers (and their Canadian colleague) stressing the importance of strengthening external support for Ukraine's resilience in Donbas; the signatories included Sweden, Denmark, the UK, the three Baltic states, Poland, Romania and the Czech Republic, but no other EU member states.[22] German foreign minister Heiko Maas still repeatedly favoured a line that moves were needed equally from 'both sides' in Donbas.

When newly elected President Zelensky offered to meet President Putin, several member states saw an opportunity to revive the peace accords. France, Germany and the Finnish presidency in late 2019 pushed Zelensky hard to accept the so-called 'Steinmeier formula' – a plan named after the German president that proposed moving ahead with autonomy for the two occupied territories in an intricate sequencing with local elections. Many other member states were concerned that this ceded too much to Russia. Ukrainian citizens protested against Zelensky for conceding too much ground and admonished the EU for allowing separatists to keep hold of territory they had gained through violence. The first Normandy meeting for three years was held in December 2019, amid hopes that the two sides would agree to compromise. No breakthrough was made, however, as Zelensky stuck to the line that Ukraine needed to regain control of its borders prior to separatist autonomy. Despite pre-meeting fears to the contrary, President Macron and Chancellor Merkel supported the Ukrainian president. Adding further support, in 2020 the UK signed a new strategic partnership with Ukraine that included direct military cooperation to help the Kiev government hold its line in the conflict.

EU policy has been one of conflict containment, not conflict transformation. Figure 11.3 shows the situation on the ground at the end of the 2010s. Russia largely welcomed the aim to freeze the Donbas conflict, as this reduced violence but kept status questions unresolved and allowed Moscow to maintain its influence over Ukrainian internal politics.[23] Ukrainians criticised the EU for prioritising mediation and bridge-building initiatives, as if the conflict were between rival internal factions rather than an external invasion of a sovereign state.[24] The EU supported Ukraine's territorial integrity and the eventual reintegration of occupied areas but also insisted it accept far-reaching self-governance for separatist-held zones. The EU implicitly made its offer of support conditional on Ukraine accepting it had de facto lost control of parts of its territory.[25]

Figure 11.3 Occupied territories in Ukraine

Upgrading the Eastern Partnership

The Eastern Partnership was launched in 2009, pushed in particular by Poland and Sweden. It offered Eastern partners association agreements that would include Deep and Comprehensive Free Trade Areas (DCFTAs). These required EaP states to align large numbers of their laws and regulations with those of the European Union; the EU supported this through a 'Structured approximation process'. By 2013 over 50 EaP twinning arrangements existed with various ministries and regulatory agencies. In late 2013, the situation changed dramatically. In September 2013, Armenia announced it was joining the Eurasian customs union and pulling out of the association agreement talks with the European Union. Russia imposed sanctions against Ukraine, Georgia and Moldova to dissuade them from signing their association agreements. Ukraine then dramatically pulled out of its association agreement talks. Azerbaijan also rejected an association agreement and Belarus stepped further back from engagement.

The EaP's low-key approach seemed unsuited to this new reality. The initial EaP took no apparent account of Russia's role, interests or its potential to undercut EU initiatives. In most EaP states there were disputes over territory and the EU refrained from any direct involvement in this contested 'stateness'.[26] Most notably, after a Russian intervention in the disputed Georgian enclaves of Abkhazia and South Ossetia in 2008, the EU offered even-handed mediation but avoided any direct pressure against Russian involvement. The EaP was designed around rules-transfer rather than the Union offering eastern states any security protection.[27] The EU struggled even to bring about low-politics regulatory convergence to the extent that adaptation costs were high for EaP governments.[28] The policy was designed around the EU's own internal market rules, not what was best geopolitically for the EaP region.[29] The EaP provoked geopolitical reactions from Russia, but eschewed any direct security response to these.[30]

The EU made changes to the EaP as a result of the new context after 2014. The Commission introduced a new EaP strategy that promised more high-level commitment and more foreign policy coordination with eastern states.[31] The EU would do more to promote itself as 'a diplomatic actor and provider of security' through 'more action based on diplomacy, conflict prevention and mediation'.[32] The EU added a 'Common Security and Defence Policy panel' to the EaP's multilateral track, to deepen security partnerships. It began to distinguish more systematically between the three states – Georgia, Moldova and Ukraine – that were keen to move ahead with deeper partnership and those – Armenia, Azerbaijan and Belarus – that were more ambivalent. This so-called 'differentiation' supposedly became a key means of unlocking the EaP's strategic potential.

The EU accelerated the signing of association agreements with Ukraine, Georgia and Moldova. These agreements were brought forward to June 2014, ahead of their originally estimated dates. The EU agreed visa-free travel for Ukraine and Georgia, having already granted this to Moldova. Transgovernmental networks gained momentum between the EU and Eastern partner states – although in some technical sectors more than in others.[33] The EU promised to make the 15 billion euros allocated under the European Neighbourhood Instrument for the 2014–2020 period available on terms that were 'more flexible' and with lighter forms of conditionality; it made approximation requirements more optional than legally binding. The EU promised 'new ways of working' and indicated that security and 'stabilisation' would now be the EU's highest priorities. It prioritised engagement 'with partners in the security sector' and increased its funding of cyber-security capacities across the EaP partners.[34] Figure 11.4 summarises the European Commission's EaP aid allocations during these crucial years (member state aid being in addition to these amounts).

Notwithstanding all these new commitments, the EaP upgrade was limited in many respects. The EU declined to offer EaP states a membership prospect – which is what they most wanted as a bulwark against Russian interference. Indeed, EU diplomats admitted that the crisis had made membership even more unlikely, far from the EU stepping up to use accession as a geopolitical tool. The EU did not offer a customs union or European Economic Area membership for the EaP states; these would have been difficult to implement for technical, economic and political reasons. Its overall funding for the EaP did not increase; the 2014–2020 allocation of 5 billion euros was a freeze relative to the previous five-year budget cycle. Southern member states pushed to ensure that the Ukraine crisis did not divert resources away from the southern Mediterranean, and that the latter still received two-thirds of the 15 billion-euro total ENP budget. Member state aid to the EaP region remained limited. The EaP did not offer states a direct security guarantee or even much in the way of security assistance to help partner states protect their territories and borders.

As the EaP's 2017–2020 strategy approached its end, Georgia, Moldova and Ukraine pushed for an upgrade in relations with the EU, arguing that it was now time to look beyond the DCFTAs to options like an extension of the European Economic Area or some kind of security compact. A small group of

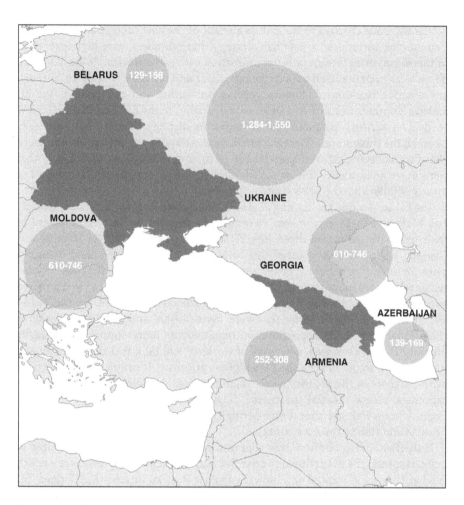

Figure 11.4 European Neighbourhood Instrument funding to EaP states, 2014–2020, million euros

Source: European Commission and External Action Service

member states, led by Sweden and some Central and Eastern European countries, agreed and pushed for a major policy boost as a riposte to Russian actions.[35] However, most member states were not willing to offer these states a higher level of strategic cooperation. In March 2020, the Commission and External Action Service proposed a new EaP framework beyond 2020 that offered merely an imprecise promise of 'deeper sectorial cooperation' for those states that wanted it.[36] An EaP summit was held online in June 2020 without making any major advances. The focus was at this stage mainly on COVID-19 issues, for which the EU provided an emergency rescue package. Baltic governments expressed frustration with those member states that continued to block more ambitious cooperation with the vanguard EaP states.[37] The EaP played no role in response to the renewed conflict between Azerbaijan and Armenia in late 2020; Turkey intervened to support Azerbaijan, Russia played a prime role in trying to end hostilities and these two governments refused to accept a post-ceasefire EU monitoring mission.

Supporting Ukraine

Beyond the broad-ranging adjustments to the EaP, EU diplomats stressed that the Union's most effective contribution to holding Russian influence at bay came through its enhanced support to Ukraine. The EU supported Ukraine to become a more resilient and efficient state from the late 1990s and with particular commitment after the 2004 popular revolt known as the Orange Revolution. The EU supported the Orange Revolution but did not play a proactive role in causing it. In the 1990s and early 2000s, member states built a cooperative relationship with Ukraine under the largely undemocratic regime of Leonid Kuchma that was seen as a bridge with Russia. When protestors rose up against that regime's attempt to manipulate election results to hand-pick Kuchma's successor, the EU offered rhetorical support and a limited amount of logistical help, with then High Representative Javier Solana trying to mediate a compromise outcome in the background.

Once the pro-democracy Orange coalition succeeded in overturning the results and taking power, the EU offered Ukraine a package of long-term assistance for institution building. Yet EU support and pressure were not enough to prevent Ukraine drifting back into a form of soft authoritarianism. Commission aid to Ukraine for 2007–2010 was double the amount disbursed in 2003–2006. The EU increased technical assistance, with the aim of strengthening accountability in public administration through twinning programmes. It opened talks for its most wide-ranging association agreement ever. The EU held back portions of its aid as the government stalled on or reversed reforms.[38] It also channelled an increasing share of its support into rule of law projects.[39]

This engagement was extensive and yet struggled to gain traction. So far did the Orange coalition lose public confidence that in 2010 Viktor Yanukovich – the Moscow-backed candidate who had been denied office in 2004 – won power in elections. He tightened executive control over the judiciary, restricted press freedom and imprisoned many members of the opposition. After concluding association agreement negotiations, the EU then put the accord on hold mainly in response to the imprisonment of opposition leader Yulia Tymoshenko. As Ukrainian democracy slowly unravelled between 2011 and 2013, EU pressure intensified. One week before the Vilnius EaP summit in November 2013, the president announced that Ukraine was pulling out of the agreement.

A small group of member states moved to get the EU to drop the demand that Tymoshenko be released; but this came too late to entice the Ukrainian government back to the agreement. Protestors took to Kiev's central Maidan square against corruption and in support of the EU agreement. During three months of protests, the EU offered additional funds and other upgrades to the association agreement in an effort to change Yanukovich's mind. Some in the EU argued this was the moment to offer full membership, as the only incentive that could make a decisive difference; but most member states remained adamantly against this. While the EU offered a few hundred million euros extra, Russia offered 15 billion dollars.

As the government cracked down with increasing brutality – on one fateful day in February 2014 army snipers killed over a hundred protestors – so the demands of the 'Euromaidan' revolt escalated. Protestors now wanted Yanukovich out and were dismayed that the EU continued to support him as the legitimate president. The EU offered little practical support to the protestors. Only a small number of funding bodies like the European Endowment for Democracy were present and willing to release short-term help for the uprising. Most EU governments kept a distance. To protestors' dismay, the EU only agreed to sanctions when the regime was already on the verge of defeat. The primary European influence came when the German, French and Polish foreign ministers went to Kiev and pressured the president into signing a power-sharing deal with members of the opposition. However, Yanukovich then abruptly fled the country. Uncomfortably, the EU had tried to keep in power a president forced to flee by Ukrainian citizens.

After Yanukovich fled, an interim administration formed and moved Ukraine towards elections in May 2014. The EU agreed a raft of new funding. Overall EU support would eventually total 11 billion euros. This included the EU's largest ever programme of macro-economic assistance. The EU offered direct budgetary support through a 355 million-euro State-Building Contract and a separate 10 million-euro package for civil society. By 2020, the EU and member states had over 400 technical assistance programmes running in Ukraine. In 2016, the EU began a 100 million-euro project to support decentralisation. It set up a Ukraine Support Group to coordinate all this support. Figure 11.5 details the range of EU support to Ukraine. An EU Advisory Mission for Civilian Security Sector Reform Ukraine

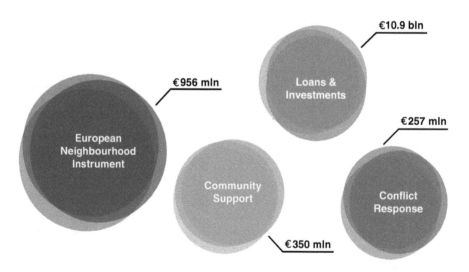

Figure 11.5 EU support package to Ukraine

Source: European External Action Service (2019a), p. 42

supported police and rule of law reform. Germany announced a new 500 million-euro package of support to Ukraine; Sweden and the UK developed more modestly funded governance initiatives.

The EU and Ukraine signed the political elements of the association agreement within days. The EU unilaterally removed many tariffs, giving Ukraine immediate, free access for many of its exports to the European market. It also promised to 'frontload' assistance, loosening conditionality and technical requirements.[40] The EU began to deliberate the possibility of integrating Ukraine into some sectors of EU integration, like energy and the digital single market. Unsurprisingly, many Ukrainians complained that all these measures were overshadowed by the EU's refusal to grant Ukraine a membership perspective. Yet it was significant that the Union's raft of post-2014 funding represented its most comprehensive support programme anywhere in the world.

The EU used conditionality in relation to corruption, arguing this was crucial to strengthening the Ukrainian state. It delayed a second tranche of its macro-economic financial assistance from late 2015 to early 2017 and delayed a third tranche from December 2017 to July 2018; it released a fourth tranche at the end of 2018. In addition, the EU attached corruption-related conditions to visa liberalisation, not granting this until 2017. The EU struck a balance: it delayed aid payments and other offers until the Ukrainian government unblocked progress on specific anti-corruption measures, but increased aid despite the overall reform process slowing after 2016.[41] The EU saw some conditionality as necessary to enhancing Ukraine's resilience, but was concerned that too much pressure could be destabilising. Many reformist voices in Ukraine complained that the EU had become too uncritically supportive of Poroshenko as his government reverted increasingly to neo-patrimonial politics.

The EU pushed to ensure that the 2019 elections were free and fair, and that the defeated Poroshenko accepted a democratic transfer of power – a major advance in Ukraine. The new quasi-populist President Zelensky paradoxically unlocked both internal reform and cooperation with the EU by replacing many of the political and state elites backed by Union programmes since 2014.[42] This opened the way for increased EU cooperation on anti-corruption and rule of law measures. Yet tensions also intensified. By this stage Ukraine was pressing strongly for an upgraded relation with the EU, which the Union refused. Concerns grew in 2020 that the new president's populist-like zeal was straining the rule of law. The EU tried to rein Zelensky back from pushing through prosecution cases against Poroshenko. It also held back 1.2 billion euros of new macro-financial assistance after the central bank governor's sacking raised doubts about the government's reform commitments; the aid was eventually released in July 2020. The impact of the EU's heavy post-2013 investment in Ukraine remained uncertain.

Eastern resilience?

Russian assertiveness and the Ukraine crisis also prompted the EU to reassess its policies in the wider EaP region after 2014. Significant geopolitical recalibration followed in each of the EaP partners.

Georgia

The EU's policy towards Georgia has been shaped both by political processes within the country and Russia's influence in Georgia and its breakaway territories of South Ossetia and Abkhazia (Figure 11.6 shows these and other contested areas in the region). The EU gave fulsome support to President Saakashvili in the 2000s, especially for his state modernisation programmes. In the brief 2008 Russo-Georgian war, the EU brokered a ceasefire agreement between the Georgian government and Russia, with French president Nicolas Sarkozy playing a prominent role. The EU pushed strongly for a free transfer of power when 2012 elections brought to power the opposition Georgian Dream coalition, built around another strongman leader, billionaire businessman Bidzina Ivanishvili. Driven by events in Ukraine, the EU then deepened relations with Georgia. It granted Georgia accession to the Energy Community, signed the association agreement in 2014 and agreed visa liberalisation in 2017. The EU was critical of the Georgian Dream government for trying to tighten control over the judiciary and the media, while providing deeper engagement in selected fields.

Yet the EU response to Russia's creeping occupation of South Ossetia and Abkhazia has been underwhelming. While Poland and Lithuania explicitly classified these as occupied regions, countries like Germany along with the EU institutions refused to do so. The EU declined to offer a framework for settling the status of the enclaves, more modestly funding low-level confidence-building measures that failed to gain traction.[43] Russia's confrontational tactics of so-called 'borderisation' intensified during 2019 and 2020; the EU was powerless to prevent this. The Union also had to adapt to complex internal tensions, as protests erupted in Georgia during summer 2019. As a means of defusing frustration over the executive's power, the EU successfully pushed the government to loosen control through a more proportional electoral system. In October 2020 the EU was critical of irregularities in elections that saw Georgian Dream return to power. The Union has sought to balance criticism and help, pushing still-needed reforms on the one hand, while showing flexibility to bolster Georgia's fragile sovereignty on the other.

Moldova

The EaP's third state with membership aspirations has faced similar challenges, including in relation to increased Russian involvement. The EU's policy towards Moldova has similarly been shaped by the Union's geopolitical interests, the country's internal political processes and Russia's influence, especially in the autonomous territory of Transnistria. After the Alliance for European Integration won power in 2009, the EU ramped up its support to Moldova. It provided a highly generous aid allocation to the country, signed an association agreement, offered a visa-free regime, worked to reduce the state's dependence on Russian oil, increased trade flows, stepped up economic cooperation with Transnistria and beefed up a border mission to stifle illegal activities there. The EU's policy of active engagement took shape in the context of increasing Russian influence in Moldova. The visa regime and association agreement were granted strategically to shore up support for the pro-EU Alliance in the 2014 elections.

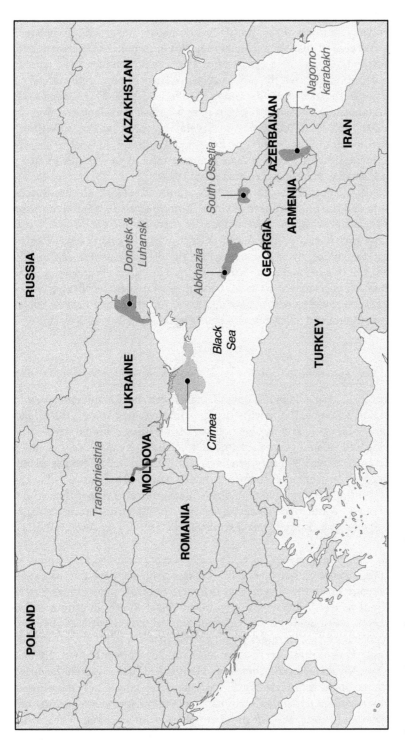

Figure 11.6 Contested territories in EaP states

Strategic interests meant that the Union initially turned a blind eye to a banking scandal involving members of the pro-EU coalition government. The EU belatedly toughened its stance by suspending budget support in response to this monumental financial scandal that drained away around 10 per cent of the country's national income in corruption. By then the pro-European alliance had lost support and the EU's reputation suffered with it. The Union then faced a broader challenge as oligarch Vlad Plahotniuc tightened his grip over Moldova and democratic norms declined in 2017 and 2018. The EU delayed several tranches of aid, including a 100 million macro-economic assistance package and funds for judicial reform. It increased critical measures after the government refused to recognise mayoral elections in Cisinau won by an opposition candidate.

In June 2019, a new coalition government was formed between the pro-Russian Socialist Party and the pro-European alliance. Plahotniuc used his influence to get the court to overturn this new government. In a tense stand-off, the EU – curiously, together with Russia – stood firm in insisting that the coalition government be allowed to take office. After Plahotniuc fled, the EU quickly released the aid it had suspended. If this seemed to represent a notable pro-democratic success, however, the coalition government soon fell and the pro-Russian Socialist party took power. The EU continued to release new aid into 2020, but the political switch left the direction of European policy uncertain once again.

Armenia

In September 2013, Armenia pulled out of its talks with the EU and opted for joining the Eurasian Economic Union with Russia. After this surprise step, the EU pursued a notably pragmatic and flexible policy. Despite being rebuffed, it allocated Armenia increased aid and technical assistance. Realising its inability to compete with Russia as Armenia's security provider, the EU pursued a lower-level rapprochement based on economic relations. Armenia struggled to balance its increasingly fragile political-strategic panorama with a desire to stay reasonably close to Europe. Armenia's conflict with Azerbaijan over the Nagorno-Karabakh region along with its fear of Turkish hostility made the country reliant on Russian security.

In 2017, the Union signed a tailor-made Comprehensive and Enhanced Partnership Agreement with Armenia. This became politically sensitive, as a series of popular revolts led to the government being ejected from power in May 2018. The EU did not actively support these so-called Velvet Revolution protests, but when the regime was already on the back foot pressed for a negotiated change of government. Democratic reformers were angered that the EU did not offer any upgrade in relations or visa liberalisation after the 2018 breakthrough. The new prime minister, Nikol Pashinyan, complained that the EU had accepted the outgoing regime's creeping authoritarianism in the hope of dragging it away from Russia. While Russia remained Armenia's main partner, the EU introduced several new financing schemes to assist the reform-oriented government.[44] Yet, at the end of 2020 the EU did little to help Armenia as it lost territory to Azerbaijan in and around Nagorno-Karabakh. While President Macron was especially vocal in his backing for Armenia against Turkey-backed Azerbaijan, this did not come with any operational assistance during the six-week flare-up.

Belarus

President Lukashenka's unrelenting authoritarianism resulted in years of EU sanctions and tension between the EU and Belarus. In one of its most geopolitical shifts, the EU began to reassess its Belarus strategy after the Crimea annexation. Concerned over Russian recidivism, Belarus in turn showed more interest in cooperation with the European Union. After Lukashenka released political prisoners, the EU lifted restrictive measures against all but four Belarusian officials in early 2016. The EU widened bilateral cooperation with Belarus through a Single Support Framework aid package that doubled annual funds to (a still modest) 30 million euros. This funded Belarusian technical agencies to adopt EU standards, supported twinning initiatives and boosted network-building initiatives among civil society organisations in the country. The EU signed a visa facilitation agreement with Belarus in early 2020 and at this stage negotiated upgraded 'partnership priorities'.

This rapprochement then screeched to a halt after the regime brutally clamped down against opposition leaders and protestors during and after elections in August 2020. The EU imposed several rounds of sanctions on over 50 regime officials, including Lukashenko himself; Baltic states imposed their own separate measures. The Commission quickly released around 8 million euros of assistance to civil society actors and journalists caught up in state repression against the protests. It also considered options to move COVID-19 emergency aid away from the government, halt macro-financial assistance and suspend talks on a visa-free travel agreement. The EU was still concerned to bolster Belarusian sovereignty against the risk of Russia taking control, but Lukashenka's untamed authoritarianism made it difficult to continue support for the regime. Mindful of Russia's role in the country, the EU did not promise any major intervention to help democratic protestors in the summer of 2020; Borrell explicitly said he did not want the same degree of EU involvement as in Ukraine.[45] The EU focused on the more modest role of trying to encourage dialogue between the regime, opposition figures and Russia.

Azerbaijan

The EU's cooperation with Azerbaijan has been shaped by the country's relative autonomy from both the EU and Russia and its attractiveness as an energy supplier – the energy aspects of EU–Azerbaijan relations were covered in Chapter 8. The Azerbaijani government indicated early on that it was not interested in an association agreement or DCFTA based on harmonisation with European rules and values. Developments in Crimea made the EU keen to develop a deeper relationship with Baku. It initiated talks on a new form of agreement that would not oblige Azerbaijan to sign up to approximation with EU rules and norms. This was the first instance in which a third country itself designed the template of a bespoke agreement, rather than the EU presenting an offer. EU leaders increased engagement with the Aliyev regime despite it undertaking one of the most brutal crackdowns against civil society anywhere in the world. In response to a critical statement from the European Parliament, Baku threatened to leave the EaP altogether in 2015. EU governments and the External Action Service sought to normalise relations with Azerbaijan relations through a process of re-engagement.

In November 2018, the EU and Azerbaijan held a first Security Dialogue and agreed on a new strategic partnership negotiating framework. This was held up due to the regime's clampdown on civil society and because Azerbaijan resisted EU pressure to join the WTO. In March 2019, President Aliyev pardoned over 400 prisoners, including those whose detention had complicated the new accord. The EU now sought to accelerate the new partnership agreement. Diplomats saw Azerbaijan to be of increasing strategic importance as a gateway to Eurasia. Indeed, without waiting for the new agreement, the EU advanced on deeper strategic dialogue with Azerbaijan, trying to decouple geopolitical issues from the trade and human rights blockages. However, the flare-up between Azerbaijan and Armenia in late 2020 left the future of this strategy highly uncertain, with France especially critical of the Azerbaijani-Turkish military action that made territorial gains against Armenian forces.

Themes and analysis

The eastern region and its multiple crises have presented the Union with some of its most acute and difficult external challenges in recent years. Showing the utility of an outside-in conceptual framework, these challenges have driven the EU to fine-tune its external action in very deliberate ways. Eastern challenges have left as their legacy a different kind of European geopolitical identity. There have been several layers to the evolution of EU strategy.

First, the EU's response to Russia shifted from the logic of inclusion to one of partial exclusion. The Union largely lost any hope that the current Russian regime could be enfolded in any deep-seated way into EU cooperative initiatives or was susceptible to positive European influences. The EU became more assertive towards Russia, in at least moderate degree. Many thought the EU might retreat from the EaP area after 2014 in order to avoid being dragged into open conflict with Russia – and indeed many analysts and practitioners of realist persuasion strongly advocated this course of action.[46] The EU did not retreat, however, but sought to undercut Russian influence. Still, as the crisis evolved the EU sought to avoid being overly confrontational towards Russia. While imposing wide-ranging sanctions it has in recent years engaged with Russia on a number of global issues, with the French government in particular pushing for more such cooperation from 2019. The EU has arrived at a kind of 'containment lite' with Russia, very different from its former liberal conviction that helping to make Russia stronger would be in Europe's own self-interest.

In a second layer of response, the EU and some of its member states adjusted their foreign policy actions to influence the conflict in Ukraine. Led by France and Germany, the EU pressed for measures to contain Russian influence in eastern Ukraine and the wider region. Since the mid-2010s the EU line has been one of intricate geopolitical balance. Despite its rhetoric to the contrary, the EU de facto acquiesced to Russia's annexation of Crimea and its involvement in eastern Ukraine. Most member states judged this to be an outcome less damaging to European interests than the risk of more tension with Russia. The EU helped achieve a precarious conflict containment but not a solid foundation for resolving the conflict. The need for a short-term containment of the crisis was such that the EU largely put to one side consideration of how this outcome – favourable in many senses to Russia, while broadly protective of the rest of Ukraine – might in the longer term leave the rules of European security order somewhat more vulnerable. Echoing a strand of the conceptual framework seen throughout the book, this constituted at least a partial move away from rules-driven to context-expedient EU external action.

Third, and more indirectly, the EU stepped up its positive support to EaP states in the 2010s. This was the element of its response most in line with the Union's traditional external action toolbox. Standard inside-out analytical approaches remain more relevant in the east than to the south: the EaP developed the kind of all-encompassing range of sectoral, economic, cultural, educational and social cooperation that stalled under the Euro-Mediterranean Partnership. Yet here too the EU moved to adjust its support to the EaP eastern neighbours. It was somewhat ambivalent about the Euromaidan revolt in 2014, but in its wake rolled out its largest, widest-ranging and most institutionalised programme of support ever designed. If Ukrainian reforms remained halting, this showed the enormous difficulty of shifting countries' underlying structural problems, even with the extensive range of policy levers at the EU's disposal in the years after 2014. Yet EU support certainly helped reinforce Ukraine's pro-European path and also helped it to withstand Russian actions and incursions. In Ukraine and in other EaP states the EU's support became more strategically precise and less exclusively or reflexively grounded in the replication of EU rules and regulations. This was a case where a combined balance of outside-in and inside-out dynamics was especially consequential.

This geopolitically stratified support involved more careful thinking about liberal political values, EU conditionality and the precise nature of EU funding. In general, the EU saw tough pressure for improvements in governance standards as crucial to undercutting the structural factors that have given Russian influence a foothold. Yet the EU often overlooked the democratic infringements of nominally pro-EU governments so as not to play into the hands of pro-Russian forces.[47] The reform-oriented dimension of EU policies was framed and calibrated more instrumentally as a tool of purposive power – sometimes enhanced for this use, other times set aside where this was judged to be geopolitically optimal. The EU has struggled to get this balance right in many EaP states in recent years.

A fourth aspect of the EU response reflected more defensive and realpolitik calculation: for all the enhanced support, the EU declined fully to embrace the states on its eastern borders. It offered neither the prospect of EU accession nor major new benefits short of membership. Rather than seeking to bring the EaP states – or, at least, Georgia, Moldova and Ukraine – into the Union, it sought to keep the region as a 'middle-land' between it and a more abrasive Russia. Elements of EU responses to the post-2014 crisis suggest at least some implicit acceptance that the region should be geo-strategically managed with Russia, even though this might be anathema to the region's citizens. Certainly, EU policies to the east came to build in sensitivity to 'the Russia factor' in a way that the EaP had not previously done. In line with its famed *Sonderweg* between east and west, Germany's policy towards the EaP has in particular been based on these kinds of cautious balance.

Russia's deeper involvement in Moldova, Georgia and Ukraine was one factor that dissuaded many EU member states from any dramatically upgraded commitments to these countries. The EU has become even more reluctant in recent years to get involved in the region's conflicts beyond very light and rather non-committal forms of mediation. It has neither given the various occupied and disputed territories recognition nor pushed for their reintegration into the post-Soviet parent states. After years of crisis, the EU has not judged it desirable or feasible to offer EaP states security protection or directly safeguard their territorial integrity. In these various ways, EU policies have sat uneasily with its self-proclaimed and ostensibly distinctive identity in external action.

Finally, taken together these policy shifts in the Russia–Ukraine crisis have altered the internal dynamics of EU external action. This region provides another example of the EU's shift towards policies moulded around events-related objectives rather than the Union's institutionally embedded liberal norms and identity. One important factor in this adjustment has been the role of certain member states. In policy towards the EaP region and Russia the dynamics of renationalisation have perhaps not been as strong as in many other areas of EU external action. Yet here too a small number of member states have become more predominant actors relative to the EU institutions and they have often been influential in propelling the more ends-oriented mode of external action.

Sweden and some Central and Eastern European member states have both pushed forward EU-level interventions and engaged through national actions; many other member states have engaged with only modest commitment. The German and French lead role on the Minsk peace process has been one of the clearest examples of European influence outside a common EU framework. Many member states have been uneasy with and critical of this Franco-German influence; yet they have themselves in some sense ceded power to these two governments to limit their own exposure to the crisis. The overall EU presence in the east has come progressively to include a heavy dose of national diplomacy alongside the liberal instruments of the EU institutions. This echoes the book's wider conceptual template of national policies both driving and blunting EU external action.

Overall, the EU reacted with notable elements of strategic adjustment to the challenges generated by the eastern crises during the 2010s. While the EU did not treat the Ukraine conflict as a visceral, existential threat to the degree that Russia did, it has undoubtedly intensified its geopolitical engagement and assertiveness in the last several years. The Eastern Partnership changed from being a second-order exercise in diffusing select EU rules into being a vital protective bulwark against Russian actions. Many critics admonish the EU for having been congenitally weak towards Russian provocations. However, the Union has had some impact in containing Russia, even as Russia has in its turn revealed the limits to EU leverage. The EU has engineered a more geopolitically complex triangle of balance between itself, Russia and EaP states. The fraught politics and conflicts of the EaP region have in recent years dragged the EU towards a delicately balanced combination of liberal and less liberal approaches to geopolitics.[48]

Concluding summary

External challenges. The outside-in perspective is nowhere more germane than in the EaP region, as Russian assertiveness, Ukraine's instability and violence, and turmoil in other parts of the eastern region have crowded in on the EU's foreign policy agenda with pressing and tragic urgency.

Unity–diversity. The gravity of the eastern crises served to narrow some long-standing divides between member states on Russia policy, even if complete unity on this issue has remained elusive. The combination of national-level initiatives and EU instruments has become a more defining feature of overall European external action in the east.

Distinctive Power. Towards its east, the EU has retained many distinctive policy approaches, perhaps more so than in any other region. Yet here too more standard geopolitical approaches have also taken shape, superimposed on the EU external-governance paradigm. The Union's response to Russian actions and the Ukraine conflict has been as much about strategic balancing as commitment to the norms of liberal order.

Protective security. The EU has not acted by extending its own liberal 'security community' fully or formally into the eastern region. While some of its upgraded cooperation with EaP partners reflects a spirit of cooperative inclusion, the evident limits to EU engagement and commitment betray a partial turn to protective security.

EU influence. EU external action has been of primary and growing importance in the security challenges facing Eastern Partnership states since the early 2010s – a trend at odds with the diminution of EU power in many other regions. Nevertheless, the EU has not been influential enough to redress many of the underlying security issues in eastern Europe and on some measurements has ceded ground to Russian influence.

12 Re-casting the EU's International Influence

The concluding chapter draws together the main observations from each area of policy and relates these to the conceptual framework presented in Chapter 3 – and also revisited at the end of each thematic chapter. The preceding chapters show how EU external action has evolved over time, showing a common arc of development across different thematic and geographical areas. They also reveal important lessons about how well the EU has adjusted to position itself in relation to pressing strategic challenges. They equally suggest that trends in recent years cast doubt on some standard, widely accepted assumptions about EU external action and that a measured dose of *myth-busting* is appropriate in relation to these. The chapter sheds light on each of the five themes of the conceptual framework in turn.

External challenges

The EU has in recent years adapted to shifts in international order. It has sought to deal with global uncertainty, influence the reshaped order and address new kinds of challenges that have appeared on its foreign policy agenda. The Union's external action has in this way been obliged to deal with different levels of challenge simultaneously: at one level, overarching structural changes to the international system and indeed to the very core of what counts as external action; at another level, the emergence of particular substantive problems like conflict in its neighbourhood, the geopolitics of climate change, international terrorism and most recently the COVID-19 pandemic. The impact of both long-term structural trends and punctuated moments of crisis has become more determining and paramount.

A common thread woven through the book is that this kind of *problem-oriented* approach can tell us much about today's EU strategic decisions and that it has arguably become more salient than traditional rules- or process-oriented perspectives on European external action. The EU has moved several steps away from 'institutional external action' towards 'challenge-driven external action'. In the terms of one insider, from the early 2010s the EU shifted away from rules-based to events-based foreign policy.[1] Still, the EU has struggled coherently to implement this repositioning. While the book's different chapters reveal that the EU has undertaken far-reaching adjustment in many of its policies in response to external trends and crises, they also chronicle the limits to its reworked strategic vision. In many policy areas it is doubtful that EU external action has yet adjusted to a degree commensurate with the magnitude of global or regional changes. While external challenges may have become more significant policy drivers, the EU has preferred a reworked strategic positioning that is more cautious crouch than expansive projection.

Conventional wisdom has it that the EU is bad at agile crisis response but good at long-term visions of the underlying, structural elements of global politics. A first myth-buster may be in order here, as to some extent this seems to have inverted in recent years: the EU has responded strongly with crisis management strategies to contain immediate threats, but not moved far in rethinking a long-term vision for global politics that goes beyond simply retaining its own power and privileges. Noted experts have argued that today's agenda cannot simply be about preserving standard measures of power, but revolves around fluid networks and issues that fundamentally change the relationship between the EU and the wider international system.[2] There is relatively limited evidence that the Union has framed its response to global challenges in this way; indeed, if anything it seems to be backing away from such qualitative innovation.

Unity and diversity

The most omnipresent question applied to EU external action is whether the EU has become more united in its foreign and security policies. The last several years provide no single, clear answer to this question. In some policy areas unity has strengthened; in others it has dissolved. In still others, a mix of unity and diversity has held relatively steady. European governments have converged in their generic support for the key concepts and buzzwords that have gained prominence in recent years, like strategic autonomy, resilience and European sovereignty. Yet they tend to interpret these in ways that have reinforced their quite varied foreign policy preferences. At the same time, not all EU external action has only been subject to fissiparous rationalist calculations. In some spheres national foreign policies have still been moulded by EU-mediated identities, even as immediate external imperatives have tightened. Crucially, these constructed, shared identities have themselves shifted in recent years and European unity has increasingly clustered around adjusted external strategies.

While the degree of convergence between member states is a vital issue, there is often a danger that policy and analytical debates about EU external action get reduced to this one question. More or less every speech by every prominent EU leader or senior official has in recent years re-iterated the default line that 'we are stronger together'. Often, their arguments have then gone little beyond that. Making the case for EU cooperation almost becomes the end-point observation in itself. This book has shown across many issue areas that more Europeanised policies or a single EU voice has not always produced better policy. Much commentary on EU external action still takes the form of general laments that member states do not think the same way about particular international problems; it might indeed be better were this not the case, but the deeper question is whether convergence takes place around the right kinds of policies.

The reflexive line of 'EU actions good, national actions bad' is one ripe for myth-busting. Some governments have become more proactive foreign policy protagonists and have catalysed common European initiatives, while some EU-level leaders and institutions have shown less acuity in their global outlooks. The often-drawn assumption that EU institutions would roll out exemplary external action if only national governments ceased to meddle with their nefarious 'national interests' is not borne out by the more varied reality of recent years. Different kinds of alliances have taken shape between national and EU-level actors, with different coalitions of policy promoters and blockers across thematic areas. EU external action is increasingly multi-form: alongside common EU endeavours, sub-groupings of member states and initiatives outside the EU institutional framework have become commonplace. If foreign policy is still something of a 'poor relation' compared to other areas of deeper EU integration, one reason is that governments cannot quite decide if they want EU external action to be simply one element in their geopolitical toolbox or something more absolute.

Taking intra-EU unity as a sacrosanct end-goal can lead to analytical distortion: *sui generis* theories of coordination, collective securitisation, external governance and the like all retain much validity, and yet often leave an impression that the EU can comfort itself in its own internal convergences while the house of global geopolitics burns around it. This is, quite obviously, not to champion disunity; rather, it is to suggest that more prior focus might be needed on the substantive needs of EU external action and for analysts and policy-makers then to work back from these to assess what kinds and degree of cooperation might be helpful.

Is the EU a distinctive power?

The EU's identity as a distinctive kind of international actor has become less clear-cut in recent years. The book's chapters show the shift here is not from one absolute to another, but a matter of gradation. The EU was probably never as unique in global affairs as its own rhetoric and narratives implied. In the last decade, in many of its external actions it has come to resemble other powers and more standard models of foreign policy to a greater degree. Still, there has also been continuity within EU external action. The EU has retained many of its unique external instruments. In some areas, the EU has still wielded much influence through the extension outwards of its own laws, norms and regulations, and has continued to shape societies through the frame of its internal integration experience. It is highly significant that these kinds of EU approaches have continued to operate in an era of such visceral geopolitics, when many analysts cast profound doubts over the relevance of all such notions of inclusive and cooperative security frameworks. The Union has retained strands of liberal power somewhat against the grain of twenty-first century geopolitics.

Yet these elements of EU external action have lost some of their pre-eminence. The foregoing chapters highlight that on many emerging security challenges and in many regions of the world the Union has prioritised issues that have little to do with such supposedly quintessential EU approaches. It has veered towards modes of action that either complement or take precedence over the EU's ostensibly signature forms of liberal power. From the early 2010s many prominent analysts pointed in general terms to this increasingly mixed nature of European external action. This book reveals in some detail how in each key policy area this trend has become more consequential in the years since then. It shows the value of analytical frameworks that examine how EU institutional processes have facilitated this adjustment.

Many see this shift as overdue, while others fear the EU has begun to surrender its most valuable comparable advantages in international affairs. Many critics have long taken the Union to task for its overwhelming focus on replicating itself in societies whose norms and identities require very different and more sensitive approaches. To some degree, these criticisms have been answered. The EU has come to centre on more modest goals in most places and policy areas and its aims have become generally less ambitiously transformative – notwithstanding its rhetoric suggesting otherwise. Even if the EU was almost certainly never as inveterately multilateral or as much of a transformative power as it claimed to be, the transformative momentum of its external actions has certainly receded.

This has altered what was long seen as a core dynamic of EU external policies, namely that of Europeanisation. The book has charted how across different policy areas Europeanisation – the process of other states taking on board formal EU rules or more broadly converging around European political norms – has lost potency. It has certainly not disappeared altogether and has remained a powerful driver of policy change in a small number of countries and in some technical-regulatory domains. But what has endured is a slimmed-down or residual Europeanisation. Some third countries have, if anything, de-Europeanised. And, more broadly, the reverse dynamic has grown of the EU adjusting to others as much as others adjust to it. External Europeanisation has given way to a complex and multidirectional patchwork of cross-border influences.

This all relates to a common claim that 'the EU does not do power politics'. The EU narrative has been that the rest of the world is guilty of illiberal, raw power politics and the Union is not interest-driven enough. This was the subtext behind the new Commission's promise at the end of 2019 to be more 'geopolitical'. But this book offers a modest dose of myth-busting here, as it has shown that for quite some time before this the EU had already adopted more assertively interest-driven external action. There are many cases in recent years of the EU being hard-bitten in pursuit of its own interests, engaging in policies hardly edifying to liberal values.

It might be said the EU has inched towards a kind of hybrid geopolitics. It has increasingly combined different styles of foreign policy. Some of these are based on its own *sui generis* policy instruments as a multilateral integration club, others are far more resonant of old-style diplomacy; some are generated through EU-level measures, others are led by national governments or even non-state European actors. The EU has shown itself able and willing to operate as a fairly distinctive liberal power in one context, but act in decidedly illiberal ways in other contexts. It has adopted policies predicated on a more negotiated order – part-liberal, part-transactional. Often this has left EU external action looking ad hoc and expedient, as opposed to having a firm and rooted notion of what it actually understands by being geopolitical.

Protective power

Contrary to much commentary, the EU has not showed signs of dramatically withdrawing from the world; but it has sought a more immediately protective kind of external engagement. Protective security has become perhaps the most reverberant narrative of EU external action. Curiously, this has entailed heightened EU ambition in some outside-to-inside preventive functions, while the Union stands at least partially clear from ambitious inside-to-outside goals and third-country entanglements – notwithstanding a ritual rhetoric about the EU needing more foreign policy, more power, more influence. A common lament is that the EU has squandered power and become a passive bystander in many key challenges and crises; yet many diplomats would feel that the more self-protective and measured approach to foreign policy has been prudent insurance more than existential disaster for the Union.

In their search for a more robust protective perimeter, governments have reasoned that the EU needs to ensure a sharper demarcation between itself and the outside world. This was seen in relation to conflict, migration, terrorism, digital threats and climate-change challenges through the 2010s, while the EU's response to COVID-19 in 2020 also contained elements of protective security. Diplomats have reacted to exogenous challenges with a more self-protective mind-set, while European citizens have increasingly required this of EU policies. The EU has come to act as a physical and identity barrier against the outside world. Protective security has often meant indulging illiberalism abroad in the name of defeating illiberalism at home.

Increasingly, a quest for 'autonomy' has become the guiding leitmotif of EU external action. By definition, autonomy is about freedom from others' influence rather than influence over others. In addition, the narrative of 'European sovereignty' has been closely related to protective security. The emergent focus on – a still ill-defined – European sovereignty as the bedrock of external aims is intriguing, given that the EU's rationale for many years was to transcend the whole concept of sovereignty. This quest for European sovereignty widens possible tensions between the EU's internal and external aims: while strategic analysts insist it places a premium on size, centralisation and state-like EU power, internally citizens increasingly say they want a more flexible, locally-rooted and accountable European project.[3] The EU's challenge of combining external and internal imperatives is set to become ever-more onerous.

From other powers' vantage point there is certain irony in the EU's protective turn. While the winds of global politics were behind it, the EU preached internationalism to others; now struggling against geopolitical headwinds it seeks protection against the very world that was in part its own creation. Some stress how far the Union has slipped back into a mind-set of distinguishing itself, its own values and its own political project sharply from the rest of the world.[4] The Union has increasingly come close to equating a protection of liberal order with self-servingly shoring up its own power. Other powers might see the EU's protective security more as a risk than fillip to liberal order – a sign that illiberal forces have gained traction within Europe as much as outside it.

Does the EU still matter?

Despite all its external initiatives and adjustments, on many fronts the EU has patently failed to prevent the global context and crises from getting worse. Much of the deterioration is hardly the EU's fault. It may increasingly be beyond the Union's capacity to redirect international trends, even if its foreign policy were faultlessly designed and its unity absolute. The standard metrics for evaluating the EU's Common Foreign and Security Policy – focused on degrees of institutional coherence, convergence and coordination – begin to look less determinant for international affairs. The pendulum has swung rapidly: in previous years many worried about the EU's overly dominant hierarchical or 'neo-imperial' power; now the concern is more about the EU not even having enough power to preserve its own core sovereignty. In select areas, EU influences clearly still count for much. Yet in many instances the EU retains the mind-set and attitude of a major power but without anything approaching enough practical commitment or leverage for others to take this seriously.

Many attributes of EU 'actorness' have grown stronger in the last two decades – resources, delegations, institutional coherence, the range of policy cooperation – but in a context where this metric for supposed success no longer counts for quite so much. The same global shifts that have pushed the EU to sharpen and improve its external action are the same ones that render the Union less decisive globally. In some contexts, it is difficult to ignore just how far EU influences have been displaced by other powers, whether China, Russia, Turkey or others. While EU governments' focus on protective security entails a strategic judgement that vital interests are now best safeguarded through a more modest and defensive foreign policy, simultaneously these governments also fret that this has opened the way for others to exert power. It is difficult to see how the EU can achieve both aims: a less extended set of global engagements, without other powers gaining more influence.

Increasingly, others influence the EU at least as much as it influences global affairs. In recent years, the reshaped international order has remoulded European external action more than this has influenced the world. In the future the EU will be a receptor as much as purveyor of influence. It would be more accurate to see the EU as having become immersed at multiple levels in global affairs rather than its own pre-set policies simply working outwards into the world. In a reconfigured global order, the EU will get used to being shaped by others as much as it shapes developments beyond its own borders. It does not yet have either the conceptual orientation or the policy mechanisms to channel such outside influences to shore up cooperation and liberal values in Europe. As the EU interacts with a less liberal set of actors internally and globally, its own international identity has been remoulded, and different analytical tools will be needed to assess and explain this.[5] Analytical work on EU external action will need to engage far more with how the Union deals with countervailing powers, as the EU becomes object as much as subject of global politics.

Notes

Chapter 1

1. R. Wong (2005) 'The Role of the Member States: The Europeanization of Foreign Policy?', in C. Hill and M Smith (eds) *International Relations and the European Union*, 1ˢᵗ edition, Oxford, Oxford University Press; N. Wright (2019) *The EU's Common Foreign and Security Policy in Germany and the UK: Co-operation, Co-optation and Competition*, London, Palgrave Macmillan.
2. S. Keukelaire and T. Delreux (2014) *The Foreign Policy of the European Union*, 2ⁿᵈ edition, London, Red Globe Press; K. Smith (2014) *European Union Foreign Policy in a Changing World*, 3ʳᵈ edition, Cambridge, Polity Press; C. Hill, M. Smith and S. Vanhoonacker (eds) (2017) *International Relations and the European Union*, 3ʳᵈ edition, Oxford, Oxford University Press.
3. S. Keukeleire and T. de Bruyn (2017) 'The European Union, the BRICs and Other Powers: A New World Order?', in C. Hill, M. Smith and S. Vanhoonacker (eds) *International Relations and the European Union*, 3ʳᵈ edition, Oxford, Oxford University Press.

Chapter 2

1. For general summaries of the historical background of EU foreign policy, see S. Keukelaire and T. Delreux (2014) *The Foreign Policy of the European Union*, 2ⁿᵈ edition, London, Red Globe Press, chapter 2; K. Smith (2014) *European Union Foreign Policy in a Changing World*, 3ʳᵈ edition, Cambridge, Polity Press, chapter 2.
2. For an account of these early developments in trade policy, see S. Meunier and K. Nicolaidis (2017) 'The European Union as a Trade Power' in C. Hill, M. Smith and S. Vanhoonacker (eds) *International Relations and the European Union*, 3ʳᵈ edition, Oxford, Oxford University Press.
3. For an overview of this period, see F. Cameron (2012) *An Introduction to European Foreign Policy*, London, Routledge.
4. A trend captured in the seminal article, D. Allen and M. Smith (1990) 'Western Europe's Presence in the Contemporary International Area', *Review of International Studies*, 16/1.
5. For an overview of these issues and time period, see R. Ginsberg (2001) *The European Union in International Politics – Baptism by Fire*, New York, Rowman and Littlefield.
6. For the CFSP's early years, see M. Holland (ed) (1997) *Common Foreign and Security Policy: The Record and Reforms*, London, Pinter.
7. European Council (2003) *European Security Strategy – A Secure Europe in a Better World*, Brussels.
8. European Union (2009) *Treaty of Lisbon Amending Treaty on European Union*, Brussels.

9.   IMF figures and forecasts are online at: https://www.imf.org/external/datamapper/PPPSH@WEO/WEOWORLD/EU

10. H. Timmer and U. Dadush (2011) 'The Euro Crisis and Emerging Economies', Washington, DC, Carnegie Endowment for International Peace.

11. E. Helleiner and S. Pagliari (2011) 'The End of an Era in International Financial Regulation? A Post-crisis Research Agenda', *International Organization*, 65.

12. J. Pisani-Ferry (2011) *How to Stop Fragmentation of the Eurozone*, Brussels, Bruegel; H. Dixon (2011) 'Can Europe's Divided House Stand?', *Foreign Affairs*, November–December.

13. C. Kupchan (2012) 'Centrifugal Europe', *Survival*, 54/1.

14. J. Fischer, 'Provincial Europe', *Project Syndicate*, 31 October 2012.

15. L. van Middelaar (2012) *Le Passage à l'Europe: Histoire d'un Commencement*, Paris, Éditions Gallimard, pp. 11–13.

16. European Union (2016) *Shared Vision, Common Action: A Stronger Europe, a Global Strategy for the European Union's Foreign and Security Policy*, Brussels.

17. Concord (2019) *Aidwatch 2019*, Brussels, Concord.

18. Munich Security Conference, *Munich Security Report 2019. The Great Puzzle: Who Will Pick Up the Pieces?*, Munich, p. 14.

19. The 'European Renaissance' proposal is posted at: https://www.elysee.fr/emmanuel-macron/2019/03/04/for-european-renewal.en

20. A. Billon-Galland, T. Raines and R. Whitman (2020) *The Future of the E3: Post-Brexit Cooperation Between the UK, France and Germany*, London, Chatham House, p. 5.

21. W. Drozdiak (2020) *The Last President of Europe*, New York, Public Affairs, p. 5.

22. 'The von der Leyen Commission: Lofty Ambitions, Odd Job Titles', *Politico*, 11 September 2019.

23. Confirmation Hearing in the European Parliament, 7 October 2019; J. Borrell, 'Embracing Europe's Power', *Project Syndicate*, 8 February 2020.

24. Statement posted on the French ministry's website: https://twitter.com/francediplo/status/1247461625537482752

25. S. Bulmer and W. Paterson (2018) *Germany and the European Union: Europe's Reluctant Hegemon*, London, Red Globe Press.

26. Munich Security Conference (2020) *Zeitenwende, Wendezeiten: Special Edition of the Munich Security Report on German Foreign and Security Policy*, Munich, MSC; L. Aggestam and A. Hyde-Price (2019) 'Learning to Lead? Germany and the Leadership Paradox in EU Foreign Policy', *German Politics*, 29/1, pp. 8–24.

27. T. Bagger 'Germany's Search for a New Diplomatic Map', *Financial Times*, 23 April 2019; C. Stelzenmuller (2019) *Germany: Baffled Hegemon*, Washington, DC, Brookings; G. Hellmann (2011) 'Normatively Disarmed, but Self-Confident', *Internationale Politik*, 3.

28. Cited in S. Raine (2019) *Europe's Strategic Future: From Crisis to Coherence?*, London, International Institute for Strategic Studies Adelphi Book, p. 192.

29. N. Wright (2019) *The EU's Common Foreign and Security Policy in Germany and the UK: Co-operation, Co-optation and Competition*, London, Palgrave Macmillan.

30. J. Vaïsse (2017) 'Le passé d'un oxymora. Le débat francais de la politique etrangere', *Esprit*, November; D. Bouchard, C. Connan, J.-C. Cousseran and B. Miyet (2018) 'Le debate sur la politique etrangere francaise: l'avenir d'un oxymora', *Boulevard Exterieur*, January.

31. J. Hunt, 'Britain's Role in a Post-Brexit World', Speech in Singapore, 2 January 2019, London, International Institute for Strategic Studies.

32. Intelligence and Security Committee of Parliament (2020) *Russia*, London, House of Commons, p. 26.

33. 'UK Diplomats Told to Spurn Old EU Allies', *The Times*, 2 February 2020.
34. C. Hill (2019) *The Future of British Foreign Policy: Security and Diplomacy in a World After Brexit*, Cambridge, Polity Press.
35. G. Di Maio (2019) 'The Broken Compass of Italian Foreign Policy', Washington, DC, Brookings Institute; E. Greco (ed) (2018) *L'Italia al bivo: raporto sulla politica estera italiana*, Rome, IAI.
36. I. Molina (ed) (2020) *España en el mundo en 2020: perspectivas y desafios para el año del coronavirus*, Madrid, Elcano; I. Molina (ed) (2019) *España en el mundo en 2019: perspectivas y desafios*, Madrid, Elcano.
37. The overview of institutional processes here takes from a variety of sources, including S. Keukelaire and T. Delreux (2014) *The Foreign Policy of the European Union*, 2nd edition, London, Red Globe Press; K. Smith (2014) *European Union Foreign Policy in a Changing World*, 3rd edition, Cambridge, Polity Press, chapter 3; and F. Cameron (2012) *An Introduction to European Foreign Policy*, London, Routledge, chapter 3.
38. For detail on the early-2000s development of this security strand, see S. Biscop and R. Whitman (eds) (2013) *The Handbook of European Security*, London, Routledge.
39. Concord (2019) *Aidwatch 2019*, Brussels, Concord.

Chapter 3

1. A. Moravcsik (2017) 'Europe Is Still a Superpower', *Foreign Policy*, April; A. Moravcsik (1993) 'Preferences and Power in the European Community: A Liberal Intergovernmentalist Approach', *Journal of Common Market Studies*, 31/4.
2. For an example of this perspective, see C. Betherton and J. Vogler (2006) *The European Union as a Global Actor*, 2nd edition, London, Routledge.
3. M. E. Smith (2004) 'Toward a Theory of EU Foreign Policy Making: Multi-level Governance, Domestic Politics, and National Adaptation to Europe's Common Foreign and Security Policy', *Journal of European Public Policy*, 11.
4. J. Sperling and M. Webber (2019) 'The European Union: Security Governance and Collective Securitisation', *West European Politics*, 42/2.
5. T. Wright (2012) 'What If Europe Fails?', *Washington Quarterly*, 35/3, 23–41; A. Cottey (2012) *Security in 21st Century Europe*, 2nd edition, London, Red Globe Press, chapter 10.
6. A. Hyde-Price (2007) *European Security in the 21st Century: The Challenge of Multipolarity*, London, Routledge.
7. For an overview of these classical realist views on EU foreign policy, see F. Andreatta (2005) 'Theory and the EU's International Relations', in C. Hill and M. Smith (eds) *International Relations and the European Union*, Oxford, Oxford University Press; S. Rynning (2011) 'Realism and Common Security and Defence Policy', *Journal of Common Market Studies*, 49/1.
8. I. Manners (2002) 'Normative Power: A Contradiction in Terms?', *Journal of Common Market Studies*, 40/2; I. Manners (2008) 'The Normative Ethics of the European Union', *International Affairs*, 84/1, 45–60; S. Lucarelli and I. Manners (eds) (2006) *Values and Principles in European Union Foreign Policy*, London, Routledge; M. Tèlo (2007) *Europe: A Civilian Power? European Union, Global Governance, World Order*, London, Palgrave Macmillan; H. Sjursen (2006) 'What Kind of Power?', *Journal of European Public Policy*, 13/1.
9. C. Hill, M. Smith and S. Vanhoonacker (2017) 'International Relations and the European Union: Themes and Issues', in C. Hill, M. Smith and S. Vanhoonacker (eds) *International Relations and the European Union*, 3rd edition, Oxford, Oxford University Press, p. 12.

10. Select examples from an extensive literature on this point include: W. Wagner (2017) 'Liberal Power Europe', *Journal for Common Market Studies*, 55/6; L. Cederman (ed.) (2001) *Constructing Europe's Identity: The External Dimension*, Boulder, Lynne Rienner; M. Zürn (2000) 'Democratic Governance Beyond the Nation-State: The EU and Other International Institutions', *European Journal of International Relations*, 6/2; C. Carta and J.-F. Morin (eds) (2016) *EU Foreign Policy Through the Lens of Discourse Analysis: Making Sense of Diversity*, Farnham, Ashgate.

11. M. E. Smith (2011) 'A Liberal Grand Strategy in a Realist World? Power, Purpose and the EU's Changing Global Role', *Journal of European Public Policy*, 18/2.

12. J. Wissel (2014) 'The Structure of the European Ensemble of State Apparatuses and Its Geopolitical Ambitions', *Geopolitics*, 19/3, p. 505. More Notoriously, R. Kagan (2003) *Of Paradise and Power: America and Europe in the New World Order*, New York, Knopf.

13. S. Lavenex (2014) 'The Power of Functionalist Extension: How EU Rules Travel', *Journal of European Public Policy*, 21/6; S. Gstöhl and D. Phinnemore (eds) (2018) *The European Union, its Neighbours, and the Proliferation of 'Privileged Partnerships'*, London, Routledge.

14. C. Damro (2015) 'Market Power Europe: Exploring a Dynamic Conceptual Framework', *Journal of European Public Policy*, 22/9.

15. S. Keukelaire and T. Delreux (2014) *The Foreign Policy of the European Union*, 2nd edition, London, Red Globe Press.

16. V. Birchfield (2013) 'A Normative Power Europe Framework of Transnational Policy Formation', *Journal of European Public Policy*, 20/6.

17. J. Sperling and M. Webber (2014) 'Security Governance in Europe: A Return to System', *European Security*, 23/2; J. Zielonka (2011) 'The EU as an International Actor: Unique or Ordinary?', *European Foreign Affairs Review*, 16.

18. A. Bradford (2020) *The Brussels Effect*, New York, Oxford University Press.

19. J. Zielonka (2006) *The EU as Empire*, Oxford, Oxford University Press.

20. S. Aydin-Düzgit (2014) 'Critical Discourse Analysis in Analysing European Union Foreign Policy: Prospects and Challenges', *Cooperation and Conflict*, 49/3, pp. 354–367; K. E. Jørgensen et al. (eds) (2015) *The SAGE Handbook of European Foreign Policy*, Thousand Oaks, SAGE Publications.

21. One recent example of work on external perceptions of EU foreign policy being N. Chaban and M. Holland (eds) (2019) *Shaping the EU Global Strategy: Partners and Perceptions*, London, Palgrave Macmillan.

22. E. Barbé, O. Costa and R. Kissack (eds) (2016) *EU Policy Responses to Shifting Multilateral System*, London, Palgrave Macmillan.

23. European Union (2016) *Shared Vision, Common Action: A Stronger Europe: A Global Strategy for the European Union's Foreign and Security Policy*, Brussels.

24. S. Lucarelli (2019) 'The EU as a Securitizing Agent? Testing the Model, Advancing the Literature', *West European Politics*, 42/2.

25. S. Keukelaire and T. Delreux (2014) *The Foreign Policy of the European Union*, London, Red Globe Press, 2nd edition, p. 6.

26. E. Conceição-Heldt and S. Meunier (2014) 'Speaking with a Single Voice: Internal Cohesiveness and External Effectiveness of the EU in Global Governance', *Journal of European Public Policy*, 21/7.

27. V. Schmidt (2010) 'Taking Ideas and Discourse Seriously: Explaining Change Through Discursive Institutionalism as the Fourth New Institutionalism', *European Political Science Review*, 2/1.

28. S. Rosato (2011) 'Europe's Troubles: Power Politics and the State of the European Project', *International Security*, 35/4.

29. H. Hegemann and U. Schneckener (2019) 'Politicising European Security: From Technocratic to Contentious Politics?', *European Security*, 28/2; O. Costa (2018)

'The Politicization of EU External Relations', *Journal of European Public Policy*, 26/5.

30. C. Bickerton, D. Hodson and U. Puetter (2015) 'The New Intergovernmentalism: European Integration in the Post-Maastricht Era', *Journal of Common Market Studies*, 53/4.

31. L. Aggestam and F. Bicchi (2019) 'New Directions in EU Foreign Policy Governance: Cross-Loading, Leadership and Informal Groupings', *Journal of Common Market Studies*, 57/3.

32. U. Krotz and R. Maher (2012) 'Debating the Sources and Prospects of European Integration', *International Security*, 37/1.

33. P. Morillas (2020) 'Autonomy in Intergovernmentalism: The Role of De Novo Bodies in External Action During the Making of the EU Global Strategy', *Journal of European Integration*, 42/2.

34. S. Meunier and M. Vachudova (2018) 'Liberal Intergovernmentalism, Illiberalism and the Potential Superpower of the European Union', *Journal of Common Market Studies*, 56/7; S. Gstöhl and S. Schunz (eds) (2016) *Theorizing the European Neighbourhood Policy*, London, Routledge.

35. A. Menon (2014) 'Divided and Declining? Europe in a Changing World', *Journal of Common Market Studies*, 52, Annual Review.

36. R. Balfour (ed) (2016) *Europe's Troublemakers: The Populist Challenge to Foreign Policy*, Brussels, European Policy Centre; M. Orenstein and D. Kelemen (2017) 'Trojan Horses in EU Foreign Policy', *Journal of Common Market Studies*, 55/1; S. Meunier and M. Vachudova (2018) 'Liberal Intergovernmentalism, Illiberalism and the Potential Superpower of the European Union', *Journal of Common Market Studies*, 56/7.

37. A. Wivel and O. Wæver (2018) 'The Power of Peaceful Change: The Crisis of the European Union and the Rebalancing of Europe's Regional Order', *International Studies Review*, 20.

38. A. Cottey (2020) 'A Strategic Europe', *Journal of Common Market Studies*, 58/2; J. Rogers (2011) *A New Geography of European Power?*, Brussels, Egmont Institute, Egmont Paper 42; D. Stokes and R. Whitman (2013) 'Transatlantic Triage? European and UK Grand Strategy After the US Rebalance to Asia', *International Affairs*, 89/5; K. Hebel and T. Lenz (2016) 'The Identity/Policy Nexus in European Foreign Policy', *Journal of European Public Policy*, 23/4.

39. B. Buzan and G. Lawson (2015) *The Global Transformation: History, Modernity and the Making of International Relations*, Cambridge, Cambridge University Press, p. 285; T. Haverluk, K. Beauchemin and A. Mueller (2004) 'The Three Critical Flaws of Critical Geopolitics: Towards a Neo-classical Geopolitics', *Geopolitics*, 19/1.

40. C. Hill, M. Smith and S. Vanhoonacker (2017) 'International Relations and the European Union: Themes and Issues', in C. Hill, M. Smith and S. Vanhoonacker (eds) *International Relations and the European Union*, 3rd edition, Oxford, Oxford University Press, p. 16.

41. D. Thomas (2012) 'Still Punching Below Its Weight? Coherence and Effectiveness in European Union Foreign Policy', *Journal of Common Market Studies*, 50/3.

42. C. Hill, M. Smith and S. Vanhoonacker (2017) 'International Relations and the European Union: Themes and Issues', in C. Hill, M. Smith and S. Vanhoonacker (eds) *International Relations and the European Union*, 3rd edition, Oxford, Oxford University Press, p. 5.

43. A. Rodt, R. Whitman and S. Wolff (2015) 'The EU as an International Security Provider: The Need for a Mid-range Theory', *Global Society*, 29/2.

Chapter 4

1. C. Kupchan (2012) *No One's World: The West, the Rising Rest, and the Coming Global Turn*, New York, Oxford University Press; C. Elman and M. Jensen (2012) 'Realisms', in P. Williams (ed.) *Security Studies: An Introduction*, 2nd edition, London, Routledge; G. Rachman (2010) *Zero-Sum World: Politics, Power and Prosperity After the Crash*, London, Atlantic Books.
2. M. Jacques (2012) *When China Rules the World*, 2nd edition, London, Penguin, pp. 621–622.
3. I. Bremmer (2012) *Every Nation for Itself: Winners and Losers in a G-Zero World*, London, Portfolio Penguin.
4. C. Kupchan (2012) *No One's World: The West, the Rising Rest, and the Coming Global Turn*, New York, Oxford University Press; I. Bremmer (2012) *Every Nation for Itself: Winners and Losers in a G-Zero World*, London, Portfolio Penguin.
5. A. Linklater (1998) *The Transformation of Political Community*, Cambridge, Cambridge University Press; R. Beardsworth (2011) *Cosmopolitanism and International Relations Theory*, Cambridge, Polity Press.
6. A. Hurrell (2007) *On Global Order: Power, Values and the Constitution of International Society*, Oxford, Oxford University Press.
7. B. Maçães (2018) *The Dawn of Eurasia*, London, Penguin.
8. R. Haass (2020) 'The Pandemic Will Accelerate History Rather Than Reshape It', *Foreign Affairs*, April; D. Rodrik, 'Will Covid-19 Remake the World?', *Project Syndicate*, 6 April 2020.
9. T. Dunne and T. Flockhart (eds) (2013) *Liberal World Orders*, Oxford, Oxford University Press; G. John Ikenberry (2011) 'The Future of the Liberal World Order: Internationalism After America', *Foreign Affairs*, May/June; G. John Ikenberry (2011) *Liberal Leviathan*, Princeton, Princeton University Press; N. Barma, E. Ratner and S. Weber (2013) 'The Mythical Liberal Order', *National Interest*, March–April.
10. M. Naím (2013) *The End of Power*, New York, Basic Books.
11. EU Institute for Security Studies (2012) *Citizens in an Interconnected and Polycentric World*, Paris, EUISS.
12. P. Cerny (2010) *Rethinking World Politics: A Theory of Transnational Neo-Pluralism*, Oxford, Oxford University Press.
13. K. Jørgensen (ed) (2009) *The European Union and International Organizations*, London, Routledge.
14. S. Keukelaire and T. Delreux (2014) *The Foreign Policy of the European Union*, 2nd edition, London, Red Globe Press, p. 308.
15. European External Action Service (2019) *The European Union's Global Strategy: Three Years On, Looking Forward*, Brussels, p. 16.
16. All quotes are from European Union (2016) *Shared Vision, Common Action: A Stronger Europe, a Global Strategy for the European Union's Foreign and Security Policy*, Brussels.
17. Statement by High Representative Federica Mogherini on the International Day for Multilateralism, 23 April 2019, https://eeas.europa.eu/headquarters/head-quarters-homepage/61313/statement-high-representativevice-president-feder-ica-mogherini-international-day_en
18. Intervention at Munich Security Conference, January 2019.
19. European Union (2019) *New Strategic Agenda 2019–2024*, Brussels, p. 6.
20. H. Maas, 'Making Plans for a New World Order', *Handelsblatt*, 22 August 2018.

21. T. Benner (2019) 'What's Left of Multilateralism?', *Internationale Politik*, November–December.
22. J. Borrell, 'The Coronavirus Pandemic and the New World It Is Creating', 23 March 2020, Online blog posting at https://eeas.europa.eu/headquarters/headquarters-homepage/76379/corona-virus-pandemic-and-new-world-it-creating_en
23. As announced at https://www.auswaertiges-amt.de/en/aussenpolitik/multi-alliance-corona/2333374
24. European Commission and High Representative (2020) *Tackling Covid-19 Disinformation: Getting the Facts Right*, Join(2020)8, Brussels.
25. J. Krause and N. Ronzitti (eds) (2012) *The EU, the UN and Collective Security: Making Multilateralism Effective*, London, Routledge.
26. G. Grevi (2008) 'The Rise of Strategic Partnerships: Between Interdependence and Power Politics', in G. Grevi and A. Vasconcelos (eds) *Partnerships for Effective Multilateralism: EU Relations with Brazil, China, India and Russia*, Paris, EUISS.
27. J. Borrell, 'A Stronger European Union in a Better, Greener and Safer World – Key Principles That Will Be My Guiding Mandate', 1 December 2019, Online Blog post, at https://eeas.europa.eu/headquarters/headquarters-homepage/71265/stronger-european-union-within-better-greener-and-safer-world-key-principles-will-be-guiding_en
28. Online event run by Carnegie Europe, 9 July 2020.
29. Comments at Munich Security Conference, February 2019.
30. 'Merkel: Europe Must Unite to Stand Up to China, Russia and US', *The Guardian*, 16 May 2019.
31. Churchill Lecture by Prime Minister Mark Rutte, University of Zurich, 13 February 2019.
32. *The Economist*, 7 November 2019, see full transcript of interview with President Macron.
33. O. Waever (2018) 'A Post-Western Europe: Strange Identities in a Less Liberal World Order', *Ethics and International Affairs*, 32/1.
34. S. Lucarelli (2018) 'The EU and the Crisis of Liberal Order, at Home and Abroad', Globus Research Papers, available at www.globus.uio.no
35. Bertelsmann Foundation (2019) *EU Views*, Bertelsmann.
36. G. Grevi (2019) 'Strategic Autonomy for European Choices: The Key to Europe's Shaping Power', Brussels, European Policy Centre, p. 9.
37. 'Ireland Seeks EU Structure to Share UN Peacekeeping Information', *Irish Times*, 20 November 2018; European Parliament Research Service (2015) 'EU-UN Cooperation in Peacekeeping and Crisis Management', Briefing, p. 11; International Peace Institute (2018) *European Contributions to UN Peacekeeping Operations: Lessons Learned and the Way Forward*, Vienna, IPC, p. 4.
38. OECD (2019) *The European Union: A People Centred Agenda: An International Perspective*, Paris, OECD, p. 43.
39. 'European States Reject Divisive UN Compact on Migration', *Financial Times*, 3 December 2018.
40. B. Szewcyk (2019) 'Europe and the Liberal Order', *Survival*, 61/2, p. 46.
41. European External Action Service (2019) *The European Union's Global Strategy: Three Years On, Looking Forward*, Brussels, p. 20.
42. R. Paris (2019) 'Can Middle Powers Save the Liberal World Order?', London, Chatham House Briefing.
43. P. Pawlak (2019) 'The EU's Role in Shaping the Cyber Regime Complex', *European Foreign Affairs Review*, 24/2.
44. Speech to Ambassadors, 27 August 2018, reproduced at https://www.diplo-matie.gouv.fr/en/the-ministry-and-its-network/news/ambassadors-week/

ambassadors-week-edition-2018/article/speech-by-president-emmanuel-macron-ambassadors-conference-2018

45. E. Brattberg and B. Judah (2020) 'Forget the G7, Build the D10', *Foreign Policy*, June.
46. 'FT Interview: Emmanuel Macron Says It Is Time to Think the Unthinkable', *Financial Times*, 23 March 2020.
47. European Commission and High Representative (2021) *Communication on strengthening the EU's contribution to rules-based multilateralism*, Brussels JOIN(2021) 3.
48. Detailed by the Agence Francaise de Developpement at https://www.afd.fr/fr/actualites/france-lance-initiative-covid-19-sante-en-commun-pour-soutenir-pays-afrique
49. Detailed by the Commission at https://global-response.europa.eu/pledge_en
50. 'Poor Countries Test EU Pandemic Rhetoric', *Financial Times*, 22 April 2020.
51. M. Smith (2017) 'The European Union and the USA', in C. Hill, M. Smith and S. Vanhoonacker (eds) *International Relations and the European Union*, 3rd edition, Oxford, Oxford University Press.
52. 'Italy Wants to be Washington's Closest Partner in Europe', *The Guardian*, 18 June 2019.
53. 'China, Europe and Technology Dominate Munich Security Conference', *Financial Times*, 17 February 2020.
54. L. Cladi and A. Locatelli (2013) 'Worth a Shot: On the Explanatory Power of Bandwagoning in Transatlantic Relations', *Contemporary Security Policy*, 34/2.
55. *The Economist*, 7 November 2019. See Full Transcript of Interview with President Macron.
56. M. Smith (2021) 'European Union Diplomacy and the Trump Administration: Multilateral Strategies in a Transactional World?', in R. Haar, T. Christiansen, S. Lange and S. Vanhoonacker (eds) *The Making of European Security Policy: Between Institutional Dynamics and Global Challenges*, London, Routledge (forthcoming).
57. T. Christiansen, E. Kirchner and U. Wissenbach (2019) *The European Union and China*, London, Red Globe Press, p. 19.
58. H. Dorussen, E. Kirchner and T. Christiansen (2018) 'Security Cooperation in EU–China Relations: Towards Convergence?', *European Foreign Affairs Review*, 23/3.
59. T. Christiansen, E. Kirchner and U. Wissenbach (2019) *The European Union and China*, London, Red Globe Press, p. 73.
60. European Commission and High Representative (2019) *EU–China: A Strategic Outlook*, Brussels.
61. Remarks posted at https://eeas.europa.eu/headquarters/headquarters-home-page/59785/remarks-high-representative-vice-president-federica-mogherini-press-conference-following-eu_en
62. 'EU, China Agree on Joint Statement as Beijing Makes Last-Ditch Concessions', *Euractiv*, 10 April 2019.
63. House of Commons Foreign Affairs Committee (2019) *China and the Rules-Based International System*, 16th report of 2017–1019 Session, p. 49.
64. Churchill Lecture by Prime Minister Mark Rutte, University of Zurich, 13 February 2019.
65. W. Drozdiak (2020) *The Last President of Europe*, New York, Public Affairs, p. 138.
66. A. Small (2020) 'The Meaning of Systemic Rivalry: European and China Beyond the Pandemic', London, European Council on Foreign Relations.
67. J. Borrell, 'In Rougher Seas, the EU's Own Interests and Values Should Be Our Own Compass', Blog post, 14 June 2020, posted at https://eeas.europa.eu/headquarters/headquarters-homepage/80854/rougher-seas-eu%E2%80%99s-own-interests-and-values-should-be-our-compass_en

68. L. Ferreira-Pereira and A. Vysotskaya Guedes Vieira (2016) 'Introduction: The European Union's Strategic Partnerships: Conceptual Approaches, Debates and Experiences', *Cambridge Review of International Affairs*, 29/1.

69. S. Keukelaire and T. Delreux (2014) *The Foreign Policy of the European Union*, 2nd edition, London, Red Globe Press, p. 291.

70. Y. Lay Hwee (2011) 'Where Is ASEM Heading – Toward a Networked Approach to Global Governance?', in W. Hofmeister (ed.) *Panorama: Asia and Europe: Moving Toward a Common Agenda*, Singapore, Konrad-Adenauer-Stiftung.

71. European Commission (2018) *Elements for an EU Strategy on India*, JOIN(2018) 28.

72. European Commission and High Representative (2018) *Connecting Europe and Asia: Building Blocks for an EU Strategy*, JOIN(2018)31, Brussels.

73. T. Fallon, 'When the China Dream and the European Dream Collide', *War on the Rocks*, 7 January 2019.

74. House of Commons Foreign Affairs Committee (2019) *China and the Rules-Based International System*, 16th Report of 2017–1019 Session, p. 22.

75. A. Cottey (2019) 'Europe and China's Sea Disputes: Between Normative Politics, Power Balancing and Acquiescence', *European Security*, 28/4.

76. Opening speech by High Representative Federica Mogherini at the 1st Annual African Union-European Union ministerial meeting, 22 January 2019, at https://eeas.europa.eu/headquarters/headquarters-homepage/56937/opening-speech-high-representativevice-president-federica-mogherini-1st-annual-african-union_en

77. European Commission and High Representative (2020) *Towards a Comprehensive Strategy with Africa*, JOIN(2020)4, Brussels, p. 3.

78. European Commission (2019) *The EU and Central Asia: New Opportunities for a Stronger Partnership*, JOIN(2019)9, Brussels, p. 11.

79. T. Christiansen and S. Tsui (2017) 'The Value and the Limitations of Comprehensive Multilateralism: An EU Perspective on the Asia–Europe Meeting', *European Foreign Affairs Review*, 22/2.

80. S. Economides (2019) 'The EU, the Grand Strategy and the Challenge of Rising and Revisionist Powers', in S. Economides and J. Sperling (eds) *EU Security Strategies: Expanding the EU System of Security Governance*, London, Routledge.

81. O. Waever (2018) 'A Post-Western Europe: Strange Identities in a Less Liberal World Order', *Ethics and International Affairs*, 32/1.

82. T. Renard (2016) 'Partnerships for Effective Multilateralism? Assessing the Compatibility Between EU Bilateralism, (Inter)regionalism and Multilateralism', *Cambridge Review of International Affairs*, 29/1.

83. L. Aggestam and A. Hyde-Price (2019) 'Double Trouble: Trump, Transatlantic Relations and European Strategic Autonomy', *Journal of Common Market Studies Annual Review*, 57, pp. 114–127.

84. T. Benner (2019) 'What's Left of Multilateralism?', *Internationale Politik*, November–December.

85. S. Biscop (2019) 'How to Make Peace Last? European Strategy and the Future of the World Order', Brussels, Egmont Security Policy Brief 12.

86. L. Andersen (2019) 'Curb Your Enthusiasm: Middle Power Liberal Internationalism and the Future of the United Nations', *International Journal*, 74/1.

87. On this dynamic in US approaches to liberal order, see P. Porter (2020) *The False Promise of Liberal Order*, Cambridge, Polity Press.

88. H. Kundnani (2020) 'Europe's Sovereignty Conundrum', *Berlin Policy Journal*, May.

89. B. Szewcyk (2019) 'Europe and the Liberal Order', *Survival*, 61/2, p. 50.

90. G. Grevi (2019) 'Strategic Autonomy for European Choices: The Key to Europe's Shaping Power', Brussels, European Policy Centre.

Chapter 5

1. European Union (2016) *Bratislava Declaration and Roadmap*, Brussels, European Council.
2. SIPRI (2019) *Sipri Yearbook 2019*, Stockholm.
3. F. Tassinari (2016) 'All for None, and None for All: Life in a Broken Europe', *Foreign Affairs*, January.
4. G. Kepel (2016) *Terror in France: The Rise of Jihad in the West*, Princeton, Princeton University Press.
5. Europol (2019) *European Union Terrorism Situation and Trend Report 2019*, The Hague.
6. European Court of Auditors (2019) *Challenges to Effective EU Cybersecurity Policy*, Brussels.
7. 'Russia Deploying Coronavirus Disinformation to Sow Panic in West, EU Document Says', *Reuters*, 18 March 2020.
8. European Political Strategy Centre (2019) 'Rethinking Strategic Autonomy for the Digital Age', EPSC Strategic Note; Centre for European Policy Studies (2018) *Rethinking the EU's Cyber Defence Capabilities*, Report of CEPS Task Force, Brussels.
9. M. E. Smith (2017) *Europe's Common Security and Defence Policy: Experiential Learning and Institutional Change*, Cambridge, Cambridge University Press.
10. 'Defense Secretary Warns NATO of "Dim" Future', *New York Times*, 10 June 2011.
11. P. Serrano (2019) *The Bundle of Sticks: A Stronger European Defence to Face Global Challenges*, Madrid, Elcano Institute, p. 17.
12. SIPRI (2019) *Sipri Yearbook 2019*, Stockholm.
13. D. Fiott (2018) 'Strategic Autonomy: Towards European Sovereignty in Defence?', Paris, EUISS Brief.
14. D. Barrie, B. Barry, H. Boyd, M. Chagnaud, N. Childs, B. Giegerich, C. Mölling and T. Schütz (2018) *Protecting Europe: Meeting the EU's Military Level of Ambition in the Context of Brexit*, London, IISS.
15. 'The Netherlands Likely to Scrap NATO Spending Target', *Euractiv*, 3 June 2020.
16. See figures in D. Fiott (ed) (2020) *The CSDP in 2020*, Paris, EUISS, especially p. 8 and p. 11.
17. T. Palm and B. Crum (2019) 'Military Operations and the EU's Identity as an International Security Actor', *European Security*, 28/4, 513–534; D. Barrie, B. Barry, H. Boyd, M. Chagnaud, N. Childs, B. Giegerich, C. Mölling and T. Schütz (2018) *Protecting Europe: Meeting the EU's Military Level of Ambition in the Context of Brexit*, London, IISS.
18. A theme running through D. Fiott (ed.) (2020) *The CSDP in 2020*, Paris, EUISS. Also see S. Biscop (2019) 'Fighting for Europe: European Strategic Autonomy and the Use of Force', Brussels, Egmont Institute; S. Duke (2018) 'The Enigmatic Role of Defence in the EU: From EDC to EDU?', *European Foreign Affairs Review*, 23/1.
19. T. Latici (2020) 'What Role for the UK in the EU's Defence Labyrinth?', European Parliamentary Research Service.
20. One recent example of the many works arguing that European security has been weakened primarily by being too open to immigration and refugees is D. Murray (2017) *The Strange Death of Europe*, London, Bloomsbury.
21. 'EU Funds for Bulgaria Target Border Security', *EU Observer*, 28 September 2016.
22. European Commission (2020) *New Pact on Migration and Asylum: A Fresh Start on Migration in Europe*, Brussels, European Commission.
23. Concord (2019) *Aidwatch 2019*, Brussels, Concord, p. 21.

24. C. Castillejo (2016) 'The European Union Trust Fund for Africa: A Glimpse of the Future for EU Development Cooperation', Bonn, German Development Institute.

25. Data from the Trust Fund's website, https://ec.europa.eu/trustfundforafrica/thematic/improved-governance-and-conflict-prevention

26. L. Raineri and F. Strazzari (2019) '(B)ordering Hybrid Security? EU Stabilisation Practices in the Sahara-Sahel Region', *Ethnopolitics*, 18/4.

27. 'Bruselas concede mas ayudas a Rabat para mejorar el control migratorio', *El Pais*, 21 December 2019.

28. European Commission (2016) *First Progress Report on the Partnership Framework with Third Countries Under the European Agenda on Migration*, COM(2016) 700, Brussels, European Commission.

29. Opening speech by High Representative Federica Mogherini at the 1st Annual African Union-European Union ministerial meeting, 22 January 2019, posted at https://eeas.europa.eu/headquarters/headquarters-homepage/56937/opening-speech-high-representativevice-president-federica-mogherini-1st-annual-african-union_en

30. 'German Ministry Wants Migrants Stopped at Sea', *EU Observer*, 8 November 2016.

31. 'La entrada irregular de inmigrantes a España cae un 39% en lo que va del año', *El Pais*, 16 August 2019. E. Soler i Lecha and P. Morillas (2020) *Middle Power with Maghreb Focus: A Spanish Perspective on Security Policy in the Southern Neighbourhood*, Berlin, Friedrich Ebert Stiftung, p. 12.

32. Concord (2017) *EU Emergency Trust Fund for Africa: Partnership or Conditionality?*, Brussels, Concord.

33. European Commission (2020) *New Pact on Migration and Asylum: A Fresh Start on Migration in Europe*, Brussels, European Commission.

34. J. Black et al. (2017) *Defence and Security After Brexit*, Cambridge, RAND Europe, p. 31.

35. S. Duke (2018) 'The Enigmatic Role of Defence in the EU: From EDC to EDU?', *European Foreign Affairs Review*, 23/1, p. 67.

36. European Commission (2015) *The European Agenda on Security*, COM (2015) 185 final.

37. European Union (2016) *Shared Vision, Common Action: A Stronger Europe, a Global Strategy for the European Union's Foreign and Security Policy*, Brussels, p. 21.

38. C. Mortera-Martinez (2019) *The EU's Security Union: A Bill of Health*, London, Centre for European Reform, p. 6.

39. European Political Strategy Centre (2016) 'Towards a "Security Union": Bolstering the EU's Counter-Terrorism Response', Brussels, EPSC Strategic Notes No. 12.

40. J.-M. Ayrault and F.-W. Steinmeier, 'A Strong Europe in a World of Uncertainties', *France Diplomatie* [website], 28 June 2016.

41. C. Mortera-Martinez (2019) *The EU's Security Union: A Bill of Health*, London, Centre for European Reform, p. 12.

42. P. Dorrie, 'Europe Has Spent Years Trying to Prevent "Chaos" in the Sahel. It Failed', *World Politics Review*, 25 June 2019.

43. R. Parkes (2020) 'Reading the Runes: The Future of CSDP and AFSJ' in D. Fiott (eds) *The CSDP in 2020*, Paris, EUISS, p. 101; T. Palm and B. Crum (2019) 'Military Operations and the EU's Identity as an International Security Actor', *European Security*, 28/4; M. Riddervold (2018) *The Maritime Turn in EU Foreign and Security Policies*, London, Palgrave Macmillan.

44. European Court of Auditors, *Challenges to Effective EU Cybersecurity Policy*, Briefing paper, 2019.

45. C. Mortera-Martinez, *The EU's Security Union: A Bill of Health*, London, CER, 2019, p. 6.

46. G. Christou (2015) *Cybersecurity in the European Union: Resilience and Adaptability in Governance*, London, Palgrave Macmillan.

47. European Commission (2020) *Communication on the EU Security Union Strategy*, Com(2020) 605 final, 2020; 'EU Vows Tougher Response on Hybrid Threats', *Politico*, 30 July 2020.

48. P. Pawlak (2019) 'The EU's Role in Shaping the Cyber Regime Complex', *European Foreign Affairs Review*, 24/2, p. 182.

49. T. Renard (2018) 'EU Cyber-Partnerships: Assessing the EU Strategic Partnerships with Third Countries in the Cyber Domain', *European Politics and Society*, 19/3.

50. Amnesty International (2020) *Out of Control: Failing EU Laws for Digital Surveillance Export*, London, Amnesty International, p. 12; G. Gressel (2019) 'Protecting Europe Against Hybrid Threats', London, European Council on Foreign Relations, p. 114.

51. 'EU Pressured to Give Results of Leak Probe on China Disinformation', *Financial Times*, 21 June 2020.

52. A. Cianciara (2017) 'Stability, Security, Democracy: Explaining Shifts in the Narrative of the European Neighbourhood Policy', *Journal of European Integration*, 39/1.

53. S. Lucarelli (2019) 'The EU as a Securitising Agent? Testing the Model, Advancing the Literature', *West European Politics*, 42/2, pp. 413–436.

54. B. Stokes, R. Wike and J. Poushter (2016) *Europeans Face the World Divided*, Washington, DC: Pew Research Center; M. Goodwin, T. Raines and D. Cotts (2017) 'What Do Europeans Think About Muslim Immigration?', London, Chatham House.

55. European External Action Service (2019) *The European Union's Global Strategy: Three Years On, Looking Forward*, Brussels, p. 27.

56. V. Ntousas (2020) *Why the EU's Migration and Asylum Plan Is Flawed*, London, Chatham House.

57. P. Kingsley (2016) *The New Odyssey: The Story of Europe's Refugee Crisis*, London, Faber.

58. P. Seeberg (2017) 'Mobility Partnerships and Security Subcomplexes in the Mediterranean: The Strategic Role of Migration and the EU's Foreign and Security Policies Towards the MENA Region', *European Foreign Affairs Review*, 22/1.

59. D. Omand (2016) 'Keeping Europe Safe: Counterterrorism for the Continent', *Foreign Affairs*, September/October.

60. S. Grey (2016) *The New Spymasters*, London, Penguin, pp. 255, 282.

61. P. Dorrie, 'Europe Has Spent Years Trying to Prevent "Chaos" in the Sahel. It failed', *World Politics Review*, 25 June 2019.

62. L. Simon, 'What Is Europe's Role in Sino-American Competition?', *War on the Rocks*, 14 February 2019.

63. R. Cooper (2003) *The Breaking of Nations: Order and Chaos in the 21st Century*, London, Atlantic Books.

64. E. Barbé and P. Morillas (2019) 'The EU Global Strategy: The Dynamics of a More Politicized and Politically Integrated Foreign Policy', *Cambridge Review of International Affairs*, 32/6.

Chapter 6

1. E. Luttwark (1990) 'From Geopolitics to Geo-Economics: Logic of Conflict, Grammar of Commerce', *The National Interest*, No. 20, 17–23.
2. Figures from Eurostat, *Europe in the World, 2018 Edition*, Luxembourg, EU Publication Office, pp. 76, 83 and 86.
3. Figures from DG Trade *Statistical Guide*, July 2019, p. 21.
4. S. King (2011) *Losing Control: The Emerging Threats to Western Prosperity*, New Haven, Yale University Press, p. 232.
5. K. O'Hara and W. Hall (2018) 'Four Internets: The Geopolitics of Digital Governance', Centre for International Governance Innovation Paper 206, Waterloo, Canada.
6. 'Europe First: The EU's Digital Industrialisation Challenge', *Financial Times*, 16 December 2019.
7. European Political Strategy Centre (2019) *Rethinking Strategic Autonomy for the Digital Age*, Brussels, EPSC.
8. M. Thirwell (2010) 'The Return of Geo-Economics: Globalisation and National Security', Commentary, Lowy Institute for International Policy.
9. M. Okano-Heijmans (2012) 'Power Shift: Economic Realism and Economic Diplomacy on the Rise' in E. Fels et al. (eds) *Power in the 21st Century*, Springer.
10. WTO Secretariat (2007) *Trade Policy Review: European Communities*, Geneva, WTO.
11. Remarks at the Berlin Forum, 25 November 2019.
12. European Commission (2006) *Global Europe, Competing in the World*, Brussels.
13. Angola, Central African Republic, Chad, Congo-Brazzaville, Democratic Republic of the Congo, Djibouti, Equatorial Guinea, Ethiopia, Eritrea, Gabon, Malawi, Sao Tome and Principe, Somalia, South Sudan, Sudan and Zambia. See European Commission and High Representative (2020) *Towards a Comprehensive Strategy with Africa*, JOIN(2020)4, p. 9.
14. B. Trsoter et al. (2020) 'Delivering on Promises? The Expected Impacts and Implementation Challenges of the Economic Partnership Agreements Between the EU and Africa', *Journal of Common Market Studies*, 58/2.
15. J. Mortensen (2009) 'The Word Trade Organization and the European Union' in K. Jorgensen (ed.) *The European Union and International Organizations*, London, Routledge, p. 89.
16. House of Lords European Union Committee (2008) *Developments in EU Trade Policy*, 35th Report of 2007–2008 Session.
17. S. Everett (2007) 'Trade Policy: Time for a Rethink?' in A. Sapir (ed.) *Fragmented Power: Europe and the Global Economy*, Brussels, Bruegel, pp. 61–62.
18. European Union (206) *Shared Vision, Common Action: A Stronger Europe, a Global Strategy for the European Union's Foreign and Security Policy*, Brussels, p. 41.
19. M. Asenius (2020) 'Trade in Turbulent Times' in M. Westlake (ed.) *The European Union's New Foreign Policy*, London, Macmillan, p. 98.
20. J.-P. Lehmann, 'Absurd EU–Japan Trade Plan Underlines Doha's Failure', *Financial Times*, 20 July 2012.
21. D. Gross, 'What EU "Geopolitical" Power Will Cost', *Project Syndicate*, 6 December 2019.
22. European Commission (2018) *WTO Modernization – Concept Paper*, Brussels.
23. A. Barbone and R. Bendini (2015) *Protectionism in the G20*, European Parliament Directorate-General for External Policies, p. 23.
24. Centre for Economic Policy Research (2012) 'Débâcle: The 11th GTA Report on Protectionism'.

25. M. Nisen, 'Trade War: How 12 Major Economies Have Closed Up Since the Crisis', *Business Insider*, 18 June 2012.
26. P. Messerlin (2010) 'How the Rich OECD Nations Should Handle the Emerging Giants', *Europe's World*, Spring; F. Erixson and R. Sally (2010) *Trade, Globalisation and Emerging Protectionism Since the Crisis*, Brussels, ECIPE, pp. 8 and 12.
27. European Commission (2015) *Trade for All: Towards a More Responsible Trade and Investment Policy*, Brussels.
28. A. Bradford (2020) *The Brussels Effect*, Oxford, Oxford University Press, p. 23.
29. A. Young (2015) 'The European Union as a Global Regulator? Context and Comparison', *Journal of European Public Policy*, 22/9 – and others in this special edition.
30. The text on 'safeguard measures' is reproduced at http://trade.ec.europa.eu/doclib/docs/2017/july/tradoc_155701.pdf
31. S. Woolcock (2012) *European Union Economic Diplomacy*, Farnham, Ashgate, pp. 20, 43, 67 and 79–80.
32. European Commission (2012) *A Stronger European Industry for Growth and Economic Recovery*, Brussels, COM 582.
33. European Commission (2020) *White Paper on Levelling the Playing Field as Regards Foreign Subsidies*, COM(2020) 253.
34. European Commission and the High Representative (2020) *Report on the Generalised Scheme of Preferences Covering the Period 2018–2019*, JOIN(2020)3; I. Ioannides (2018) *The Generalised System of Preferences Regulation*, European Parliament Research Service, pp. 6–7.
35. M. Smith (2019) 'The European Union and the Global Arena: In Search of Post-Brexit Roles', *Politics and Governance*, 7/3, pp. 83–92.
36. Speech, 3 February 2020: https://www.gov.uk/government/speeches/pm-speech-in-greenwich-3-february-2020
37. M. Angel Cañete, 'Europe's New Energy Dependency', *Politico*, 6 June 2019.
38. 'Altmaier Urges EU to Protect Technology from Chinese Rivals', *Financial Times*, 18 February 2019.
39. 'EU Trade Chief Urges Tougher Defences Against Foreign Take-Overs', *Financial Times*, 16 April 2020.
40. J. Pisani-Ferry, 'Europe and the New Imperialism', *Project Syndicate*, 8 May 2019.
41. 'EU Unveils Plan to be Carbon Neutral by 2050', *Financial Times*, 12 December 2019.
42. Munich Security Conference (2020) *Zeitenwende, Wendezeiten: Special Edition of the Munich Security report on German Foreign and Security Policy*, Munich, MSC, p. 58.
43. 'The Next Epidemic: Resurgent Populism', *Politico*, 6 April 2020.
44. T. Sattich and T. Inderberg (2019) 'EU Geoeconomics: A Framework for Analysing Bilateral Relations in the European Union', *Journal of Common Market Studies*, 57/3.
45. H. Kundnani (2011) 'Germany as a Geo-Economic Power', *Washington Quarterly*, 34/3.
46. Her Majesty's Government (2011) *Trade and Investment for Growth*, London, HMG.
47. 'Perdo Sanchez apuesta por un Gobierno tecnocrata y social', *El Pais*, 11 January 2020.
48. 'The Cure Foe Coronavirus: More Trade or Less?', *Politico*, 1 April 2020.
49. M. Rutte, Investiture Speech, 'Building Bridges' November 13, 2012, www.government.nl/government/policy-statement

50. M. Okano-Heijmans (2012) 'Power Shift: Economic Realism and Economic Diplomacy on the Rise' in E. Fels et al. (eds) *Power in the 21st Century*, Springer.
51. European Commission (2018) *Elements for an EU Strategy on India*, JOIN(2018) 28, p. 8.
52. K. Vervaeke (2020) 'The European Union's Pivot to Africa' in M. Westlake (ed.) *The European Union's New Foreign Policy*, London, Macmillan, p. 170.
53. 'Macron Plays European Card on State Visit to China', *Euractiv*, 5 November 2019.
54. J. King, 'The EU Needs Its Own Security Strategy to Confront the Digital Threat', *Financial Times*, 1 February 2019.
55. 'Angela Merkel Urges EU to Seize Control of Data from US Tech Titans', *Financial Times*, 13 November 2019.
56. 'Transcript of Interview with Angela Merkel: Europe Is No Longer at the Centre of World Events', *Financial Times*, 17 January 2020.
57. European Commission (2020) *Shaping Europe's Digital Future*, COM(2020) 67; European Commission (2020) *White Paper on Artificial Intelligence: A European Approach to Excellence and Trust*, COM(2020) 65.
58. European Political Strategy Centre (2019) *Rethinking Strategic Autonomy for the Digital Age*, Brussels, EPSC, p. 14.
59. 'French Limits on Huawei 5G Equipment Amount to De Facto Ban by 2028', Reuters, 22 July 2020.
60. 'Can the EU Become Another AI Superpower?', *The Economist*, 20 September 2018.
61. 'Europe First: Taking on the Dominance of US Dollar', *Financial Times*, 5 December 2019.
62. A. Young and J. Peterson (2014) *Parochial Global Europe: Twenty-First Century Trade Politics*, Oxford, Oxford University Press.
63. A. Dür and M. Elsig (2011) 'Principals, Agents, and the European Union's Foreign Economic Policies', *Journal of European Public Policy*, 18/3.
64. B. Clift and C. Woll (2012) 'Economic Patriotism: Reinventing Control Over Open Markets', *Journal of European Public Policy*, 19/3.
65. S. Muenier and K. Nicolaidis (2017) 'The European Union as a Trade Power' in C. Hill, M. Smith and S. Vanhoonacker (eds) *International Relations and the European Union*, 3rd edition, Oxford, Oxford University Press, p. 211.
66. K. Meissner (2018) *Commercial Realism and EU Trade Policy: Competing for Economic Power in Asia and the Americas*, London, Routledge.
67. A. Sbragia (2010) 'The EU, the US and Trade Policy: Competitive Interdependence in the Management of Globalization', *Journal of European Public Policy*, 17/3.
68. S. Meunier and K. Nicolaidis (2019) 'The Geopoliticization of European Trade and Investment Policy', *Journal of Common Market Studies*, 57, Annual review.
69. European Political Strategy Centre (2019) *Rethinking Strategic Autonomy for the Digital Age*, Brussels, EPSC, p. 15.
70. European Council on Foreign Relations (2014) *European Foreign Policy Scorecard 2013*, London, ECFR, pp. 28–29.
71. M. Sandbu, 'Europe Must Find Its Will to Power', *Financial Times*, 20 June 2019.

Chapter 7

1. F. Schimmelfennig and U. Sedelmeier (2004) 'Governance by Conditionality. EU Rule Transfer to the Candidate Countries of Central and Eastern Europe', *Journal of European Public Policy*, 11/4; S. Levitsky and L. Way (2006) 'Linkage Versus Leverage. Rethinking the International Dimension of Regime Change',

Comparative Politics, 38/4; S. Grimm (2019) 'Democracy Promotion in EU Enlargement Negotiations: More Interaction, Less Hierarchy', *Democratization*, 26/5, pp. 851–868.

2. C. Powell (2007) *Revisiting Spain's Transition to Democracy, Barcelona*, Barcelona, IEMed; C. Powell (2001) 'International Aspects of Democratization. The Case of Spain' in L. Whitehead (ed.) *The International Dimensions of Democratization. Europe and the Americas,* Oxford: Oxford University Press; M. Carvallero and K. Kornetis (eds) (2019), *Rethinking Democratisation in Spain, Greece and Portugal*, London, Palgrave Macmillan.

3. M. Matlak, F. Schimmelfennig and T. Wozniakowski (eds) (2018) *Europeanization Revisited: Central and Eastern Europe in the European Union*, Florence, EUI; Democratic Progress Institute (2016) *The Role of European Union Accession in Democratisation Processes*, London; K. Smith (2004) *The Making of EU Foreign Policy: The Case of Eastern Europe*, London, Macmillan.

4. F. Schimmelfennig (2001) 'The Community Trap: Liberal Norms, Rhetorical Actions and the Eastern Enlargement of the European Union', *International Organization*, 55/1.

5. European Union (2016) *Shared Vision, Common Action: A Stronger Europe, a Global Strategy for the European Union's Foreign and Security Policy*, Brussels, p. 24.

6. J. Dzankic, S. Keil and M. Kmezic (eds) (2018) *The Europeanisation of the Western Balkans: A Failure of EU Conditionality?*, London, Routledge.

7. E. Fouere (2019) 'The EU's Re-engagement with the Western Balkans: A New Chapter Long Overdue', Policy Brief 2019/1, Brussels, Centre for European Policy Studies, p. 5.

8. For an overview of these trends, see I. Ioannides (2018) *An Evaluation of EU Peace-Building in the Western Balkans*, European Parliament Research Service, p. 6.

9. E. Usanmaz (2018) 'Successful Crisis Management? Evaluating the Success of the EU Missions in the Western Balkans', *European Foreign Affairs Review*, 23/3.

10. E. Fouere (2019) 'The EU's Re-engagement with the Western Balkans: A New Chapter Long Overdue', Policy Brief 2019/1, Brussels, Centre for European Policy Studies, p. 2.

11. European Commission (2018) *A Credible Enlargement Perspective for and Enhanced EU Engagement with the Western Balkans*, COM(2018) 65.

12. Polish Ministry of Foreign Affairs, 'Joint Statement of the Foreign Ministers on the EU's Commitment to the Western Balkan's European Integration', 11 June 2019, posted at: https://www.gov.pl/web/diplomacy/joint-statement-of-the-foreign-ministers-on-the-eu-commitment-to-the-western-balkans-european-integration

13. *The Economist*, 7 November 2019, See Full Transcript of Interview with President Macron.

14. '6 Countries Write to Juncker to Support EU Enlargement Reform', *Politico*, 20 November 2019.

15. D. Bechev (2017) *Rival Power: Russia in South-East Europe*, New Haven, Yale University Press.

16. European Commission (2020) *Enhancing the Enlargement Process – A Credible EU Perspective for the Western Balkans*, COM(2020) 57.

17. European Commission, *2020 Communication on Enlargement Policy*, COM(2020) 660.

18. For an overview of this period and the early 2010s, see N. Tocci and S. Aydin-Duzgit (2015) *Turkey and the European Union*, London, Red Globe Press.

19. Varieties of Democracy (2018) *Democracy for All? V-Dem Annual Democracy Report 2018*, Gothenburg; Freedom House (2018) *Democracy in Crisis Freedom in the World Report 2018*, Washington, DC.
20. B. Weber (2016) *Time for a Plan B: The European Refugee Crisis, the Balkan Route and the EU–Turkey Deal*, Berlin, Democratization Policy Council.
21. R. Youngs (2020) *New Directions for EU Civil Society Support*, Brussels, Carnegie Europe.
22. Zihnioğlu, Ö (2020) *EU-Turkey Relations: Civil Society and Depoliticisation*, London, Routledge, pp. 114–115.
23. European Commission (2013) *Guidelines for EU Support to Civil Society Enlargement Countries 2014–2020*; European Commission (2014) *Instrument for Pre-accession Indicative Strategy Paper for Turkey 2014–2020*, p. 19.
24. Zihnioğlu, Ö (2020) *EU-Turkey Relations: Civil Society and Depoliticisation*, London, Routledge.
25. 'Macron Says Time for Turkey to Clarify Ambiguous Stance on Islamic State', *Reuters*, 3 December 2019.
26. 'Turkey Says EU Funding Cuts Will Not Affect It's Drilling Off Cyprus', *Reuters*, 16 July 2019.
27. S. Economides (2020) *From Fatigue to Resistance: EU Enlargement and the West Balkans*, Dahrendorf Forum Paper 17.
28. L. Cooley (2019) *The European Union's Approach to Conflict Resolution: Transformation or Regulation in the Western Balkans?*, London, Routledge.
29. A. Kaliber and E. Kaliber (2019) 'From De-Europeanisation to Anti-Western Populism: Turkish Foreign Policy in Flux', *International Spectator*, 54/4, 1–16; B. Saatcloglu (2016) 'De-Europeanisation in Turkey: The Case of the Rule of Law', *South European Politics and Society*, 21/1.

Chapter 8

1. Ongoing updates to these predictions are at: https://climateactiontracker.org/global/temperatures/
2. Intergovernmental Panel on Climate Change (2019) *Global Warming of 1.5 Degrees Celsius*, IPCC Special Report, Geneva.
3. Intergovernmental Panel on Climate Change (2014) *Mitigation of Climate Change. Contribution of Working Group III to the Fifth Assessment Report of the Intergovernmental Panel on Climate Change*, Cambridge: Cambridge University Press; A. Moran et al. (2018) *The Intersection of Global Fragility and Climate Risks*, Washington, DC, United States Agency for International Aid; F. Gemenne et al. (2014) 'Climate and Security: Evidence, Emerging Risks and a New Agenda', *Climate Change*, 123/1, pp. 1–9; Foresight (2011) *International Dimensions of Climate Change*, London, UK Government Office for Science.
4. Centre for Climate and Security (2020) *A Security Threat Assessment of Global Climate Change*, Washington, DC.
5. Presentation by Professor Johan Rockstrom, Berlin Climate and Security Conference, 23 June 2020.
6. C. Church and A. Crawford (2018) *Green Conflict Minerals*, Winnipeg, International Institute for Sustainable Development.
7. IRENA (2019) *Commission on the Geopolitics of Energy Transition, a New World: The Geopolitics of Energy Transition*, Irena.

8. The 'lifeboat' argument is associated with the seminal J. Lovelock (2009) *The Vanishing Face of Gaia: A Final Warning*, London, Penguin. One early example of the latter argument is German Advisory Council on Global Change (2011) *World in Transition: A Social Contract for the Great Transformation*, Berlin.

9. https://ec.europa.eu/eurostat/cache/infographs/energy/bloc-2c.html

10. BP (2018). *BP Energy Outlook 2018*.

11. S. Oberthür and C. Kelly (2008) 'EU Leadership in International Climate Policy: Achievements and Challenges', *The International Spectator*, 43/3.

12. For a general account of this development of EU climate policy, see J. Vogler, 'The Challenge of the Environment, Energy and Climate Change' in C. Hill, M. Smith and S. Vanhoonackr (eds) *International Relations and the European Union*, 3rd edition, Oxford, Oxford University Press, 2017.

13. Figures from EU website at https://ec.europa.eu/clima/policies/ets_en

14. See European Commission's dedicated website on International Climate Finance, at: https://ec.europa.eu/clima/policies/international/finance_en

15. 'Europe Is Stealing Jungle from Us, Claim Pygmies', *The Times*, 21 August 2019.

16. G. Escribano (2019) 'The Geopolitics of Renewable and Electricity Cooperation Between Morocco and Spain', *Mediterranean Politics*, 24/5.

17. European Commission (2019) *The European Green Deal*, COM(2019) 640.

18. S. Far and R. Youngs (2015) *Energy Union and EU Global Strategy*, Stockholm, Swedish Institute for European Policy Studies.

19. M. Arias Cañete (2018) *Speech at the 4th EU Energy Summit: International Geopolitical Uncertainties: Brakes or Accelerators for the EU Energy Transition?*, Brussels, European Commission Press Corner, 12 April.

20. European Commission and the High Representative (2008) *Climate Change and International Security*; R. Youngs (2014) *Climate Change and European Security*, London, Routledge.

21. K. Zwolski and C. Kaunert (2011) 'The EU and Climate Security: A Case of Successful Norm Entrepreneurship?', *European Security*, 20/1.

22. Council of the European Union (2010) *European Council Conclusions*: http://www.consilium.europa.eu/ueDocs/cms_Data/docs/pressData/en/ec/113591

23. Council of the European Union (2011) *Council Conclusions on Climate Diplomacy*, 3106/11. http://ec.europa.eu/clima/events/0052/council_conclusions_en.pdf

24. European External Acton Service (2012) *Developing an EU Policy Towards the Arctic Region: Progress Since 2008 and Next Steps*, JOIN(2012)19, direct quote from p. 11.

25. European External Action Service (2013) *EU Climate Diplomacy for 2015 and Beyond: Reflection Paper*, Brussels.

26. For details see R. Youngs (2014) *Climate Change and European Security*, London, Routledge.

27. S. Jermy (2011) *Strategy for Action*, London, Knightstone Publishing, p. 148.

28. Fetzek, S. and L. van Schaik (2018) *Europe's Responsibility to Prepare: Managing Climate Security Risks in a Changing World*, Washington, DC: Center on Climate and Security.

29. European Commission (2018) *A Clean Planet for All: A European Strategic Long-Term Vision for a Prosperous, Modern, Competitive and Climate Neutral Economy*, COM(2018) 773, p. 21.

30. Council of the European Union (2019) *Council Conclusions on Climate Diplomacy*, 6153/19.

31. European External Action Service (2019) *The European Union's Global Strategy: Three Years On, Looking Forward*, Brussels, pp. 28 and 40.

32. European Commission (2019) *The European Green Deal*, COM(2019) 640.

33. F. Ducrotté (2012) 'The Impact of Climate Change on International Security: Prospects for an Environmental Dimension in CSDP Missions', *European Security Review*, November, p. 6.
34. European Parliament Foreign Affairs Committee (2012) *The Role of the CSDP in Case of Climate-Driven Crises and Natural Disasters*, Brussels, European Parliament, pp. 4 and 7–8.
35. A. Froggart and M. Levi (2009) 'Climate and Energy Security Policies and Measures: Synergies and Conflicts', *International Affairs*, 85/6, pp. 1129–1141.
36. S. Droge (2018) 'Climate and Security Revisited', Berlin, SWP Comment.
37. L. Bergamaschi and N. Sartori (2018) *The Geopolitics of Climate: Transatlantic Dialogue*, Rome, Istituto Affari Internazionali, p. 8.
38. Council of the EU (2018) *Foreign Affairs Council Conclusions on Climate Diplomacy*, 6125/18.
39. European Court of Auditors (2017) *Landscape Review: EU Action on Energy and Climate Change*, Brussels.
40. L. Bergamaschi, N. Mabey, C. Born and A. White (2019) *Managing Climate Risk for a Safer Future: A New Resilience Agenda for Europe*, London, E3G.
41. D. Depledge and T. Feakin (2012) 'Climate Change and International Institutions: Implications for Security', *Climate Policy*, 12/1, 82.
42. European Commission (2020) *Critical Raw Materials for Strategic Technologies and Sectors in the EU: A Foresight Study*, Brussels, European Commission.
43. 'Five Eyes Alliance Could Expand in Scope to Counteract China', *The Times*, 29 July 2020.
44. J. Richert (2017) 'From Single Voice to Coordinated Polyphony EU Energy Policy and the External Dimension', *European Foreign Affairs Review*, 22/2.
45. K. Szulecki and K. Westphal (2014) 'The Cardinal Sins of European Energy Policy: Non-governance in an Uncertain Global Landscape', *Global Policy*, 5/1, 38–51; V. Birchfield and J. Duffield (eds) (2011) *Toward a Common European Union Energy Policy*, London, Palgrave Macmillan.
46. European Union (2015) *A Framework Strategy for a Resilient Energy Union with a Forward-Looking Climate Change Policy*, COM (2015), 80; S. Far and R. Youngs (2015) *Energy Union and EU Global Strategy*, Stockholm, Swedish Institute for European Policy Studies.
47. European Union (2015) *A Framework Strategy for a Resilient Energy Union with a Forward-Looking Climate Change Policy*, COM (2015), 80 final European Commission, p. 18.
48. A. Prontera (2017) *The New Politics of Energy Security in the European Union and Beyond. States, Markets, Institutions*, London, Routledge; A. Goldthau and N. Sitter (2015) *A Liberal Actor in a Realist World. The European Union Regulatory State and the Global Political Economy of Energy*, Oxford, Oxford University Press; A. Herranz-Surrallés (2016) 'An Emerging EU Energy Diplomacy? Discursive Shifts, Enduring Practices', *Journal of European Public Policy*, 23/9.
49. 'Turkstream Line: Russian Tightens Its Grip on Europe's Gas Supplies', *The Times*, 9 January 2020.
50. A. Herranz-Surrallés (2018) 'Thinking Energy Outside the Frame? Reframing and Misframing in Euro-Mediterranean Energy Relations', *Mediterranean Politics*, 23/1, pp. 122–141.
51. D. Stein (2019) *Impact of the European Court of Justice's Opal Decision*, Washington, DC, Atlantic Council.
52. European Parliament Research Service (2019) *Intergovernmental Agreements in the Field of Energy*, Brussels, European Parliament.

53. European Commission (2018) *A Clean Planet for All: A European Strategic Long-Term Vision for a Prosperous, Modern, Competitive and Climate Neutral Economy*, COM(2018) 773, p. 8.
54. M. Siddi (2019) 'The EU's Botched Geopolitical Approach to External Energy Policy: The Case of the Southern Gas Corridor', *Geopolitics*, 24/1.
55. Climate Diplomacy Report (2020) *The Geopolitics of Decarbonisation: Reshaping European Foreign Relations*, Berlin, Adelphi.
56. 'Merkel Faces Calls to Scrap Nord Stream 2 After Navalny Poisoning', *Financial Times*, 4 September 2020.
57. D. Huber (2020) *The New European Commission's Green Deal and Geopolitical Language: A Critique from a Decentring Perspective*, Rome, IAI.
58. A. Goldthau and N. Sitter (2020) 'Power, Authority and Security: The EU's Russian Gas Dilemma', *Journal of European Integration*, 41/7.
59. J. Richert (2017) 'From Single Voice to Coordinated Polyphony EU Energy Policy and the External Dimension', *European Foreign Affairs Review* 22/2.
60. S. Hofmann and U. Staeger (2019) 'Frame Contestation and Collective Securitisation: The Case of EU Energy Policy', *West European Politics*, 42/2.

Chapter 9

1. Economist Intelligence Unit (2020) *Democracy Index 2019 – A Year of Democratic Setbacks and Popular Protests*, London, EUI.
2. Freedom House (2020) *Freedom in the World 2020 – A Leaderless Struggle for Democracy*, Washington, DC, Freedom House.
3. Varieties of Democracy (2020) *Democracy Report 2020: Autocratization Surges – Resistance Grows*, Gothenburg, V-Dem.
4. Economist Intelligence Unit (2019) *Democracy Index 2018 – Me Too?*, London, EIU.
5. A. Lührmann and S. Lindberg (2019) 'A Third Wave of Autocratization Is Here: What Is New About It?', *Democratization*, 26/7.
6. Reporters without Borders (2018) *RSF Index 2018: Hatred of Journalism Threatens Democracies*, Washington, DC.
7. A. Poppe, J. Leininger and J. Wolff (2019) 'Introduction: Negotiating the Promotion of Democracy', *Democratization*, 26/5.
8. European Commission (2011) *Increasing the Impact of EU Development Policy: An Agenda for Change*, COM(2011) 637.
9. For more detail on these innovations, see F. Gomez, C. Muguruza and J. Wouters (eds) (2018) *EU Human Rights and Democratisation Policies: Achievements and Challenges*, London, Routledge.
10. Council of the European Union (2019) *Council Conclusions on Democracy*, 12836/19.
11. European Commission and the High Representative (2020) *EU Action Plan on Human Rights and Democracy 2020–2024*, JOIN(2020)5.
12. The Commission's list of all EU sanctions is at https://www.sanctionsmap.eu/#/main; See also S. Raine (2019) *Europe's Strategic Future: From Crisis to Coherence?*, London, International Institute for Strategic Studies, p. 122.
13. 'UK to Begin Crackdown on Human Rights Abusers', *Financial Times*, 10 January 2020.
14. S. Besch and B. Oppenheim (2019) *Up in Arms: Warring Over the EU's Arms Exports Regime*, London, Centre for European Reform, p. 9.

15. European Commission and the High Representative (2020) *Report on the Generalised Scheme of Preferences Covering the Period 2018–2019*, JOIN(2020)3; I. Ioannides (2018) *The Generalised System of Preferences Regulation*, Brussels, European Parliament Research Service.

16. Notification at Government of the Netherlands, 'Letter on Sanctions Against Iran on the Grounds of Undesirable Interference', 8 January 2019.

17. K. Godfrey and R. Youngs (2019) *Towards a New EU Democracy Strategy*, Brussels, Carnegie Europe, p. 6.

18. Economist Intelligence Unit (2020) *Democracy Index 2019 – A Year of Democratic Setbacks and Popular Protests*, London, EUI.

19. M. Russell (2018) *Uzbekistan Comes in from the Cold*, Brussels, European Parliament Research Service.

20. A move criticised by Human Rights Watch, 'EU: Postpone Vote on Vietnam Free Trade Agreement', 10 January 2019, at https://www.hrw.org/news/2019/01/10/eu-postpone-vote-vietnam-free-trade-agreement

21. K. Kinzelbach (2015) *The EU Human Rights Dialogues with China: Quiet Diplomacy and Its Limits*, London, Routledge.

22. 'Prague Mayor Condemns China, Unveils Taipei Partnership', *France, 24*, 12 January 2020.

23. 'Declaration by the High Representative on Behalf of the EU on the Announcement by China's National People's Congress Spokesman on Hong Kong', 22 May 2020, posted at https://www.consilium.europa.eu/en/press/press-releases/2020/05/22/declaration-by-the-high-representative-on-behalf-of-the-european-union-on-the-announcement-by-china-s-national-people-s-con-gress-spokesperson-regarding-hong-kong/

24. 'As Australia Clashes with China, the EU Lies Low', *Politico,* 31 May 2020.

25. S. Besch and B. Oppenheim (2019) *Up in Arms: Warring Over the EU's Arms Exports Regime*, London, Centre for European Reform.

26. S. Feldstein (2019) 'How Artificial Intelligence Is Reshaping Repression', *Journal of Democracy*, 30/1, 40–52.

27. J. Borrell, 'The Coronavirus Pandemic and the New World It Is Creating', Blog post, 23 March 2020, at https://eeas.europa.eu/headquarters/headquarters-home-page/76379/corona-virus-pandemic-and-new-world-it-creating_en

28. C. Hackenhesch (2018) *The EU and China in African Authoritarian Regimes*, London, Palgrave Macmillan.

29. European External Action Services (2019) *EU-Kenya Relations*, Brussels, EEAS.

30. 'Can France Ever Leave Africa? Airstrikes in Chad Raise an Old Question', *New York Times*, 14 February 2019.

31. 'La France reprend sa relation bilaterale avec le Burundi', *Deutsche Welle*, 22 July 2019.

32. 'EU Divided Over Conditionality of Aid', *Euractiv*, 27 January 2015.

33. E. dos Santos Oliviera (2019) *An Assessment of the Substance of EU Democracy Promotion in Ethiopia*, Bruges, College of Europe.

34. European Partnership for Democracy (2019) *Louder than Words? Connecting the Dots of European Democracy Support*, Brussels, EPD, p. 62.

35. European Commission (2011) *Increasing the Impact of EU Development Policy: An Agenda for Change*, COM(2011) 637.

36. European Partnership for Democracy (2019) *Louder than Words? Connecting the Dots of European Democracy Support*, Brussels: EPD, p. 118; B. von Ow-Freytag (2018) *Filling the Void: Why the EU Must Step up Support to Russian Civil Society*, Martens Centre for European Studies, pp. 17–18.

37. I. Zamfir (2018) *Democracy Support in EU External Policy*, European Parliament Research Service Briefing, p. 7.

38. S. Lavenex (2016) 'On the Fringes of the European Peace Project: The Neighbourhood Policy's Functionalist Hubris and Political Myopia', *British Journal of Politics and International Relations*, 19/1, pp. 63–76; K. Muhina (2018) 'Administrative Reform Assistance and Democracy Promotion: Exploring the Democratic Substance of the EU's Public Administration Reform Principles for the Neighbourhood Countries', *Democratization*, 25/4, 673–691.

39. A. Mungiu-Pippidi (2019) *Europe's Burden: Promoting Good Governance Across Borders*, Cambridge, Cambridge University Press, pp. 48 and 53.

40. Details of these initiatives are at: www.Protectdefenders.eu

41. Federal Ministry for Economic Cooperation and Development (BMZ) (2017) 'A Marshall Plan with Africa', at: https://www.bmz.de/en/countries_regions/marshall_plan_with_africa/index.html

42. Sida (2018) *Strategy for Sweden's Development Cooperation in the Areas of Human Rights Democracy and the Rule of law 2018–2022*, Stockholm, Swedish Development Agency.

43. Danida (2011) *The Right to a Better Life: Strategy for Denmark's Development Cooperation*, Copenhagen, Danish Development Agency.

44. J. Their (2020) *A Force for Good in the World: Placing Democratic Values at the Heart of the UK's International Strategy*, London, Westminster Foundation for Democracy, p. 15.

45. Department for International Development (2019) *Governance for Growth, Stability and Inclusive Development*, London, DfID.

46. C. Anderson and M. de Tollenaere (2019) *Development Assistance Flows for Governance 2008–2017*, Paris, OECD DAC Network on Governance, p. 15.

47. The list of projects can be found on the trust Fund's website, at: https://ec.europa.eu/trustfundforafrica/thematic/improved-governance-and-conflict-prevention; https://privacyinternational.org/long-read/4291/surveillance-disclosures-show-urgent-need-reforms-eu-aid-programmes

48. For more information, see European Endowment for Democracy (2018) *Annual Report 2018: Supporting People Striving for Democracy*, Brussels, EED.

49. E. Newman and C. Stefan (2020) 'Normative Power Europe? The EU's Embrace of the Responsibility to Protect in a Transitional World Order', *Journal of Common Market Studies*, 58/2.

50. The list of IcSP projects can be accessed at: https://icspmap.eu/

51. N. Koenig (2016) *EU Security Policy and Crisis Management: A Quest for Coherence*, London, Routledge.

52. European Commission (2020) *EU Emergency Trust Fund for Africa: Mali*, Brussels; G. Faleg and C. Palleschi (2020) *African Strategies: European and Global Approaches Towards Sub-Saharan Africa*, Paris, EU Institute for Security Studies, pp. 35–36.

53. G. Faleg and C. Palleschi (2020) *African Strategies: European and Global Approaches Towards Sub-Saharan Africa*, Paris, EU Institute for Security Studies, pp. 35–36.

54. O. Hassan (2019) 'The Evolution of the European Union's Failed Approach to Afghanistan', *European Security*, 29/1, 74–95.

55. A. Juncos and S. Blockmans (2018) 'The EU's Role in Conflict Prevention and Peacebuilding: Four Key Challenges', *Global Affairs*, 4/2; F. Ejdus and A. Juncos (2017) 'Reclaiming the Local in EU Peacebuilding: Effectiveness, Ownership, and Resistance', *Contemporary Security Policy*, 39/1, 4–27.

56. J. Joseph and A. Juncos (2019) 'Resilience as an Emergent European Project? The EU's Place in the Resilience Turn', *Journal of Common Market Studies*, 57/5.

57. E. Fanoulis (2018) 'The EU's Democratization Discourse and Questions of European Identity', *Journal of Common Market Studies*, 56/6.
58. For example, in European Commission (2017) *EU Action Plan on Human Rights and Democracy (2015–2019): Mid-Term Review*, Brussels, Commission.
59. T. Theuns (2019) 'The Legitimacy of Free Trade Agreements as Tools of EU Democracy Promotion', *Cambridge Review of International Affairs*, 32/1.
60. A. Sepos (2018) 'EU Support of Polyarchy? The Case of Morocco', *European Foreign Affairs, Review*, 23/4.
61. European Partnership for Democracy (2019) *Louder than Words? Connecting the Dots of European Democracy Support*, Brussels, EPD, p. 75.

Chapter 10

1. R. del Sarto, H. Malmvig and E. Soler (2019) *Interregnum: The Regional Order in the Middle East and North Africa After 2011*, MENARA project report.
2. S. Heydemann (2018) *Beyond Fragility: Syria and the Challenges of Reconstruction in Fragile States*, Washington, DC, Brookings.
3. Interview with President Sarkozy, *L'Express*, 3 May 2011.
4. Her Majesty's Government (2010) *A Strong Britain in an Age of Uncertainty*, London, HMG.
5. European Commission and the High Representative (2011) *A Partnership for Democracy and Shared Prosperity in the Southern Mediterranean*, JOIN(2011)200; European Commission (2011) *A New Response to a Changing Neighbourhood*, COM(2011) 303.
6. European Commission and the High Representative (2012) *Delivering on a New Neighbourhood Policy*, JOIN(2012) 14.
7. T. Carothers (2012) *Democracy Policy Under Obama: Revitalization or Retreat?*, Washington, DC, Carnegie Endowment for International Peace; K. Archick and D. Mix (2013) *The United States and Europe: Responding to Change in the Middle East and North Africa*, Washington, DC, Congressional Research Service.
8. R. Boserup and F. Tassinari (2012) 'The Return of Arab Politics and Europe's Chance to Engage Anew', *Mediterranean Politics*, 17/1.
9. R. Youngs (2014) *Europe in the New Middle East: Opportunity or Exclusion?*, Oxford, Oxford University Press, p. 93.
10. European Commission (2012) *Joint Staff Working Document, Implementation of the European Neighbourhood Policy in 2011: Statistical Annex*, SWD(2012) 122 final, p. 35.
11. A. Driss (2011) 'Tunisia and the EU' in Bertelsmann Foundation, *The Future of the Mediterranean, Europe in Dialogue*, Gutersloh, Bertelsmann, p. 78.
12. Euro-Mediterranean Network of Economic Studies (2017) *Trade and Investment in the Mediterranean: Country and Regional Perspectives*, EMNES Studies, 2, p. 16.
13. European Commission (2011) *Euro-Med 2030: Long-Term Challenges for the Mediterranean Union*, Brussels, Report of Expert Group, pp. 87 and 99.
14. R. Roccu and B. Voltolini (2018) 'Security and Stability Reframed, Selective Engagement Maintained? The EU in the Mediterranean After the Arab Uprisings', *Mediterranean Politics*, 23/1, 182–195.
15. European Commission (2011) *A Dialogue for Migration, Mobility and Security with the Southern Mediterranean Countries*, Brussels, COM(2011) 292; European Commission (2011) *Communication on Migration*, COM(2011) 248.

16. G. Tsourapas (2019) 'The Syrian Refugee Crisis and Foreign Policy Decision-Making in Jordan, Lebanon, and Turkey', *Journal of Global Security Studies*, 4/4.

17. S. Lehne and F. Siccardi (2020) *Where in the World Is the EU Now?*, Brussels, Carnegie Europe.

18. A. Dandashly (2018) 'EU Democracy Promotion and the Dominance of the Security–Stability Nexus', *Mediterranean Politics*, 23/1.

19. E. Cohen-Hadria (ed.) (2018) *The EU-Tunisia Privileged Partnership*, Euromesco Joint Policy Study.

20. C. Teevan (2019) 'The EU, Morocco, and the Stability Myth', *Sada Journal*, Carnegie Endowment for International Peace; A. Sepos (2018) 'EU Support of Polyarchy? The Case of Morocco', *European Foreign Affairs Review*, 23/4; 'El Supremo decidira la legalidad de 30 milliones entregados a Marruecos para frenar la inmigracion irregular', *El Pais*, 20 July 2020.

21. 'Pedro Sánchez viajará por primera vez a Argelia en abril', *El Pais*, 4 March 2020.

22. 'France's Macron Returns to Beirut, Urges Political Reform After New Lebanon PM Named', *Deutsche Welle*, 1 September 2020; 'Macron on Lebanon: It's a Risky Bet I Am Making', *Politico*, 2 September 2020.

23. European Commission (2017) *Report on the Implementation of the ENP Policy Review*, JOIN(2017) 18.

24. V. Durac (2018) 'Counterterrorism and Democracy: EU Policy in the Middle East and North Africa After the Uprisings', *Mediterranean Politics*, 23/1, pp. 103–121.

25. C. Portela (2012) *The EU's Sanctions Against Syria: Conflict Management by Other Means*, Brussels, Egmont Institute.

26. European Union (2015) *Strategic Orientation Document for the EU Regional Trust Fund in Response to the Syrian Crisis*, Brussels; European Union (2016) *EU Regional Trust Fund in Response to the Syrian Crisis: Factsheet*, Brussels, European Union, p. 4; N. Koenig (2017) 'Libya and Syria: Inserting the European Neighbourhood Policy in the European Union's Crisis Response Cycle', *European Foreign Affairs Review*, 22/1, pp. 19–38; European Commission and the High Representative (2011) *Elements for an EU Strategy for Syria*, JOIN(2017)11.

27. A list of UK aid contracts for Syria is at: https://www.contractsfinder.service.gov.uk/Notice/8801cf18-e1cb-4e80-89b6-8bed2deb33a7

28. F. Brown (2018) *Dilemmas of Stabilization Assistance: The Case of Syria*, Washington, DC, Carnegie Endowment for International Peace.

29. Her remarks to the conference are at: https://eeas.europa.eu/headquarters/headquarters-homepage/59564/remarks-hrvp-mogherini-closing-session-days-dialogue-third-brussels-conference-supporting_en

30. P. Costello (2020) 'Values and Interests in Post-Lisbon European Union Foreign Policy' in M. Westlake (ed.) *The European Union's New Foreign Policy*, London, Macmillan.

31. Chatham House Libya Working Group (2012) *Libya: Turning the Page*, London, Chatham House.

32. S. Ekiz (2018) 'EU Strategy in Libya: Discourses vs Actions', *European Foreign Affairs Review*, 23/3, 405–426; 'EU's Policy of Helping Libya Intercept Migrants Is Inhuman, Says UN', *The Guardian*, 14 November 2017.

33. House of Commons Foreign Affairs Select Committee (2016) *Libya: Examination of Intervention and Collapse and the UK's Future Policy Options*, London, House of Commons.

34. House of Commons Foreign Affairs Select Committee (2016) *Libya: Examination of Intervention and Collapse and the UK's Future Policy Options*, London, House of Commons.

35. 'Trafficked and Abused: Libya's Migrants Caught in the Business of War', *Financial Times*, 3 May 2020.
36. F. Wehrey and W. Lacher (2018) 'The Wrong Way to Fix Libya', *Foreign Affairs*, June; International Crisis Group (2016) *The Libyan Political Agreement: Time for a Reset*, Brussels, ICG.
37. 'Declaration by the High Representative on Behalf of the EU on the Situation in Libya', 11 April 2019, at: https://www.consilium.europa.eu/en/press/press-releases/2019/04/11/declaration-by-the-high-representative-federica-mogher-ini-on-behalf-of-the-eu-on-the-situation-in-libya/
38. 'France Will Not Tolerate Turkey's Role in Libya', *Reuters*, 22 June 2020.
39. 'EU Draws up Options for Boots on the Ground in Libya', *Politico*, 1 October 2020.
40. See contributions in A. Dessi and V. Ntousas (eds) (2019) *Europe and Iran in a Fast-Changing Middle East*, Rome, IAI.
41. R. Alcaro (2018) *Between a Rock and a Hard Place: Europe's Uncertain Role in Middle Eastern Geopolitics*, Rome, IAI.
42. B. Oppenheim (2019) *You Never Listen to Me: The European-Saudi Relationship After Kashoggi*, London, Centre for European Reform.
43. C. Adebahr (2020) *Europe Needs a Regional Strategy on Iran*, Brussels, Carnegie Europe.
44. 'MEPP: Statement by the High Representative on the US Initiative', 4 February 2020, at: https://eeas.europa.eu/headquarters/headquartershomepage_en/73960/MEPP:%20Statement%20by%20the%20High%20Representative/Vice-President%20Josep%20Borrell%20on%20the%20US%20initiative
45. B. Oppenheim, 'Annexation Will Plunger Israel's Relations with the EU into Existential Crisis', *Haaretz*, 11 June 2020.
46. K. Kausch (2018) 'Rethinking Europe's Comparative Advantage in the Mediterranean' in I.E. Med, *Mediterranean Yearbook 2018*, Barcelona, IEMed.
47. F. Mogerhini, 'The Middle East and the EU: New Realities, New Policies', speech to Menara conference, Brussels 6 March 2019, at https://eeas.europa.eu/headquar-ters/headquarters-homepage/59180/speech-high-representativevice-president-federica-mogherini-final-conference-menara-and_en
48. Interview with ECFR, January 2019, https://www.ecfr.eu/article/commentary_shaping_europes_present_and_future
49. J. Ojendal, H. Leonardsson and M. Lundqvist (2017) *Local Peace-Building – Challenges and Opportunities*, Stockholm, EBA; O. Richmond (2016) *Peace Formation and Political Order in Conflict Affected Societies*, Oxford, Oxford University Press; B. Jones, M. Elgin-Crossart and J. Esberg (2012) *Pathways Out of Fragility: The Case for A Research Agenda on Inclusive Political Settlements in Fragile States*, New York, Center on International Cooperation.
50. R. Alcaro (2018) *Europe and Iran's Nuclear Crisis: Lead Groups and EU Foreign Policy-Making*, London, Palgrave Macmillan.
51. S. Colombo, M. Otte, E. Soler and N. Tocci (2019) *The Art of the (Im)possible: Sowing the Seeds for the EU's Constructive Engagement in the Middle East and North Africa*, Final report Menara project, p. 12.

Chapter 11

1. B. Lo (2015) *Russia and the New World Disorder*, London, Chatham House; A. Monaghan (2013) 'Putin's Russia: Shaping a Grand Strategy?', *International Affairs*, 89/5; R. Allison (2014) 'Russian "Deniable" Intervention in Ukraine: How and Why Russia Broke the Rules', *International Affairs*, 90/6.
2. S. Fischer (2014) *Escalation in Ukraine*, Berlin, SWP; W. Russell Mead (2014) 'The Return of Geopolitics', *Foreign Affairs*, May/June.
3. D. Trenin (2014) *The Ukraine Crisis and the Resumption of Great Power Rivalry*, Moscow, Carnegie Russia.
4. F. Heisbourg (2015) 'Preserving Post-Cold War Europe', *Survival*, 57/1, p. 34.
5. A. Moshes (2015) *The War and Reforms in Ukraine, Can It Cope with Both?*, Finnish Institute for International Affairs.
6. L. Simon (2013) 'The Spider in Europe's Web? French Grand Strategy from Iraq to Libya', *Geopolitics*, 18/2.
7. K. Raik (2016) 'Liberalism and Geopolitics in EU–Russia Relations: Rereading the Baltic Factor', *European Security*, 25/2.
8. T. Forsberg (2016) 'From Ostpolitik to Frostpolitik? Merkel, Putin and German Foreign Policy Towards Russia', *International Affairs*, 92/1.
9. L. Kulesa (ed.) (2014) *Is a New Cold War Inevitable? Central European Views on Rebuilding Trust in the Euro-Atlantic Region*, Warsaw, PISM.
10. EU trade statistics are at: https://ec.europa.eu/trade/policy/countries-and-regions/countries/russia/
11. T. Romanova (2016) 'Sanctions and the Future of EU–Russian Economic Relations', *Europe-Asia Studies*, 68/4.
12. A. Getmanchuk (2015) *Ukraine-NATO: A Hidden Integration or Undeclared Neutrality?*, Kiev, Institute for World Policy.
13. M. Emerson (2014) *Russia's Economic Interests and the EU's DCFTA with Ukraine*, Brussels, Centre for European Policy Studies.
14. W. Jakobik (2015) 'A Return to Business as Usual', *New Eastern Europe*, 29 October.
15. Organisation for Security and Cooperation in Europe (2015) *Back to Diplomacy: Final Report and Recommendations of the Panel of Eminent Persons on European Security as a Common Project*, Vienna.
16. P. Remler (2019) *Russia and Cooperative Security in Europe: Times Change, Tactics Remain*, Washington, DC, Carnegie Endowment for International Peace.
17. 'Macron's Grand Vision for a Modern French Enlightenment', *The Times*, 23 August 2019.
18. 'France's Macron Makes Russia a Top Priority', *Euractiv*, 28 August 2019.
19. *The Economist*, 7 November 2019, See full transcript of interview with President Macron.
20. A. Wilson (2014) *Ukraine Crisis: What It Means for the West*, Yale University Press.
21. L. Linkevcius, 'Security Before Politics in Eastern Ukraine', *Wall Street Journal*, 27 January 2016.
22. 'The West Must Not Abandon Crimea and Ukraine to Russian Aggression', *The Guardian*, 28 February 2019.
23. P. Remler (2019) *Russia and Cooperative Security in Europe: Times Change, Tactics Remain*, Washington, DC, Carnegie Endowment for International Peace.
24. See survey carried out in O. Burlyuk (2014) *The Role of Culture in Reconciliation in the Ukraine Crisis*, Brussels, More Europe Policy Paper.

25. A. Getmanchuk and S. Solodkyy (2016) *Ukraine–Germany: How to Turn Situational Partnership into Priority One*, Kiev, Institute for World Policy, p. 9.

26. G. Sasse (2013) 'Linkages and the Promotion of Democracy: The EU's Eastern Neighbourhood', *Democratization*, 20/4; N. Babayan (2014) *Democratic Transformation and Obstruction: The European Union, United States and Russia in the South Caucasus*, London, Routledge.

27. E. Korosteleva (2013) 'Evaluating the Role of Partnership in the European Neighbourhood Policy: The Eastern Neighbourhood', *Eastern Journal of European Studies*, 4/2; E. Korosteleva (2012) *The European Union and Its Eastern Neighbours: Towards a More Ambitious Partnership?*, London, Routledge.

28. J. Langbein (2014) 'European Union Governance Towards the Eastern Neighbourhood: Transcending or Redrawing Europe's East–West Divide?', *Journal of Common Market Studies*, 52/1.

29. K. Wolczuk (2014) *Ukraine and the EU: Turning the Association Agreement into a Success Story*, Brussels, European Policy Centre.

30. T. Forsberg and H. Haukkala (2016) 'Could It Have Been Different? The Evolution of the EU-Russian Conflict and Its Alternatives' in C. Nitoiu (ed.) *Avoiding a New 'Cold War': The Future of EU-Russia Relations in the Context of the Ukraine Crisis*, London, LSE Ideas Report, p. 12.

31. Leaked extracts of the paper were posted by the *Financial Times* at http://blogs.ft.com/brusselsblog/files/2014/02/20-points-on-Eastern-Partnership.pdf

32. European Commission and the High Representative (2014) *Neighbourhood at the Crossroads: Implementation of the European Neighbourhood Policy in 2013*, JOIN(2014) 12. Quotes from pp. 2 and 17.

33. K. Shyrokykh and D. Rimkute (2019) 'EU Rules Beyond Its Borders: The Policy-Specific Effects of Transgovernmental Networks and EU Agencies in the European Neighbourhood', *Journal of Common Market Studies*, 57/4.

34. European Commission (2017) *Eastern Partnership – 20 Deliverables for 2020: Focusing on Key Priorities and Tangible Results*, Brussels, Commission Joint Staff Working Document.

35. P. Havlicek, 'Eastern Partnership: In a Dismal State or a New Beginning?', *Euractiv*, 6 December 2017.

36. European Commission and the High Representative (2020) *Eastern Partnership Policy Beyond 2020*, Join(2020)7, p. 4.

37. High level think-tank online event on the future of the Eastern Partnership, organised by German Council on Foreign Relations and European Commission, 19 June 2020.

38. E. Kaca (2014) *A New Pact for Ukraine: Making EU Aid Work*, Warsaw, Polish Institute for International Affairs, 2014.

39. O. Burlyuk (2014) 'An Ambitious Failure: Conceptualising the EU Approach to Rule of Law Promotion (in Ukraine)', *Hague Journal on the Rule of Law*, 6/1; O. Burlyuk (2014) 'A Thorny Path to the Spotlight: The Rule of Law Component in EU External Policies and EU–Ukraine Relations', *European Journal of Law Reform*, 1, pp. 26–46.

40. European Commission and the High Representative (2014) *Neighbourhood at the Crossroads: Implementation of the European Neighbourhood Policy in 2013*, JOIN(2014) 12, p. 3.

41. K. Parandii (2019) *The EU's Anti-corruption Conditionalities in Ukraine*, Bruges, College of Europe.

42. M. Minakov (2020) *Democratisation and Europeanisation in 21st Century Ukraine*, Brussels, CEPS.

43. G. Harpaz (2017) 'The Causes of the EU's Ineffectual Contribution to Resolution of the Abkhazian and South Ossetian Conflicts', *European Foreign Affairs Review*, 22/2.
44. S. Secrieru and S. Saari (eds) (2019) *The Eastern Partnership a Decade On: Looking Back, Thinking Ahead*, Paris, EUISS.
45. 'Borrell: Lukashenko es como Maduro. No le reconocemos pero hay que tratarle', *El Pais*, 23 August 2020.
46. One prominent example being J. Mearsheimer (2014) 'Why the Ukraine Crisis Is the West's Fault: The Liberal Delusions That Provoked Putin', *Foreign Affairs*, 93/5.
47. S. Kudelia (2018) 'Ukraine's Emerging Security State', *Current History*, 117 (801).
48. An extended discussion of this assessment is in R. Youngs (2017) *Europe's Eastern Crisis: The Geopolitics of Asymmetry*, Cambridge, Cambridge University Press.

Chapter 12

1. L. van Middelaar (2019) *Alarums and Excursions: Improvising Politics on the European Stage*, London, Agenda.
2. A. Giddens (2014) *Turbulent and Mighty Continent: What Future for Europe?*, Cambridge, Polity Press, p. 15 and ch 4.
3. For a theoretical discussion of inward- and outward-facing legitimacy, see O. Costa (2019) 'The Politicization of EU External Relations', *Journal of European Public Policy*, 26/5.
4. C. Kinnvall (2016) 'The Postcolonial Has Moved into Europe: Bordering, Security and Ethno-Cultural Belonging', *Journal of Common Market Studies*, 54/1.
5. S. Klose (2018) 'Theorizing the EU's Actorness: Towards an Interactionist Role Theory Framework', *Journal of Common Market Studies*, 56/5.

Bibliography

Adebahr C. (2020) *Europe Needs a Regional Strategy on Iran*, Brussels, Carnegie Europe

Aggestam L. and F. Bicchi (2019) 'New Directions in EU Foreign Policy Governance: Cross-Loading, Leadership and Informal Groupings', *Journal of Common Market Studies*, 57/3, 515–532

Aggestam L. and A. Hyde-Price (2019a) 'Double Trouble: Trump, Transatlantic Relations and European Strategic Autonomy', *Journal of Common Market Studies Annual Review*, 57, 114–127

Aggestam L. and A. Hyde-Price (2019b) 'Learning to Lead? Germany and the Leadership Paradox in EU Foreign Policy', *German Politics*, 29/1, 8–24

Alcaro R. (2018a) *Between a Rock and a Hard Place: Europe's Uncertain Role in Middle Eastern Geopolitics*, Rome, IAI

Alcaro R. (2018b) *Europe and Iran's Nuclear Crisis: Lead Groups and EU Foreign Policy-Making*, London, Palgrave Macmillan

Allen D. and M. Smith (1990) 'Western Europe's Presence in the Contemporary International Area', *Review of International Studies*, 16/1, 19–37

Allison R. (2014) 'Russian "Deniable" Intervention in Ukraine: How and Why Russia Broke the Rules', *International Affairs*, 90/6, 1255–1297

Andersen L. (2019) 'Curb Your Enthusiasm: Middle Power Liberal Internationalism and the Future of the United Nations', *International Journal*, 74/1, 47–64

Anderson C. and M. de Tollenaere (2019) *Development Assistance Flows for Governance 2008–2017*, Paris, OECD DAC Network on Governance

Andreatta F. (2005) 'Theory and the EU's International Relations', in C. Hill and M. Smith (eds) *International Relations and the European Union*, Oxford, Oxford University Press

Archick K. and D. Mix (2013) *The United States and Europe: Responding to Change in the Middle East and North Africa*, Washington, DC, Congressional Research Service

Asenius M. (2020) 'Trade in Turbulent Times', in M. Westlake (ed) *The European Union's New Foreign Policy*, London, Macmillan

Aydin-Düzgit S. (2014) 'Critical Discourse Analysis in Analysing European Union Foreign Policy: Prospects and Challenges', *Cooperation and Conflict*, 49/3, 354–367

Ayrault J.-M. and F.-W. Steinmeier (2016) 'A Strong Europe in a World of Uncertainties', *France Diplomatie* [website], 28 June 2016

Babayan N. (2014) *Democratic Transformation and Obstruction: The European Union, United States and Russia in the South Caucasus*, London, Routledge

Bagger T. (2019) 'Germany's Search for a New Diplomatic Map', *Financial Times*, 23 April 2019

Balfour R. (ed) (2016) *Europe's Troublemakers: The Populist Challenge to Foreign Policy*, Brussels, European Policy Centre

Barbé E. and P. Morillas (2019) 'The EU Global Strategy: The Dynamics of a More Politicized and Politically Integrated Foreign Policy', *Cambridge Review of International Affairs*, 32/6, 753–770

Barbé E., O. Costa and R. Kissack (eds) (2016) *EU Policy Responses to Shifting Multilateral System*, London, Palgrave Macmillan

Barbone A. and R. Bendini (2015) *Protectionism in the G20*, European Parliament Directorate-General for External Policies

Barma N., E. Ratner and S. Weber (2013) 'The Mythical Liberal Order', *National Interest*, March–April

Barrie D., B. Barry, H. Boyd, M. Chagnaud, N. Childs, B. Giegerich, C. Mölling and T. Schütz (2018) *Protecting Europe: Meeting the EU's Military Level of Ambition in the Context of Brexit*, London, IISS

Beardsworth R. (2011) *Cosmopolitanism and International Relations Theory*, Cambridge, Polity Press

Bechev D. (2017) *Rival Power: Russia in South-East Europe*, Yale, Yale University Press

Benner T. (2019) 'What's Left of Multilateralism?', *Internationale Politik*, November–December

Bergamaschi L. and N. Sartori (2018) *The Geopolitics of Climate: Transatlantic Dialogue*, Rome, IAI

Bergamaschi L., N. Mabey, C. Born and A. White (2019) *Managing Climate Risk for a Safer Future: A New Resilience Agenda for Europe*, London, E3G

Bertelsmann Foundation (2019) *EU Views*, Gütersloh, Bertelsmann

Besch S. and B. Oppenheim (2019) *Up in Arms: Warring Over the EU's Arms Exports Regime*, London, Centre for European Reform

Bickerton C., D. Hodson and U. Puetter (2015) 'The New Intergovernmentalism: European Integration in the Post-Maastricht Era', *Journal of Common Market Studies*, 53/4, 703–722

Billon-Galland A., T. Raines and R. Whitman (2020) *The Future of the E3: Post-Brexit Cooperation Between the UK, France and Germany*, London, Chatham House

Birchfield V. (2013) 'A Normative Power Europe Framework of Transnational Policy Formation', *Journal of European Public Policy*, 20/6, 907–922

Birchfield V. and J. Duffield (eds) (2011) *Toward a Common European Union Energy Policy*, London, Palgrave Macmillan

Biscop S. (2019a) *Fighting for Europe: European Strategic Autonomy and the Use of Force*, Brussels, Egmont Institute

Biscop S. (2019b) 'How to Make Peace Last? European Strategy and the Future of the World Order', Brussels, Egmont Security Policy Brief 12

Biscop S. and R. Whitman (eds) (2013) *The Handbook of European Security*, London, Routledge

Black J. et al (2017) *Defence and Security After Brexit*, Cambridge, RAND Europe

Borrell J. (2019) 'A Stronger European Union in a Better, Greener and Safer World – Key Principles That Will Be My Guiding Mandate', 1 December 2019, Online Blog post, at https://eeas.europa.eu/headquarters/headquarters-homepage/71265/stronger-european-union-within-better-greener-and-safer-world-key-principles-will-be-guiding_en

Borrell J. (2020a) 'In Rougher Seas, the EU's Own Interests and Values Should Be Our Own Compass', Blog post, 14 June 2020, posted at https://eeas.europa.eu/headquarters/headquarters-homepage/80854/rougher-seas-eu%E2%80%99s-own-interests-and-values-should-be-our-compass_en

Borrell J. (2020b) 'The Coronavirus Pandemic and the New World It Is Creating', 23 March 2020, Online Blog Posting, at https://eeas.europa.eu/headquarters/headquarters-homepage/76379/corona-virus-pandemic-and-new-world-it-creating_en

Borrell J. (2020c) 'Embracing Europe's Power', *Project Syndicate*, 8 February 2020

Boserup R. and F. Tassinari (2012) 'The Return of Arab Politics and Europe's Chance to Engage Anew', *Mediterranean Politics*, 17/1, 97–103

Bouchard D., C. Connan, J.-C. Cousseran and B. Miyet (2018) 'Le debate sur la politique etrangere francaise: l'avenir d'un oxymora', *Boulevard Exterieur*, January

BP (2018) *BP Energy Outlook 2018*

Bradford A. (2020) *The Brussels Effect*, New York, Oxford University Press

Brattberg E. and B. Judah (2020) 'Forget the G7, Build the D10', *Foreign Policy*, June

Bremmer I. (2012) *Every Nation for Itself: Winners and Losers in a G-Zero World*, London, Portfolio Penguin

Bretherton C. and J. Vogler (2006) *The European Union as a Global Actor*, London, Routledge

Brown F. (2018) *Dilemmas of Stabilization Assistance: The Case of Syria*, Washington, DC, Carnegie Endowment for International Peace

Bulmer S. and W. Paterson (2018) *Germany and the European Union: Europe's Reluctant Hegemon*, London, Red Globe Press

Burlyuk O. (2014a) 'A Thorny Path to the Spotlight: The Rule of Law Component in EU External Policies and EU-Ukraine Relations', *European Journal of Law Reform*, 1, 26–46

Burlyuk O. (2014b) 'An Ambitious Failure: Conceptualising the EU Approach to Rule of Law Promotion (in Ukraine)', *Hague Journal on the Rule of Law*, 6/1, 26–46

Burlyuk O. (2014c) *The Role of Culture in Reconciliation in the Ukraine Crisis*, Brussels, More Europe Policy Paper

Buzan B. and G. Lawson (2015) *The Global Transformation: History, Modernity and the Making of International Relations*, Cambridge, Cambridge University Press

Cameron F. (2012) *An Introduction to European Foreign Policy*, London, Routledge

Cañete M. Arias (2018) *Speech at the 4th EU Energy Summit: International Geopolitical Uncertainties: Brakes or Accelerators for the EU Energy Transition?*, Brussels, European Commission Press Corner, 12 April

Cañete M. Arias 'Europe's New Energy Dependency', *Politico*, 6 June 2019

Carothers T. (2012) *Democracy Policy Under Obama: Revitalization or Retreat?*, Washington, DC, Carnegie Endowment for International Peace

Carta C. and J.-F. Morin (eds) (2016) *EU Foreign Policy Through the Lens of Discourse Analysis: Making Sense of Diversity*, Farnham, Ashgate

Carvallero M. and K. Kornetis (eds) (2019) *Rethinking Democratisation in Spain, Greece and Portugal*, London, Palgrave Macmillan

Castillejo C. (2016) *The European Union Trust Fund for Africa: A Glimpse of the Future for EU Development Cooperation*, Bonn, German Development Institute

Cederman L. (ed) (2001) *Constructing Europe's Identity: The External Dimension*, Boulder, Lynne Rienner

Centre for Climate and Security (2020) *A Security Threat Assessment of Global Climate Change*, Washington, DC, Centre for Climate and Security

Centre for Economic Policy Research (2012) *Débâcle: The 11th GTA Report on Protectionism*, London, CEPR

Centre for European Policy Studies (2018) *Rethinking the EU's Cyber Defence Capabilities*, Report of CEPS Task Force, Brussels

Cerny P. (2010) *Rethinking World Politics: A Theory of Transnational Neo-pluralism*, Oxford, Oxford University Press

Chaban N. and M. Holland (eds) (2019) *Shaping the EU Global Strategy: Partners and Perceptions*, London, Palgrave Macmillan

Chatham House Libya Working Group (2012) *Libya: Turning the Page*, London, Chatham House

Christiansen T. and S. Tsui (2017) 'The Value and the Limitations of Comprehensive Multilateralism: An EU Perspective on the Asia-Europe Meeting', *European Foreign Affairs Review*, 22/2, 233–252

Christiansen T., E. Kirchner and U. Wissenbach (2019) *The European Union and China*, London, Red Globe Press

Christou G. (2015) *Cybersecurity in the European Union: Resilience and Adaptability in Governance*, London, Palgrave Macmillan

Church C. and A. Crawford (2018) *Green Conflict Minerals*, Winnipeg, International Institute for Sustainable Development

Cianciara A. (2017) 'Stability, Security, Democracy: Explaining Shifts in the Narrative of the European Neighbourhood Policy', *Journal of European Integration*, 39/1, 49–62

Cladi L. and A. Locatelli (2013) 'Worth a Shot: On the Explanatory Power of Bandwagoning in Transatlantic Relations', *Contemporary Security Policy*, 34/2, 374–381

Clift B. and C. Woll (2012) 'Economic Patriotism: Reinventing Control Over Open Markets', *Journal of European Public Policy*, 19/3, 307–323

Climate Diplomacy Report (2020) *The Geopolitics of Decarbonisation: Reshaping European Foreign Relations*, Berlin, Adelphi

Cohen-Hadria E. (ed) (2018) *The EU–Tunisia Privileged Partnership*, Euromesco Joint Policy Study

Colombo S., M. Otte, E. Soler and N. Tocci (2019) *The Art of the (Im)possible: Sowing the Seeds for the EU's Constructive Engagement in the Middle East and North Africa*, Final report Menara Project

Conceição-Heldt E. and S. Meunier (2014) 'Speaking with a Single Voice: Internal Cohesiveness and External Effectiveness of the EU in Global Governance', *Journal of European Public Policy*, 21/7, 961–979

Concord (2017) *EU Emergency Trust Fund for Africa: Partnership or Conditionality?*, Brussels, Concord

Concord (2019) *Aidwatch 2019*, Brussels, Concord

Cooley L. (2019) *The European Union's Approach to Conflict Resolution: Transformation or Regulation in the Western Balkans?*, London, Routledge

Cooper R. (2003) *The Breaking of Nations: Order and Chaos in the 21st Century*, London, Atlantic Books

Costa O. (2018) 'The Politicization of EU External Relations', *Journal of European Public Policy*, 26/5, 790–802

Costa O. (2019) 'The Politicization of EU External Relations', *Journal of European Public Policy*, 26/5, 790–802

Cottey A. (2012) *Security in 21st Century Europe*, London, Red Globe Press

Cottey A. (2019) 'Europe and China's Sea Disputes: Between Normative Politics, Power Balancing and Acquiescence', *European Security*, 28/4, 473–492

Cottey A. (2020) 'A Strategic Europe', *Journal of Common Market Studies*, 58/2, 276–229

Council of the European Union (2010) *European Council Conclusions*: http://www.con-silium.europa.eu/ueDocs/cms_Data/docs/pressData/en/ec/113591

Council of the European Union (2011) *Council Conclusions on Climate Diplomacy*, 3106/11

Council of the European Union (2018) *Foreign Affairs Council Conclusions on Climate Diplomacy*, 6125/18

Council of the European Union (2019a) *Council Conclusions on Climate Diplomacy*, 6153/19

Council of the European Union (2019b) *Council Conclusions on Democracy*, 12836/19

Damro C. (2015) 'Market Power Europe: Exploring a Dynamic Conceptual Framework', *Journal of European Public Policy*, 22/9, 1336–1354

Dandashly A. (2018) 'EU Democracy Promotion and the Dominance of the Security–Stability Nexus', *Mediterranean Politics*, 23/1, 62–82

Danida (2011) *The Right to a Better Life: Strategy for Denmark's Development Cooperation*, Copenhagen, Danish Development Agency

del Sarto R., H. Malmvig and E. Soler (2019) *Interregnum: The Regional Order in the Middle East and North Africa after 2011*, MENARA Project Report

Democratic Progress Institute (2016) *The Role of European Union Accession in Democratisation Processes*, London, Democratic Progress Institute

Department for International Development (2019) *Governance for Growth, Stability and Inclusive Development*, London, DfID

Depledge D. and T. Feakin (2012) 'Climate Change and International Institutions: Implications for Security', *Climate Policy*, 12/1, 73–84

Dessi A. and V. Ntousas (eds) (2019) *Europe and Iran in a Fast-Changing Middle East*, Rome, IAI

DG Trade (2019) *Statistical Guide*, July 2019

Di Maio G. (2019) *The Broken Compass of Italian Foreign Policy*, Washington, DC, Brookings Institute

Dixon H. (2011) 'Can Europe's Divided House Stand?', *Foreign Affairs*, November–December

Dorrie P. (2019) 'Europe Has Spent Years Trying to Prevent "Chaos" in the Sahel. It Failed', *World Politics Review*, 25 June 2019

Dorussen H., E. Kirchner and T. Christiansen (2018) 'Security Cooperation in EU–China Relations: Towards Convergence?', *European Foreign Affairs Review*, 23/3, 287–304

dos Santos Oliviera E. (2019) *An Assessment of the Substance of EU Democracy Promotion in Ethiopia*, Bruges, College of Europe

Driss A. (2011) 'Tunisia and the EU', in Bertelsmann Foundation (ed) *The Future of the Mediterranean, Europe in Dialogue*, Gutersloh, Bertelsmann

Droge S. (2018) 'Climate and Security Revisited', Berlin, SWP Comment

Drozdiak W. (2020) *The Last President of Europe*, New York, Public Affairs

Ducrotté F. (2012) 'The Impact of Climate Change on International Security: Prospects for an Environmental Dimension in CSDP Missions', *European Security Review*, November

Duke S. (2018) 'The Enigmatic Role of Defence in the EU: From EDC to EDU?', *European Foreign Affairs Review*, 23/1, 63–80

Dunne T. and T. Flockhart (eds) (2013) *Liberal World Orders*, Oxford, Oxford University Press

Dür A. and M. Elsig (2011) 'Principals, Agents, and the European Union's Foreign Economic Policies', *Journal of European Public Policy*, 18/3: 323–338

Durac V. (2018) 'Counterterrorism and Democracy: EU Policy in the Middle East and North Africa After the Uprisings', *Mediterranean Politics*, 23/1, 103–121

Dzankic J., S. Keil and M. Kmezic (eds) (2018) *The Europeanisation of the Western Balkans: A Failure of EU Conditionality?*, London, Routledge

Economides S. (2019) 'The EU, the Grand Strategy and the Challenge of Rising and Revisionist Powers', in S. Economides and J. Sperling (eds) *EU Security Strategies: Expanding the EU System of Security Governance*, London, Routledge

Economides S. (2020) *From Fatigue to Resistance: EU Enlargement and the West Balkans*, Dahrendorf Forum Paper 17

Economist Intelligence Unit (2019) *Democracy Index 2018 – Me Too?*, London, EIU

Economist Intelligence Unit (2020) *Democracy Index 2019 – A Year of Democratic Setbacks and Popular Protests*, London, EUI

Ejdus F. and A. Juncos (2017) 'Reclaiming the Local in EU Peacebuilding: Effectiveness, Ownership, and Resistance', *Contemporary Security Policy*, 39/1, 4–27

Ekiz S. (2018) 'EU Strategy in Libya: Discourses vs Actions', *European Foreign Affairs Review*, 23/3, 405–426

Elman C. and M. Jensen (2012) 'Realisms', in P. Williams (ed) *Security Studies: An Introduction*, 2nd edition, London, Routledge

Emmerson M. (2014) *Russia's Economic Interests and the EU's DCFTA with Ukraine*, Brussels, Centre for European Policy Studies

Erixson F. and R. Sally (2010) *Trade, Globalisation and Emerging Protectionism Since the Crisis*, Brussels, ECIPE

Escribano G. (2019) 'The Geopolitics of Renewable and Electricity Cooperation Between Morocco and Spain', *Mediterranean Politics*, 24/5, 674–681

EU Institute for Security Studies (2012) *Citizens in an Interconnected and Polycentric World*, Paris, EUISS

Euro-Mediterranean Network of Economic Studies (2017) *Trade and Investment in the Mediterranean: Country and Regional Perspectives*, EMNES Studies, 2

European Commission (2006) *Global Europe, Competing in the World*, Brussels, European Commission

European Commission (2011a) *A Dialogue for Migration, Mobility and Security with the Southern Mediterranean Countries*, Brussels, COM(2011) 292

European Commission (2011b) *Communication on Migration*, COM(2011) 248

European Commission (2011c) *A New Response to a Changing Neighbourhood*, COM(2011) 303

European Commission (2011d) *Euro-Med 2030: Long-Term Challenges for the Mediterranean Union*, Brussels, Report of Expert Group

European Commission (2011e) *Increasing the Impact of EU Development Policy: An Agenda for Change*, COM(2011) 637

European Commission (2012a) *A Stronger European Industry for Growth and Economic Recovery*, Brussels, COM 582

European Commission (2012b) *Joint Staff Working Document, Implementation of the European Neighbourhood Policy in 2011: Statistical Annex*, SWD(2012) 122 final

European Commission (2013) *Guidelines for EU Support to Civil Society Enlargement Countries 2014–2020*, Brussels, European Commission

European Commission (2014) *Instrument for Pre-accession Indicative Strategy*, Paper for Turkey 2014–2020

European Commission (2015a) *The European Agenda on Security*, COM (2015) 185 final

European Commission (2015b) *Trade for All: Towards a More Responsible Trade and Investment Policy*, Brussels, European Commission

European Commission (2016) *First Progress Report on the Partnership Framework with Third Countries Under the European Agenda on Migration*, COM(2016) 700, Brussels, European Commission

European Commission (2017a) *Eastern Partnership – 20 Deliverables for 2020: Focusing on Key Priorities and Tangible Results*, Brussels, Commission Joint Staff Working Document

European Commission (2017b) *EU Action Plan on Human Rights and Democracy (2015–2019): Mid-Term Review*, Brussels, Commission

European Commission (2017c) *Report on the Implementation of the ENP Policy Review*, JOIN(2017)18

European Commission (2018) *EU Emergency Trust Fund for Africa Annual Report 2018*, Brussels, European Commission

European Commission (2018a) *A Clean Planet for All: A European Strategic Long-Term Vision for a Prosperous, Modern, Competitive and Climate Neutral Economy*, COM(2018) 773

European Commission (2018b) *A Credible Enlargement Perspective for and Enhanced EU Engagement with the Western Balkans*, COM(2018) 65

European Commission (2018c) *Elements for an EU Strategy on India*, JOIN(2018) 28

European Commission (2018d) *WTO Modernization – Concept Paper*, Brussels, European Commission

European Commission (2019a) *Client and supplier countries of the EU27 in merchandise trade*, Brussels, DG Trade

European Commission (2019a) *The EU and Central Asia: New Opportunities for a Stronger Partnership*, JOIN(2019)9, Brussels, p. 11

European Commission (2019b) *The European Green Deal*, COM(2019) 640

European Commission (2020a) *Communication on the EU Security Union Strategy*, Com(2020) 605 final

European Commission (2020b) *EU Emergency Trust Fund for Africa: Mali*, Brussels, European Commission

European Commission (2020c) *White Paper on Levelling the Playing Field as Regards Foreign Subsidies*, COM(2020) 253

European Commission (2020d) *Shaping Europe's Digital Future*, COM(2020) 67

European Commission (2020e) *White Paper on Artificial Intelligence: A European Approach to Excellence and Trust*, COM(2020) 65

European Commission (2020f) *Communication on Enlargement Policy*, COM(2020) 660

European Commission and High Representative (2018) *Connecting Europe and Asia: Building Blocks for an EU Strategy*, JOIN(2018)31, Brussels

European Commission and High Representative (2019) *EU-China: A Strategic Outlook*, Brussels, European Commission and High Representative

European Commission and High Representative (2020a) *Towards a Comprehensive Strategy with Africa*, JOIN(2020)4

European Commission and High Representative (2020b) *Tackling Covid-19 Disinformation: Getting the Facts Right*, Join(2020)8

European Commission and High Representative (2008) *Climate Change and International Security*

European Commission and High Representative (2011a) *A Partnership for Democracy and Shared Prosperity in the Southern Mediterranean*, JOIN(2011)200

European Commission and High Representative (2011b) *Elements for an EU Strategy for Syria*, JOIN(2017)11

European Commission and High Representative (2012) *Delivering on a New Neighbourhood Policy*, JOIN(2012)14

European Commission and High Representative (2014) *Neighbourhood at the Crossroads: Implementation of the European Neighbourhood Policy in 2013*, JOIN(2014)12

European Commission and High Representative (2020a) *Eastern Partnership Policy Beyond 2020*, JOIN(2020)7

European Commission and High Representative (2020b) *EU Action Plan on Human Rights and Democracy 2020–2024*, JOIN(2020)5

European Commission and High Representative (2020c) *Report on the Generalised Scheme of Preferences Covering the Period 2018–2019*, JOIN(2020)

European Council (2003) *European Security Strategy – A Secure Europe in a Better World*, Brussels, European Council

European Council on Foreign Relations (2014) *European Foreign Policy Scorecard 2013*, London, ECFR

European Court of Auditors (2017) *Landscape Review: EU Action on Energy and Climate Change*, Brussels, European Court of Auditors

European Court of Auditors (2019) *Challenges to Effective EU Cybersecurity Policy*, Brussels, European Court of Auditors

European Endowment for Democracy (2018) *Annual Report 2018: Supporting People Striving for Democracy*, Brussels, EED

European External Action Service (2012) *Developing an EU Policy Towards the Arctic Region: Progress Since 2008 and Next Steps*, JOIN(2012)19

European External Action Service (2013) *EU Climate Diplomacy for 2015 and Beyond: Reflection Paper*, Brussels, European External Action Service

European External Action Service (2019a) *The European Union's Global Strategy: Three Years On, Looking Forward*, Brussels, European External Action Service

European External Action Service (2019b) *EU-Kenya Relations*, Brussels, EEAS

European Parliament Foreign Affairs Committee (2012) *The Role of the CSDP in Case of Climate-Driven Crises and Natural Disasters*, Brussels, European Parliament

European Parliament Research Service (2015) 'EU-UN Cooperation in Peacekeeping and Crisis Management', Brussels, European Parliament

European Parliament Research Service (2019) *Intergovernmental Agreements in the Field of Energy*, Brussels, European Parliament

European Partnership for Democracy (2019) *Louder than Words? Connecting the Dots of European Democracy Support*, Brussels: EPD

European Political Strategy Centre (2016) 'Towards a "Security Union": Bolstering the EU's Counter-Terrorism Response', Brussels, EPSC Strategic Notes No. 12

European Political Strategy Centre (2019) *Rethinking Strategic Autonomy for the Digital Age*, Brussels, EPSC

European Union (2009) *Treaty of Lisbon Amending Treaty on European Union*, Brussels, European Union

European Union (2015a) *A Framework Strategy for a Resilient Energy Union with a Forward-Looking Climate Change Policy*, COM (2015), 80

European Union (2015b) *Strategic Orientation Document for the EU Regional Trust Fund in Response to the Syrian Crisis*, Brussels, European Union

European Union (2016a) *Bratislava Declaration and Roadmap*, Brussels, European Council

European Union (2016b) *EU Regional Trust Fund in Response to the Syrian Crisis: Factsheet*, Brussels, European Union

European Union (2016c) *Shared Vision, Common Action: A Stronger Europe: A Global Strategy for the European Union's Foreign and Security Policy*, Brussels, European Union

European Union (2019) *New Strategic Agenda 2019–2024*, Brussels, European Union

European Union (2019) The European Union's Global Strategy Three Years On, Looking Forward, Brussels, European External Action Service

Europol (2019) *European Union Terrorism Situation and Trend Report 2019*, The Hague, Europol

Eurostat, *Europe in the World, 2018 Edition*, Luxembourg, EU Publication Office

Everett S. (2007) 'Trade Policy: Time for a Rethink?', in A. Sapir (ed) *Fragmented Power: Europe and the Global Economy*, Brussels, Bruegel

Faleg G. and C. Palleschi (2020) *African Strategies: European and Global Approaches Towards Sub-Saharan Africa*, Paris, EU Institute for Security Studies

Fallon T. (2019) 'When the China Dream and the European Dream Collide', *War on the Rocks*, 7 January 2019

Fanoulis E. (2018) 'The EU's Democratization Discourse and Questions of European Identity', *Journal of Common Market Studies*, 56/6, 1362–1375

Far S. and R. Youngs (2015) *Energy Union and EU Global Strategy*, Stockholm, Swedish Institute for European Policy Studies

Feldstein S. (2019) 'How Artificial Intelligence Is Reshaping Repression', *Journal of Democracy*, 30/1, 40–52

Ferreira-Pereira L. and A. Vysotskaya Guedes Vieira (2016) 'Introduction: The European Union's Strategic Partnerships: Conceptual Approaches, Debates and Experiences', *Cambridge Review of International Affairs*, 29/1, 3–17

Fetzek, S. and L. van Schaik (2018) *Europe's Responsibility to Prepare: Managing Climate Security Risks in a Changing World*, Washington, DC, Center on Climate and Security

Fiott D. (2018) *Strategic Autonomy: Towards European Sovereignty in Defence?*, Paris, EUISS Brief

Fiott D. (ed) (2020) *The CSDP in 2020*, Paris, EUISS

Fischer J. (2012) 'Provincial Europe', *Project Syndicate*, 31 October 2012

Fischer S. (2014) *Escalation in Ukraine*, Berlin, SWP

Foresight (2011) *International Dimensions of Climate Change*, London, UK Government Office for Science

Forsberg T. (2016) 'From Ostpolitk to Frostpolitik? Merkel, Putin and German Foreign Policy Towards Russia', *International Affairs*, 92/1, 21–42

Forsberg T. and H. Haukkala (2016) 'Could It Have Been Different? The Evolution of the EU–Russian Conflict and Its Alternatives', in C. Nitoiu (ed) *Avoiding a New 'Cold War': The Future of EU–Russia Relations in the Context of the Ukraine Crisis*, London, LSE Ideas Report

Fouere E. (2019) 'The EU's Re-engagement with the Western Balkans: A New Chapter Long Overdue', Policy Brief 2019/1, Brussels, Centre for European Policy Studies

Freedom House (2018) *Democracy in Crisis Freedom in the World Report 2018*, Washington, DC, Freedom House

Freedom House (2020) *Nations in Transit*, Washington DC, Freedom House

Freedom House (2020) *Freedom in the World 2020 – A Leaderless Struggle for Democracy*, Washington, DC, Freedom House

Froggart A. and M. Levi (2009) 'Climate and Energy Security Policies and Measures: Synergies and Conflicts', *International Affairs*, 85/6, 1129–1141

Gemenne F. et al (2014) 'Climate and Security: Evidence, Emerging Risks and a New Agenda', *Climate Change*, 123/1, 1–9

German Advisory Council on Global Change (2011) *World in Transition: A Social Contract for the Great Transformation*, Berlin, German Advisory Council on Global Change

Germanwatch (2019) *Global Climate Risk Index 2019*, Bonn

Getmanchuk A. (2015) *Ukraine–NATO: A Hidden Integration or Undeclared Neutrality?*, Kiev, Institute for World Policy

Getmanchuk A. and S. Solodkyy (2016) *Ukraine–Germany: How to Turn Situational Partnership into Priority One*, Kiev, Institute for World Policy

Giddens A. (2014) *Turbulent and Mighty Continent: What Future for Europe?*, Cambridge, Polity Press

Ginsberg R. (2001) *The European Union in International Politics – Baptism by Fire*, New York, Rowman and Littlefield

Godfrey K. and R. Youngs (2019) *Towards a New EU Democracy Strategy*, Brussels, Carnegie Europe

Goldthau A. and N. Sitter (2015) *A Liberal Actor in a Realist World. The European Union Regulatory State and the Global Political Economy of Energy*, Oxford, Oxford University Press

Goldthau A. and N. Sitter (2020) 'Power, Authority and Security: The EU's Russian Gas Dilemma', *Journal of European Integration*, 41/7, 111–127

Gomez F., C. Muguruza and J. Wouters (eds) (2018) *EU Human Rights and Democratisation Policies: Achievements and Challenges*, London, Routledge

Goodwin M., T. Raines and D. Cotts (2017) 'What Do Europeans Think About Muslim Immigration?', London, Chatham House

Greco E. (ed) (2018) *L'Italia al bivo: raporto sulla politica estera italiana*, Rome, IAI

Gressel G. (2019) Protecting Europe Against Hybrid Threats, London, European Council on Foreign Relations

Grevi G. (2008) 'The Rise of Strategic Partnerships: Between Interdependence and Power Politics', in G. Grevi and A. Vasconcelos (eds) *Partnerships for Effective Multilateralism: EU Relations with Brazil, China, India and Russia*, Paris, EUISS

Grevi G. (2019) *Strategic Autonomy for European Choices: The Key to Europe's Shaping Power*, Brussels, European Policy Centre

Grey S. (2016) *The New Spymasters*, London, Penguin

Grimm S. (2019) 'Democracy Promotion in EU Enlargement Negotiations: More Interaction, Less Hierarchy', *Democratization*, 26/5, 851–868

Gross D. 'What EU "Geopolitical" Power Will Cost', *Project Syndicate*, 6 December 2019

Gstöhl S. and D. Phinnemore (eds) (2018) *The European Union, Its Neighbours, and the Proliferation of 'Privileged Partnerships'*, London, Routledge

Gstöhl S. and S. Schunz (eds) (2016) *Theorizing the European Neighbourhood Policy*, London, Routledge

Haass R. (2020) 'The Pandemic Will Accelerate History Rather than Reshape It', *Foreign Affairs*, April

Hackenhesch C. (2018) *The EU and China in African Authoritarian Regimes*, London, Palgrave Macmillan

Harpaz G. (2017) 'The Causes of the EU's Ineffectual Contribution to Resolution of the Abkhazian and South Ossetian Conflicts', *European Foreign Affairs Review*, 22/2, 253–270

Hassan O. (2019) 'The Evolution of the European Union's Failed Approach to Afghanistan', *European Security*, 29/1, 74–95

Haverluk T., K. Beauchemin and A. Mueller (2004) 'The Three Critical Flaws of Critical Geopolitics: Towards a Neo-classical Geopolitics', *Geopolitics*, 19/1, 19–39

Havlicek P. (2017) 'Eastern Partnership: In a Dismal State or a New Beginning?', *Euractiv*, 6 December 2017

Hebel K. and T. Lenz (2016) 'The Identity/Policy Nexus in European Foreign Policy', *Journal of European Public Policy*, 23/4, 473–491

Hegemann H. and U. Schneckener (2019) 'Politicising European Security: From Technocratic to Contentious Politics?', *European Security*, 28/2, 133–152

Heisbourg F. (2015) 'Preserving Post-Cold War Europe', *Survival*, 57/1, 31–48

Helleiner E. and S. Pagliari (2011) 'The End of an Era in International Financial Regulation? A Post-crisis Research Agenda', *International Organization*, 65, 169–200

Hellmann G. (2011) 'Normatively Disarmed, but Self-Confident', *Internationale Politik*, 3, 45–51

Her Majesty's Government (2010) *A Strong Britain in an Age of Uncertainty*, London, HMG

Her Majesty's Government (2011) *Trade and Investment for Growth*, London, HMG

Herranz-Surrallés A. (2016) 'An Emerging EU Energy Diplomacy? Discursive Shifts, Enduring Practices', *Journal of European Public Policy*, 23/9, 1386–1405

Herranz-Surrallés A. (2018) 'Thinking Energy Outside the Frame? Reframing and Misframing in Euro-Mediterranean Energy Relations', *Mediterranean Politics*, 23/1, 122–141

Heydemann S. (2018) *Beyond Fragility: Syria and the Challenges of Reconstruction in Fierce States*, Washington, DC, Brookings

Hill C. (2019) *The Future of British Foreign Policy: Security and Diplomacy in a World After Brexit*, Cambridge, Polity Press

Hill C., M. Smith and S. Vanhoonacker (2017a) 'International Relations and the European Union: Themes and Issues', in C. Hill, M. Smith and S. Vanhoonacker, *International Relations and the European Union*, 3rd edition, Oxford, Oxford University Press

Hill C., M. Smith and S. Vanhoonacker (eds) (2017b) *International Relations and the European Union*, 3rd edition, Oxford, Oxford University Press

Hofmann S. and U. Staeger (2019) 'Frame Contestation and Collective Securitisation: The Case of EU Energy Policy', *West European Politics*, 42/2, 323–345

Holland M. (ed) (1997) *Common Foreign and Security Policy: The Record and Reforms*, London, Pinter

House of Commons Foreign Affairs Committee (2019) *China and the Rules-Based International System*, 16th Report of 2017–2019 Session

House of Commons Foreign Affairs Select Committee (2016) *Libya: Examination of Intervention and Collapse and the UK's Future Policy Options*, London, House of Commons

House of Lords European Union Committee (2008) *Developments in EU Trade Policy*, 35th Report of 2007–2008 Session

Huber D. (2020) *The New European Commission's Green Deal and Geopolitical Language: A Critique from a Decentring Perspective*, Rome, IAI

Hunt J. (2019) 'Britain's Role in a Post-Brexit World', Speech in Singapore, 2 January 2019, London, International Institute for Strategic Studies

Hurrell A. (2007) *On Global Order: Power, Values and the Constitution of International Society*, Oxford, Oxford University Press

Hyde-Price A. (2007) *European Security in the 21st Century: The Challenge of Multipolarity*, London, Routledge

Ikenberry G. John (2011a) 'The Future of the Liberal World Order: Internationalism After America', *Foreign Affairs*, May/June

Ikenberry G. John (2011b) *Liberal Leviathan*, Princeton, Princeton University Press

Intelligence and Security Committee of Parliament (2020) *Russia*, London, House of Commons

Intergovernmental Panel on Climate Change (2014) *Mitigation of Climate Change. Contribution of Working Group III to the Fifth Assessment Report of the Intergovernmental Panel on Climate Change*, Cambridge, Cambridge University Press

Intergovernmental Panel on Climate Change (2019) *Global Warming of 1.5 Degrees Celsius*, IPCC Special Report, Geneva

International Crisis Group (2016) *The Libyan Political Agreement: Time for a Reset*, Brussels, ICG

International Peace Institute (2018) *European Contributions to UN Peacekeeping Operations: Lessons Learned and the Way Forward*, Vienna, IPC

Ioannides I. (2018a) *An Evaluation of EU Peace-Building in the Western Balkans*, Brussels, European Parliament Research Service

Ioannides I. (2018b) *The Generalised System of Preferences Regulation*, Brussels, European Parliament Research Service

IRENA (2019) *Commission on the Geopolitics of Energy Transition, a New World: The Geopolitics of Energy Transition*, Irena

Jacques M. (2012) *When China Rules the World*, 2nd edition, London, Penguin

Jakobik W. (2015) 'A Return to Business as Usual', *New Eastern Europe*, 29 October

Jermy S. (2011) *Strategy for Action*, London, Knightstone Publishing

Jones B., M. Elgin-Crossart and J. Esberg (2012) *Pathways Out of Fragility: The Case for A Research Agenda on Inclusive Political Settlements in Fragile States,* New York, Center on International Cooperation

Jørgensen K. (ed) (2009) *The European Union and International Organizations*, London, Routledge

Jørgensen K. et al (eds) (2015) *The SAGE Handbook of European Foreign Policy*, Thousand Oaks, SAGE Publications

Joseph J. and A. Juncos (2019) 'Resilience as an Emergent European Project? The EU's Place in the Resilience Turn', *Journal of Common Market Studies*, 57/5, 995–1012

Juncos A. and S. Blockmans (2018) 'The EU's Role in Conflict Prevention and Peacebuilding: Four Key Challenges', *Global Affairs*, 4/2, 131–140

Kaca E. (2014) *A New Pact for Ukraine: Making EU Aid Work*, Warsaw, Polish Institute for International Affairs

Kagan R. (2003) *Of Paradise and Power: America and Europe in the New World Order*, New York, Knopf

Kaliber A. and E. Kaliber (2019) 'From De-Europeanisation to Anti-Western Populism: Turkish Foreign Policy in Flux', *International Spectator*, 54/4, 1–16

Kausch K. (2018) 'Rethinking Europe's Comparative Advantage in the Mediterranean', in IE Med (ed) *Mediterranean Yearbook 2018*, Barcelona, IEMed

Kepel G. (2016) *Terror in France: The Rise of Jihad in the West*, Princeton, Princeton University Press

Keukeleire S. and T. de Bruyn (2017) 'The European Union, the BRICs and Other Powers: A New World Order?', in C. Hill, M. Smith and S. Vanhoonacker (eds) *International Relations and the European Union*, 3rd edition, Oxford, Oxford University Press

Keukelaire S. and T. Delreux (2014) *The Foreign Policy of the European Union*, 2nd edition, London, Red Globe Press

King S. (2011) *Losing Control: The Emerging Threats to Western Prosperity*, New Haven, Yale University Press

King J. (2019) 'The EU Needs Its Own Security Strategy to Confront the Digital Threat', *Financial Times*, 1 February 2019

Kingsley P. (2016) *The New Odyssey: The Story of Europe's Refugee Crisis*, London, Faber

Kinnvall C. (2016) 'The Postcolonial Has Moved into Europe: Bordering, Security and Ethno-cultural Belonging', *Journal of Common Market Studies*, 54/1, 152–168

Kinzelbach K. (2015) *The EU Human Rights Dialogues with China: Quiet Diplomacy and Its Limits*, London, Routledge

Klose S. (2018) 'Theorizing the EU's Actorness: Towards an Interactionist Role Theory Framework', *Journal of Common Market Studies*, 56/5, 1144

Koenig N. (2016) *EU Security Policy and Crisis Management: A Quest for Coherence*, London, Routledge

Koenig N. (2017) 'Libya and Syria: Inserting the European Neighbourhood Policy in the European Union's Crisis Response Cycle', *European Foreign Affairs Review*, 22/1, 19 38

Korosteleva E. (2012) *The European Union and its Eastern Neighbours: Towards a More Ambitious Partnership?*, London, Routledge

Korosteleva E. (2013) 'Evaluating the Role of Partnership in the European Neighbourhood Policy: The Eastern Neighbourhood', *Eastern Journal of European Studies*, 4/2, 11–36

Krause J. and N. Ronzitti (eds) (2012) *The EU, the UN and Collective Security: Making Multilateralism Effective*, London: Routledge

Krotz U. and R. Maher (2012) 'Debating the Sources and Prospects of European Integration', *International Security*, 37/1, 178–99

Kudelia S. (2018) 'Ukraine's Emerging Security State', *Current History*, 117/801, 264–270

Kulesa L. (ed) (2014) *Is a New Cold War Inevitable? Central European Views on Rebuilding Trust in the Euro-Atlantic Region*, Warsaw, PISM

Kundnani H. (2011) 'Germany as a Geo-Economic Power', *Washington Quarterly*, 34/3, 31–45

Kundnani H. (2020) 'Europe's Sovereignty Conundrum', *Berlin Policy Journal*, May

Kupchan C. (2012a) 'Centrifugal Europe', *Survival*, 54/1, 111–118

Kupchan C. (2012b) *No One's World: The West, the Rising Rest, and the Coming Global Turn*, New York, Oxford University Press

Langbein J. (2014) 'European Union Governance Towards the Eastern Neighbourhood: Transcending or Redrawing Europe's East-West Divide?', *Journal of Common Market Studies*, 52/1, 157–174

Latici T. (2020) 'What Role for the UK in the EU's Defence Labyrinth?', European Parliamentary Research Service

Lavenex S. (2014) 'The Power of Functionalist Extension: How EU Rules Travel', *Journal of European Public Policy*, 21/6, 885–903

Lavenex S. (2016) 'On the Fringes of the European Peace Project: The Neighbourhood Policy's Functionalist Hubris and Political Myopia', *British Journal of Politics and International Relations*, 19/1, 63–76

Lay Hwee Y. (2011) 'Where Is ASEM Heading—Toward a Networked Approach to Global Governance?', in W. Hofmeister (ed) *Panorama: Asia and Europe: Moving Toward a Common Agenda*, Singapore, Konrad-Adenauer-Stiftung

Lehmann J.-P. (2012) 'Absurd EU–Japan Trade Plan Underlines Doha's Failure', *Financial Times*, 20 July 2012

Lehne S. and F. Siccardi (2020) *Where in the World Is the EU Now?*, Brussels, Carnegie Europe

Levitsky S. and L. Way (2006) 'Linkage Versus Leverage. Rethinking the International Dimension of Regime Change', *Comparative Politics*, 38/4, 379–400

Linkevcius L. (2016) 'Security Before Politics in Eastern Ukraine', *Wall Street Journal*, 27 January 2016

Linklater A. (1998) *The Transformation of Political Community*, Cambridge, Cambridge University Press

Lo B. (2015) *Russia and the New World Disorder*, London, Chatham House

Lovelock J. (2009) *The Vanishing Face of Gaia: A Final Warning*, London, Penguin

Lucarelli S. (2018) 'The EU and the Crisis of Liberal Order, at Home and Abroad', Globus Research Papers, available at www.globus.uio.no

Lucarelli S. (2019) 'The EU as a Securitising Agent? Testing the Model, Advancing the Literature', *West European Politics*, 42/2, 413–436

Lucarelli S. and I. Manners (eds) (2006) *Values and Principles in European Union Foreign Policy*, London, Routledge

Lührmann A. and S. Lindberg (2019) 'A Third Wave of Autocratization Is Here: What Is New About It?', *Democratization*, 26/7, 1095–1113

Luttwark E. (1990) 'From Geopolitics to Geo-economics: Logic of Conflict, Grammar of Commerce', *The National Interest*, 20, 17–23

Maas H. (2018) 'Making Plans for a New World Order', *Handelsblatt*, 22 August 2018

Maçães B. (2018) *The Dawn of Eurasia*, London, Penguin

Manners I. (2002) 'Normative Power: A Contradiction in Terms?', *Journal of Common Market Studies*, 40/2, 235–258

Manners I. (2008) 'The Normative Ethics of the European Union', *International Affairs*, 84/1, 45–60

Matlak M., F. Schimmelfennig and T. Wozniakowski (eds) (2018) *Europeanization Revisited: Central and Eastern Europe in the European Union*, Florence, EUI

Mearsheimer J. (2014) 'Why the Ukraine Crisis Is the West's Fault: The Liberal Delusions That Provoked Putin', *Foreign Affairs*, 93/5, 77–89

Meissner K. (2018) *Commercial Realism and EU Trade Policy: Competing for Economic Power in Asia and the Americas*, London, Routledge

Menon A. (2014) 'Divided and Declining? Europe in a Changing World', *Journal of Common Market Studies*, 52, Annual Review, 5–24

Messerlin P. (2010) 'How the Rich OECD Nations Should Handle the Emerging Giants', *Europe's World*, Spring

Meunier S. and K. Nicolaidis (2017) 'The European Union as a Trade Power', in C. Hill, M. Smith and S. Vanhoonacker (eds) *International Relations and the European Union*, 3rd edition, Oxford, Oxford University Press

Meunier S. and K. Nicolaidis (2019) 'The Geopoliticization of European Trade and Investment Policy', *Journal of Common Market Studies*, 57, Annual Review, 103–113

Meunier S. and M. Vachudova (2018) 'Liberal Intergovernmentalism, Illiberalism and the Potential Superpower of the European Union', *Journal of Common Market Studies*, 56/7, 1631–1647

Minakov M. (2020) *Democratisation and Europeanisation in 21st Century Ukraine*, Brussels, CEPS

Mogerhini F. (2019) 'The Middle East and the EU: New Realities, New Policies', Speech to Menara Conference, Brussels, 6 March 2019, at https://eeas.europa.eu/head-quarters/headquarters-homepage/59180/speech-high-representativevice-president-federica-mogherini-final-conference-menara-and_en

Molina I. (ed) (2019) *España en el mundo en 2019: perspectivas y desafíos*, Madrid, Elcano

Molina I. (ed) (2020) *España en el mundo en 2020: perspectivas y desafíos para el anio del coronavirus*, Madrid, Elcano

Monaghan A. (2013) 'Putin's Russia: Shaping a Grand Strategy?', *International Affairs*, 89/5, 1221–1236

Moran A. et al (2018) *The Intersection of Global Fragility and Climate Risks*, Washington, DC, United States Agency for International Aid

Moravcsik A. (1993) 'Preferences and Power in the European Community: A Liberal Intergovernmentalist Approach', *Journal of Common Market Studies*, 31/4, 473–524

Moravcsik A. (2017) 'Europe Is Still a Superpower', *Foreign Policy*, April

Morillas P. (2020) 'Autonomy in Intergovernmentalism: The Role of De Novo Bodies in External Action During the Making of the EU Global Strategy', *Journal of European Integration*, 42/2, 231–246

Mortensen J. (2009) 'The World Trade Organization and the European Union', in K. Jorgensen (ed) *The European Union and International Organizations*, London, Routledge

Mortera Martinez C. (2019) *The EU's Security Union: A Bill of Health*, London, Centre for European Reform

Moshes A. (2015) *The War and Reforms in Ukraine, Can It Cope with Both?*, Helsinki, Finnish Institute for International Affairs

Muenier S. and K. Nicolaidis (2017) 'The European Union as a Trade Power', in C. Hill, M. Smith and S. Vanhoonacker (eds) *International Relations and the European Union*, 3rd edition, Oxford, Oxford University Press

Muhina K. (2018) 'Administrative Reform Assistance and Democracy Promotion: Exploring the Democratic Substance of the EU's Public Administration Reform Principles for the Neighbourhood Countries', *Democratization*, 25/4, 673–691

Mungiu-Pippidi A. (2019) *Europe's Burden: Promoting Good Governance Across Borders*, Cambridge, Cambridge University Press

Munich Security Conference, *Munich Security Report 2019. The Great Puzzle: Who Will Pick up the Pieces?*, Munich

Munich Security Conference (2020) *Zeitenwende, Wendezeiten: Special Edition of the Munich Security Report on German Foreign and Security Policy*, Munich, MSC

Murray D. (2017) *The Strange Death of Europe*, London, Bloomsbury

NATO (2019) *Defence expenditure of NATO countries 2013-2019*, Press Release 123, Brussels, NATO

Naím M. (2013) *The End of Power*, New York, Basic Books

Newman E. and C. Stefan (2020) 'Normative Power Europe? The EU's Embrace of the Responsibility to Protect in a Transitional World Order', *Journal of Common Market Studies*, 58/2, 472–490

Nisen M. (2012) 'Trade War: How 12 Major Economies Have Closed Up Since the Crisis', *Business Insider*, June 18, 2012

Notification at Government of the Netherlands (2019) 'Letter on Sanctions Against Iran on the Grounds of Undesirable Interference', 8 January 2019

Ntousas V. (2020) *Why the EU's Migration and Asylum Plan Is Flawed*, London, Chatham House

O'Hara K. and W. Hall (2018) 'Four Internets: The Geopolitics of Digital Governance', Centre for International Governance Innovation Paper 206, Waterloo, Canada

Oberthür S. and C. Kelly (2008) 'EU Leadership in International Climate Policy: Achievements and Challenges', *The International Spectator*, 43/3, 35–50

OECD (2019) *The European Union: A People Centred Agenda: An International Perspective*, Paris, OECD

Ojendal J., H. Leonardsson and M. Lundqvist (2017) *Local Peace-Building –Challenges and Opportunities*, Stockholm, EBA

Okano-Heijmans M. (2012) 'Power Shift: Economic Realism and Economic Diplomacy on the Rise', in E. Fels et al (eds) *Power in the 21st Century*, Berlin, Springer

Omand D. (2016) 'Keeping Europe Safe: Counterterrorism for the Continent', *Foreign Affairs*, September/October

Oppenheim B. (2019) *You Never Listen to Me: The European–Saudi Relationship After Khashoggi*, London, Centre for European Reform

Oppenheim B. (2020) 'Annexation Will Plunge Israel's Relations with the EU into Existential Crisis', *Haaretz*, 11 June 2020

Orenstein M. and D. Kelemen (2017) 'Trojan Horses in EU Foreign Policy', *Journal of Common Market Studies*, 55/1, 87–102

Organisation for Security and Cooperation in Europe (2015) *Back to Diplomacy: Final Report and Recommendations of the Panel of Eminent Persons on European Security as a Common Project*, Vienna, Organisation for Security and Cooperation in Europe

Palm T. and B. Crum (2019) 'Military Operations and the EU's Identity as an International Security Actor', *European Security*, 28/4, 513–534

Parandii K. (2019) *The EU's Anti-corruption Conditionalities in Ukraine*, Bruges, College of Europe

Paris R. (2019) *Can Middle Powers Save the Liberal World Order?*, London, Chatham House Briefing

Parkes R. (2020) 'Reading the Runes: The Future of CSDP and AFSJ', in D. Fiott (eds) *The CSDP in 2020*, Paris, EUISS

Pawlak P. (2019) 'The EU's Role in Shaping the Cyber Regime Complex', *European Foreign Affairs Review*, 24/2, 167–186

Pisani-Ferry J. (2011) *How to Stop Fragmentation of the Eurozone*, Brussels, Bruegel

Pisani-Ferry J. (2019) 'Europe and the New Imperialism', *Project Syndicate*, 8 May 2019

Polish Ministry of Foreign Affairs (2019) 'Joint Statement of the Foreign Ministers on the EU's Commitment to the Western Balkan's European integration', 11 June 2019, posted at: https://www.gov.pl/web/diplomacy/joint-statement-of-the-foreign-ministers-on-the-eu-commitment-to-the-western-balkans-european-integration

Poppe A., J. Leininger and J. Wolff (2019) 'Introduction: Negotiating the Promotion of Democracy', *Democratization*, 26/5, 759–776

Portela C. (2012) *The EU's Sanctions Against Syria: Conflict Management by Other Means*, Brussels, Egmont Institute

Portela, C. (2019) *A Blacklist Is (Almost) Born: Building a Resilient Human Rights Sanctions Regime*, Paris, EUISS

Porter P. (2020) *The False Promise of Liberal Order*, Cambridge, Polity Press

Powell C. (2001) 'International Aspects of Democratization. The Case of Spain', in L. Whitehead (ed) *The International Dimensions of Democratization. Europe and the Americas*, Oxford, Oxford University Press

Powell C. (2007) *Revisiting Spain's Transition to Democracy, Barcelona*, Barcelona, IEMed

Prontera A. (2017) *The New Politics of Energy Security in the European Union and Beyond. States, Markets, Institutions*, London, Routledge

Rachman G. (2010) *Zero-Sum World: Politics, Power and Prosperity After the Crash*, London, Atlantic Books

Raik K. (2016) 'Liberalism and Geopolitics in EU–Russia Relations: Rereading the Baltic Factor', *European Security*, 25/2, 237–255

Raine S. (2019) *Europe's Strategic Future: From Crisis to Coherence?*, London, International Institute for Strategic Studies Adelphi Book

Raineri L. and F. Strazzari (2019) '(B)ordering Hybrid Security? EU Stabilisation Practices in the Sahara-Sahel Region', *Ethnopolitics*, 18/4, 544–559

Remler P. (2019) *Russia and Cooperative Security in Europe: Times Change, Tactics Remain*, Washington, DC, Carnegie Endowment for International Peace

Renard T. (2016) 'Partnerships for Effective Multilateralism? Assessing the Compatibility Between EU Bilateralism, (Inter)regionalism and Multilateralism', *Cambridge Review of International Affairs*, 29/1, 18–35

Renard T. (2018) 'EU Cyber-Partnerships: Assessing the EU Strategic Partnerships with Third Countries in the Cyber Domain', *European Politics and Society*, 19/3, 321–337

Reporters Without Borders (2018) *RSF Index 2018: Hatred of Journalism Threatens Democracies*, Washington, DC

Richert J. (2017) 'From Single Voice to Coordinated Polyphony EU Energy Policy and the External Dimension', *European Foreign Affairs Review*, 22/2, 213–232

Richmond O. (2016) *Peace Formation and Political order in Conflict Affected Societies*, Oxford, Oxford University Press

Riddervold M. (2018) *The Maritime Turn in EU Foreign and Security Policies*, London, Palgrave Macmillan

Roccu R. and B. Voltolini (2018) 'Security and Stability Reframed, Selective Engagement Maintained? The EU in the Mediterranean After the Arab Uprisings', *Mediterranean Politics*, 23/1, 182–195

Rodrik D. 'Will Covid-19 Remake the World?', *Project Syndicate*, 6 April 2020

Rodt A., R. Whitman and S. Wolff (2015) 'The EU as an International Security Provider: The Need for a Mid-range Theory', *Global Society*, 29/2, 149–155

Rogers J. (2011) *A New Geography of European Power?*, Brussels, Egmont Institute, Egmont Paper 42

Romanova T. (2016) 'Sanctions and the Future of EU–Russian Economic Relations', *Europe–Asia Studies*, 68/4, 774–796

Rosato S. (2011) 'Europe's Troubles: Power Politics and the State of the European Project', *International Security*, 35/4, 45–86

Russell M. (2018) *Uzbekistan Comes in from the Cold*, Brussels, European Parliament Research Service

Russell Mead W. (2014) 'The Return of Geopolitics', *Foreign Affairs*, May/June

Rutte M. (2012) Investiture Speech, 'Building Bridges', November 13, 2012, www.government.nl/government/policy-statement

Rynning S. (2011) 'Realism and Common Security and Defence Policy', *Journal of Common Market Studies*, 49/1, 23–42

Saatcloglu B. (2016) 'De-Europeanisation in Turkey: The Case of the Rule of Law', *South European Politics and Society*, 21/1, 133–146

Sandbu M. (2019) 'Europe Must Find Its Will to Power', *Financial Times*, 20 June 2019

Sasse G. (2013) 'Linkages and the Promotion of Democracy: The EU's Eastern Neighbourhood', *Democratization*, 20/4, 553–591

Sattich T. and T. Inderberg (2019) 'EU Geoeconomics: A Framework for Analysing Bilateral Relations in the European Union', *Journal of Common Market Studies*, 57/3, 502–514

Sbragia A. (2010) 'The EU, the US and Trade Policy: Competitive Interdependence in the Management of Globalization', *Journal of European Public Policy*, 17/3, 368–382

Schimmelfennig F. (2001) 'The Community Trap: Liberal Norms, Rhetorical Actions and the Eastern Enlargement of the European Union', *International Organization*, 55/1, 47–80

Schimmelfennig F. and U. Sedelmeier (2004) 'Governance by Conditionality. EU Rule Transfer to the Candidate Countries of Central and Eastern Europe', *Journal of European Public Policy*, 11/4, 661–679

Schmidt V. (2010) 'Taking Ideas and Discourse Seriously: Explaining Change Through Discursive Institutionalism as the Fourth New Institutionalism', *European Political Science Review*, 2/1, 1–25

Secrieru S. and S. Saari (eds) (2019) *The Eastern Partnership a Decade On: Looking Back, Thinking Ahead*, Paris, EUISS

Seeberg P. (2017) 'Mobility Partnerships and Security Subcomplexes in the Mediterranean: The Strategic Role of Migration and the EU's Foreign and Security Policies Towards the MENA Region', *European Foreign Affairs Review*, 22/1, 91–110

Sepos A. (2018) 'EU Support of Polyarchy? The Case of Morocco', *European Foreign Affairs Review*, 23/4, 521–548

Serrano P. (2019) *The Bundle of Sticks: A Stronger European Defence to Face Global Challenges*, Madrid, Elcano Institute

Shyrokykh K. and D. Rimkute (2019) 'EU Rules Beyond Its Borders: The Policy-Specific Effects of Transgovernmental Networks and EU Agencies in the European Neighbourhood', *Journal of Common Market Studies*, 57/4, 749–767

Sida (2018) *Strategy for Sweden's Development Cooperation in the Areas of Human Rights Democracy and the Rule of Law 2018–2022*, Stockholm, Swedish Development Agency

Siddi M. (2019) 'The EU's Botched Geopolitical Approach to External Energy Policy: The Case of the Southern Gas Corridor', *Geopolitics*, 24/1, 124–144

Simon L. (2013) 'The Spider in Europe's Web? French Grand Strategy from Iraq to Libya', *Geopolitics*, 18/2, 403–434

Simon L. (2019) 'What Is Europe's Role in Sino-American Competition?', *War on the Rocks*, 14 February 2019

SIPRI (2019) *SIPRI Yearbook 2019*, Stockholm, SIPRI

Sjursen H. (2006) 'What Kind of Power?', *Journal of European Public Policy*, 13/1, 169–181

Small A. (2020) *The Meaning of Systemic Rivalry: European and China Beyond the Pandemic*, London, European Council on Foreign Relations

Smith M.E. (2004) 'Toward a Theory of EU Foreign Policy Making: Multi-level Governance, Domestic Politics, and National Adaptation to Europe's Common Foreign and Security Policy', *Journal of European Public Policy*, 11, 740–745

Smith M.E. (2011) 'A Liberal Grand Strategy in a Realist World? Power, Purpose and the EU's Changing Global Role', *Journal of European Public Policy*, 18/2, 144–163

Smith K. (2014) *European Union Foreign Policy in a Changing World*, 3rd edition, Cambridge, Polity Press

Smith M. (2017a) 'The European Union and the USA', in C. Hill, M. Smith and S. Vanhoonacker (eds) *International Relations and the European Union*, 3rd edition, Oxford, Oxford University Press

Smith M.E. (2017b) *Europe's Common Security and Defence Policy: Experiential Learning and Institutional Change*, Cambridge, Cambridge University Press

Smith M. (2019) 'The European Union and the Global Arena: In Search of Post-Brexit Roles', *Politics and Governance*, 7/3, 83–92

Smith M. (2021) 'European Union Diplomacy and the Trump Administration: Multilateral Strategies in a Transactional World?', in R. Haar, T. Christiansen, S. Lange and S. Vanhoonacker (eds) *The Making of European Security Policy: Between Institutional Dynamics and Global Challenges*, London, Routledge (forthcoming)

Soler i Lecha E. and P. Morillas (2020) *Middle Power with Maghreb Focus: A Spanish Perspective on Security Policy in the Southern Neighbourhood*, Berlin, Friedrich Ebert Stiftun

Sperling J. and M. Webber (2014) 'Security Governance in Europe: A Return to System', *European Security*, 23/2, 126–144

Sperling J. and M. Webber (2019) 'The European Union: Security Governance and Collective Securitisation', *West European Politics*, 42/2, 228–260

Stein D. (2019) *Impact of the European Court of Justice's Opal Decision*, Washington, DC, Atlantic Council

Stelzenmuller C. (2019) *Germany: Baffled Hegemon*, Washington, DC, Brookings

Stokes D. and R. Whitman (2013) 'Transatlantic Triage? European and UK Grand Strategy After the US Rebalance to Asia', *International Affairs*, 89/5, 1087–1107

Stokes B., R. Wike and J. Poushter (2016) *Europeans Face the World Divided,* Washington, DC, Pew Research Center

Szewcyk B. (2019) 'Europe and the Liberal Order', *Survival*, 61/2, 33–52

Szulecki K. and K. Westphal (2014) 'The Cardinal Sins of European Energy Policy: Non-governance in an Uncertain Global Landscape', *Global Policy*, 5/1, 38–51

Tassinari F. (2016) 'All for None, and None for All: Life in a Broken Europe', *Foreign Affairs*, January

Teevan C. (2019) 'The EU, Morocco, and the Stability Myth', *Sada Journal*, Carnegie Endowment for International Peace

Tèlo M. (2007) *Europe: A Civilian Power? European Union, Global Governance, World Order*, London, Palgrave, Macmillan

Their J. (2020) *A Force for Good in the World: Placing Democratic Values at the Heart of the UK's International Strategy*, London, Westminster Foundation for Democracy

Theuns T. (2019) 'The Legitimacy of Free Trade Agreements as Tools of EU Democracy Promotion', *Cambridge Review of International Affairs*, 32/1, 3–21

Thirwell M. (2010) 'The Return of Geo-Economics: Globalisation and National Security', Commentary, Lowy Institute for International Policy

Thomas D. (2012) 'Still Punching Below Its Weight? Coherence and Effectiveness in European Union Foreign Policy', *Journal of Common Market Studies*, 50/3, 457–474

Timmer H. and U. Dadush (2011) *The Euro Crisis and Emerging Economies*, Washington, DC, Carnegie Endowment for International Peace

Tocci N. and S. Aydin-Duzgit (2015) *Turkey and the European Union*, London, Red Globe Press

Trenin D. (2014) *The Ukraine Crisis and the Resumption of Great Power Rivalry*, Moscow, Carnegie Russia

Trsoter B. et al (2020) 'Delivering on Promises? The Expected Impacts and Implementation Challenges of the Economic Partnership Agreements Between the EU and Africa', *Journal of Common Market Studies*, 58/2, 365–383

Tsourapas G. (2019) 'The Syrian Refugee Crisis and Foreign Policy Decision-Making in Jordan, Lebanon, and Turkey', *Journal of Global Security Studies*, 4/4, 464–481

UNHCR (2019) *Refugee and migrants arrival summary data*, Geneva, UNHCR

Usanmaz E. (2018) 'Successful Crisis Management? Evaluating the Success of the EU Missions in the Western Balkans', *European Foreign Affairs Review*, 23/3, 381–404

Vaisse J. (2017) 'Le passé d'un oxymora. Le debat francais de la politique etrangere', *Esprit*, November

van Middelaar L. (2012) *Le Passage à l'Europe: Histoire d'un Commencement*, Paris, Éditions Gallimard

van Middelaar L. (2019) *Alarums and Excursions: Improvising Politics on the European Stage*, London, Agenda

Varieties of Democracy (2018) *Democracy for All? V-Dem Annual Democracy Report 2018*, Gothenburg

Varieties of Democracy (2020) *Democracy Report 2020: Autocratization Surges – Resistance Grows*, Gothenburg, V-Dem

Vervaeke, K (2020) 'The European Union's Pivot to Africa', in M. Westlake (ed) *The European Union's New Foreign Policy*, London, Macmillan

Vogler J. (2017) 'The Challenge of the Environment, Energy and Climate Change', in C. Hill, M. Smith and S. Vanhoonackr (eds) *International Relations and the European Union*, 3rd edition, Oxford, Oxford University Press

von Ow-Freytag B. (2018) *Filling the Void: Why the EU Must Step Up Support to Russian Civil Society*, Brussels, Martens Centre for European Studies

Waever O. (2018) 'A Post-Western Europe: Strange Identities in a Less Liberal World Order', *Ethics and International Affairs*, 32/1, 75–88

Wagner W. (2017) 'Liberal Power Europe', *Journal for Common Market Studies*, 55/6, 1398–1212

Weber B. (2016) *Time for a Plan B: The European Refugee Crisis, the Balkan Route and the EU–Turkey Deal*, Berlin, Democratization Policy Council

Wehrey F. and W. Lacher (2018) 'The Wrong Way to Fix Libya', *Foreign Affairs*, June

Wilson A. (2014) *Ukraine Crisis: What It Means for the West*, Yale , Yale University Press

Wissel J. (2014) 'The Structure of the EU-ropean Ensemble of State Apparatuses and Its Geopolitical Ambitions', *Geopolitics*, 19/3, 490–513

Wivel A. and O. Wæver (2018) 'The Power of Peaceful Change: The Crisis of the European Union and the Rebalancing of Europe's Regional Order', *International Studies Review*, 20, 317–325

Wolczuk K. (2014) *Ukraine and the EU: Turning the Association Agreement into a Success Story*, Brussels, European Policy Centre

Wong R. (2005) 'The Role of the Member States: The Europeanization of Foreign Policy?', in C. Hill and M. Smith, *International Relations and the European Union*, 1st edition, Oxford, Oxford University Press

Woolcock S. (2012) *European Union Economic Diplomacy*, Farnham, Ashgate

World Economic Forum (2019) *The EU's trading partners*, WEF Chart of the Day

Wright T. (2012) 'What If Europe Fails?', *Washington Quarterly*, 35/3, 23–41

Wright N. (2019) *The EU's Common Foreign and Security Policy in Germany and the UK: Co-operation, Co-optation and Competition*, London, Palgrave Macmillan

WTO Secretariat (2007) *Trade Policy Review: European Communities*, Geneva, WTO

Young A. (2015) 'The European Union as a Global Regulator? Context and Comparison', *Journal of European Public Policy*, 22/9, 1233–1252

Young A. and J. Peterson (2014) *Parochial Global Europe: Twenty-First Century Trade Politics*, Oxford, Oxford University Press

Youngs R. (2014a) *Climate Change and European Security*, London, Routledge

Youngs R. (2014b) *Europe in the New Middle East: Opportunity or Exclusion?*, Oxford, Oxford University Press

Youngs R. (2017) *Europe's Eastern Crisis: The Geopolitics of Asymmetry*, Cambridge, Cambridge University Press

Youngs R. (2020) *New Directions for EU Civil Society Support*, Brussels, Carnegie Europe

Youngs R. and O. Zihnioğlu (2021) 'EU aid policy in the Middle East and North Africa: politicization and its limits', *Journal of Common Market Studies*, volume 29.

Zamfir I. (2018) *Democracy Support in EU External Policy*, European Parliament Research Service Briefing

Zielonka J. (2006) *The EU as Empire*, Oxford, Oxford University Press

Zielonka J. (2011) 'The EU as an International Actor: Unique or Ordinary?', *European Foreign Affairs Review*, 16, 281–301

Zihnioğlu, Ö (2020) *EU–Turkey Relations: Civil Society and Depoliticisation*, London, Routledge

Zürn M. (2000) 'Democratic Governance Beyond the Nation-State: The EU and Other International Institutions', *European Journal of International Relations*, 6/2, 183–221

Zwolski K. and C. Kaunert (2011) 'The EU and Climate Security: A Case of Successful Norm Entrepreneurship?', *European Security*, 20/1, 21–43

Index

Lightning Source UK Ltd.
Milton Keynes UK
UKHW020153200522
403281UK00003B/144